Programming with Python

T.R. Padmanabhan

Programming with Python

 Springer

T.R. Padmanabhan
Amrita University
Coimbatore, Tamil Nadu
India

ISBN 978-981-10-9832-1   ISBN 978-981-10-3277-6   (eBook)
DOI 10.1007/978-981-10-3277-6

Printed on acid-free paper

This Springer imprint is published by Springer Nature
The registered company is Springer Nature Singapore Pte Ltd.
The registered company address is: 152 Beach Road, #22-06/08 Gateway East, Singapore 189721, Singapore

Dedicated

To

Maya and Roshan

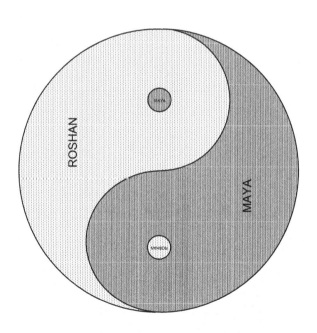

Preface

People, not withstanding caste, creed, gender, ethnic diversities, nationalities, are interacting intensely in the recent decades identifying commonalities, accommodating differences, making common cause. Python stands out as a shining outcome of such distributed but focused co-ordination. It started with an idea—'Simplicity at lofty heights (*my view*)'—that occurred to Guido van Rossum, who continues to be the accepted *benevolent dictator for life* (BDFL) for Python community. It is not that anyone can join this bandwagon and contribute; as it is not that easy. You can suggest a contribution but its pros and cons are discussed in an open forum through the net and (in the accepted shape) it enters the 'Holy Book' as PEP (Python Enhancement Proposal). The (open) Holy Book continues to grow in size shedding better light. It is a thrill to know how well it is evolving and to 'feel' or participate in its lustre. Python shines with the layers for its use—simple for the novice, versatile for the programmer, added facilities for the developer, openness for a 'Python sculptor'. It has a varied and versatile data structure, a vast library, a huge collection of additional resources, and above all OPENNESS. So embrace Python —the language by the people, of the people, for the people.

Definitely this is not justification enough for another book on Python. The variety of data structures and the flexibility and vastness of the modules in the Python library are daunting. The most common features of Python have been dealt with in this book bringing out their subtleties; their potential and suitability for varied use through illustrations. Nothing is glossed over. One can go through the illustrative examples, repeat them in toto, or run their variants at one's own pace and progress. The matter has been presented in a logical and graded manner. Some of the exercises at the ends of chapters are pedagogical. But many of them call for more efforts—perhaps candidates for minor projects. Concepts associated with constructs like *yield, iterator, generator, decorator, super* (inheritance), *format* (Python 3) are often considered to be abstract and difficult to digest. A conscious effort has been made to explain these through apt examples. The associated exercises complement these in different ways. Any feedback by way of corrections, clarifications, or any queries are welcome (blog: nahtap.blogspot.com).

I am grateful to Prof. K. Gangadharan of Amrita University to have opened my eyes to the openness of open systems. This book is an offshoot of this. In many ways, I am indebted to my students and colleagues over the decades; discussions with them, often spurred by a query, have been immensely helpful in honing my understanding and clarifying concepts. Implicitly the same is reflected in the book as well. I thank Suvira Srivastav and Praveen Kumar for steering the book through the Processes in Springer.

Lastly (but not priority wise) my thanks are due to my wife Uma for her unwavering and sustained accommodation of my oddities.

Coimbatore, India   T.R. Padmanabhan

Contents

About the Author

Dr. T.R. Padmanabhan was formerly professor emeritus at Amrita Vishwa Vidyapeetham, Coimbatore. He taught at the IIT Kharagpur, before doing R&D for private companies for several years. He is a senior member of the IEEE and a fellow of both the Institution of Engineers (IEI) and the Institution of Electronics and Telecommunication Engineers (IETE). He has previously published books with Wiley, Tata McGraw-Hill, and Springer Verlag.

Chapter 1
Python–A Calculator

Computer languages have so far been of the 'interpreted' or the 'compiled' type. Compiled languages (like 'C') have been more common. You prepare a program, save it (the debugged version), and (when needed) call it for running (or execution). Prior to running, the compiler compiles the program as a whole. In the interpreted versions (like Basic) you give a command, it is executed then and there (interpreted).

Python functions in both the forms; basically you run it in the interpreter mode. When needed, written and ready to run 'modules'/'functions' can be called up to join the interpreted sequence.

Let us consider the interpreted functioning. Python running environment can be opened by typing in 'python3' and following it by the '↵' (enter) key entry. Python environment opens and the python prompt −'>>>'—appears at the left end of the screen. The basic information regarding the version of python precedes this. We can safely ignore this, at least, for the present.

One of the simplest yet powerful uses of Python is to do calculations—as with a calculator. Let us go through an interactive session in Python (Rossum and Drake 2014). The session details are reproduced in Fig. 1.1 in the same order. The numerals in the sequence are not in the screen per se but have been added at the right end to facilitate explanations. Throughout this book an integer within square brackets—as '[1]'—refers to the line in the interpreted sequence under discussion. Let us understand the sequence in Fig. 1.1 by going through the sequence in the same order. You keyed in '3 + 4' in [1]—as you do with a calculator—and pressed the enter key. Python carried out the algebra you desired and returned the result as '7' which appears in line [2]—the next line. Having completed the assigned task— as a calculator—Python proceeds to the next line and outputs the prompt sign −'>>>' [3]—as though it says 'I am ready for the next assignment'. You continue the session—as calculator—through the steps shown. The following can be understood from the sequence shown:

© Springer Nature Singapore Pte Ltd. 2016
T.R. Padmanabhan, *Programming with Python*,
DOI 10.1007/978-981-10-3277-6_1

```
trp@trp-Veriton-Series:~$ python3
Python 3.4.2 (default, Oct 30 2014, 15:27:09)
[GCC 4.8.2] on linux
Type "help", "copyright", "credits" or "license" for more
information.
>>> 3+4                          [1]
7                                [2]
>>> 4-7                          [3]
-3                               [4]
>>> 7*3                          [5]
21                               [6]
>>> 4-7*3                        [7]
-17                              [8]
>>> 21/3                         [9]
7.0                              [10]
>>> 8+4*2-2*7                    [11]
2                                [12]
>>> 8+4*2-4/2                    [13]
14.0                             [14]
>>> 4--2                         [15]
6                                [16]
>>> 4-3.0                        [17]
1.0
>>> 4      +      9              [18]
13
>>> 4 +
9
13                               [19]
>>> 4+                           [20]
  File "<stdin>", line 1
    4+
      ^
SyntaxError: invalid syntax
>>>  4+9                         [21]
  File "<stdin>", line 1
    4+9
      ^
```

Fig. 1.1 A Python Interpreter sequence illustrating simple operations

- The basic algebraic operations—addition, subtraction [3] and [4], multiplication [5] and [6], and division [8] and [9]—are carried out through the associated symbols—'+', '−', '*', and '/'—respectively.
- Negative numbers are identified by the presence of the '−' symbol preceding the number. '−' is interpreted as one identifying a negative number or as the operator signifying subtraction based on the context. [14] and [15] clarify this: $4 − − 2$ is interpreted as $4 − (−2)$.
- With the '+', '−', and '*' operators if the two arguments involved are integers, the result is an integer and is output as such. If either one of the arguments is a

floating point number, the output is automatically displayed in floating point mode—as can be seen from [16] and [17].

- With the '/' operation the result is automatically shown in floating point mode even if the remainder (obtained when an integer dividing another) is zero as in [8] and [9]; same is true of algebraic chains involving division—as can be seen from lines [12] and [13].

- Algebra involving a mix of integer(s) and floating point number(s) is automatically interpreted as algebra with floating point numbers—as in lines [16] and [17].

- Spaces between the numbers (variables) and operators are ignored by the Interpreter [18]. An extreme case of this is in [19] where the space left after the addition operator is such that the next number is fed in the following line (of the terminal). Python still interprets it properly.

- However if you attempt to feed the number after '↵' (enter) i.e., the enter key is pressed before feeding the next number (second argument for the + operator) Python treats it as the end of the command line and returns an error—as in [20]. ('Yes, you have specified an add operation without keying in the second argument').

- In Python indentations at the left end have a specific significance. Indentations are used to group a set of statements belonging to an operation (explained later). Hence the space preceding the first character of a statement is treated as such a specific indentation. It's wrong usage in line [21] returns an error. The same is clarified through Fig. 1.2.

- A few additional points are clarified through the Python session details in Fig. 1.3. The opening message from the Interpreter with the Python version number and the copyright notice are deleted in all the session details reproduced hereafter.

- Comments can be inserted whenever desired. All literals following a '#' literal in a line are treated as forming a comment. [1] forms a full line comment. [2] has a full line comment following a line of Python code. Python interpreter ignores the comment and proceeds with the execution of the code. The comments in

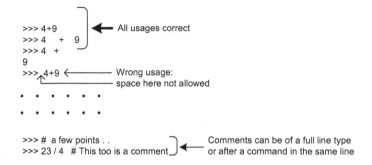

Fig. 1.2 Extract from a Python Interpreter sequence showing an erroneous insertion of 'space' at start of a command line

```
>>> #A few points on operators is in order here        [1]
...
>>> 23/4    #This is also a comment                    [2]
5.75
>>> #The operator '//' returns the floored quotient
...
>>> 23//4                                              [3]
5
>>> 23//4.2                                            [4]
5.0
>>> 23%4 # '%' is the remainder operator               [5]
3
>>> 23%4.2                                             [6]
1.999999999999991
>>> 5*4.2+1.999999999999991                            [7]
23.0
>>> 23///4.2                                           [8]
  File "<stdin>", line 1
    23///4.2
         ^
SyntaxError: invalid syntax
>>> 4**3                                               [9]
64
>>> 64**0.3333333
3.999999445482294
>>> 64**.333334
4.000011090370264
>>> 4+(3**2)/2                                         [10]
8.5
>>> 4+3**2/2                                           [11]
8.5
>>> (4+3**2)/2                                         [12]
6.5
>>>
```

Fig. 1.3 A Python Interpreter sequence bringing out additional calculator type operations

Python (as in any other computer language) are only for the user's understanding.

The operator '//' returns the floor value of the quotient of a division operation. Division of 23 by four in [3] yields five as the quotient and '5' is an integer here. Division of 23 by 4.2 in [4] also yields '5' as the quotient as 5.0 which is in floating point mode. The interpreter interprets the result to be in floating point form due to the divisor being in floating point form.

A clarification regarding number representation is in order here. Integers can be entered and represented as such; '+12' as well as '12' is taken as the positive integer 12—the positive sign before the integer is optional. But '−12' is taken as a negative number, the negative sign preceding a negative number being mandatory.

'%' is the remainder operator. [5] is an example where integer '23' is divided by integer '4' to yield integer '3' as the remainder. But division of 23 by 4.2 yields 1.9999999999999991—a floating point number as remainder as seen in [6]. The algebra in [7] confirms the floor and remainder results of division of 23 by 4.2. '///' is not a defined operation; its use (naturally) results the interpreter returning a syntax error as seen in [8]. '**' is the operator to raise a number to the power of another number [9]. 4^3 is returned as 64; by way of confirmation $64^{0.333}$ and $64^{0.3334}$ are evaluated and shown in the succeeding lines.

The parentheses pair '()' can be used for grouping to avoid ambiguity/confusion. [10] evaluates $4 + 3^2/2$ and gives the result as 8.5. In fact even if we do not use the parentheses here the algebra will be done as desired as in [11]. The operational precedence rules in Python will be followed by the interpreter (more of it later). However inserting the parentheses and avoiding confusion is always desirable. Note that $4 + 3^2/2$ (= 8.5) and $(4 + 3^2)/2$ (= 6.5)—as in [12]—are different. Proper use of parentheses avoids confusion.

Reference

van Rossum G, Drake FL Jr (2014) Python tutorial. Python software foundation

Chapter 2
Algebra with Variables

Python Interpreter working as a basic calculator was explained in the opening chapter. Working in the calculator mode can be done with variables as well. Variables, their types, and different basic operations with them are discussed here.

2.1 Variables

One can define variables, assign values to them, and do algebra. Consider the sequence in Fig. 2.1. [1] has a variable with assigned name 'a'. It has been assigned the integral value '3'. There is no need to assign a variable 'tag' or assign a type to it. From the statement in [1] Python understands all these. In [2] we are putting a query to Python 'What is 'a'? Python interpreter returns the value assigned to 'a'. In [3] we are passing on the query 'What type of object is this entity 'a'?'. The interpreter returns with the clarification that 'a' belongs to the class of objects termed 'int' (integer). Such type queries can be made whenever desired to understand the class (identity) of any object.

In [4] a variable has been given the name **Aa** and it is assigned the integral value '4'. In general a variable can be given a name—called 'Identifier'—as a sequence of ASCII characters excluding the two—'$' and '?'. The preferred practice is to use Identifiers for variables as well as other entities that we use in a language like Python such that the variable/entity can be easily identified from it. The constraints in the selection here are

- The first character has to be a small or a capital letter or '_' (underscore).
- The characters '$' and '?' cannot be used in an Identifier.
- The Identifier should not begin or end with a pair of underscores. In fact these are reserved for specific use (described later).
- A specific set of combinations of letters is used as 'keywords' in Python (van Rossum and Drake 2014a). These are to be avoided as Identifiers. Table 2.1

© Springer Nature Singapore Pte Ltd. 2016
T.R. Padmanabhan, *Programming with Python*,
DOI 10.1007/978-981-10-3277-6_2

```
>>> a = 3                [1]      >>> d1, e1 = 4.2, 5.3        [14]
>>> a                    [2]      >>> d1, e1 = e1, d1
3                                 >>> d1
>>> type(a)              [3]      5.3
<class 'int'>                     >>> e1
>>> Aa = 4               [4]      4.2
>>> Aa*2                          >>> d1, e1 = e1, d1-2        [15]
8                                 >>> d1
>>> b = 4.1              [5]      4.2
>>> type(b)                       >>> e1
<class 'float'>                   3.3
>>> c = a+b              [6]      >>> d3, e3 = d2*e2, d2/e2   [16]
>>> c                             >>> d3
7.1                               22.8484
>>> type(c)              [7]      >>> e3
<class 'float'>                   1.0
>>> d = c*c-a**2-b**2    [8]      >>> d2 = e2 = 4.78          [17]
>>> d                             >>> d2
24.599999999999998                4.78
>>> a1=4                 [9]      >>> e2
>>> _b = 5                        4.78
>>> c_ = (a1 - _b)**3            >>> d3+=1                    [18]
>>> c_-1                          >>> d3
>>> type(c_)                      23.8484
<class 'float'>                   >>> e3-=2                    [19]
>>> d, e = 5.1, 9        [10]     >>> e3
>>> d                             -1.0
5.1                               >>> d3/=2                    [20]
>>> type(d)              [11]     >>> d3
<class 'float'>                   11.9242
>>> e                             >>> d3*=2                    [21]
9                                 >>> d3
>>> type(e)              [12]     23.8484
<class 'int'>                     >>> d3 *= e3                 [22]
>>> d_e = d/e            [13]     >>> d3
>>> d_e                           -23.8484
0.5666666666666667                >>>
>>> type(d_e)
<class 'float'>
```

Fig. 2.1 A Python Interpreter sequence involving variables and assignments

is the set of all the keywords in Python. Avoiding their use directly or in combinations is healthy programming practice. Same holds good of 'built-in' function names such as abs, repr, chr, divmod, float, and so on.

b in [5], **c** in [6], and **d_e** in [13] are other examples of such Identifiers. Identifiers are case sensitive; **a** and **A** are different variables. [5] defines a variable **b** and assigns a value 4.1 to it. Python automatically takes b as a floating point variable and assigns the value 4.1 to it. The same is clarified by the 'type (**b**)' query and the clarification offered by Python in the two lines following. Algebra with variables can be carried out as with integers. In [6] the values of **a** and **b** are

Table 2.1 The set of keywords in Python

False	class	finally	is	return
None	continue	for	lambda	try
True	def	from	nonlocal	while
and	del	global	not	with
as	elif	if	or	yield
assert	else	import	pass	
break	except	in	raise	

added and assigned to a new variable **c**. Once again there is no need for a separate declaration, type clarification, and so on. [7] and [8] in the following lines clarify this. 'Chain' algebra can be carried out and assigned to variables—if necessary new ones—as can be seen from [8] and the following lines. [9] and the following lines are further examples of this. [10] has two variables assigned values in a sequence. Such sequential assignments can be done for any number of variables. Python will decide the type of variable and assign values to them conforming to the sequence specified. The type queries [11] and [12] and the Python responses in the lines that follow clarify this. In [13] **d_e** is assigned the value (**d/e**). '**d**' being a floating point variable—with value 5.1 as can be seen from [10]—**d_e** is automatically taken as a floating point variable and assigned the result. The query and response that follow confirm this. **d1** and **e1** are assigned values 4.2 and 5.3 in [14]. The following lines reassign values to them. Note that the assignments to **d1** and **e1** have been interchanged without the use of an intermediate temporary storage. This is not limited/restricted to numerical assignments alone. In [15] the new value of **e1** is **d1**-2 with d1 having the value prior to the present assignment. [16] is another example of multiple assignments done concurrently. The Python execution sequence following confirms this. In [17] **d2** and **e2** are assigned the same value of −4.78. Such sequence of assignments is also possible. The combination operator '+=' in [18] assigns a new value to **d3** as **d3 = d3 + 1**. Same holds good of the combination operators '−=', '*=', and '/=' as can be seen from [19], [20], [21], and [22] and the query-response sequences following these.

Table 2.2 Operators in Python: Algebraic operators are listed in order of ascending priorities

Algebraic operators	Symbol	Operation performed	Logical/bit operators	Symbol	Operation performed
	+	Addition		~	Complement
	−	Subtraction		&	Logical AND
	*	Multiplication		|	Logical OR
	/	Division		∧	Logical XOR
	//	Floored quotient		≫	Right shift (bits)
	%	Remainder		≪	Left shift (bits)
	**	Exponentiation			

In addition the combination operators—+=, −=, *=, /=, //=, %=, **=, &=, |=, ~=, ≫=, and ≪= are also available

```
>>> a=3.2                              4.78539444560216
>>> b =_                   [1]         >>> hc = complex(3.1, 4.2)
>>> b                                        [15]
3.2                                    >>> hc
>>> c = b*2                            (3.1+4.2j)
>>> c                                  >>> complex(a,aa)    [16]
6.4                                    (-3.2+3.2j)
>>> d = 9-_                 [2]        >>> he = complex(a) [17]
>>> d                                  >>> he
2.5999999999999996                     (-3.2+0j)
>>> e = 4+3j                [3]        >>> type(he)             [18]
>>> f = e*2                 [4]        <class 'complex'>
>>> f                                  >>> hk = hc.conjugate()
(8+6j)                                       [19]
>>> e**2                    [5]        >>> hk
(7+24j)                                (3.1-4.2j)
>>> g-e                     [6]        >>> hr = hk.real       [20]
(3+21j)                                >>> hr
>>> h = 2.1-4.3j            [7]        3.1
>>> h*3                     [8]        >>> hi = hk.imag       [21]
(6.300000000000001-                    >>> hi
12.899999999999999j)                   -4.2
>>> i = h**2                [9]        >>> type(hi)           [22]
>>> i                                  <class 'float'>
(-14.079999999999998-18.06j)           >>> a, b = 3, 4
>>> i**0.5                  [10]       >>> pow(b,a)           [23]
(2.099999999999996-4.3j)               64
>>> ii = _*2               [11]       >>> pow(b,3.0)         [24]
>>> ii                                 64.0
(4.19999999999999-8.6j)                >>> pow(b,-a)          [25]
>>> (i**0.5)*2             [12]       0.015625
(4.19999999999999-8.6j)                >>> pow(b,a,5)         [26]
>>> a = -3.2                           4
>>> aa = abs(a)            [13]       >>> g = pow(13,11)    [27]
>>> aa                                 >>> g
3.2                                    1792160394037
>>> ha = abs(h)           [14]       >>> g%17
>>> ha                                 4
                                       >>> pow(13,11,17)     [28]
                                       4
```

Fig. 2.2 A Python Interpreter sequence with algebraic operations and simple functions with numbers

The operators used in algebra and the operations they signify are given in Table 2.2 (van Rossum and Drake 2014b). The combination operators are also given in the table.

The underscore symbol '_' plays a useful role in interactive sessions. It is assigned the last 'printed' expression. Referring to the sequence in Fig. 2.2, in [1] it is the numerical value—that is 3.2—in the preceding line. b is assigned this value of 3.2. b carries this value for subsequent algebraic steps. [2] is an instance of using '_' where it is used in an algebraic expression.

2.2 Complex Quantities

Python has the provision to handle complex numbers and variables. [3] assigns the value 4 + 3*j* to **e**. Here 3*j* signifies the imaginary component of the number. Algebra can be carried out with complex numbers with equal ease—in the same manner as real numbers. [4], [5], and [6] represent such algebra where the real imaginary parts of the variables/numbers and the expected results—are all integers. [7], [8], [9], and [10] show cases where the complex numbers involved have the real and imaginary parts in floating point form. The results too have the real and imaginary parts in floating point form. [11] is another example of the use of '_'—to use the last result in the current line without the need to retype. [12] confirms the correctness of the computation with [11].

2.3 Common Functions with Numbers

Python has a number of built-in functions (van Rossum and Drake 2014b); each function accepts the specified arguments, executes the routines concerned and returns the result (if and as desired). Functions are discussed in detail later. Here we introduce a few of the built-in functions useful directly in the calculator type of work. abs(**a**) returns the absolute value of a specified as argument. [13] is an instance of the absolute value of −3.2 returned as 3.2. [14] returns the absolute value of the complex number **h** with assigned value in [7] as 2.1 − 4.3j that is 4.78539444560216. complex() is another built-in function. It takes two arguments —**x** and **y**—in the same order and returns the complex quantity **x** + **y***j*. [15] is an example of the direct use of complex() function to form the complex number 3.1 + 4.2*j* taking 3.1 and 4.2 as the arguments. [16] is another example confirming this. If only one argument is specified in the complex() function it is implicitly taken as the real component and the imaginary part is automatically taken as zero. [17] is an illustration of this usage as can be seen from the lines following. The conjugate of a complex quantity is obtained as in [19]—**he** representing the complex conjugate of **hc**. In [20] and [21] **hk**.real and **hk**.imag return the real and imaginary components of **hk** and assign them to the variables **hr** and **hi** respectively. The following line confirms that **hr** is a floating point number (the same is true of **hi** also). The function pow(**a**, **b**) returns **a**^{b}—the same as **a** ** **b**. Here **a** and **b** can be integers or floating point numbers. **a**^{b} is an integer if and only if **a** and **b** are integers and **b** is positive. These can be seen from [22] to [25]. The function pow(**a**, **b**, **c**) returns (**a** ** **b**) % **c** as can be seen from [26]. [27] is another illustration of this at a slightly longer integer level. The sequence computes (13^{11}) % 17 in two steps—a longer route. [28] achieves the same in a single step. Figure 2.3 shows the possibilities and constraints in the use of pow() in a compact form.

pow(x, y, [z])

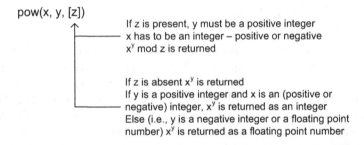

If z is present, y must be a positive integer
x has to be an integer – positive or negative
x^y mod z is returned

If z is absent x^y is returned
If y is a positive integer and x is an (positive or
negative) integer, x^y is returned as an integer
Else (i.e., y is a negative integer or a floating point
number) x^y is returned as a floating point number

Fig. 2.3 Different possibilities and constraints of pow() function execution

When doing numerical work sometimes it becomes necessary to convert an integer into floating point mode. Similarly a floating point number may have to be approximated to an integer. The relevant functions and their use are illustrated through the Python Interpreted sequence in Fig. 2.4. **x** is a floating point number with value 4.3 and **y** an integer with value 3 as assigned in [1]. As can be seen from [2] **z** = **y**^{x}. **y**—an integer is raised to the power of a floating point number; the result seen from [3] is a floating point number. int(**x**) is assigned the value of the integral part of **x**—namely 4. Hence **z** = **y**$^{int(x)}$ is an (positive) integral power of an integer; the result is an integer as can be seen from [4]. The integer y is converted into floating point mode by [5] returning the assigned value 3.0; note that the numerical value remains unaltered. This floating point number is raised to the powers of **x** and int(**x**) respectively in [6]. Both the results—in [7] and [8] are in floating point mode. These may be compared with the corresponding values in [3] and [4] obtained earlier. The function **z** = int(**x**) retains the integral part of **x** and ignores the fractional part. Even if the fractional part exceeds 0.5, it is ignored; the

```
>>> x, y = 4.3, 3                               [1]
>>> z1, z2 = y**x, y**int(x)                     [2]
>>> z1                                           [3]
112.62152279558863
>>> z2                                           [4]
81
>>> float(y)                                     [5]
3.0
>>> z3, z4 = float(y)**x, float(y)**int(x)       [6]
>>> z3                                           [7]
112.62152279558863
>>> z4                                           [8]
81.0
>>> int(4.7)                                     [9]
4
>>>
```

Fig. 2.4 Illustration of conversions between floating point numbers and integers

Table 2.3 Common functions with numbers

Function—form	Result
abs(**x**)	Returns the absolute value of **x**
complex(**a**, **b**)	Returns the complex number a + bj
x.conjugate	Returns the complex conjugate of x
x.real	Returns the real part of the complex number x
x.imag	Returns the imaginary part of the complex number x
pow(**x**, **y**, **z**)	Returns x ** y if z is absent; returns (x ** y) % z if z in present
int(**x**)	Returns the integral part of x
float(**x**)	Converts the integer x into a floating point number with the same value

operation done by int() is not a rounding off. [9] confirms this. Table 2.3 summarizes the functions with numbers discussed here. Additional functions are introduced later.

The basic operators in Python for doing algebra as well as for forming algebraic expressions are given in Table 2.2. They are listed in the table in the order of their priorities (specifically the operators in descending order of priorities are—**, %, //, /, *, −, and +). Thus in any algebraic chain '**'—if present—will be evaluated first; then '%' and so on. '+' operation is the last one to be carried out. The Python Interpreter sequence in Fig. 2.5 illustrates these. 3 *+ 4 in [1] is fairly clear; the integer 3 is multiplied by the positive integer +4 to yield the integer 12 as the result. A clearer way of specifying this is shown to the right (after the '#' symbol) as 3 * (+4). Similarly 12/−4 in [2] is interpreted as division of integer 12 by the negative integer −4 with −3.0 as the result. Once again 12/(−4) shown at the right is clearer. With 12 + 5 * 8 in [3] the '*' operation gets priority over the '+' operation; hence 5 * 8 is done first and the result (40) added to 12 subsequently to yield 52 as the result. 12 + (5 * 8) shown at the right avoids any ambiguity. Note that

```
>>> 3*+4              [1]#3*(+4)
12
>>> 12/-4             [2]#12/(-4)
-3.0
>>> 12+5*8            [3]#12+(5*8)
52
>>> 60/5*3            [4]#(60/5)*3
36.0
>>> 60/5*3//2         [5]#(60/5)*3)//2
18.0
>>> 4+-77/7           [6]#+(-77/11)
-7.0
>>> 4*5-77/11+7*2     [7]#(4*5)-(77/11)+(7*2)
27.0
```

Fig. 2.5 Representative algebra involving multiple operations and their priorities

(12 + 5) * 8 is different from this. With 60/5 * 3 the division operation (/) gets priority over the multiplication operation (*); hence the expression is evaluated as (60/5) * 3 (=36.0) as clarified at the right. Similarly 60/5 * 3//2 in [5] is evaluated as ((60/5) * 3)//2 to yield 18.0. With 4 * 5 – 77/11 + 7 * 2 in [7] division (77/11 = 7.0), multiplications—4 * 5 (20) and 7 * 2 (=14), subtraction (20 – 7.0 = 13.0), and addition—13.0 + 14 (=27.0) are carried out in that order. The expression evaluated is (4 * 5)—(77/11) + (7 * 2) as shown in the right. Since the division 77/11 always returns a floating point number the final result (algebra involving a mixture of integers and floating point numbers) yields a floating number.

Algebraic expressions can be made compact by conforming to the priorities of operators. However as a practice, it is better to use parentheses (though superfluous) and clarify the desired sequence and avoid room for ambiguity.

2.4 Logical Operators

The logical operators in Table 2.2 operate bit-wise on integers. The Python Interpreter sequence in Fig. 2.6 illustrates their use. **a** in [1] and **b** in [2] are 10110_2 (binary equivalent of the decimal number 22) and 10101_2 (binary equivalent of the decimal number 21) respectively. **a|b** in [3] is 10111_2 which is 23 in decimal form. The other operations too can be verified similarly.

Fig. 2.6 Illustration of use of logical operators

```
>>> a = 22                    [1]
>>> b = 21                    [2]
>>> a|b                       [3]
23
>>> a & b                     [4]
20
>>> a^b                       [5]
3
>>> (~a) & (~b)               [6]
-24
>>> a << 2                    [7]
88
>>> b >> 2                    [8]
5
>>>
```

2.5 Strings and Printing

A string is a type of 'object' in Python. Any character sequence can form a string. Strings can be useful in taking output as printouts and in presenting any entity in/from Python. Figure 2.7 is a Python interpreted sequence to demonstrate basic operations with strings (van Rossum and Drake 2014c). String 'great' is assigned to the identifier **s1**. [2] and the line following it confirm this. Similarly **s2** in [3] is a string. Strings can be combined conveniently using the addition operator—'+'. **s3** defined in [4] is such a combination as can be seen from [5] and the output

```
>>> s1 = 'great'                                              [1]
>>> type(s1)                                                  [2]
<class 'str'>
>>> s2 = 'day'                                                [3]
>>> s3 = s1+s2                                                [4]
>>> s3                                                        [5]
'greatday'
>>> s4 = s1 + ' ' + s2                                        [6]
>>> s4
'great day'
>>> s5 = s4*3                                                 [7]
>>> s5
'great daygreat daygreat day'
>>> s5 = s4 + '! '                                            [8]
>>> s6 = s5*3
>>> s6
'great day! great day! great day! '
>>> print(s1)                                                 [9]
great
>>> a = 35                                                    [10]
>>> print(a)                                                  [11]
35
>>> a, b, c = 10, 21.3, True                                  [12]
>>> print(a, b, c)                                            [13]
10 21.3 True
>>> b = 11
>>> c = a*b                                                   [14]
>>> repr(c)                                                   [15]
'385'
>>> type(repr(c))                                             [16]
<class 'str'>
>>> print('Product of a and b is' + '=' + repr(c))           [17]
Product of a and b is=385
>>> print('Product of a and b is' + '=' + repr(a*b))         [18]
Product of a and b is=385
>>> print('Product of a and b is' + ' = ' + repr(a*b))       [19]
Product of a and b is = 385
```

Fig. 2.7 Illustration of basic operations with strings

following. In Python the operator '+' is used in the sense of combining two entities but not restricted to mean the addition of two numbers alone. Such an extended concept is true of other operators as well as many functions as well. These will be explained duly.

s4 in [6] is a more elegant 'good day' than **s3**. Here the white space—' '—a string of single character has been interposed between 'good' and 'day'; the three strings—**s1**('good'), the white space string ' ', and **s2** ('day') have been combined using the '+' operator to form the string **s4** ('good day'). The '*' operator can be used with a string to repeat a desired sequence (imposition!). **s5** in [7] is an example. It has been refined in [8] and the repeated sequence reproduced as **s6** in a more elegant manner as can be seen from [8].

Entities in Python (like strings) can be output/displayed by invoking the `print` () function. The `print(`**s1**`)` in [9] is possibly the simplest form of use of `print()` function. Any string can be directly output in this manner. Objects which can be output directly too can be printed in this manner. **a** has been assigned the integer value 35 in [10] (hence **a** is of `Type int`); it is output in [11] through `print(`**a**`)`. **a**, **b**, and **c** have been assigned values 10, 21.3 and `True` respectively in [12]; in turn they are of type `int`, `float`, and `Boolean`. They are output directly in the same sequence with the print command `print(`**a**, **b**, **c**`)` in [13]. Numbers, values of variables, and the like have to be converted into string form before they can be output through the print function. The function `repr()` achieves such a conversion into a string form which can be directly used as input to the `print()` function. **c** as specified in [14] forms the product of **a**(=35) and **b**(=11). To get it (value of 385) printed out it is converted into string form through `repr(`**c**`)` in [15]. [16] confirms this. Its value is printed out in [17]. **a** * **b** or any other such algebraic sequence—its value—can be directly converted into a string—avoiding the use of the intermediate temporary variable **c**—for output as done in [18] and [19].

2.6 Exercises

1. Evaluate the following:

   (a) 0.2 + 2.3 − 9.7 + 11.2
   (b) 4.2 − 2.3 + 9.7 − 11.2
   (c) 4.2 − 2.3 + 9.7 * 11.2
   (d) 4.2 − 2.3 + 9.7/11.2
   (e) (4.2/2.3) * (9.7/11.2)
   (f) (4.2/2.3) ** (9.7/11.2)
   (g) 97 % 3, pow(97, 3, 23), pow(3, 97, 23)

2. **AA** = 'Mary had a little lamb'. '**AA**' is a string here. Assign different names to each word in **AA** (**b1**, **b2**, …), combine them in different combinations, and print out.

3. Evaluate the following:

   (h) $((((3 ** 2) ** 2) ** 2) ** 0.5) ** 0.5) ** 0.5$: these types of expressions are
        evaluated to ascertain the accuracy/speed achieved/possible with numerical
        methods/computers.

   (i) $((((0.3 ** 0.5) ** 0.5) ** 0.5) ** 0.5) ** 0.5$

   (j) $((((3 ** 0.5) ** 0.5) ** 0.5) ** 0.5) ** 0.5$

   (k) $\dfrac{1}{1+\dfrac{1}{1+\dfrac{1}{1+\frac{1}{4}}}}$

   (l) $\dfrac{1}{1-\dfrac{1}{1-\dfrac{1}{1-\frac{1}{4}}}}$

References

van Rossum G, Drake FL Jr (2014a) The Python language reference. Python software foundation
van Rossum G, Drake FL Jr (2014b) The Python library reference. Python software foundation
van Rossum G, Drake FL Jr (2014c) Python tutorial. Python software foundation

Chapter 3
Simple Programs

As was seen in the last two chapters basic algebraic operations are carried out in Python as with a simple calculator. More involved operations call for preparation of programs and working with them. The program structure in Python has to conform to specific syntactic rules. These are to be religiously followed to ensure that Python interprets the program for subsequent execution (van Rossum and Drake 2014).

3.1 Basic Program Structure

Even the simplest of programs calls for a sequence of computations/activities to be executed with its associated constraints (Guttag 2013). Let us take such a simple program by way of illustration.

Example 3.1 Compute the sum of n_r natural numbers.

The steps [1]–[5] in the sequence in Fig. 3.1 achieve this for $n_r = 12$; the result is output—[6] and the related output in the following line. Any other (positive) integral value can be assigned to n_r and the corresponding sum computed in the same manner.

Figure 3.2 aids the understanding of the program and its working. 'while' is a keyword. 'while i:' tests the value of i; as long as it is True—that is it is non-zero—the group of statements following is executed. The colon ':' following i signifies this. This set of statements forming the group is to be indented with respect to the beginning of the line (incidentally in Python such a group is often referred to as a 'suite'). The indentation can be achieved through tabs or spaces. But all the statements within the group should have the same indentation—done consistently with tabs or spaces (preferably spaces). One line left free after the group [4] and [5] here—signifies the end of the group. In the specific program here if i (equal to n_r) at the start is non-zero, it is added to the sum [4] and decremented [5]. The sequence continues until i becomes zero; i.e., n_r (12), $n_r - 1$ (11), $n_r - 2$ (10), … 2, and 1 are

© Springer Nature Singapore Pte Ltd. 2016
T.R. Padmanabhan, *Programming with Python*,
DOI 10.1007/978-981-10-3277-6_3

```
>>> sum, Nr = 0, 12                                    [1]
>>> i = Nr                                             [2]
>>> while i:                                           [3]
...     sum += i                                       [4]
...     i -= 1                                         [5]
...
>>> print('The sum of all natural numbers up to
(and inclusive of) ' + repr(Nr) + ' is ' +
repr(sum))                                             [6]
The sum of all natural numbers up to (and
inclusive of) 12 is 78
>>> l1, l2, n = 100, 200, 13                           [7]
>>> j = l1
>>> while j < l2:                                      [8]
...     if j%n == 0:                                   [9]
            print(repr(j) + ', ')                      [10]

...     j += 1                                         [11]

...
104,
117,
130,
143,
156,
169,
182,
195,                                                   [12]
```

Fig. 3.1 Python Interpreter sequence for Examples 3.1 and 3.2

all successively added to the sum. Once the loop operation is over the program proceeds to the following line [6] and continues execution. Here the values of n_r and sums are printed out. The simplicity of the loop structure is striking. There is no need to put parentheses around the condition to be tested, no need to identify the group by enclosing it within curly brackets and so on. The group may have as many executable statements as desired. The whole condition is checked after every execution of the group sequence.

Example 3.2 Identify all the numbers in the interval {100 to 200} which are divisible by 13 and output them.

The 6-line program from [7]–[11] achieves this; it is a bit more involved compared to the previous one. The program accepts three integers—**l1** (lower limit), **l2** (upper limit), and a specified number **n**—and prints out all the numbers between **l1** and **l2** which are divisible by **n**. **j**—a dummy/running variable—is assigned the value of the lower limit to start with. Two successive checks are done on **j**. First check whether **j** < l2; if so enter the loop/continue within the loop execution. Within the loop 1 check whether **j** is divisible by **n**. If so enter loop 2 and execute it. Else do not enter loop 2/keep away from it. Loop 2 here demands a single action—print the value of the number and proceed to the next line. Once you

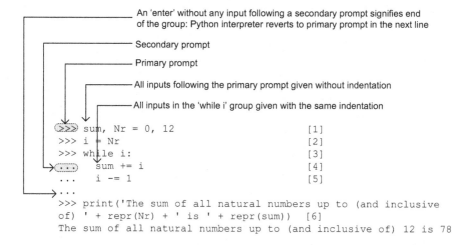

Fig. 3.2 Structure of the program for the sequence [1]–[6] in Fig. 3.1 (Example 3.1)

exit loop 2, you are back in loop 1. Increment the value of j [11]. This forms the last line of the program within loop 1. In the specific case here all numbers in the interval—100–200—that are divisible by 13 are printed out in the same sequence as they are encountered.

The program brings out a number of additional aspects of Python.

- Loop 2 is within loop 1. All statements within loop 2 form a sub-group. (Incidentally loop 2 has only a single statement here.) They appear with the same indentation within loop 1 (see Fig. 3.3).
- 'if' is a keyword. It is used to check a condition and execute a loop if the condition is satisfied.
- The operator '==' checks whether the values of quantities on either side are identical. Specifically here if j%n is zero, j%n == 0 is true (or 1); if it is non-zero, it is false (or 0).

Fig. 3.3 Structure of the program for the sequence [7]–[11] in Fig. 3.1 (Example 3.2)

```
>>> l1, l2, n = 100, 200, 13        [7]
>>> j = l1
>>> while j < l2:                   [8]
...     if j%n == 0:                [9]
...         print(repr(j) + ', ')   [10]

...     j += 1                      [11]
```

104,

Inner loop (loop 2)
Outer loop (loop 1)
Main program

Fig. 3.4 The sequence in
Fig. 3.3 with its loop 2 being
in a single line

```
>>> 11, 12, n = 100, 200, 13
>>> j = 11
>>> while j < 12:
...     if j%n == 0:print(repr(j) + ', ')
...     j += 1
...
104,
117,
130,
143,
156,
169,
182,
195,
>>>
```

Incidentally if a loop has only a single statement in it, the same can follow the condition on the same line. The Python Interpreter sequence is as in Fig. 3.4.

Any normal/useful program will require a sequence of activities (representing the corresponding executable statements) to be carried out. The sequence will be linked through specific conditional decisions (as in the two small illustrations above). It is necessary to conceive of the overall computation, fully understand the same, represent it in a clear logical sequence and then do the program coding. Such a structured representation is conveniently done in 'pseudo-code' form. It is good programming practice to represent the program in pseudo-code form and then proceed with the coding proper. The pseudo code for a program with one conditional loop within is shown in Fig. 3.5a; Example 3.1 can be seen to be of this type. The pseudo-code in Fig. 3.5b has two conditional loops—loop 2 being executed within loop 1; Example 3.2 can be seen to be of this type. The following are noteworthy here:

- Any sequence of executions which does not involve conditional checks is represented by one/a few statements. The suite of these statements together constitutes one logical block to be executed. 'begin' and 'end' signify the beginning and the end of the block/suite.
- Every logical block is entered after a conditional check. To clarify this, the logical block is identified through a definite indent on the left of the parent block.
- For successive logical checks followed by corresponding logical blocks similar indentations are used.

In general the pseudo code of a program may involve a number of conditional loops in a sequence; some of these loops may have single or multiple loops within in cascaded/sequential forms. A number of such pseudo code structures appear with the examples to follow here as well as in subsequent chapters.

(a)

```
Statement 1
Statement 2
 .  .  .  .
 .  .  .  .
Statement i
 while (condition):
        Start loop
        Statement i+1
        Statement i+2
         .  .  .  .

         .  .  .  .
        Statement i+j
        End loop
Statement i+j+1
 .  .  .  .
 .  .  .  .
Statement last
```

(b)

```
Begin
Statement 1
Statement 2
 .  .  .  .
 .  .  .  .
Statement i
 while (condition):
        Begin loop1
        Statement i+1
        Statement i+2
         .  .  .  .

         .  .  .  .
        Statement i+j
        Statement i+j+1
                Begin loop2
                Statement i+j+2
                Statement i+j+3
                 .  .  .  .

                 .  .  .  .
                Statement i+j+k
                Statement
i+j+k+1
                End loop2
        Statement i+j+k+3
         .  .  .  .

         .  .  .  .
        Statement i+j+k+1
        Statement i+j+l+1
        End loop1
Statement i+j+l+2
 .  .  .  .
 .  .  .  .
Statement last
End
```

Fig. 3.5 a Pseudo codes for the sequence in Fig. 3.1: **a** First example and **b** Second example

The pseudo code representation of the program enables the programmer to conceive of the program in its totality, identify the conditions and activities at the highest level and represent it in a compact form. Subsequently each of the activities identified can be looked into separately and split into separate connected conditional blocks (See Fig. 3.6). The process can be continued as much as necessary; finally each block in the representation can be coded separately. All such coded blocks can be combined conforming to the representations at different stages and finally the overall program can be realized. This is the 'top down' approach used for the program. The approach has many advantages:

Fig. 3.6 'Top down' approach to pseudo code representation

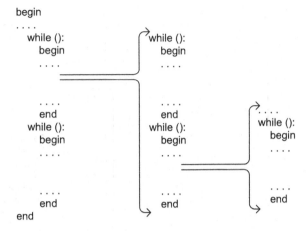

- Visualization of the program in the proper perspective—in terms of major blocks and their connections/links at the top level.
- Identification of the activities at each block, their connections, and sequences.
- Clarity in visualization and program realization.
- Easiness in testing and debugging: each of the identified smallest blocks can be programmed, tested, and debugged separately and blocks combined in a step by step manner.
- With large programs different segments can be developed individually, and (if necessary) separately by different groups. All segments can be knitted together with the least interface problems.

3.2 Flow Chart

Flow chart is an alternate form of representation of computer programs. Each identified activity in a program is represented as a block and the program conceived as a group of blocks connected through lines and arrows representing program flow. Figure 3.7 shows a simple flow chart. Start and stop—the beginning and end of the program are represented with respective circles. Inputs and outputs are identified through double-line oblong enclosures shown. Executable groups of statements are represented by rectangular blocks. The flow chart in Fig. 3.7 has four such executable block segments. The diamond (or a rhombus in its place) is a decision block. It represents a condition to be tested and the resulting branching. There may be two or more branches on the output side of a conditional block. A decision/branching is a key element in a flow chart. It steers the program

Fig. 3.7 A typical flowchart
structure

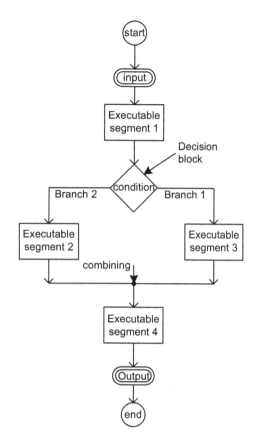

conforming to the logical process desired. The blocks are connected through lines
with arrows showing directions of program flow. In general a program represented
by a flow chart progresses downwards. The flowcharts for the two examples considered earlier are shown in Fig. 3.8.

Flow charts of programs encountered in practice can be much more involved—
involving a number of decision blocks, and executable blocks. Well thought out
programs can be represented as well organized flow charts. In turn it helps the
coding and execution considerably.

The choice of a pseudo code or a flowchart for a program is purely a subjective
one. When embarking on preparing a program for a task, the need to clearly
conceive the program task, and represent it in the form of a flow chart or a pseudo
code with full logic flow and interlinking fully clarified, need hardly be stressed.

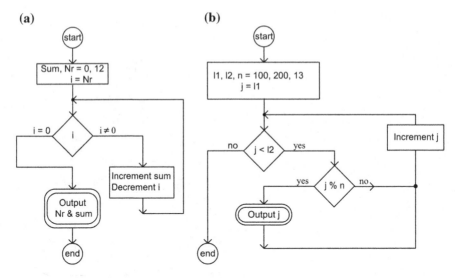

Fig. 3.8 Flowcharts for **a** Example 3.1 and **b** Example 3.2

3.3 Conditional Operations

A select set of keywords helps to test conditions and steer program. Their usage is brought out through a set of examples here.

Example 3.3 Output the sum of squares of the first eight odd integers.

The segment [1]–[4] in the python Interpreter sequence in Fig. 3.9 computes the desired sum—sum of squares of the eight odd integers starting with 1—and outputs the same (=680). Here n is a counter—initialized to 8 and counting is done downwards until n is zero. The loop starting with 'while' is executed as long as n ≠ 0; 'while' is a keyword here. n = 0 is interpreted as 'False' and causes termination of the loop execution. The flow chart for the program is shown in Fig. 3.10; it can be seen to be similar to the flowchart in Fig. 3.8a as far as functional blocks and program flow are concerned. In the print statement [3] the function repr(**sm**) converts **sm** to a printable string. It is concatenated with the string 'the required sum is' and the combination output in a convenient form. [4] is possibly a simpler print version. The print function outputs the string and sn directly.

'True' and 'False' are keywords; they are the Boolean values equivalent to 1 and 0 respectively. Their use is illustrated through the following example.

Example 3.4 Identify the first seven positive integers and output the sum of their cubes.

The routine [5]–[8] in the sequence in Fig. 3.9 obtains the desired sum and outputs the same. As in the previous program n counts down from 8. a is assigned the 'True' value initially. The loop execution continues as long as the status of a

```
>>> n, m, sm = 8, 1, 0                                    [1]
>>> while n:        #Add squares of the first 8           [2]
...     sm += m*m   # odd numbers
...     m += 2      #Print out the sum
...     n -= 1
...
>>> print('The required sum is ' + repr(sm))             [3]
The required sum is 680
>>> print('The required sum is ', sm)                    [4]
The required sum is  680
>>> a, n, m, sm = True, 8, 7, 0                           [5]
>>> while a:           #Get the sum of the cubes         [6]
...     sm += m*m*m    #of the first 8 positive
...     n -= 1         #integers divisible by 7
...     m += 7
...     if n == 0:a = False                               [7]
...
>>> print('The required sum is ' + repr(sm))             [8]
The required sum is 444528
```

Fig. 3.9 Python Interpreter sequence for Examples 3.3 and 3.4

Fig. 3.10 Flowchart for
Example 3.3 (Interpreter
sequence [1]–[4] in Fig. 3.9)

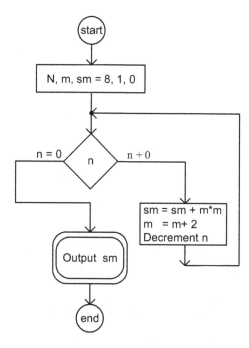

remains True. It is changed to False in the loop when n becomes zero [7]. [7]
illustrates the use of keyword 'if'. Like 'while', the 'if' statement checks for a
condition; on the condition being satisfied, the statement (group of statements)
following is (are) executed. The condition being tested is whether n == 0. If the

```
>>> a = True                                                [1]
>>> n = sm = 0   #Total number of positive integers
>>> while a is True:# below 200 divisible by 11         [2]
...     sm += 1
...     n += 11
...     if n >200: a = False                            [3]
...
>>> print("The required sum is " + repr(sm-1))          [4]
The required sum is 18
>>> b, sn = 100, 0   #numbers between 100 and 1000 which are
        [5]
>>> while b < 1000: # divisible by 11 as well as 13  [6]
...     if (b% 11 == 0) and (b% 13 == 0):               [7]
...         sn += 1
...         print('sn = '+ repr(sn) + ', b =' + repr(b) + ';
')                                                      [8]
...     b += 1
...
sn = 1, b =143;
sn = 2, b =286;
sn = 3, b =429;
sn = 4, b =572;
sn = 5, b =715;
sn = 6, b =858;
>>> n = 29    # What is the smallest number greater      [9]
>>> while True:# than 10,000 which is a power of 29? [10]
...     n *=29
...     if n > 10000:break                              [11]
...
>>> print('The desired number is ' + repr(n))
The desired number is 24389
>>>
```

Fig. 3.11 Python Interpreter sequence for Examples 3.5, 3.6, and 3.7

condition is true—that is n is zero—the statement specified is executed (**a** is assigned the value False). In turn execution terminates here. The sum (444,528) is output following line [8]. The flowchart is similar to that in Fig. 3.10 and is not shown separately.

The Python Interpreter sequence in Fig. 3.11 illustrates use of some additional features basic to Python programs, again through examples.

Example 3.5 What is the total number of positive integers below 200 which are divisible by 11?

The routine [1]–[4] in Fig. 3.11 obtains this number. There are altogether 18 of these numbers as can be seen from the line following [4]. The program is also an illustration for the use of keyword 'is'.

Here the condition 'a' being true is being tested in [2] with the use of 'is'. The block of three executable statements up to [3] is executed as long as **a is** True. As soon as **a** = False the loop execution stops. The operation 'is not' can be used similarly. 'a is not b' has value 'True' as long as **a** and **b** are not identical.

Example 3.6 Identify all the numbers between 100 and 1000 which are divisible by 11 and 13 and output them.

The program sequence [5]–[8] in Fig. 3.11 identifies and outputs these numbers. The condition that the number represented by **b** is divisible by 11 (**b**%11 == 0) as well as by 13 (**b**%13 == 0) is tested using the single condition in [7]. It uses the logical operator 'and'—a keyword; **p** and **q** is True only if **p** is True and simultaneously **q** is also True. The logical operator 'or' can be used in a similar manner. **p or q** is True if either **p** is True or **q** is True.

Example 3.7 Identify the smallest number greater than 10000 which is a power of 29.

The routine follows from [9] in Fig. 3.11. Starting with 29 we take its successive powers. The process is continued without break until the number crosses the value 10000. Once this value is crossed execution breaks out of the loop as specified by [11]. '**break**'—a keyword—exits from the current loop on the specified condition being true. '**while True**' is always true: hence in the absence of the conditional break statement within, the loop execution will continue ad infinitum. Incidentally the desired number here is $24,389(=29^3)$.

Example 3.8 Obtain the sum of the cubes of all positive integers in the range [0, 10] which have 3 as a factor.

The segment [1]–[4] in the Python Interpreter sequence in Fig. 3.12 is the relevant program. This simple example also illustrates the use of the 'range()' function.

The scope of the range function is clarified in Fig. 3.13. range() specifies a sequence of integers—often used to carry out an iteration as done here. The first integer signifies the start for the range and the second one its termination. The first can be absent in which case the default value is taken as zero. The third stands for the interval for the range; if absent the default interval value is taken as unity. All the three integers can be positive or negative. The range specification should be realizable.

range(5), range(0, 5), range (0, 5, 1) all these specify the range {0, 1, 2, 3, 4}.
range (−2, 3, 1) and range (−2, 3) specify the same range {−2, −1, 0, 1, 2}
range (10, −5, −2) implies the range {10, 8, 6, 4, 2, 0, −2, −4}.
range (2, 4, −1) is erroneous.

In the context here the suite of executable statements—in fact the single one in [2]: sm += i^3 is executed over a specified range—namely 0–10 with an interval of 3. The routine outputs the sum $3^3 + 6^3 + 9^3$ as can be seen from [3]. [4] also achieves the same output. Both are shown here to bring out the fact that a string can be specified through '...' or "...".

```
>>> sm = 0 # Sum up the cubes of all positive integers  [1]
>>> for i in range(0, 10, 3): sm += i**3 #up to10,divisible
by3                                                         [2]
...
>>> print("the sum - 3**3 + 6**3 + 9**3 = ", sm)            [3]
the sum - 3**3 + 6**3 + 9**3 =  972
>>> print('the sum - 3**3 + 6**3 + 9**3 = ', sm)            [4]
the sum - 3**3 + 6**3 + 9**3 =  972
>>> for n in range(2,10): #Identify all even & odd numbers
                                                            [5]
...    if n%2 == 0:                                         [6]
...       print(n, " : an even number", )
...       continue                                          [7]
...    print(n, " : an Odd number", )                       [8]
...
2  : an even number
3  : an Odd number
4  : an even number
5  : an Odd number
6  : an even number
7  : an Odd number
8  : an even number
9  : an Odd number
>>> for n in range(2,10):                                   [9]
...    if n%2 == 0:
...       print(n, " : an even number", )
...    print(n, " : a number", )
...
2  : an even number
2  : a number
3  : a number
4  : an even number
4  : a number
5  : a number
6  : an even number
6  : a number
7  : a number
8  : an even number
8  : a number
```

Fig. 3.12 Python Interpreter sequence for Examples 3.8 and 3.9

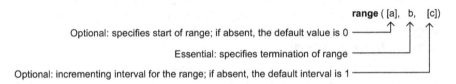

range ([a], b, [c])

Optional: specifies start of range; if absent, the default value is 0

Essential: specifies termination of range

Optional: incrementing interval for the range; if absent, the default interval is 1

Fig. 3.13 Structure and scope of range() in Python: Note that **a**, **b**, and **c** should be integers or functions which return an integer

Example 3.9 In the range [2, 10] identify the integers as 'odd' or 'even' and output accordingly.

The sequence [5]–[8] in Fig. 3.12 executes the desired task. It also illustrates the use of the keyword 'continue'. The outer loop is executed for all m in the range 2–10. If (n%2 == 0)—that is n is an even number—the value is output as an 'even number'. Then the routine continues with the loop—ignoring the sequence following. This is implied by 'continue'. Of course if n is odd, (n%2 == 0) is not satisfied and the loop execution continues with the rest of the executable lines. Here the number concerned is output as an 'odd number'. If the 'continue' is replaced by 'break' the loop will terminate after the first execution following satisfaction of condition (n% == 0)—after the first even number (=2) is output. The program has been repeated as a sequence following [9] with 'continue' being absent. Here the even numbers are output with an 'even number' tag. Apart from this they are also output with tag 'number' since line [8] is also executed here. The program is included here to clarify the role of the keyword—'continue'.

3.4 Iterative Routines

Consider the quadratic equation

$$px^2 + qx + r = 0$$

where p, q, and r are constants. The solutions can be directly obtained using the formula

$$x = \frac{-q \pm \sqrt{q^2 - 4pr}}{2p}$$

If $p = 1$, $q = -3$, and $r = 2$, we get 1 and 2 as the possible solutions. There are a number of situations where a solution cannot be obtained directly in this manner. A widely adopted procedure is to select an appropriate iterative method of solving such equations (Kreyszig 2006). Let us illustrate this through an example.

Example 3.10 Find the cube root of 10.

It is implicitly assumed here that we do not have access to log tables or calculator based procedures which yield the cubic root directly. We fall back on a 'trial and error' approach—a binary search. The procedure involves the following steps:

1. Let **a** = 10—**a** is assigned the value of the number whose cube root we seek.
2. Starting with **b** = 1, get b3 as b^3.
3. Increment **b** and get its cube. Do this successively until b^3 exceeds **a**.
4. Now we know that the cube root of **a** lies between the last value of **b** and that of **b** − 1. Let **b1** = **b** − 1 and **b2** = **b**. This completes the first part of the iteration.
5. Compute **bm**—the mean of **b1** and **b2** as **bm** = (**b1** + **b2**)/2.

6. Obtain **bm**³. If **bm**³ > **a**, we know that the cube root of **a** lies between **b1** and **bm**. Assign **bm** to **b2** as **b2** = **bm**. Proceed to step 8.
7. If **bm**³ ≤ **a** in step 6, we know that the cube root of **a** lies between **bm** and **b2**. Assign **bm** to **b1** as **b1** = **bm**.
8. If **bm** and **b1** (or **bm** and **b2**) are sufficiently close, we take **bm** as the cube root value with the desired level of accuracy; else we go back to step 5.
9. The iterative procedure outlined above is depicted in flowchart form in Fig. 3.14. The Python code for the example is in Fig. 3.15.—[1]–[6]. The result is in [7]. We have introduced a counter—'**n**'—in the routine to keep track of the number of iterations gone through. If n exceeds a preset limit we terminate the program. Here the limit has been set as 20. When execution is completed we get the desired cube root of **a** as 2.1552734375; the solution is after 10 iterative cycles.

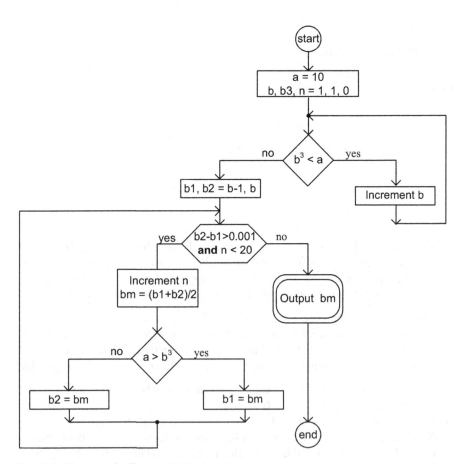

Fig. 3.14 Flowchart for Example 3.10

```
>>> a = 10                                                   [1]
>>> b, b3, n = 1, 1, 0                                       [2]
>>> while b3 < a:                                            [3]
...      b +=1
...      b3 = b**3

>>> b1, b2 = b-1, b
>>> while (b2 - b1 > 0.001) and (n < 20):                    [4]
...      n += 1
...      bm = (b1 + b2)/2.0
...      if a > bm**3:b1 = bm                                [5]
...      else: b2 = bm                                       [6]

>>> print('bm = ', bm, ', n = ', n, ',a = ', a)[7]
bm =   2.1552734375 , n =   10 ,a =   10
>>> b, b3, n = 1, 1, 0                                       [8]
>>> while b3 < a:                                            [9]
...      b +=1
...      b3 = b**3

>>> b1, b2 = b-1, b                                          [10]
>>> while (abs(b3-a)/a > 0.001) and (n < 20):                [11]
...      n += 1
...      bm = (b1 + b2)/2.0
...      if a > b3: b1 = bm                                  [12]
...      else: b2 = bm                                       [13]

>>> print('bm = ', bm, ', n = ', n, ',a = ', a)
bm =   2.154296875 , n =   9 ,a =   10
```

Fig. 3.15 Python iterative sequence for Example 3.10

The routine also illustrates the use of keyword—'else'. else is always used in combination with if to steer a routine through one or the other alternative code groups. The iteration process—reduction in the search range of solution in successive iteration cycles gone through is depicted in Fig. 3.16. The following are noteworthy here:

- The approach followed is of a 'divide and conquer' type; with each successive step the search range is halved. In turn the % error or indecision in the value of the cube root obtained is also halved.
- Since $2^{-10} = 1/1024$, the condition $b1 - b2 \leq 0.001$ (=1/1000) is achieved in 10 successive iterations. Hence $n = 10$ when the iteration stops.
- If ε denotes the accuracy specified ($\varepsilon = 0.001$ here), as ε reduces the number of iterative cycles required to achieve the specified accuracy increases. In fact the number of iterative cycles required is $\lceil -\log_2\varepsilon \rceil$.
- Beyond a limit the cumulative effect of truncation errors will dominate, preventing further improvement in accuracy (error propagation is not of direct interest to us here).
- $2.1552734375^3 - 10 = 0.01168391$. The fractional error in the cube value is $0.001168391 = 0.117\%$.

Iteration cycle   Search range

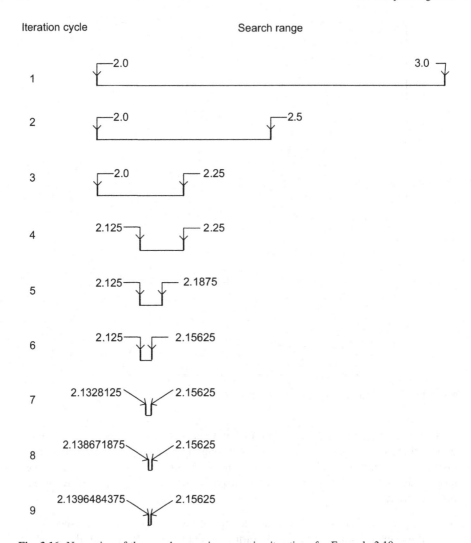

Fig. 3.16 Narrowing of the search range in successive iterations for Example 3.10

- The program is run with the termination condition altered to that in [11] in Fig. 3.15. The accuracy for termination is specified in terms of the cube value (in contrast to the last case where it was in terms of the cube root value). The program stops after nine iterations. The cube root value obtained is 2.154296875. Correspondingly the fractional error is $|(2.154296875^3 - 10)|/ 10 = 0.0001919$.

As mentioned earlier the successive bifurcation procedure outlined here can be used to seek solution for a variety of equations. More often we seek solutions for x such that $f(x) = 0$ where $f(x)$ is a specified function of x. For the above case

$f(x) = 10 - x^3$. In all these cases we should have a clear prior idea of the possible range of solutions and the number of solutions in the range. This is to prevent a 'wild-goose-chase' situation.

The sequence in Fig. 3.17 is a slightly altered approach to the problem in Example 3.10. Here the search interval in every iterative cycle is reduced to 1/3rd of the preceding one—[1] and [4]. As in the preceding case starting with one, b is successively incremented until a value of **b** whose cube exceeds **a** is identified. The desired cube root of **a** lies between **b** − 1 and **b**. This base interval is divided into three equal intervals ([1] and [2])—**ba** to **bb**, **bb** to **bc** and bc to b itself. a is compared with ba^3, bb^3, and bc^3 and the interval where it lies is identified. This forms the base interval for the start of the next iteration. It is again divided into three equal segments—[4]—(each of length 1/3rd of the previous case) and ba, bb, and bc reassigned to the respective new segment boundary values. The iterative cyclic process is continued until the interval is close enough to zero. The acceptable interval limit specified to stop iteration here [3] is 0.0001. The cube root value is obtained in eight iterations; its value is 2.154448000812884 · 2.154448000812884^3 − 10 = 0.00018535 is the error in the cube value.

The example here also illustrates the use of keyword—elif (stands for 'else if')—[5]. The condition chain—if … elif…elif … elif…else … can be used judiciously to test multiple conditions and steer a routine to respective code segments.

The iteration termination has been specified here in terms of accuracy in the root value. If necessary it can be specified in terms of the same in the cube value as was done earlier in the approach using bifurcation of the intervals.

```
>>> while b3 < a:
...     b +=1
...     b3 = b**3
...
>>> d = 1/3                                         [1]
>>> ba, bb, bc, = b-1, b-2*d, b - d                 [2]
>>> bb3, bc3 = bb**3, bc**3
>>> while (bc-bb > 0.0001) and (n < 20):            [3]
...     n += 1
...     d = (bc - bb)/3                             [4]
...     if a < bb3:
...         bb, bc  = ba+d, ba+2*d
...     elif a < bc3:                               [5]
...         ba, bb, bc = bb, bb+d, bb+2*d
...     else:                                       [6]
...         ba, bb, bc = bc, bc+d, bc+2*d
...     bb3, bc3 = bb**3, bc**3
...
>>> print('bb = ', bb, ', n = ', n, ',a = ', a)
bb =   2.154448000812884 , n =   8 ,a =   10
```

Fig. 3.17 Python Interpreter sequence with the altered approach for Example 3.10

3.5 Exercises

1. $x = \left(\sum_{i=2}^{6} |i|^j \right)^{1/j}$: Write a Python program to evaluate x for:

    a. $j = 1, 3, 10, 30, 100$
    b. $j = -1, -3, -10, -30, -100$
    c. $j = 1, 1/3, 1/10, 1/30, 1/100$
    d. $j = -1, -1/3, -1/10, -1/30, -1/100$

    All the above represent norms of vectors in finite dimensional linear spaces (of dimension 5). The vector component values have been taken as 2, 3, 4, 5, and 6. If j increases in the positive direction the larger magnitude gets more weight; eventually as j tends to infinity only the largest magnitude prevails. As j decreases from one, difference in contributions from components become less pronounced; in the limit as j tends to zero, all components are given equal weight. For negative values of j smaller magnitudes prevail over the larger ones with behavior characteristics as above. Choice of j helps to focus on selected characteristics of spaces

2. Write a Python program to evaluate the following iteratively. Continue the iteration until the change due to the last element as a fraction of the latest value is less than 10^{-6}:

    a. $x = 1 + \frac{1}{1!} + \frac{1}{2!} + \frac{1}{3!} + \frac{1}{4!} \ldots$
    b. $f(x) = 1 + \frac{x}{1!} + \frac{x^2}{2!} + \frac{x^3}{3!} + \frac{x^4}{4!} \ldots$ for $x = -0.1, -0.3, +0.1, +1.0, +3.0, +10.0$
    c. $f(x)(= \sin x) = \frac{x}{1!} - \frac{x^3}{3!} + \frac{x^5}{5!} - \frac{x^7}{7!} \ldots$ for $x = -0.1, -0.3, +0.1, +1.0, +3.0, +10.0$
    d. $f(x)(= \cos x) = 1 - \frac{x^2}{2!} + \frac{x^4}{4!} - \frac{x^6}{6!} + \frac{x^8}{8!} \ldots$ for $x = -0.1, -0.3, +0.1, +1.0, +3.0, +10.0$

3. Write a Python program to evaluate $5.1^{7.2}$, $5.1^{-7.2}$, $5.1^{1/7.1}$, $5.1^{-1/7.1}$. Use $5.1^{7.2} = 5.1^7 * 5.1^{0.2}$. Compute $5.1^{0.2}$ iteratively and multiply it by 5.1^7. To get x^{-y} evaluate x^y and take its reciprocal.

4. Modify the program for Example 3.9 as indicated below, run the same, and comment on the results:

    a. Use break in place of continue.
    b. Use the if... else combination.
    c. Swap the odd and even segments and do the above.

5. Numerical methods of solving equations (even in a single variable) take various forms. Unless one has a fairly clear idea of the nature/region of the solution sought things may go haywire. As an example consider the solution of the quadratic in x: $x^2 - x - 1 = 0$. The two solutions are $0.5(1 \pm \sqrt{5})$. One approach to solving for x is as follows:

$$y(x) = x + 1 \tag{3.1}$$

$$y(x) = x^2 \tag{3.2}$$

Start with a value for x, substitute it in (3.1) to get y. Use this value of y in (3.2) and solve for next approximate value of x. Continue this iteratively until the difference in successive values of x is within the acceptable limit. If x does not converge within a specified number of iterations, give up! Write a program to solve the given equation for x. Start with $x = 0$ as initial value. Solution of (3.2) yields two values for x; proceed with both.

Write a program to solve for x starting with (3.2) and try it with initial value $x = 0$.

6. Consider the cubic equation $y(x) = x^3 + ax^2 + bx + c = 0$. Since $y(0) = c$, $y(x)$ has a real root with a sign opposite that of c. If c is positive, one can evaluate y for different values of x (say -0.1, -1.0, -10.0, -100.0) until y is negative. Then a negative root can be obtained following the algorithm in Example 3.10. If c is negative a similar procedure can be followed with positive values of x to extract a positive root. The remaining roots can be obtained by solving the remaining quadratic factor. Write a program to solve a cubic polynomial. Solve the cubic for the sets of values—(1.0, 1.0, 1.0), (1.0, 1.0, -1.0), (1.0, 10.0, 10.0), (1.0, 10.0, -10.0), and (1.0, -10.0, 10.0), of the set (a, b, c).

7. Newton-Raphson method: the method solves $y(x) = o$ for x using a first degree polynomial approximation of y as

$$y_1 = y_0 + \left.\frac{dy}{dx}\right|_{x_0} \delta x$$

where y_0 is the value of y at $x = x_0$. With $y_1 = 0$ we have

$$\delta x = -\frac{y_0}{\left.\frac{dy}{dx}\right|_{x_0}}$$

With $x_1 = x_0 + \delta x$ evaluate next y. Continue iteratively until difference in successive values of x is within tolerance specified. Write a Python program for the general case (Make room for iteration failure with an upper limit to the number of iterations). Solve $e^{-x} - 2\cos x = 0$ in the interval $(0, \pi/2)$. Apply the method to get the cube root of 10.

8. With (x_1, y_1) and (x_2, y_2) as two points on a straight line in the (x, y) plane, equation of the straight line through the two points is

$$y = y_1 + \frac{y_2 - y_1}{x_2 - x_1}(x - x_1) \tag{3.3}$$

Solving this for $y = 0$ yields the solution x_0. The procedure can be extended to solve $y(x) = 0$ for x.

Get two points (x_1, y_1) and (x_2, y_2) as on the curve with y_1 and y_2 being of opposite signs. Form (3.3) and get x_3. Evaluate y_3 by substituting in the given function. If y_1 and y_3 are of different signs, form the equation similar to (3.3) for next iteration using (x_1, y_1) and (x_3, y_3); else use (x_2, y_2) and (x_3, y_3) for it. Continue the iteration until solution (or its failure!). Write a Python program for the iterative method. Solve the equations in Exercise (7) above.

9. An amount of c rupees is deposited every month in a recurring deposit scheme for a period of y years. Annual interest rate is $p\%$. Write a program to get the accumulated amount at the end of the deposit period with compounding done at the end of every year. Write a program to get the accumulated amount if the compounding is done monthly. Get the accumulated amounts for $c = 100$, $p = 8$, and $y = 10$.

10. A bank advances an amount of d rupees to a customer at $p\%$ compound interest. He has to repay the loan in equated monthly installments (EMI) for y years. Write a program to compute the EMI (EMI based loan repayment is the reverse of the recurring deposit scheme). Get the EMI for $d = 10,000$, $p = 10$, and $y = 10$.

11. Depreciation:

   a. In 'straight line depreciation' if an item (of machinery) is bought for p rupees and its useful life is y years the annual depreciation is p/y rupees.
   b. In 'double declining balance' method if the annual depreciation is $d\%$, the book value of the item at the end of y years is $(1 - (d/100))^y$ times its bought out value. The annual reduction in book value is the depreciation.
   c. In 'Sum of years digit' method of depreciation, with y as the useful life in years of an item form s as the sum of integers up to (and including) y. The depreciation in the xth year is (x/s) times the bought out value.

   Write programs to compute depreciation by all the three methods. With $p = 80,000$, $y = 10$, $d = 10$, get the depreciation and the book values at the end of each year for five years.

12. Copper wire (tinned) is used as the 'fuse wire' to protect electrical circuits. With d mm as the diameter of the wire used, the fusing current I_f is $80 \times d^{1.5}$ amperes. Adapt the program in Example 3.10 to get the fusing current for a given d. For the set of values of $d - \{0.4, 0.6, 0.8, 1.0, 1.2\}$ get the fusing currents.

13. *Coffee Strength Equalization*: Amla has three identical tumblers—A, B, and C. Each is 80 % full. A has coffee decoction and B and C have milk. She has to prepare three tumblers of coffee of equal amount and equal strength (accurate to 1%) without the aid of any other vessel. From A she pours coffee into B and C and fills them; after this she goes through a similar cyclic pouring sequence—B to C, C to A, A to B and so on. How many times does she have to do this to get the required set? Solve this through a Python program.

14. *Recurring Deposits and Equated Monthly Installment repayment of loan amount*: a fixed amount of Rs 100/- is deposited every month in a recurring

deposit scheme of a bank. The annual interest rate is r %. Write programs to do the following:

Compounding is done monthly; calculate the equivalent monthly simple interest rate.

With interest compounded every month calculate the maturity amount after y years.

With interest compounded annually calculate the maturity value of the amount. Note that the problem of taking a loan and returning it as EMIs is the same as the recurring deposit scheme run in the reverse direction.

References

Guttag JV (2013) Introduction to computation and programming using Python. MIT Press, Massachusetts

Kreyszig E (2006) Advanced engineering mathematics, 9th edn. Wiley, New Jeresy

van Rossum G, Drake FL Jr (2014) The Python library reference. Python software foundation

Chapter 4
Functions and Modules

Programming and running programs mostly follow definite patterns. A program is often run repeatedly with different sets of data that too on different occasions/days. Programs have to be stored and rerun. Sometimes a program calls for a modification and a rerun in the modified form. Some situations call for the use of a code segment repeatedly in a program. All these are facilitated in Python through the use of 'functions' and 'modules' (Rossum and Drake 2014).

4.1 Functions

Functions are entities which accept one or more arguments as inputs, execute a specific code block, and return the result of execution of the specified code block to the parent.

Example 4.1 Form a Python function to return the harmonic mean of all the numbers in the interval [100, 200] which are divisible by **a**. Get the harmonic mean for **a** = 9.

m_h—the harmonic mean of $n_1, n_2, n_3, \ldots n_k$—is given by (Sullivan 2008)

$$m_h = \frac{1}{\sum_{i=1}^{k} \frac{1}{n_i}} \qquad (4.1)$$

The desired code block for the function is in Fig. 4.1. The function definition has its first statement starting with the keyword def. It is followed by the name of the function (with a gap of one or two spaces for clarity). All the input arguments are specified within the parentheses. The ':'—colon—at the end implies that the code block of the defined function follows. The code block is indented with respect to def by a definite amount (2 to 4 spaces). Preferably the first line in the code block here is a string—a statement stating the scope of the function. This is not

© Springer Nature Singapore Pte Ltd. 2016
T.R. Padmanabhan, *Programming with Python*,
DOI 10.1007/978-981-10-3277-6_4

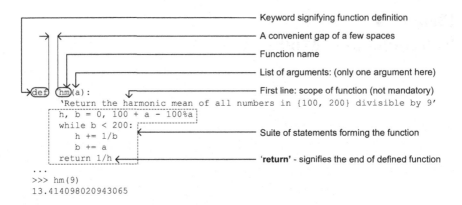

Keyword signifying function definition
A convenient gap of a few spaces
Function name
List of arguments: (only one argument here)
First line: scope of function (not mandatory)
Suite of statements forming the function
'return' - signifies the end of defined function

```
def hm(a):
    'Return the harmonic mean of all numbers in {100, 200} divisible by 9'
    h, b = 0, 100 + a - 100%a
    while b < 200:
        h += 1/b
        b += a
    return 1/h
...
>>> hm(9)
13.414098020943065
```

Fig. 4.1 Structure of a function in Python

mandatory. But its inclusion is preferred (for reasons to be clarified later). The code body forming the function follows. return—a keyword—is the last statement in any function. The completed output is returned to the calling program. In the specific case here **hm** (**a**) returns the desired harmonic mean value—the harmonic mean of all the numbers divisible by **a** in the interval [100, 200]. The function is coded in Python interpreter as shown in Fig. 4.2. **hm**(9) signifies calling of the function **hm** (**a**) with argument **a** = 9. It returns the desired **hm** value—[1].

hm(**a** = 9) is a more flexible form of the above function—[2]. The argument **a** has been given a value of 9 (default value). Calling the function without specifying any argument or its value returns the hm value for the default value of **a** (=9 here)—[3]. Calling it with any other value of the argument returns the corresponding hm value—as can be seen from [4] and [5] which return the function values for 11 and 13 respectively.

To bring out the function details in its versatile form let us consider another example.

Example 4.2 Do the coding for a function that returns $a^{1/p}$ to the desired accuracy. Run it for $a = 50$ and $p = 4$. The accuracy in the computed value has to be better than 0.2%.

A function root_1() has been defined and the code for it given in Fig. 4.3. Along with the results of specific interpreted runs. root_1() can be seen to be a versatile variant of cube root routine in Example 3.10. Here we obtain the pth root of **a**. i is the initial search step size—that is we start with b = 1 and increase it successively by i until b^p exceeds a. We start the iteration cycles with the interval—{b, b – i} and proceed with successive bifurcation of the interval. The iterations stop when the desired accuracy—**delta**—is achieved or the number of iteration cycles reaches the specified limit nn. The iterative process is the same as in Example 3.10.

```
>>> def  hm(a):
        'Return the harmonic mean of all numbers in {100,
200} divisible by 9'
...        h, b = 0, 100 + a - 100%a
...        while b < 200:
...            h += 1/b
...            b += a
...        return 1/h


...
>>> hm(9)                                                      [1]
13.414098020943065
>>> def  hm(a=9):                                              [2]
...        h, b = 0, 100 + a - 100%a
...        while b < 200:
...            h += 1/b
...            b += a
...        return 1/h
...
  >>> hm()                                                     [3]
13.414098020943065
>>> hm(11)                                                     [4]
16.513049663029967
>>> hm(13)                                                     [5]
17.92184242238757
>>>
```

Fig. 4.2 A Python function to get the harmonic mean as in Example 4.1

The function **root_1** has been made versatile in a few respects—essentially by redefining the argument list. Figure 4.4 brings out the flexibility with possible options. Referring to the figure the relevant details are as follows:

- The function defined can have as many arguments as desired.
- If any argument is assigned a value in the function definition it will be the default value of the argument in the function evaluation. During a function call if this argument is left out the default value will be used for the function call. In the specific case here all the arguments have been assigned values in [1] in Fig. 4.3. **root_1** has been called in [3] without specifying any value; the default values will be used by the Python Interpreter for all the arguments and the program will be run. The result is in [4]. The other quantities in the printout conform to the listing of **root_1**() in Fig. 4.3.
- If a value is specified for any argument during the function call the default value will be overrun and the specified value used in the program run.
- **root_1** has been called with a specific set of values for the arguments [5]— different from the default values specified in [1]; the result is in [6].

```
>>> def  root_1(a = 10, p = 3, delta = 0.001, nn = 20, i
= 1):                                                    [1]
...       b, bp, n = 1, 1, 0
...       while bp < a:
...            b += i
...            bp = b**p
...       b1, b2 = b - i, b
...       while (b2 - b1 > delta) and (n < nn):
...            n += 1
...            bm = (b1 + b2)/2.0
...            if a > bm**p:b1 = bm
...            else: b2 = bm
...       print('bm = ', bm, ', p = ', p, 'n = ', n, ', a
= ', a)
...       return                                         [2]
...
>>> root_1()                                             [3]
bm =  2.1552734375 , p =   3 n =   10 , a =   10 [4]
>>> root_1(20, 5, 0.002, 25, 3)                          [5]
bm =  1.82177734375 , p =   5 n =   11 , a =   20 [6]
>>> root_1(p = 5, a = 20, delta = 0.002, i = 3, nn = 20)
                                                         [7]
bm =  1.82177734375 , p =   5 n =   11 , a =   20 [8]
>>>
```

Fig. 4.3 Python Interpreter sequence for Example 4.2

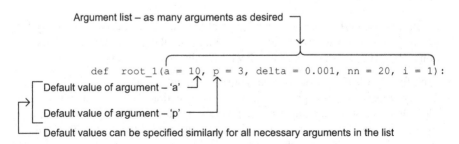

Fig. 4.4 Argument list possibilities for function definition in Python

- When a function is called the argument list order is not a rigid constraint. If the order remains unchanged only the values of the arguments need be fed as in [5] here; else the arguments can be fed in any order as done in [7]. The corresponding results are in [8].

If the function is desired to compute a quantity and return the same will be done as was the case in Example 4.1 ('return 1/**h**'). But if the function need not return anything specific it is indicated by a 'return' statement as in [8] here. The Interpreter will complete execution of the function and return to the main program.

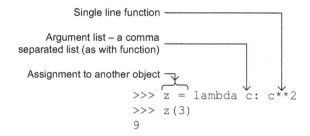

Fig. 4.5 Use of **lambda** in anonymous function definitions

4.1.1 Lambda Function

Many situations call for the use of single line functions. The keyword 'lambda' facilitates this in a compact form. It defines an anonymous function of the specified arguments. The function output can be assigned to any desired object to suit the context. The details are brought out through a simple example in Fig. 4.5. The function here has a single argument—**c**. It—the one line function—evaluates c^2 and assigns it to **z**. **z** is evaluated for the argument value of three (as nine) in the following line. The Python Interpreter sequence in Fig. 4.6 further illustrates the use of lambda. **z** is evaluated for the argument value four (as sixteen) in [5] and [6]. **z** has been assigned to **a** and **b** and evaluated for argument values of two and four (as four and sixteen) in [5] and [6] respectively.

[7] is an example where lambda is a function of two arguments—**x** and **y**. (**x**/**y**) is evaluated and assigned to **zz**. The ratio (4/5) is evaluated as **zz**(4,5) in [8]—

Fig. 4.6 A Python Interpreter sequence for the illustration of use of **lambda**

```
>>> z = lambda c: c**2   [1]
>>> z(3)                 [2]
9
>>> z(4)                 [3]
16
>>> a = z                [4]
>>> a(2)                 [5]
4
>>> b = z(4)             [6]
>>> b
16
>>> zz = lambda x,y:x/y[7]
>>> zz(4,5)              [8]
0.8
>>> def yy(x,y):         [9]
...     return x/y       [10]
...
>>> yy(4,5)              [11]
0.8
```

(=0.8). The equivalent function definition in terms of **yy** and its evaluation for the argument set (4,5)—**yy**(4,5)—follow in [9] to [11]. The simpler (and more compact) implementation using lambda is more convenient in many situations.

4.1.2 Recursion

Some routines require a code sequence to be repeatedly executed with a successively increasing/decreasing parameter set. Such recursive routines can be coded compactly by the program calling itself.

Example 4.3 Write a Python program to compute $(1/n!)$ and execute it for $n = 3$.

The Python Interpreter code for $(1/n!)$ in Fig. 4.7 has been evaluated for $n = 4$ as 0.041666 and for $n = 5$ as 0.0083333 in [2] and [3] respectively. The recursive

```
>>> def  in_ftr(n):                                              [1]
...    i, x = 0, 1
...    while i < n:
...       i += 1
...       x /= i
...    return x
...
>>> in_ftr(4)                                                    [2]
0.041666666666666664
>>> in_ftr(5)                                                    [3]
0.008333333333333333
>>>
>>> def  in_ft1(n):                                              [4]
...    if n == 0:#reciprocal of n! - using recurrence [5]
...       return 1
...    else:
...       return in_ft1(n-1)/n                                   [6]
...
>>> in_ftr1(4)
0.041666666666666664
>>> in_ftr1(5)
0.008333333333333333
>>> def nf_inv(n):                                               [7]
...    print('desired number is ', in_ft1(n))                    [8]
...    return
>>> nf_inv(4)
desired number is  0.041666666666666664
>>> nf_inv(5)
desired number is  0.008333333333333333
```

Fig. 4.7 A Python Interpreter sequence for the illustration of recursion

routine for (1/n!) follows from [4]. If n = 0 the function returns unity (0!). For all succeeding values of *n* the routine calls itself recursively from the preceding value of *n* and evaluates (1/n!) as (1/(n − 1!))/n.

The code sequence from [7] illustrates an instructive aspect of functions. Two functions can be defined separately in a Python Interpreter sequence. The latter can call the former within it as is done here. Of course being an illustrative example this routine has only one executable statement within it to compute—calling and printing out the output. But a practical situation can be more involved. A function can call any of the previously defined functions, within itself any number of times. This makes room for a well-structured programming approach. A main program can be composed of a number of smaller programs—if necessary repeatedly used. Each such smaller program can be coded separately and then called within the major program. Such 'calls within calls' can be done as many times as required.

The arguments used in a function definition can be of any type without restrictions as long as they are meaningfully used within the function. Example 4.4 is an illustration where a function is used as an argument in the definition of another function.

Example 4.4 Obtain the sum of the cube roots of all the integers from 3 to 8 (inclusive).

The function demb_1 in the demb module returns the cube root of a given number. The routine is reproduced in Fig. 4.8. The algorithm used in the function **root_1** for Example 4.2 is followed to extract the cube root here. The 0th element of the returned tuple is the cube root [1]. The function **aa**() [2] in Fig. 4.8 accepts three arguments—**bb** as a function, and **c** and **d** as two numbers. The function **bb** (**jj**) is evaluated for all numbers from **c** to **d** at intervals of unity and **bb[jj][0]**—the 0th element of the returned tuple—is summed up and returned. The function **aa**() is called in [3] with **demb.demb_1** as the function argument and 3 and 8 as the two numbers. 10.46875 is the desired sum. It is verified by direct computation in [3].

4.1.3 Nested Functions

One function can have other functions defined within it. If necessary such a daughter function can be returned for use outside. A few toy examples considered in the Python Interpreter sequence in Fig. 4.9 illustrate some possibilities. snn(x) in [1] is defined as a function which computes sin(x) using the series (Sullivan 2008)

$$\sin x = x - \frac{x^3}{3!} - \frac{x^5}{5!} + \frac{x^7}{7!} - \frac{x^9}{9!} + \dots \tag{4.2}$$

ntht(x, mm) has been defined as a function [2] inside **snn(x)**. It computes a term in the series of (4.2) recursively. $sx = x - \frac{x^3}{3!} - \frac{x^5}{5!}$ is computed as a first approximation of sin(x) [5]. Subsequent terms are computed and added to **sx**

```
def demb_1(a):
#get cube root of a through binary segmentation
# a should be a number > 1
#Termination on achieving root value with accuracy
   b, b3, n = 1, 1, 0
   while b3 < a:
     b +=1
     b3 = b**3
#Cube root of a lies between b & b-1
   b1, b2 = b-1, b
   while (b2 - b1 > 0.001) and (n < 20):
      n += 1
      bm = (b1 + b2)/2.0
      if a > bm**3:b1 = bm
      else: b2 = bm
   return ([bm, n, a])                                        [1]

>>> def aa(bb, c, d):                                         [2]
...     jj, smm = c, 0.0
...     while jj <= d:
...        smm += bb(jj)[0]
...        jj += 1
...     return smm
...
>>> aa(demb.demb_1, 3, 8)                                     [3]
10.46875
>>>
3**(1/3)+4**(1/3)+5**(1/3)+6**(1/3)+7**(1/3)+8**(1/3) [4]
10.469678344556833
>>>
```

Fig. 4.8 A Python Interpreter sequence illustrating a function forming an argument input for another function

repeatedly until the fractional addition from the next term is negligible [6]. sin(x) and the number of terms $((nn + 1)/2)$ is the number of terms used for the approximate computation) are returned in [7]. sin(0.2), sin(0.3), sin(0.4) are computed using **snn** [8]. The values obtained here can be compared with those computed directly using math.sin (x) [9]. As demanded by the context any number/type of functions can be defined within another function in this manner.

ffa() is defined in [10] to return function **ffb** [12]. Here **ffb** () has been defined within **ffa**() itself as another function to return sin(**xx**), **xx** being the argument. [13] has **ffa** assigned to **bb**. It is confirmed as a function in [14]. **bb**() in [15] is a function local to **ffa** [16] consistent with def in [10]. With 0.3 as argument **bb**() (assigned to **cc** and) is evaluated as sin(0.3) [17]. **faa** () in [19] returns a more involved function **fbb**. Function **fbb** [20] as defined here accepts two arguments—**xx** and **nn**. **bb** is sin(**x**) or cos(**x**) depending on whether **nn** = 1 or 2. For all other values of **nn**, **bb**[21] is tan(**x**). As an illustration all these cases have been used in

```
>>> def snn(x):                                          [1]
...    def ntht(x, mm):                                  [2]
...       if mm == 1: return x
...       else:return - ntht(x, mm-2)*x*x/(mm*(mm-1))
...    sx, nn = 0, 1                                      [3]
...    while True:
...       ntrm = ntht(x, nn)                              [4]
...       nn += 2
...       if nn < 6:sx += ntrm                            [5]
...       else:
...        if abs(ntrm/sx)< 1.0e-15:break                 [6]
...        continue
...    return sx, nn                                      [7]
...
>>> snn(0.2), snn(0.3), snn(0.4)                          [8]
((0.19866666666666669, 15), (0.2955, 15),
(0.38933333333333336, 17))
>>> from math import sin
>>> sin(0.2), sin(0.3),sin(0.4)                           [9]
(0.19866933079506122, 0.29552020666133955,
0.3894183423086505)
>>> def ffa():                                           [10]
...    def ffb(xx):
...       import math
...       return math.sin(xx)                            [11]
...    return ffb                                        [12]
...
>>> bb = ffa                                             [13]
>>> bb                                                   [14]
<function ffa at 0x7fcc404cfbf8>
>>> bb()                                                 [15]
<function ffa.<locals>.ffb at 0x7fcc404cfc80>
>>> cc = bb()                                            [16]
>>> cc(0.3)                                              [17]
0.29552020666133955
>>> ffa()(0.3)                                           [18]
0.29552020666133955
>>> def faa():                                           [19]
...    def fbb(xx, nn):                                  [20]
...       import math
...       if   nn == 1:bb = math.sin(xx)
...       elif nn == 2:bb = math.cos(xx)
...       else:bb = math.tan(xx)
...       return bb                                      [21]
...    return fbb                                        [22]
...
>>> cc = faa                                             [23]
>>> dd = cc()                                            [24]
>>> dd(0.3, 3), dd(0.3, 2), dd(0.3, 1)                   [25]
(0.30933624960962325, 0.955336489125606,
0.29552020666133955)
```

Fig. 4.9 A Python Interpreter sequence illustrating use of nested functions

[25] to return sin(0.3), cos(0.3), and tan(0.3) respectively. The example illustrates the possibility of defining functions, doing a set of operations with them, and returning a more comprehensive and encompassing function.

4.1.4 Nested Scope

Any object in its environment in Python (like a variable, a function and c.) can be read for its value using proper references. The value can be altered and reassigned in the same environment when possible. Declaring an object as 'global' or 'nonlocal' makes it possible to change the scope of access of the object for reading or reassigning in different ways (Rossum and Drake 2014). The possibilities are discussed here through small examples involving numbers.

a1 is a number with an assigned value (=3.1) in [1] in the Python Interpreter sequence in Fig. 4.10. Function **ff1** accepts **b1** as an argument [2] and returns **a1** $\times$ **b1**. With **b1** = 2, **ff1**(2) returns 6.2 in [3]. When **ff1** is called Python searches for **a1** within **ff1** first; if not available here the scope of search is widened to the immediate outer domain. In the specific case here **a1** is available there with an assigned value of 3.1. With this value of **a1**, **a1** $\times$ **b1** is computed and returned. If **a1** is not available there either, the search continues in the next outer domain and so on. If **a1** were not available after all such possibilities are exhausted, an error is returned and execution terminated. The process of search for availability of any object in this manner is automatic. It obviates the need for redefining or reassigning.

ff2 [4] has **a1** = 3.0 as an assignment and returns **a1** $\times$ **b2**. Hence the function **ff2**(3) in [5] returns 6.0. **a1** within **ff2**() is different from **a1** in [1]; the two have separate identities. **a1** within **ff2** () is automatically destroyed as one exits **ff2**(). **a1** outside **ff2**() remains intact (with a value of 3.1) as seen from [6]. In case a variable (or any object for that matter) defined within a function is to be available outside, it has to be declared as global as done in [8]—within the function definition of **ff3**() (See also Exercise 5.6). As many entities as desired can be declared as global in this manner. With an assigned value of 4 for **a2**, **ff3**(2) has been evaluated as 8.0 and returned in [9]. **a2** is accessed in the following line and its value confirmed as 4.0—the last value assigned to it. **a3** = 44 in [10]. **a3** has been declared as global in [12] within function **dem_f3**() [11]. The assigned value is 55. **a3** is accessed in [13] (outside the function definition of **dem_f3**()). Its value remains unaffected at 44. But after **dem_f3**() is called [14] **a3** becomes global. Its value is 55 assigned within the function call; [15] confirms this.

```
>>> a1 = 3.1          [1]
>>> def ff1 (b1):     [2]          >>> b1, b2, b3 = 10, 20, 30[16]
...    return a1*b1                >>> def dem_b0():
...                                ...     b3 = 31            [17]
>>> ff1(2)            [3]          ...     def dem_b1():       [18]
6.2                               ...         nonlocal b3     [19]
>>> def ff2(b2):      [4]          ...         b3 = 32         [20]
...    a1 = 3.0                    ...         global b2       [21]
...    return a1*b2                ...         b2 = 22         [22]
...                                ...         print('f1:','b1=',b1,'b2=',b2,'b3=',b3)
>>> ff2(2)            [5]          [23]
6.0                               ...         return
>>> a1                [6]          ...     print('f2:','b1=',b1,'b2=',b2,'b3 =',b3)
3.1                               [24]
>>> def ff3(b3):      [7]          ...     dem_b1()
...    global a2      [8]          [25]
...    a2 = 4.0                    ...     print('f3:','b1=',b1,'b2=',b2,'b3=',b3)
...    return a2*b3                [26]
...                                ...     return
>>> ff3(2)            [9]          ...
8.0                               >>> print('f4:','b1=',b1,',b2=',b2,',b3=',b3)
>>> a2                            [27]
4.0                               f4: b1=10,b2=20,b3=30
>>> a3 = 44           [10]         >>> dem_b0()                      [28]
>>> def dem_f3():     [11]         f2: b1=10,b2=20,b3=31             [29]
...    global a3      [12]         f1: b1=10,b2=22,b3=32             [30]
...    a3 = 55                     f3: b1=10,b2=22,b3=32             [31]
...    print(a3/10.0)              >>> print('f5:','b1=',b1,'b2=',b2,'b3=',b3)
...    return                      [32]
...                                f5: b1=10,b2=22,b3=30             [33]
>>> a3                [13]         >>>
44
>>> dem_f3()          [14]
5.5
>>> a3                [15]
55
```

Fig. 4.10 A Python Interpreter sequence illustrating the use of global and nonlocal declarations

The keyword nonlocal adds a different dimension to nested scopes especially when more than two levels are involved. The function **dem_b0**() [17] illustrates this. **b1**, **b2**, and **b3** are assigned values 10, 20, and 30 respectively in [16]. **b3** is assigned the value of 31 in [17]—within **dem_b0**(). Another function **dem_b1**() has been declared within **dem_b0**() itself. **b3** has been declared as nonlocal here. It refers to **b3** of the 'parent' scope (the immediately preceding level) and binds it. **b3** has been given a new value of 32 [20] within **dem_b1**(). This value will be valid within **dem_b1** () as well as within **dem_b0**() (until a new assignment for it if the same is made). **b2** has been declared global [21] and assigned the value 22 in [22]. **dem_b1**() is called within **dem_b0**() itself in [25]. The set of print statements in different domains and the sequences clarify the role/scope of the objects at different levels. The flags **f1**, **f2**, ... **f5** identify the print levels. Table 4.1 summarizes the scope of different variables and reasons for the changes in their values.

Table 4.1 The prints in the same sequence as in the execution sequence in Fig. 4.10: for brevity only the flags are retained in the column in the left

Identification of printed line	Details and reasons for the printed values for **b1**, **b2**, **b3**
f4 [27]	**b1**, **b2**, **b3** values as assigned in [16] before function **dem_b0**() is called in [28]
f2 [29]	When **dem_b0**() is called, after **b3** = 31, the only other executable statement within it [24] is executed; **b3** = 31—its assigned value in [17]; **b1** and **b2** remain unaltered
f1 [30]	Subsequent to [24] **dem_b1** () is called within **dem_b0**(). **b2** and **b3** have been declared as `nonlocal` and `global` respectively. They are assigned values of 22 and 32 [20] and [22]. These values are reflected here
f3 [20]	Since no new assignments have been made **b1**, **b2**, and **b** retain their values as above
f5 [32]	As in all previous cases **b1** remains unchanged at 10. **b2** being a global object the last assigned value (=22—though two levels inside) is retained. **b3** was `nonlocal`. The assigned value of 32 in [20] is valid only within **dem_b0**(). Once you come out **b3** used there is destroyed. **b3** (an altogether different object) as assigned in [16] has retained its value

4.2 Modules

A function defined and used in a Python Interpreter sequence is lost when you quit the Python session. It is desirable to save a function developed, tested, and debugged for later use. Such reuse can be direct or indirect for use within another function defined/used later. This is facilitated by the use of 'module' in Python. In general a module is a file containing a set of definitions (of functions) and statements. It is saved with the extension '.py'. A module can be generated in a text editor and saved wherever desired. Let us consider the routine of Example 4.2. The function defined for the pth root has been saved in a module in the current directory with the name—'**solun.py**'—as shown in Fig. 4.11. The only content of the module **solun.py** is the function **root_1**. The Python Interpreter sequence in Fig. 4.12 uses this module to run **root_1**. The module can be invoked with the command—' `import` **solun**'—as in [1]. With that the defined function is available for the interpreter for execution. The command **solun.root_1**() in [2] executes the function **root_1** from the module (and outputs the cube root of 10) as can be seen from the result in the following line. With the argument value for **a** as 100, the function is again called and executed in [3] with **p**, **nn**, **delta** and **i** retaining their default values. The cube root extraction with **i** = 8 in [4] takes 13 iterative cycles to achieve the same accuracy.

The function has been assigned to **rt** in [6]. With this the whole function can be accessed directly for execution using **rt**. The query—**solun.root_1**—in [5] returns the information—**<function root_1 at 0x7f4b60fcab70>**—that it is a function (starting) at memory location **0x7f4b60fcab70**. The query—**rt**—also returns an

```
def  root_1(a = 10, p = 3, delta = 0.001, nn = 20, i = 1):
     'pth root of a - thru\' successive bifurcation'
#delta is the acceptable accuracy
#p is the exponent - integer
#nn is the maximum number of iterations acceptable
#i is the initial interval used for searching
     b, bp, n = 1, 1, 0
     while bp < a:
       b += i
       bp = b**p
     b1, b2 = b - i, b
     while (b2 - b1 > delta) and (n < nn):
       n += 1
       bm = (b1 + b2)/2.0
       if a > bm**p:b1 = bm
       else: b2 = bm
     print('bm = ', bm, ', p = ', p, 'n = ', n, ', a = ', a)
     return
```

Fig. 4.11 A Python module with the function in Example 4.2 as its content

```
>>> import solun                                           [1]
>>> solun.root_1()                                         [2]
bm =   2.1552734375 , p =   3 n =   10 , a =   10
>>> solun.root_1(a=100)                                    [3]
bm =   4.6416015625 , p =   3 n =   10 , a =   100
>>> solun.root_1(a=100, i=8)                               [4]
bm =   4.6416015625 , p =   3 n =   13 , a =   100
>>> solun.root_1                                           [5]
<function root_1 at 0x7f4b60fcab70>
>>> rt = solun.root_1                                      [6]
>>> rt
<function root_1 at 0x7f4b60fcab70>
>>> rt(a = 200)                                            [7]
bm =   5.8486328125 , p =   3 n =   10 , a =   200
>>> rt(a=200, i=8)                                         [8]
bm =   5.8486328125 , p =   3 n =   13 , a =   200
>>> solun.root_1(a=200, i=25)                              [9]
bm =   5.848480224609375 , p =   3 n =   15 , a =   200
>>> er1, er2 = 5.8486328125**3 - 200,
5.848480224609375**3 - 200                                 [10]
>>> er1
0.0612920792773366
>>> er2
0.045633992110282406
```

Fig. 4.12 Python Interpreter sequence invoking the module in Fig. 4.8

identical information; a clarification that **rt** too refers to (points to) the same function. However the access to **root_1** here is easier than using '**solun.root_1**' (involves less key strokes effort?). The cube root of 200 has been obtained successively in [7], [8], and [9] using function **rt**. In [7] the search starts with the basic range [5, 6] since 200 lies between 5^3 (=125) and 6^3 (=216). The corresponding ranges for [8] and [9] are [1, 9] and [1, 25] respectively. In turn the number iteration cycles for completion of execution increases to n = 13 and n = 15 respectively. Incidentally the error value with [9] is less (at 0.04563) than in [7] or [8] (at 0.06129).

If the module to be imported is not in the current directory it can be imported by calling it from the source directory. '**alpha_1.py**' is a Python module in the directory '**demo_s**'. It is imported with the command—'from **demo_s** import **alpha_1**' in [1] in the Python sequence in Fig. 4.14. The module at the time of import is in Fig. 4.13a. **a** has been assigned a value 11.3; **b, c**, and **d** are assigned values in terms of **a**. **a** will be assigned the value (of 11.3) and **b, c**, and **d** computed conforming to their definitions in Fig. 4.13a at the time of import; these are done once for all. To access **a**, it has to be specified as '**alpha_1.a**'(a simple '**a**' implies the entity called '**a**' in the main running sequence (if at all it exists). The other quantities within **alpha_1** can be accessed similarly [2]. An additional line has been added to **alpha_1.py** and the file saved as shown in Fig. 4.13b. An attempt to access **dd** as '**alpha_1.dd**' fails [3] since the import was effected prior to the addition of the line involving **dd**.

The 'imp' module in Python facilitates a renewal. To use this, the imp module has to be imported [4]. A subsequent 'imp.reload(**alpha_1**)' loads **alpha_1** afresh [5]. In the present case **a** will be assigned the value 11.3 itself afresh. **b, c**, and **d** too will be computed afresh. **dd** will be assigned the value of d^3 conforming to its assignment in Fig. 4.13b. **alpha_1.dd** can be accessed and its value displayed as can be seen from [6]. In Fig. 4.13c **alpha_1.py** has been enhanced further. A function **avr_var**() to compute the average value and the variance of the five quantities—**a, b, c, d**, and **dd**—and display them has been added. As earlier an attempt to use the function [7] fails because the already imported version of the module is not aware of this addition. Once again **alpha_1.py** has to be refreshed through the command 'imp.reload(**alpha_1**)' as in [8]. Subsequent access of **alpha_1.avr_var**() is successful as can be seen from [9].

The function **avr_var_1**() added in Fig. 4.13d uses the values assigned to **a, b, c, d**, and **dd** at the time of reload to compute the average value and variance. Here the same function as the earlier one is repeated with the five inputs **a1, a2, a3**, a4, and **a5**. **alpha_1** is again reloaded [10]. The numerical values for **a, b, c, d**, and **dd** obtained above are assigned to the set and avr and var computed again separately. The values here [11] are identical to those following [9] (Fig. 4.14).

The executable statements in a module are useful to initialize the variable values/objects prior to their use in functions defined subsequently in the same module as was done in the trivial/illustrative example here.

An alternative to 'reload' operation explained above is to quit the running Python sequence and start another one afresh. The new 'import' imports the

(a)

```
a = 11.3
b = a/3
c = b*b
d = c*2
```

(b)

```
a = 11.3
b = a/3
c = b*b
d = c*2
dd = d**3
```

(c)

```
a = 11.3
b = a/3
c = b*b
d = c*2
dd = d**3

def avr_var():
    'Alternate average & varaince of 5 numbers'
    av = (a + b + c + d + dd)/5
    var = (a-av)**2 + (b-av)**2 +(c-av)**2 +(d-av)**2
+(dd-av)**2
    var = var/5
    print ('average = ', av, ': variance = ', var)
    return
```

(d)

```
a = 11.3
b = a/3
c = b*b
d = c*2
dd = d**3

def avr_var():
    'Alternate average & varaince of 5 numbers'
    av = (a + b + c + d + dd)/5
    var = (a-av)**2 + (b-av)**2 +(c-av)**2 +(d-av)**2
+(dd-av)**2
    var = var/5
    print ('average = ', av, ': variance = ', var)
    return

def avr_var_1(a1, a2, a3, a4, a5):
    'Average & varaince of 5 numbers'
    av1 = (a1 + a2 + a3 + a4 + a5)/5
    var1 = (a1-av1)**2 + (a2-av1)**2 +(a3-av1)**2 +(a4-
av1)**2 +(a5-av1)**2
    var1 = var1/5
    print ('average = ', av1, ': variance = ', var1)
    return
```

Fig. 4.13 Four successive stages in the development of the module alpha_1.py

```
>>> from demo_s import alpha_1                              [1]
>>> alpha_1.a, alpha_1.b, alpha_1.c, alpha_1.d             [2]
(11.3, 3.766666666666667, 14.18777777777778,
28.37555555555556)
>>> alpha_1.dd                                             [3]
Traceback (most recent call last):
  File "<stdin>", line 1, in <module>
AttributeError: 'module' object has no attribute 'dd'
>>> import imp                                             [4]
>>> imp.reload(alpha_1)                                    [5]
<module 'demo_s.alpha_1' from
'/home/trp/demo_s/alpha_1.py'>
>>> alpha_1.dd                                             [6]
22847.20716169
>>> alpha_1.avr_var():                                     [7]
  File "<stdin>", line 1
    alpha_1.avr_var():
                    ^
SyntaxError: invalid syntax
>>> imp.reload(alpha_1)                                    [8]
<module 'demo_s.alpha_1' from
'/home/trp/demo_s/alpha_1.py'>
>>> alpha_1.avr_var()                                      [9]
average =  4580.967432338 : variance =  83413942.07028815
>>> imp.reload(alpha_1)                                    [10]
<module 'demo_s.alpha_1' from
'/home/trp/demo_s/alpha_1.py'>
>>> alpha_1.avr_var_1(11.3, 3.766666666666667,
14.18777777777778, 28.37555555555556, 22847.20716169) [11]
average =  4580.967432338 : variance =  83413942.07028815
>>>
```

Fig. 4.14 Python Interpreter sequence testing and developing successive stages of the module alpha_1.py

updated version of **alpha_1.py**. This process is attractive only if one, two, or three modules have been imported for the session. In the case of long running sequences with a number of imported modules present, a reload is preferable.

Example 4.5 The infinite series for exp(x) (Sullivan 2008) is:

$$\exp(x) = \sum_{n=0}^{\infty} \frac{x^n}{n!}$$

Prepare a Python routine to evaluate exp(x). Evaluate exp(0.5) and exp(j0.5). Use the infinite series expansions for sin(x) and cos(x) and develop the routines for them. Evaluate sin(0.5) and cos(0.5) to confirm the value of exp(0.5j).

(a)

```
def  xprx(x):
 'compute exp(x)'
 y, z, i = 1.0, 1.0, 1
 while True:
   z *= x/i
   i += 1
   if abs(z)< 1.0e-10: break
   else: y += z
 return y
```

(b)

```
def  xcsx(x):
 'compute cos(x)'
 y, z, i = 1, 1, 1
 while True:
   z *= -x*x/(i*(i+1))
   i += 2
   if abs(z)< 1.0e-10: break
   else: y += z
 return y
```

(c)

```
def  xsnx(x):
  'compute sin(x)'
  y, z, i = x, x, 2
  while True:
    z *= -x*x/(i*(i+1))
    i += 2
    if abs(z)< 1.0e-10: break
    else: y += z
  return y
```

(d)

```
def  xprx(x):
  'compute exp(x)'
  y, z, i = 1.0, 1.0, 1
  while True:
    z *= x/i
    i += 1
    if abs(z)< 1.0e-10: break
    else: y += z
  return y

def  xsnx(x):
  'compute sin(x)'
  y, z, i = x, x, 2
  while True:
    z *= -x*x/(i*(i+1))
    i += 2
    if abs(z)< 1.0e-10: break
    else: y += z
  return y

def  xcsx(x):
  'compute cos(x)'
  y, z, i = 1, 1, 1
  while True:
    z *= -x*x/(i*(i+1))
    i += 2
    if abs(z)< 1.0e-10: break
    else: y += z
  return y
```

Fig. 4.15 Routines for Example 4.5 **a** Routine for exp(x) **b** Routine for cos(x) **c** Routine for sin (x) **d** Module **trgf** with the routines for exp(x), cos(x), and sin(x)

The nth term in the series for exp(x) can be expressed in terms of the $(n-1)$th term as

$$\frac{x^n}{n!} = \frac{x^{n-1}}{(n-1)!} \frac{x}{n}.$$

Hence the nth term can be evaluated by multiplying the $(n-1)$th by x/n. With this the code for exp(x) is given in Fig. 4.15a. The summation is continued until the value of the new term is less than 10^{-10}.

The series for cos x is

$$\cos x = \sum_{n=0}^{\infty} (-1)^n \frac{x^{2n}}{(2n)!}$$

It has only the terms involving even powers of x—with the alternate terms being negative. Each term is evaluated from the previous one by multiplying it by $-x^2/i(i+1)$. Here again the summation is continued until the contribution from the new term becomes less than 10^{-10}. The code for the function is in Fig. 4.15b. The infinite series expansion for sin x is

$$\sin x = \sum_{n=0}^{\infty} (-1)^n \frac{x^{2n+1}}{(2n+1)!}$$

The code for sin x is done on the same lines as that for cos x; it is in Fig. 4.15c. The functions xprx(),xcsx(), and xsnx() are for exp(x), cos(x), and sin (x) respectively. They are all in the module **trgf.py** (trigonometric functions).

The module has been imported into the Python Interpreter session reproduced in Fig. 4.16 in [1]. exp(0.5j), cos(0.5), and sin(0.5), have been evaluated using the respective functions—**trgf.xprx**, **trgf.xcsx**, and **trgf.xsnx** in [2], [4], and [6] respectively. One can see that exp(0.5j) [3] is equal to cos(0.5) [5] + j sin(0.5) [7]. exp(0.5) has been evaluated in [8]. **trgf.xprx** has again been used to evaluate e [9] as exp(1).

```
>>> from demo_s import trgf                    [1]
>>> aa = trgf.xprx(0+0.5j)                      [2]
>>> aa                                          [3]
(0.8775825618898637+0.4794255386164159j)
>>> bb = trgf.xcsx(0.5)                         [4]
>>> bb                                          [5]
0.8775825618898637
>>> cc = trgf.xsnx(0.5)                         [6]
>>> cc                                          [7]
0.4794255386164159
>>> trgf.xprx(0.5)                              [8]
1.6487212706873655
>>> trgf.xprx(1)                                [9]
2.7182818284467594
>>>
```

Fig. 4.16 Python Interpreter sequence for Example 4.5

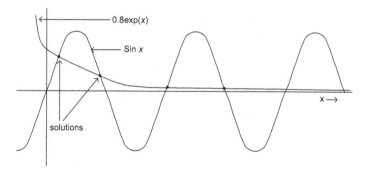

Fig. 4.17 Sketches of functions 0.8exp(−x) and sin x showing the solutions for Example 4.6

Example 4. 6 Through a Python program get a solution of $0.8e^{-x} - \sin x = 0$ with the constraint $0.1 < x < \pi/2$.

The functions 0.8exp(−x) and sin x are shown sketched in Fig. 4.17. All the solutions are seen to be for positive values of x; All of them are in the intervals $\{2n\pi, (2n + 1)\pi\}$ for all integral values of n from zero onwards. The specified interval has only one solution in it.

The program is in the function **solna()** in the module **solun.py** shown in Fig. 4.18. The algorithm used is similar to that used in **Example** 4.2 for root extraction through successive bifurcation. Starting with **c** = 0.1, **y(x)** = 0.8exp(−x) —sin x is evaluated at intervals of 0.1 until the value of y becomes negative. This freezes the search interval of 0.1—from **c1** to **c2**—in [4]. The interval is successively bifurcated and the search narrowed down until the desired accuracy is achieved. The functions for exp(x) and sin(x) are in the module **trgf** in the directory **demo_s**. Hence the module **trgf** is imported into the present module [1] from the source directory. Any module can be imported into another module and items defined therein used in this manner. The functions **trgf.xprx** and **trgf.xsnx** have been assigned to **y1** and **y2** in [2]. Through the single line function definition using lambda y is defined as 0.8exp(x)—sin(x) in [3]. The iteration sequence following is similar to that in Fig. 4.3. The flowchart in Fig. 3.14 is applicable here; the condition (0.8exp(x)—sin(x) < 0) is to be used in place of (a > b³). The module has a simple additional function **cff()** defined within it. It calls the function **solna()**, assigns its output (i.e., the value of x returned in [6]) and prints it out. Since the function **solna** is within the same module, such calling is possible. Any function in a module can call any other function and defined entities within the same module in this manner (**cff()** has been introduced here merely to illustrate this).

The Python sequence for the example is in Fig. 4.18. The interpreter execution sequence is as follows:

- The function to solve 0.8 exp(x)—sin(x) = 0 is **solna()**. It is in module **slnss** which is in the directory **demo_s. slnss** is imported specifying the path.
- **solna()** is executed.

```
from demo_s import trgf                                    [1]
def solna(a = 0.8, d = 0.0001):
    'solve cexp(-x) - sin(x) = 0 for 0< x < 1.6'
    y1, y2  = trgf.xprx, trgf.xsnx                         [2]
    y = lambda x: a*y1(-x) - y2(x)                         [3]
    c, e, cm, n = 0.1, 0.1, 0, 0
    while True:
        if y(c) < 0: break
        else: c += e
    c2, c1 = c, c - e                                      [4]
    while c2 - c1 > d and n < 20:
        n += 1
        cm = (c1 + c2)/2.0
        if y(cm) > 0.0: c1 = cm
        else: c2 = cm
    print('x = ', cm, ', a = ', a, 'n = ', n)              [5]
    return cm                                              [6]

def  cff():
    'print cos(x) for x such that cexp(x) - sin(x) = 0
for 0< x < 1.6'                                            [7]
    aa = solna()
    print('aa = ', aa)
    return
```

Fig. 4.18 Module **slnss.py** for Example 4.6

- Referring to in Fig. 4.18, in the process of execution the values of **x**, **a**, and **n** are 'printed out'.
- The value of x (as **cm**) is output as completion of execution of **slns.solna**()— conforming to step 2 above.
- The function **slnss.cff**() is called.
- **slnss.cff**() in turn calls and executes **slnss.solna**(). As part of execution of **slnss.solna**(), **x**, **a**, and **n** are 'printed out'.
- The value of x (as **cm**) is output once again as completion of execution of **slns.solna**().

```
>>> from demo_s import   slnss                        [1]
>>> slnss.solna()                                     [2]
x =  0.50419921875 , a =  0.8 n =  10                 [3]
0.50419921875                                         [4]
>>> slnss.cff()                                       [5]
x =  0.50419921875 , a =  0.8 n =  10                 [6]
aa =  0.50419921875                                   [7]
>>>
```

Fig. 4.19 Python Interpreter sequence for Example 4.6

The default values for **a** and **d** have been used in this example. **a** exp(*x*)—sin (*x*) can be solved in a similar manner for any other value of the constant **a**. Desired accuracy can be achieved by suitably redefining the value of **d** (Fig. 4.19)

```
>>> import math
>>> a1, a2 = math.exp(0.5),
math.exp(-0.5)              [1]
>>> a1, a2                  [2]
(1.6487212707001282,
0.6065306597126334)
>>> c1, c2, c3, c4 =
math.exp(1e-5)-1, math.exp(-
1e-5)-1, math.expm1(1e-5),
math.expm1(-1e-5)          [3]
>>> c1, c2, c3, c4         [4]
(1.0000050000069649e-05,
9.999950000172397e-06,
1.0000050000166668e-05, -
9.999950000166666e-06)
>>> c1*c2                  [5]
-9.999999999992047e-11
>>> c3*c4                  [6]
-1.0000000000083335e-10
>>> d1, d2, d3 =
math.log(11),
math.log(11,10),
math.log(10)              [7]
>>> d1, d2, d3            [8]
(2.397852727983707,
1.041392685158225,
2.302585092994046)
>>> math.log10(11) #compare
with math.log(11,10)
obtained earlier
1.041392685158225
>>> d2*d3                 [9]
2.397852727983707
>>> e1, e2, e3 =
math.log(1e-6),
math.log1p(1e-
6),1+math.log(1e-6)       [10]
```

```
>>> e1, e2, e3            [11]
(-13.815510557964274,
9.999995000003334e-07, -
12.815510557964274)
>>> f1, f2, f3 =
math.log2(1e3),
math.log2(1e6),
math.log2(1e9)            [12]
>>> f1, f2, f3
(9.965784284662087,
19.931568569324174,
29.897352853986263)
>>> n1, n2, n3 = 1000,
1000000, 1000000000
>>> g1, g2, g3 =
n1.bit_length(),
n2.bit_length(),
n3.bit_length()           [13]
>>> g1, g2, g3
(10, 20, 30)
>>> h1, h2, h3, h4, h5,
h6=math.pow(2,3),math.pow(2,
-3),math.pow(-
2,3),math.pow(-2,-3),2**3,(-
2)**3
>>> h1, h2, h3, h4, h5, h6
                          [14]
(8.0, 0.125, -8.0, -0.125,
8, -8)
>>> j1, j2 = math.sqrt(2),
math.sqrt(math.pow(math.sqrt
(2),2))                   [15]
>>> j1, j2
(1.4142135623730951,
1.4142135623730951)
>>> a1, a2 = math.pi, math.e
                          [16]
>>> a1, a2
(3.141592653589793,
2.718281828459045)
>>>
```

Fig. 4.20 Python Interpreter sequence to illustrate the access details of exponential and related functions in the math module

4.2.1 *Built-in Modules*

Python has a number of built-in functions. They are always available for use. Use of some of them in a limited form has been explained earlier (more of this later). A number of built-in modules are also available—like `math` and `random`. They can be imported and the functions within used by programmers as was done with the defined modules here.

4.2.2 *Math Module*

The `math module` in Python has a set of commonly encountered mathematical functions (In fact these are all in Standard C). The functions here are for real numbers. The arguments of these functions can also be other functions which return numbers as outputs. Values of the commonly encountered constants—π and e—are available and are accessed as `math.pi` and `math.e` (See [16] in Fig. 4.20).

The functions in the `math module` have been organized and their scope given in Tables 4.2, 4.3, 4.4, 4.5. Their uses are illustrated through the Python Interpreter sequences in Figs. 4.20, 4.21, 4.22, 4.23.

Table 4.2 Exponential and related functions: illustrations for use are in the Python Interpreter sequence in Fig. 4.20

Access	Scope	Reference
`math.exp (a)`	Returns $\exp(a)$	[1], [2]
`math.expm1 (a)`	Returns $(\exp(a) - 1)$:preferable when a is close to zero. Results are compared in [3], [4], and [5]	[3], [4], [5], [6]
`math.log (a)`	Returns the natural log of a	[7]
`math.log1p (a)`	Returns the natural log of $(1 + a)$: useful when a is close to 0. [10] and [11] compare results with use of log a.	[10],[11]
`math.log2 (a)`	Returns $\log_2 a$: $\lceil log_2 a \rceil$ is the number of bits in a in binary form as can be seen from [12] and [13]	[12], [13]
`math.log10 (a)`	Returns $\log_{10} a$:	[7]
`math.log (a,b)`	Returns $\log_a b$: $\log_e 11 = \log_{10} 11 \ \log_e 10$—verified by [9]	[7], [8], [9]
`math.sqrt (a)`	Returns $\sqrt{a}$:	[15]
`math.pow (a,b)`	Returns a^b: [15] verifies $\sqrt{\sqrt{2}^2} = 2$	[14], [15]

'Reference' denotes the relevant lines in it

Table 4.3 Trigonometric and related functions: illustrations for use are in the Python Interpreter sequence in Fig. 4.21

Access	Scope—all argument values are in radians	Reference
math.cos (a)	Returns cos a	[1],[2]
math.sin (a)	Returns sin a	[3], [4]
math.tan (a)	Returns tan a	[5],[6], [7],[8]
math. hypot(a, b)	Returns the value of the hypotenuse of right-angled triangle with a and b as sides	[9], [10]
math. degrees (a)	Returns value of a in degrees	[11], [12]
math. radians (a)	Returns value of a in radians	[13], [14]
math.acos (a)	Returns value of acos (a) in radians	[15], [16]
math.asin (a)	Returns value of asin (a) in radians	
math.atan (a)	Returns value of atan(a) in radians	
math. atan2 (a/b)	Returns value of atan(a) in radians in the range -π to +π—the quadrant being decided by the signs of a (sin) and b(cos)	

'Reference' denotes the relevant lines in it

Table 4.4 Hyperbolic functions: illustrations for use are in the Python Interpreter sequence in Fig. 4.22

Access	Scope	Reference
math.cosh (a)	Returns cosh a	[1],[2]
math.sinh (a)	Returns sinh a	[5], [6]
math.tanh (a)	Returns tanh a—[11] and [12] verify tanh(a) = sinh (a)/cosh(a)	[9],[10], [11], [12]
math.acosh (a)	Returns value of acosh (a)	[3], [4]
math.asinh (a)	Returns value of asinh (a)	[7],[8]
math.atanh (a)	Returns value of atanh(a)	[14],[15]

'Reference' denotes the relevant lines in it

Table 4.5 Additional functions in math: illustrations for use are in the Python Interpreter sequence in Fig. 4.23

Access	Scope	Reference
math.ceil(a)	Returns the ceiling—the smallest integer $\geq a$	[1]
math.floor(a)	Returns the floor—largest integer $\leq a$	[2]
math.copysign (x,y)	Returns a number having the sign of y and absolute value of x	[3]
math.fabs(a)	Returns the absolute value of (a)	[4]
math.factorial (a)	Returns $a!$	[5]
math.fmod(x, y)	Returns x mod (y)—use these with floating point numbers and $x\%y$ with integers	[6]
math.frexp (a)	Returns a as a mantissa-exponent (m, e) pair such that $a = m*(2**e)$	[7]
math.ldexp (m, e)	Returns $m*(2**e)$	[8]
math.fsum(a)	Returns the sum of elements in **a** (a tuple/list or similar sequence of numbers). Sum(a) is discussed later (in Chapter 5).	[9], [10], [11]
math.modf(a)	Returns (m, e) pair representing a in the floating point format	[12]
Math.trunc(a)	Truncates a as an integer and returns the same	[13]

'Reference' denotes the relevant lines in it

4.3 Exercises

1. As a generalization of the method used in Example 4.6, write a generic Python program to solve for x such that $f(x) = 0$.
2. Use the trifurcation method used with Example 3.10 to solve $0.8e^{-x} - \sin x = 0$.
3. Write a generic program to solve for x such that $f(x) = 0$ using the trifurcation method.
4. Solve the following for x, using the bifurcation and the trifurcation methods:

   a. In the interval $\{0, \pi/2\}$ such that $2\sin 0.9x = \tan x$.
   b. In the interval $\{0, \pi\}$ such that $1 + \cos x = x^3$.
   c. In the interval $\{0, -2\}$ such that $x^2 + 0.5\, x^2 \sin x - 1 = 0$

5. Use the routine to compute $a^{-1/p}$ and write a program to compute $\sum_{i=1}^{b} a^{-1/i}$. Evaluate the sum for a = 2 and b = 10.
6. A number of infinite series, infinite products, and infinite fractions are available for the evaluation of π. A few are reproduced here (Zwillinger 2003):

```
>>> import math
>>> b1, b2, b3, b4, b5, b6 =
math.cos(0.3),math.cos(30),m
ath.cos(-0.3),math.cos(-
30),math.cos(math.fmod(30,
2*a1)),math.cos(math.fmod(-
30,2*a1))                    [1]
>>> b1, b2, b3, b4, b5, b6
                            [2]
(0.955336489125606,
0.15425144988758405,
0.955336489125606,
0.15425144988758405,
0.15425144988758502,
0.15425144988758502)
>>> c1, c2, c3, c4, c5, c6 =
math.sin(0.3),
math.sin(30),math.sin(-
0.3),math.sin(-30),
math.sin(math.fmod(30,
2*a1)),math.sin(math.fmod(-
30,2*a1))                    [3]
>>> c1, c2, c3, c4, c5, c6
                            [4]
(0.29552020666133955, -
0.9880316240928618, -
0.29552020666133955,
0.9880316240928618, -
0.9880316240928616,
0.9880316240928616)
>>> d1, d2, d3, d4, d5, d6 =
math.tan(0.3),
math.tan(30),math.tan(-
0.3),math.tan(-30),
math.tan(math.fmod(30,
2*a1)),math.tan(math.fmod(-
30,2*a1))                    [5]
>>> d1, d2, d3, d4, d5, d6
                            [6]
(0.30933624960962325, -
6.405331196646276, -
0.30933624960962325,
6.405331196646276, -
6.405331196646235,
6.405331196646235)
>>> e1, e2, e3, e4, e5, e6 =
c1/b1, c2/b2, c3/b3, c4/b4,
c5/b5, c6/b6                 [7]
>>> e1, e2, e3, e4, e5, e6
                            [8]
```

```
(0.3093362496096232, -
6.4053311966462765, -
0.3093362496096232,
6.4053311966462765, -
6.405331196646235,
6.405331196646235)
>>> f1, f2, f3, f4 =
math.hypot(3,4),
math.hypot(3,-4),
math.hypot(12,5),
math.hypot(12,-5)           [9]
>>> f1, f2, f3, f4          [10]
(5.0, 5.0, 13.0, 13.0)
>>> g1, g2, g3, g4 =
math.degrees(0.3),
math.degrees(30),math.degre
es(-0.3),math.degrees(-30)
                            [11]
>>> g1, g2, g3, g4          [12]
(17.188733853924695,
1718.8733853924696, -
17.188733853924695, -
1718.8733853924696)
>>> h1, h2, h3, h4 =
math.radians(g1),math.radia
ns(g2),math.radians(g3),mat
h.radians(g4)               [13]
>>> h1, h2, h3, h4          [14]
(0.3, 30.0, -0.3, -30.0)
>>> j1, j2, j3, j4, j5, j6
= math.acos(b1),
math.acos(b3),
math.asin(c1),
math.asin(c3),
math.atan(d1),
math.atan(d3)               [15]
>>> j1, j2, j3, j4, j5, j6
                            [16]
(0.30000000000000016,
0.30000000000000016, 0.3, -
0.3, 0.3, -0.3)
>>> k1, k2, k3, k4 =
math.atan2(c1, b1),
math.atan2(c3, b3),
math.atan2(c1, -
b1),math.atan2(-c3, b3)[17]
>>> k1, k2, k3, k4          [18]
(0.3, -0.3,
2.8415926535897933, 0.3)
>>>
```

Fig. 4.21 Python Interpreter sequence to illustrate the access details of trigonometric and related functions in the math module

```
>>> l1, l2, l3, l4, l5 = 0,        >>> q1, q2, q3, q4, q5 =
1, 2, -1, -2                        math.tanh(l1),
>>> m1, m2, m3, m4, m5 =           math.tanh(l2),
math.cosh(l1), math.cosh(l2),      math.tanh(l3),
math.cosh(l3), math.cosh(l4),      math.tanh(l4),
math.cosh(l5)              [1]      math.tanh(l5)              [9]
>>> m1, m2, m3, m4, m5    [2]      >>> q1, q2, q3, q4, q5 [10]
(1.0, 1.5430806348152437,          (0.0, 0.7615941559557649,
3.7621956910836314,                0.9640275800758169, -
1.5430806348152437,                0.7615941559557649, -
3.7621956910836314)                0.9640275800758169)
>>> n1, n2, n3, n4, n5 =           >>> r1, r2, r3, r4        [11]
math.acosh(m1),math.acosh(m2)      (1.1752011936438014,
,math.acosh(m3),math.acosh(m4      1.8134302039235095, -
),math.acosh(m5)          [3]      1.1752011936438014, -
>>> n1, n2, n3, n4, n5    [4]      1.8134302039235095)
(0.0, 1.0, 2.0, 1.0, 2.0)          >>> r1, r2, r3, r4, r5 =
>>> o1, o2, o3, o4, o5 =           o1/m1, o2/m2, o3/m3, o4/m4,
math.sinh(l1), math.sinh(l2),      o5/m5                     [12]
math.sinh(l3), math.sinh(l4),      >>> r1, r2, r3, r4, r5 [13]
math.sinh(l5)              [5]      (0.0, 0.7615941559557649,
>>> o1, o2, o3, o4, o5    [6]      0.964027580075817, -
(0.0, 1.1752011936438014,          0.7615941559557649, -
3.626860407847019, -               0.964027580075817)
1.1752011936438014, -              >>> s1, s2, s3, s4, s5 =
3.626860407847019)                 math.atanh(q1),math.atanh(q
>>> p1, p2, p3, p4, p5 =           2),math.atanh(q3),math.atan
math.asinh(o1),math.asinh(o2)      h(q4),math.atanh(q5)      [14]
,math.asinh(o3),math.asinh(o4      >>> s1, s2, s3, s4, s5[15]
),math.asinh(o5) [7]               (0.0, 0.9999999999999999,
>>> p1, p2, p3, p4, p5 [8]         2.0000000000000004, -
(0.0, 1.0, 2.0, -1.0, -2.0)        0.9999999999999999, -
                                   2.0000000000000004)
                                   >>>
```

Fig. 4.22 Python Interpreter sequence to illustrate the access details of hyperbolic functions in the math module

Leibniz Series:

$$\frac{\pi}{8} = \frac{1}{1 \times 3} + \frac{1}{5 \times 7} + \frac{1}{9 \times 11} + ..$$

arctan(1.0):

$$\pi = \sum_{n=0}^{\infty} \frac{8}{16 \times n^2 + 16 \times n + 3}$$

```
>>> import math
>>> math.ceil(4.2), math.ceil(-4.2), math.ceil(0.42e1)   [1]
(5, -4, 5)
>>> math.floor(4.2),math.floor(-4.2),math.floor(0.42e1)  [2]
(4, -5, 4)
>>> math.copysign(4.2, -1), math.copysign(4.2,+0.0),
math.copysign(0.42e1, 1)                                 [3]
(-4.2, 4.2, 4.2)
>>> math.fabs(4.2), math.fabs(-4.2),math.fabs(-0.42e1)   [4]
(4.2, 4.2, 4.2)
>>> math.factorial(3), math.factorial(7)                 [5]
(6, 5040)
>>> math.fmod(47, 5), math.fmod(47,7), math.fmod(-47,7)  [6]
(2.0, 5.0, -5.0)
>>> math.frexp(2.0), math.frexp(-2.0), math.frexp(2.625),
math.frexp(0.2)                                          [7]
((0.5, 2), (-0.5, 2), (0.65625, 2), (0.8, -2))
>>> math.ldexp(0.5,2),math.ldexp(-
0.5,2),math.ldexp(0.65625,2),math.ldexp(0.8,-2)          [8]
(2.0, -2.0, 2.625, 0.2)
>>> aa = (2.5, -1.24, 2.346, 4.321)
>>> sum(aa), math.fsum(aa)                               [9]
7.927, 7.927
>>> bb = [0.1, 0.01, 0.11, 0.111]
>>> sum(bb), math.fsum(bb)                               [10]
(0.331, 0.331)
>>> bb = (0.1, 0.1, 0.1, -0.3)
>>> sum(bb), math.fsum(bb)                               [11]
(5.551115123125783e-17, 2.7755575615628914e-17)
>>> math.modf(2.5), math.modf(-1.24), math.modf(-0.42e-1)
                                                         [12]
```

Fig. 4.23 Python Interpreter sequence to illustrate the access details of functions in the math module detailed in Table 4.5

Nilakantha:

$$\pi = 3 + \frac{1}{2 \times 3 \times 4} + \frac{1}{4 \times 5 \times 6} + \frac{1}{6 \times 7 \times 8} + \cdots$$

Spigot:

$$\pi = \sum_{n=0}^{\infty} \frac{1}{16^n} \times \left(\frac{4}{8n+1} - \frac{2}{8n+4} - \frac{1}{8n+5} - \frac{1}{8n+6} \right)$$

Prepare programs to evaluate the value of π using each of the above series and test each.

7. Parity Check: Parity Checking is commonly carried out in Data Communication and Storage and Retrieval Systems (Padmanabhan 2007). With a binary stream odd parity check returns a one bit if the number of 1-bits in the stream is odd; else it returns a zero bit. Write a program to do parity checking (Hint: Starting with $p = 0$ with n as the given integer

while n:
$p^{\wedge} = n \& 1$
   $n \gg 1$
Adapt the above suite).

References

Padmanabhan TR (2007) Introduction to microcontrollers and their applications. Alpha science international ltd, Oxford

Rossum Gv, Drake FL Jr (2014) The Python library reference. Python software foundation

Sullivan M (2008) Algebra & trigonometry, 8th edn. Pearson Prentice hall, New Jersey

Zwillinger D (ed) (2003) Standard mathematical tables and formulae. Chapman & Hall/CRC, New York

Chapter 5
Sequences and Operations with Sequences

The possibility of representing sequences in different ways is one of the unique features of Python. The functions and methods available to process them add an additional dimension to their use. Sequences and operations (Rossum and Drake 2014) with them is the focus of this chapter.

5.1 String

A '**string**' is a collection of characters. Usually a word, a phrase, a sentence, or a paragraph is represented as a **string**. The full set of characters forming the **string** appears within single quotes, double quotes or triple quotes. In other words any set of characters put within quotes–single, double, or triple–is interpreted as a **string** in the Python environment. The Python Interpreter sequence in Fig. 5.1 brings out the basic features of strings and '**tuple**'s (discussed in the next section). When put within single or double quotes—[1] and [2]—the whole string has to be within a single line. When it extends beyond one line the string has to be necessarily within triple quotes [4]. Single line strings too can appear within triple quotes [3]. Incidentally the lines in **s4** [4] have been aligned by inserting spaces (white characters) wherever necessary. Each character in a string has an associated address—starting with zero. **s1**[0:7] in [5] signifies the set of the first seven characters of **s1**–0 to 7 (exclusive). This character set is assigned to **b1**. Similar character sets have been assigned to **b2**, **b3**, and **b4**. Each of these is a string on its own right. [7] and [8] return the information that **s1** is a string and **b1** (on its own right) is a string. A string is an immutable sequence–in the sense that characters in it cannot be altered or deleted; nor can one insert a character into an existing string. Various **string** related operations are discussed later.

© Springer Nature Singapore Pte Ltd. 2016
T.R. Padmanabhan, *Programming with Python*,
DOI 10.1007/978-981-10-3277-6_5

```
>>> s1 = 'Twinkle twinkle little star'                          [1]
>>> s2 = "Twinkle twinkle little star"                          [2]
>>> s3 = '''Twinkle twinkle little star'''                      [3]
>>> s4 = '''Twinkle twinkle little star                         [4]
...         How I wonder what you are!
...         Up above the world so high
...         Like a diamond in the sky'''
>>> b1, b2, b3, b4 = s1[0:7],s2[15:22], s3[23:27],
s4[28:62]                                                        [5]
>>> b1, b2, b3, b4                                               [6]
('Twinkle', ' little', 'star', '         How I wonder what
you are!')
>>> type(s1)                                                    [7]
<class 'str'>
>>> type(b4)                                                    [8]
<class 'str'>
>>> c = b1, b2, b3, b4                                          [9]
>>> type(c)                                                     [10]
<class 'tuple'>
>>> c[0][1:5]                                                   [11]
'wink'
>>> type(c[0][1:5])                                            [12]
<class 'str'>
>>> d = c,(s1, s4)                                             [13]
>>> type(d)                                                    [14]
<class 'tuple'>
>>> print(d[1][1])                                            [15]
Twinkle twinkle little star
        How I wonder what you are!
        Up above the world so high
        Like a diamond in the sky
>>> e = b1, b2, b3                                             [16]
>>> f = e,32                                                   [17]
>>> f
(('Twinkle', ' little', 'star'), 32)
>>> g = f,3.2e1                                                [18]
>>> g                                                          [19]
((('Twinkle', ' little', 'star'), 32), 32.0)
>>> g[0][1]                                                    [20]
32
>>> g[1]                                                       [21]
32.0
>>> g[0][0][1:3]                                               [22]
(' little', 'star')
>>> g[0][0][1][1:4]                                            [23]
'lit'
>>> x = 3.2                                                    [24]
>>> bb = x*x,                                                  [25]
>>> bb                                                         [26]
(10.240000000000002,)
>>> type(bb)                                                   [27]
<class 'tuple'>
>>> bb*2                                                       [28]
(10.240000000000002, 10.240000000000002)
>>> bb[0]*2                                                   [29]
20.480000000000004
```

Fig. 5.1 Python Interpreter sequence to explain **string** and **tuple**

5.2 Tuple

A 'tuple' is an immutable sequence. It is essentially a set of comma separated elements. **c** in [9] is such a **tuple**—as can be seen from [10]. Each element in this tuple is a string. The tuple comprising of **b1, b2, b3,** and **b4** can be specified as **b1, b2, b3, b4** or (**b1, b2, b3, b4**). When Python outputs a tuple it is within parentheses. As can be seen from [8] the element **c**[0] in the tuple **c** is **b1**—the 7-character string '**Twinkle**'. Hence **c**[0][1:5]—the set of four characters starting with **w** is '**wink**' [11]. This set itself is a string [12]. The **tuple c** has been concatenated with another tuple of two elements **s1** and **s2** as in [13] to form **d**— again a **tuple**. **d** is a tuple of five elements (**b1, b2, b3, b4,** (**s1, s4**)). Hence **d**[1] [1] is **s4**—the 4-line poem—as can be seen from [15]. **d**[1][1] being printable it has been output through [15]. It has been reproduced faithfully—first line directly and the following three lines with the respective white spaces preceding (as in [4]). **e** as defined in [16] is a tuple of three strings. **f** in [17] is a tuple of two elements—**e** and an integer—32 as defined by [17]. The floating point number 32.0 has been added as an additional element to **e** to form the new tuple **g** as in [18]. Figure 5.2 depicts the structure of **g** and shows how different elements and sub-elements in it can be represented/culled. **g**[0][0][1:3] is a tuple of two strings—'**little**' and '**star**' [22] while g[0][0][1][1:4] is a string of three characters [23].

As mentioned at the outset a **tuple** is a comma separated set of elements. A single element with a comma following is a **tuple** too. With **x** = 3.2 [24] **bb** in [25] is such a **tuple** (a singleton)—as is evident from [26] and confirmed in [27]. bb being a tuple bb * 2 [28] becomes a tuple with the element repeated. **bb**[0] * 2 [29] is **x** * **x** (=20.48). Various additional operations with **tuples** are discussed later.

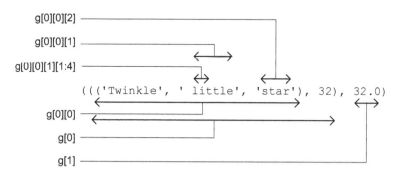

Fig. 5.2 Element g [19] in the sequence in Fig. 5.1 showing the structure and identity of different elements referred

5.3   List

list is a versatile and mutable sequence. Elements in a **list** can be changed or deleted. Additional elements can be added to the **list**. In the Python sequence in Fig. 5.3 **h** is a simple list of three elements [1]—all of them being integers. They are enclosed in square brackets signifying a '**list**'. **h1**—as is obvious from its definition [2]—is a tuple of three floating point numbers. **h1** has been combined with **h** to form the list **hl**—[3], [4], [5]. Though **hl** has two elements—the first [6] being a

```
>>> h= [25, 32, 47]                                        [1]
>>> h1 = 2.5, 3.2, 4.7                                      [2]
>>> hl = [h,h1]                                             [3]
>>> hl                                                      [4]
[[25, 32, 47], (2.5, 3.2, 4.7)]
>>> type(hl)                                                [5]
<class 'list'>
>>> type(hl[0])                                             [6]
<class 'list'>
>>> type(hl[1])                                             [7]
<class 'tuple'>
>>> hll = [h, h1, 44]                                       [8]
>>> hll[2]                                                  [9]
44
>>> type(hll[2])                                            [10]
<class 'int'>
>>> j =
{'Rama':21,'Ramya':19,'Shyam':18,'Latha':'girl'}[11]
>>> j
{'Latha': 'girl', 'Shyam': 18, 'Rama': 21, 'Ramya': 19}
>>> type(j)                                                 [12]
<class 'dict'>
>>> j['Latha']                                             [13]
'girl'
>>> type(j['Latha'])                                        [14]
<class 'str'>
>>> type(j['Rama'])
<class 'int'>                                               [15]
>>> print(j)                                                [16]
{'Latha': 'girl', 'Shyam': 18, 'Rama': 21, 'Ramya': 19}
>>> k = {'Rama', 'Ramya', 'Shyam', 'Latha'}               [17]
>>> k
{'Latha', 'Shyam', 'Rama', 'Ramya'}
>>> type(k)                                                 [18]
<class 'set'>
>>>
```

Fig. 5.3 Python Interpreter sequence to explain the concepts of list, dictionary, and set

list and the second [7] a **tuple**, **hll**—is a **list** of three elements—**h1**, **h2**, and integer 44—[8] and [9]. [10] confirms the third element in **hll**—**hll**[2]—to be an integer. Different operations with lists and the elements in them are discussed later.

5.4 Dictionary

Any person is characterized by a set of attributes, characteristics, and so on. These can be personal physical data (height, weight, colour of eyes …), behavioral characteristics (unselfish, extrovert, dynamic, open, …), academic details(Master degree holder, specialized in anthropology, …), professional standing (marketing, years of experience in sales, …), and so on. All these together can form an 'object' with an identifying tag—may be her name—associated. Such information for a number of individuals together can be represented as a **dictionary** in Python. For each individual in the **dictionary** the tag can be the '**key**' and the collection of all information related to her represented in a structured manner—the '**value**'. This dictionary here is a convenient platform for representation and any further processing of the information in it. Generalizing the concept any collection of information which can be grouped and conveniently compartmentalized can form a **dictionary** with each group (**value**) having a unique identity tag as its **key**.

A **dictionary** is an associative memory. It comprises of a set of key-value pairs within braces. **j** in [11] is a simple dictionary. '**Rama**' is a key; against this the integer 21 is stored. Here 21 signifies **Rama's** age. Any other item (object) that can be identified with the key '**Rama**' can be in its place or clubbed with it in an identified sequence. The same holds good of the other three entries in **j** also. '**Ramya**', '**Shyam**', and '**Latha**' too are keys. 19 & 18—the ages of **Ramya** and **Shyam** are stored against their names. '**girl**' –The information that she is a girl—is stored against **Latha**. The keys in a dictionary are tags used to identify, access, and modify the stored contents. The key has to be an immutable item—typically a string as here. It can also be a number. Once a key-value pair has been entered into a dictionary the key cannot be changed. The value can be accessed as with [13], [14] or [15]. The value can be altered or redefined. A key-value pair can be deleted. A new key-value pair can be added. Procedures with dictionary are discussed later.

5.5 Set

set is a simple data type. A collection of unordered and comma-separated items within curly brackets constitutes a **set**—[17] & [18]. No item in a set is repeated. Being an unordered set the items in a set have no locational significance. Hence they cannot be accessed by specific addresses. Set can be used for membership testing or eliminating duplicate entries. A limited number of operations are possible with **set**s.

Example 5.1 Count the number of vowels and the number of words in

"*Make me, oh God, the prey of the lion, ere You make the rabbit my prey*" (Gibran 1926).

Also count the number of the letters 'a' and 'b' in the above quote—irrespective of it being small letter or capital letter.

vow1(ss) in the module **dem_wr** reproduced in Fig. 5.4 is the Python program for counting the number of vowels in the string 'ss'. **vls** is a **set** with all the vowels—small and capital letters together ten in number—as its members [1]. The function **len**(ss) represents (in [2]) the number of items in **ss**. In the present context **ss** is a **string** and **len**(ss) is the number of characters in ss. Every character in **ss** starting from **ss**[0] to **ss**[**len**(ss)-1]—i.e., the last one, is examined successively. If it matches any entry in **vls** (that is if it is a vowel), **c**—a counter—is incremented [3]. The **c** value at the end of counting is returned. The final count value of **c** is the number of vowels in **ss**.

The Python Interpreter sequence in Fig. 5.5 has **s1** as the given sequence [1]. **len**(**s1**) gives the number of characters in **s1** as 71 [2]. With **s1** as input **vow1**() is run [3]. The number of vowels in **s1** is seen to be 21.

```
def vow1 (ss):
    'No of vowels in strings'
    c = 0
    vls = {'a', 'e', 'i', 'o', 'u', 'A', 'E', 'I', 'O',
'U'}                                                        [1]
    for i in range(len(ss)):                               [2]
        if ss[i] in vls: c += 1                            [3]
    return c

def wrd2(ss):
    'No of words in ss'
    noalpha = {' ', ',','.'}                               [4]
    w, l = 0, len(ss)
    for i in range(l-1):
        if (ss[i] not in noalpha) and (ss[i+1] in noalpha):
w += 1                                                      [5]
        return w

def wrd1(ss):

    'No. of a /b in ss'
    na, nb = 0, 0
    aA, bB = {'a','A'}, {'b', 'B'}                         [6]
    for i in range(len(ss)):
        if ss[i] in aA: na += 1                            [7]
        elif ss[i] in bB:nb += 1                           [8]
    return (na, nb)                                        [9]
```

Fig. 5.4 Python Interpreter sequence for Example 5.1

```
>>> from demo_5 import dem_wr
>>> s1='Make me, oh God, the prey of the lion, ere You
make the rabbit my prey.'                               [1]
>>> len(s1)                                             [2]
71
>>> dem_wr.vowl(s1)                                     [3]
21
>>> dem_wr.wrd2(s1)                                     [4]
16
>>> dem_wr.wrd1(s1)                                     [5]
(3, 2)
>>>
```

Fig. 5.5 Module **dem_wr.py** with the Python routines for Example 5.1

An examination of **s1** shows that a letter followed by a blank space, a comma, or a full stop signifies a word ending. **wrd2(ss)** in the module **dem_wr** in Fig. 5.4 counts such character pairs and returns this number as the word count. In the sequence in Fig. 5.5 **wrd2**() has been called with **s1** as input. The program returns 16 as the number of words in **s1** [4].

wrd1(ss) in Fig. 5.4 counts the number of occurrences of the letters 'a' and 'b' in **ss** separately. Every letter in **ss** is checked for its presence in the set **na** [6]; if present the count in **na**—number of 'a's present—is incremented [7]; else a similar check is made for 'b' and if necessary **nb**—number of 'b's present—is incremented [8]. On completion of the check **na** and **nb** are returned as a **tuple** [9].

In the Python sequence in Fig. 5.5 **wrd1**() has been called with **s1** as input [5]; the **tuple** (3, 2) shows **s1** to have three 'a's and two 'b's.

5.6   Operators with Sequences

A number of operators, built-in functions, and methods are available with sequences (Zhang 2015). These are discussed in stages here, in the sections following, and the next chapter.

5.6.1   *All and Any*

all and **any** functions facilitate repeated testing for being **true** or **false**. **x == a and x == b and x == c** can be implemented compactly using **all** by testing **x == l for all l in {a, b, c}**. Similarly x == **a or x == b or x == c** can be tested compactly using **any**.

Example 5.2 Identify all the numbers in the range {100, 200} which do not have any of the numbers in {2, 3, 5, 7, 11, 13, 17} as a factor.

```
def alltst(ab, ae):
   'return all numbers in range(ab, ae) which are not
divisible by any in s'
   s = (2, 3, 5, 7, 11, 13, 17)                           [1]
   k = []
   for  j in range(ab,ae):
       if all(j%l for l in s):k.append(j)                 [2]
   return k

def anytst(lb):
   'test for any failures'
# la is the list of students who failed in the class
# lb: given list
#Check whether any in given list has failed
   la = 'a', 'b', 'c', 'd', 'e'                            [3]
   for j in lb:
       if any( j is k for k in la):                       [4]
           print (j+' failed')
       else: print (j+' passed')                          [5]
   return
```

Fig. 5.6 Module **dem_all.py** with the Python routines for Examples 5.2 and 5.3

The routine is the function **alltst(ab, ae)** in the module **dem_all.py** repro-duced in Fig. 5.6. **S** = (2, 3, 5, 7, 11, 13, 17) is a tuple of the given numbers [1] in the function. For any **j**, the test **all(j%l for l in s)** in [2], tests whether **j** is divisible by very one of the elements in **s**. If none of them divides **j**, the condition (**j%l for l in s**) is **True**. If this condition is satisfied this specific **j** value is added (appended) to the **list k**. The appending is done at the right end of **k**. It increases the number of elements in **k** by one. The test is done for all **j** values in the specified range (**ab, ae**).

[2] also brings out the generality of **for** in its use. **for l in s** implies for all entries **in s**. Here **s** can be a **tuple**, **list** and so on; but all of them should be of the same **type**. It should also match the **type** of **j** here. These are implied in the use of **for** in the context.

[1] in the Python Interpreter sequence in Fig. 5.7 executes the routine for the desired range—{100–200}. The output is the **list** in [2].

Use of the method **append**() has been illustrated here. '**aa.append(b)**' is a command to add item **b** to **aa**. Here **aa** is a **list**; **b** can be any entity. It will be appended to **aa**—that is added to **aa** as its last element. In turn the number of elements in **aa** increases by one.

Example 5.3 A list of students who failed in an examination is given as **la**. A second list of students **lb** is input. Check to see whether anyone in **lb** has failed.

The function **anytst(lb)** in the module **dem_all.py** in Fig. 5.6 serves the purpose. [4] checks whether **j** matches any entry in **la**—that is the name '**j**' is

```
>>> from demo_5 import dem_all
>>> dem_all.alltst(100, 200)                                    [1]
[101, 103, 107, 109, 113, 127, 131, 137, 139, 149, 151,
157, 163, 167, 173, 179, 181, 191, 193, 197, 199]        [2]
>>> p = 'c', 'e', 'g', 'h'                                      [3]
>>> dem_all.anytst(p)
c failed
e failed
g passed
h passed
>>>
```

Fig. 5.7 Python Interpreter sequence for Examples 5.2 and 5.3

present in the failed list [3]; if so **j** is declared 'failed' in the output; else **j** is declared 'passed'. It is done for every entry in **lb** as can be seen from [4].

The Python Interpreter sequence in Fig. 5.7 specifies a student list **p** in [3]. Status of all the students in **p** is tested and the desired results output in the following lines.

5.6.2 sum *and* eval

The built-in function **sum**() takes a sequence and returns the numerical sum of the items in it. All the items in the sequence are to be numbers. [2] in the Python Interpreter sequence in Fig. 5.8 uses the **sum** function and computes the mean value of the numbers in **ll**. The function **sum**() is a bit more general than the way it is used here. It accept two arguments; **sum(a, b)** should have **a** as a sequence of numbers. **b** should be reducible to a number and forms the bias—**b** is added to the sum of the elemental values of **a**. If **b** is absent the bias—its default value—is taken as zero—as in the example here. [3] illustrates the more generalized use of **sum**().

The **eval**() function in its simplest form accepts any expression as a **string** and evaluates it. [4] is a trivial example; **a1**—as evaluated here—is sin 0.3. **x1** has been assigned the numerical value 1.2 in [5]. **a2** in [6] does the evaluation of sin (0.3 + 0.1*$x1$) using this value of **x1**. With **x2** = 0.4 in [7] **a3** is evaluated in [8] as ($x1^2 + x2^2$). The expression to be evaluated can be any built-in function or a user-defined (if necessary imported) function; all its arguments have to be assigned values beforehand for **eval**() as used here. [9] illustrates a more general use of **eval**(). All the arguments used in **eval**() are made available through a **dictionary** forming the second argument of **eval**(). Here **a4** is evaluated as ($x3^2 + x4^2$)—**x3** and **x4** being assigned numerical values of 0.2 and 0.4 respectively through the **dictionary**. In short **eval('alpha', beta)** evaluates and returns the expression **'alpha'** as follows:

```
>>> ll = (31, 42, 87, 55, 95, 68)                              [1]
>>> sum(ll)/len(ll)                                            [2]
63.0
>>> sum(ll, -63*6)                                             [3]
0
>>> import math
>>> a1 = eval('math.sin(0.3)')                                 [4]
>>> a1
0.29552020666133955
>>> x1=1.2                                                      [5]
>>> a2 = eval('math.sin(0.3+0.1*x1)')                          [6]
>>> a2
0.40776045305957015
>>> x2=0.4                                                      [7]
>>> a3 = eval('x1**2 + x2**2')                                 [8]
>>> a3
1.6
>>> a4 = eval('x3**2+x4**2',{'x3':0.2, 'x4':0.4})              [9]
>>> a4
0.20000000000000004
```

Fig. 5.8 Python Interpreter sequence illustrating use of **sum**() and **eval**()

- If **beta** is present it has to be a dictionary: values of all arguments used in **alpha** are to be supplied through **beta**.
- If **beta** is absent **eval**('**alpha**') takes the argument values assigned beforehand and evaluates **alpha**. If any argument remains unassigned an error is returned.

5.7 Iterator

We have seen that sequences like **string**, **tuple**, and **list** have a number of elements within, each with its own positional identity. In a program often one has to carry out a set of operations for each of the members of the sequence. Identifying prime numbers in a sequence of numbers, checking for the presence of 'Ram' or 'imp' in a name, counting the number of letters in a string, calculation of the grade point average of a student, calculating the ex-factory cost of the products made in a factory are examples. Any sequence with such elements in it for which one or a set of operations can be carried out is an 'iterable'. An '**iterator**' is associated with an iterable; it points to a specific location in the iterable (Ramalho 2014). As and when required the data in the specific location concerned is accessed and used for processing. The access here is on a 'on demand' basis and the full data is not called expect when specifically demanded. The **iter**() function generates an iterator directly from an iterable. The Python Interpreter sequence in Fig. 5.9 clarifies the concepts associated with **iter**() function. **lt** in [1] is a **list** with a set of five distinct elements in it. **lt** is an iterable. The function **iter**(**lt**) returns an iterator **a1** from **lt** [2]. **lt**[0], **lt**[2],

```
>>> lt = ['Ram', 32, '32',          >>> a10, a12, a14 =
3.2, '3.2']                 [1]      iter(lt[0]), iter(lt[2]),
>>> a1= iter(lt)            [2]      iter(lt[4])                [12]
>>> a10 = iter(lt[0])       [3]      >>> next(a10), next(a12),
>>> a11 = iter(lt[1])       [4]      next(a14)                  [13]
Traceback (most recent call          ('R', '3', '3')
last):                               >>> next(a10), next(a12),
  File "<stdin>", line 1, in         next(a14)                  [14]
<module>                             ('a', '2', '.')
TypeError: 'int' object is           >>> next(a10), next(a14)[15]
not iterable                         ('m', '2')
>>> a12 = iter(lt[2])       [5]      >>> next(a10), next(a14)[16]
>>> a13 = iter(lt[3])       [6]      Traceback (most recent call
Traceback (most recent call          last):
last):                                 File "<stdin>", line 1, in
  File "<stdin>", line 1, in         <module>
<module>                             StopIteration
TypeError: 'float' object is         >>> from demo_5 import fp1
not iterable                         [17]
>>> a14 =  iter(lt[4])      [7]      >>> a1 = 'Tenderness and
>>> a14                              kindness are not signs of
<str_iterator object at              weakness and despair, but
0x7fe667a33d30>                      manifestations of strength
>>> next(a10), next(a12),            and resolution.'           [18]
next(a14)                   [8]      >>> c1 = fp1.ctw(a1)       [19]
('R', '3', '3')                      >>> c1
>>> next(a10), next(a12),            16
next(a14)                   [9]      >>> a2 = 'Are you awake
('a', '2', '.')                      now?'
>>> next(a10), next(a12),            >>> fp1.ctw(a2)            [20]
next(a14)                  [10]      4
Traceback (most recent call          >>> a1= iter(lt)          [21]
last):                               >>> next(a1,'z')          [22]
  File "<stdin>", line 1, in         'Ram'
<module>                             >>> next(a1,'z'),
StopIteration                        next(a1,'z'), next(a1,'z'),
>>> next(a10), next(a14)[11]         next(a1,'z')
Traceback (most recent call          32, '32', 3.2, '3.2'
last):                               >>> next(a1,'z')          [23]
  File "<stdin>", line 1, in         'z'
<module>                             >>> next(a1,'z')
StopIteration                        'z'
                                     >>>
```

Fig. 5.9 Python Interpreter sequence—demonstration of **iter** () function

and **lt**[4] are **string**s; each is an iterable with a distinct character set within. [3], [5], and [7] return respective **iterator**s as **a10**, **a12**, and **a14** respectively. **lt** [1] is an integer and **lt** [3] is a floating point number; neither is iterable. Attempts to extract an **iterator** from these fails ([4], [6]) and **TypeError** is raised.

The function **next**() returns the **next** iterable item from the iterable starting from the 0th one. **next(a10)**, **next(a12)**, and **next(a14)** in [8] return the respective iterable values as '**R**', '**3**', and '**3**' respectively. [9] advances to the subsequent **set**—that is those with index 1. Repeat of the attempt to access the **next** iterator value fails in the case of **a12** [10] and '**StopIteration**' is raised. One more attempt to access the next set of values (4th one) will return '**StopIteration**' with **a10** and **a14** as well [11]. Being wiser with the above we make fresh attempts in [12] by reassigning **a10**, **a12**, and **a14** afresh. The repeated accesses of the **next** element continue until the iterator **lists** are exhausted.

Example 5.4 Extract the number of words in the quote

'Tenderness and kindness are not signs of weakness and despair, but manifestations of strength and resolution.' using the **iter**() function.

The relevant program **ctw** () (module **fp1**) is in Fig. 5.10. The logic for word extraction is the same as that in Example 5.1. The non-alphabetic character **list**—**noalpha**—has been enhanced here by adding '**?**' to it [1]. Both **x1** and **x2** are iterations of the **string qt**. But with [3] **x1** and **x2** are the successive iterator values (characters) in the iterable—quote here. [4] tests for word ending and increments the word count when a word is identified. The quote of interest here is assigned to **a1** in [18] in Fig. 5.9. **fp1.ctw (a1)**—[19] in Fig. 5.9 can be seen to return the final word count in the given quote as 16.

As another illustration the number of words in the string **a2** is counted through **fp1.ctw (a2)** and returned (=4) in [20].

The general version of **next** () takes two arguments. The first is the iterator. The second one—a default element—is optional. If present when the iterator range is exhausted the default is returned. The illustrations thus far omitted the second argument. **a1** in [21] in Fig. 5.9 is the iterator for **lt**. Line [22] returns the successive elements of **lt** until **lt** is exhausted. Subsequent lines—[23] onwards—return '**z**'—the default quantity specified.

```
def ctw(qt):
    'Count the no. of words in a quote -use iter()'
    noalpha = {' ', ',','.', '?'}                        [1]
    x1, x2, c = iter(qt), iter(qt), 0                    [2]
    next(x2)                                             [3]
    for j in range(len(qt)-1):
        a, b = next(x1), next(x2)
        if a not in noalpha and b in noalpha: c += 1     [4]
    return c
```

Fig. 5.10 Python program for Example 5.4

5.8   Iterator Functions

A number of functions are available to generate an iterator directly from iterables. The simpler ones are discussed here.

The **enumerate**() function operates on an iterable. It identifies each element of the iterable with its positional address, forms a pair, and returns an iterator for this pair. The iterator can be used to form corresponding sequences like a **dictionary**, a **list**, or a **tuple**. Figure 5.11 shows an illustrative Python Interpreter sequence. **mm**—[1]—is a list of items—single character strings. **list** (**enumerate**(**mm**)) enumerates **mm** and returns it as a **list** [2]. The **list** has as many **tuples** as elements of **mm**. Each **tuple** is a pair with the sequentially assigned address (Serial Number) and the element of **mm** as its content. **m1** in [3] is a **list** of integers. **tuple**(**enumerate**(**m1**)) in [4] returns a **tuple** with similar content—set of **tuples** each with the serial no. and the parent sequence element in [3] as its contents. Similarly [5] returns the enumerated sequence as a **dictionary** since a dictionary has been specified here; the serial number is the **key** and the item pointed by the iterator the value. The starting number for the enumeration in **enumerate**() function can be specified if desired; if specified enumeration starts from this number as in [6], [7], and [8].

The **map** built-in function is an iterator for mapping one sequence into another. The mapping conforms to a defined function. The structure of **map** () is shown in Fig. 5.12. **map** takes at least two arguments; the first is the function used for the mapping—specified without any argument. It can be a built-in function or a user defined one. The second argument is the sequence to be mapped. If the function takes two or more arguments, an equal number of sequences is to be specified—all of the same length. Figure 5.13 shows an illustrative Python Interpreted sequence. **a** in [1] is a function which returns the square of **x**. [2] uses the function **a** to transform the **tuple** (2, 3, 4) into a list **b**—its elements being the respective

```
>>> mm = ['a', 'b', 'c', 'd', 'e']                        [1]
>>> list (enumerate(mm))                                   [2]
[(0, 'a'), (1, 'b'), (2, 'c'), (3, 'd'), (4, 'e')]
>>> m1 = [22,33,44,55]                                     [3]
>>> tuple(enumerate(m1))                                   [4]
((0, 22), (1, 33), (2, 44), (3, 55))
>>> dict(enumerate(m1))                                    [5]
{0: 22, 1: 33, 2: 44, 3: 55}
>>> list(enumerate(m1,2))                                  [6]
[(2, 22), (3, 33), (4, 44), (5, 55)]
>>> tuple(enumerate(m1,3))                                 [7]
((3, 22), (4, 33), (5, 44), (6, 55))
>>> dict(enumerate(m1,-3))                                 [8]
{0: 55, -1: 44, -3: 22, -2: 33}
```

Fig. 5.11 Python Interpreter sequence to illustrate use of **enumerate**() function

squares ([4, 9, 16]) in [3]; here the **iterator map**(**a**, (2, 3, 4)) is directly converted into the list **b**. Function **aa** in [4] accepts two arguments—**x** and **y**—components of a vector—and returns the vector magnitude—(Euclidean norm).

In turn **bb** in [5] uses the x-component sequence (6, 5, 4) and the y-component sequence (2, 6, 7) to compute and return the corresponding sequence of magnitudes as a **tuple** in [6]. [7] illustrates the use of the built-in function **pow**() with two arguments. The resulting **list** [7] is $[7^2, 5^3, 3^{-2}]$. Similarly [8] (using three arguments) returns $7^2\%11$, $5^3\%11$, and $3^4\%11$ as the **list** [5, 4, 4]. Note that in all these cases, all the arguments must be sequences—and sequences of the same length. Further the number of sequences should match the number of arguments for the function.

Example 5.5 Form the scalar product of the vectors **a** = [1,2,3,4,5], and **c** = [2, −3, 5, 7, −0.5].

In the Python interpreter sequence in Fig. 5.13 **mul**[10] is defined as a **lambda** function which multiplies the arguments **x** and **y**. **map**(**mul**, **a**, **c**) in [11] is an **iterator** of the product of components of the vectors **a** and **c**. Their sum as **d** (=**sum**(**map**(**mul**, **a**, **c**)) is the vector product [11]. **d** has been evaluated as 36.5 [12].

The mapping can be useful in other ways also. **fc** in [3] in the module **demap** (Fig. 5.14) is **tuple** of two functions. They return the square and the cube of **x** and **y** respectively. [4] accepts an argument **z** and returns **vv** with z^2 and z^3 as its elements. The function set **fc** forms the sequence argument here. [14] in Fig. 5.13 uses the map for **vv**(2) to return the **list** $[2^2, 2^3]$.

Example 5.6 A set of numbers is given—(31, 42, 87, 55, 95, 68). Get their mean and variance.

The Python program is **meva**() in Fig. 5.14 in the module **demap**. bb in [5] is the number of elements in the input sequence dd. med in [6] gives the mean value of the elements of the sequence **dd**. The function **list**(**map**(**sq**, **dd**) forms a **list** with the squares of the items in **dd** as its elements. The mean of their sum is formed and **med**^{2} subtracted from it to get the variance (**vr**). This conforms to the definition of variance as (Decoursey 2003)

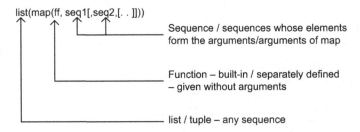

Fig. 5.12 Structure of **map**()—typical use

```
>>> a = lambda x: x**2                                         [1]
>>> b = list(map(a, (2,3,4)))                                  [2]
>>> b                                                          [3]
[4, 9, 16]
>>> aa = lambda x, y:(x**2 + y**2)**0.5                        [4]

>>> bb = tuple(map(aa, [6,5,4], [2,6,7]))                      [5]
>>> bb                                                         [6]
(6.324555320336759, 7.810249675906654, 8.06225774829855)
>>> list(map(pow, (7, 5, 3), (2, 3, -2)))                      [7]
[49, 125, 0.1111111111111111]
>>> list(map(pow, (7, 5, 3), (2, 3, 4),(11, 11, 11)))         [8]
[5, 4, 4]
>>> a, c = [1,2,3,4,5], [2, -3, 5,7, -0.5]                     [9]
>>> mul = lambda x, y: x*y                                     [10]
>>> d = sum(map(mul, a,c))                                     [11]
>>> d                                                         [12]
36.5
>>> from demo_5 import demap                                   [13]
>>> list(demap.vv(2))                                         [14]
[4, 8]
>>> ll = (31, 42, 87, 55, 95, 68)                             [15]
>>> demap.meva(ll)                                           [16]
(63.0, 525.666666666667)
```

Fig. 5.13 Python Interpreter sequence to illustrate use of **map**() function

```
sq = lambda x: x**2                                           [1]
cu = lambda y: y**3                                           [2]
fc = (sq,cu)                                                  [3]
#Return square & Cube of r - use of 'map'
def vv(r): return map(lambda z: z(r), fc)                    [4]
def meva(dd):
    'With dd as a sequence of numbers, return their
mean & variance'
    bb = len(dd)                                             [5]
    med = sum(dd)/bb                                         [6]
    vr = sum(list(map(sq,dd)))/bb - med**2                  [7]
    return med, vr                                          [8]
```

Fig. 5.14 Another Python Interpreter sequence to illustrate use of **map**() function

$$var(x_i) = \frac{\sum x_i^2}{n} - x_{mean}$$

The mean and variance together is returned as a **tuple** (**med**, **vr**) in [8]. Reverting to the Python Interpreter sequence in Fig. 5.13, the **tuple ll** in [15] is the given sequence of numbers. The function **meva** is called with this as argument in [16] and (mean, variance) pair is returned.

The **zip**() function accepts a number of iterables as input and returns an iterator of tuples. The *j*th returned element has the *j*th elements of all the iterable inputs. The Python interpreter sequence of Fig. 5.15 illustrates its features. **a** is a list of five integers [1] and **b** a string of five characters [2]. **e** [3] **zip**s the two, treating the characters in **b** as a **tuple** of characters and outputs the **list** of all the five **tuple**s so formed [4].

[5] and [6] form another illustration of the use of **zip**(); **p**, **q**, and **r** are identical iterators with **range**(0,10)—that is 0–9 inclusive. **zip**(**p**, **q**, **r**) is the iterator of corresponding **tuple**s—*j*th **tuple** being (*j*, *j*, *j*). This lot of ten **tuple**s is returned as a **list** in [6].

Example 5.7 The marks obtained by five students—Kishore, Sanjay, Siva, Asha, and Nisha in the subjects—physics, chemistry, maths, mechanics, english—are available as respective **list**s. Rearrange the **list** with separate groups of names and marks in individual subjects.

The information given with students' names and subjects is in Fig. 5.16. **sa** in [7] in Fig. 5.15 constitutes a **list** of **tuple**s—**s1**, **s2**, **s3**, **s4**, **s5**—each representing the data for one student. This single element **tuple** (**sa**) is zipped [8]

```
>>> a = [1,2,3,4,5]                                [1]
>>> b = 'truth'                                    [2]
>>> e = list(zip(a,b))                             [3]
>>> e                                              [4]
[(1, 't'), (2, 'r'), (3, 'u'), (4, 't'), (5, 'h')]
>>> p = q = r = range(10)                          [5]
>>> p
range(0, 10)
>>> list(zip(p,q,r))                               [6]
[(0, 0, 0), (1, 1, 1), (2, 2, 2), (3, 3, 3), (4, 4,
4), (5, 5, 5), (6, 6, 6), (7, 7, 7), (8, 8, 8), (9,
9, 9)]
>>> from demo_5 import marks1
>>> sa = marks1.ss                                 [7]
>>> aa = zip(sa)                                   [8]
>>> ab = list(aa)                                  [9]
>>> ab                                             [10]
[((['Kishore', 75, 66, 91, 87, 76],), (['Sanjay', 81,
62, 95, 91, 62],), (['Siva', 41, 51, 45, 39, 52],),
(['Asha', 88, 78, 97, 83, 72],), (['Nisha', 50, 61,
68, 40, 81],)]
>>> list(zip(sa[0], sa[1], sa[2], sa[3],sa[4]))[11]
[('Kishore', 'Sanjay', 'Siva', 'Asha', 'Nisha'),
(75, 81, 41, 88, 50), (66, 62, 51, 78, 61), (91, 95,
45, 97, 68), (87, 91, 39, 83, 40), (76, 62, 52, 72,
81)]
```

Fig. 5.15 Python Interpreter sequence to illustrate use of **zip**() function

```
dta = 'name', 'physics', 'chemistry', 'maths', 'mechanics',
'english'                                                    [1]
dta = 'name', 'phy.', 'chem.', 'math.', 'mechn.', 'engl.'
s1 = 'Kishore', 75, 66, 91, 87, 76                           [2]
s2 = 'Sanjay', 81, 62, 95, 91, 62
s3 = 'Siva', 41, 51, 45, 39, 52
s4 = 'Asha', 88, 78, 97, 83, 72
s5 = 'Nisha', 50,61, 68, 40, 81
ss = s1, s2, s3, s4, s5
s6 = 'Karthik', 77, 78, 79, 80, 81
s7 = 'Sarani', 76, 78, 82, 83, 84
s8 = 'Karun', 85, 86, 87, 88, 89
s9 = 'Kala', 90, 86, 91, 92, 93
s10 = 'Lan', 65, 86, 66, 67, 68
st = [s6, s7, s8, s9, s10]
```

Fig. 5.16 Contents of module **marks1.py** in demo_5 folder

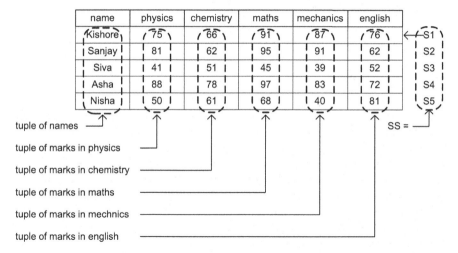

Fig. 5.17 Formation of **tuple**s of names and marks in physics, … from the **tuple SS** (Example 5.7)

and produced as a **list** [9], [10]. [11] has these five sequences—as inputs. When zipped as a list we get the names, marks in Physics and so on as separate lists. Figure 5.17 illustrates the process.

filter() as an iterator function can be used with any sequence to extract subsequences conforming to specific conditions. **filter (alpha, beta)** takes two arguments. The second one—**beta**—is a sequence to be filtered. The first—**alpha** —is a function to decide the filtering; only if this function evaluates to **True** for an item in **beta**, that item is 'eligible' for the iterative action. [1] and [2] in Fig. 5.18 form a simple illustration for the use of **filter**(). **h** in [1] is a **tuple** of names.

```
>>> h = ('Ram', 'Maya', 'Sri', 'Dhan', 'Dhanush')        [1]
>>> list(filter(lambda k:len(k)>3, h))                    [2]
['Maya', 'Dhan', 'Dhanush']
>>> a = tuple(filter(lambda k:(k%7)==0, range(100)))      [3]
>>> a
(0, 7, 14, 21, 28, 35, 42, 49, 56, 63, 70, 77, 84, 91,
98)
>>> list(map(lambda k:k/7, a))                            [4]
[0.0, 1.0, 2.0, 3.0, 4.0, 5.0, 6.0, 7.0, 8.0, 9.0, 10.0,
11.0, 12.0, 13.0, 14.0]
>>>
```

Fig. 5.18 Python Interpreter sequence to illustrate use of **filter**() function

filter(lambda k: len(k) > 3, h) returns an iterator. Only those names in **h** longer than 3 are selected here. [2] forms the full **list** of such names in **h**. [3] is another example; in the range of integers $\{0, 99\}$, those divisible by 7 are selected and returned as a **tuple**—**a**. Every one of these in **a** is divided by 7 and the resultant list of quotients formed is in [4].

5.9   Generators

A **generator** is a 'half-way' function with input arguments (if any); it returns an **iterator**. The **iterator** can be used to get the successive values of the function, to form a sequence like a **list**, and so on. **y** [2] in the Python Interpreter sequence in Fig. 5.19 is an illustration of a **generator** in its simplest form. For the argument a1[1] it forms an **iterator** with $x*x$ as its values for **x** in **a1**. [3] shows that **y** is a **generator** object. **next(y)** in [4] returns the value (of $x*x$) for the first **x** in **a1** (=2). The subsequent values are returned sequentially until the list of elements in **a1** is exhausted. **next(y)** in [5] at this stage returns 'StopIteration'. **list(y)** in [6] returns an empty list.

The same generator is again assigned to **yy** in [7]. **next(yy)** returns the first value. The following **list(yy)** [9] returns the rest of the values as a list. An expression within parentheses as in [2]/[7] is an **iterator**; but the same within brackets directly forms the corresponding list itself. Formation of **yy** in [10] once again and the **list**s in [11] confirm this.

The **generator** is essentially a reusable function; it forms a loop to create the elements of the output list. The comprehensive form of the expression forming a generator is shown in Fig. 5.20. The syntax is the general one for 'compre-hension'. It can be the basis for forming a **list** too. **z** in [12] is such a more general **generator**. With the elements in **a1** being numbers, **z** will return the iterator for x^2, x^2, or $0.25*x$ depending on whether $x < 3$, $x > 3$, or $x = 3$ respectively. **list(z)** [13] confirms this. **zz** in [14] is another **generator** of the

```
>>> a1 = (2, 3, 4)                                           [1]
>>> y = (x*x for x in a1)                                    [2]
>>> y                                                        [3]
<generator object <genexpr> at 0x7f2dba508ee8>
>>> next(y), next(y), next(y)                                [4]
4, 9, 16
>>> next(y)                                                  [5]
Traceback (most recent call last):
  File "<stdin>", line 1, in <module>
StopIteration
>>> list(y)                                                  [6]
[]
>>> yy = (x*x for x in a1)                                   [7]
>>> next(yy)                                                 [8]
4
>>> list(yy)                                                 [9]
[9, 16]
>>> yy = (x*x for x in a1)                                   [10]
>>> [x*x for x in a1], list(yy)                              [11]
([4, 9, 16], [4, 9, 16])
>>> z = (x*x if x<3 else x*x*x if x>3 else 0.25*x for x
in a1)                                                       [12]
>>> z
<generator object <genexpr> at 0x7f2dba508f78>
>>> list(z)                                                  [13]
[4, 27, 1.0]
>>> zz = ('jj is small; ' if jj<3 else 'jj is large; ' if
jj>3 else 'jj is 3; ' for jj in a1)                          [14]
>>> list(zz)
['jj is small; ', 'jj is 3; ', 'jj is large; ']             [15]
>>> mm = 'aA1bB2cC3dD4'                                      [16]
>>> import string                                            [17]
>>> gg = (c.upper() if c in string.ascii_lowercase else c
for c in mm)                                                 [18]
>>> gg                                                       [19]
<generator object <genexpr> at 0x7f2dba510558>
>>> ''.join(gg)                                              [20]
'AA1BB2CC3DD4'
>>> a2 = (-1, 1, 0.5)                                        [21]
>>> list(x*y for x in range(4) for y in a2)
                              [22]
[0, 0, 0.0, -1, 1, 0.5, -2, 2, 1.0, -3, 3, 1.5]
>>>
```

Fig. 5.19 Python Interpreter sequence to illustrate the concepts of **generator**

same type. It returns specified string statements depending on the value of the argument [15]. Note that the order of elements in the returned list is the same as their order in the argument **a1**.

Fig. 5.20 Structure of a   exp   for   (exp)   for   if . . . . . .
generator in Python
                                    ←—— Minimal ——→

                                    ←—— More general ——→ ——→ With additional **for** / **if** parts

mm in [16] is a **string** of ASCII characters. The **module string** is
imported [17] to facilitate formation of the **generator gg** [18]. **gg**—when
invoked—replaces the lower case characters in **mm** with the respective upper case
counterparts but leaves all other characters unchanged. ' '.**join**(**gg**) in [20] is the
new and altered version of **mm**.

a2[21] is a **tuple** of three numbers; "**x*y for x in range**(4) **for y in a2**"
in [22] is a **generator** using a succession of two '**for**'s. The **list** in [22] is
formed for every value in **range**(4) for every value in **a2** (with a total of 12
elements). Note that evaluation starts with the leftmost **for** which is the case
always.

5.10   Hashing

In information systems storage, updation, retrieval, and comparison of various
items stored, is a challenging task—all the more so in a dynamic environment when
the number of quantities involved becomes large. The concept of hashing plays a
key role here. In a computer environment the hash value of an entity is a name tag
assigned to it by the computer system (Shyamala et al. 2011). All such name tags
are numbers—its size may extend to 16 bits in a 16-bit machine and 32 bits in a
32-bit machine. Consider a storage where the items are stored in a **dict**—each
item being identified by its own **key**. The storage forms hash values of the keys and
uses them as their tags. Any search for comparison, duplication check, deletion etc.,
is carried out by the computer using the hash value as the basis. The algorithm used
for hashing has to satisfy a set of basic requirements:

- It should use all the information available in the item to form the hash value.
- The hashing function should return the same hash value for an entity whenever
  it is evaluated.
- The hash values of two different entities should be different (and bear no correlation to each other) even if the two entities are only marginally different.
- Hash values of numbers can be numbers: two numbers (integer, rational, float)
  having the same value should hash to the same value.
- Chances of two different entities hashing to the same hash value should have a
  very low (negligible) probability.

The **hash** () function in Python can be used to form hash values of different
entities. The Python Interpreter sequence in Fig. 5.21 illustrates its use. **aa** in [1] is
a **tuple** of **string**s. Its hash value is obtained in [2]. The same **tuple** is

```
>>> aa= ('a1', 'b2', 'c3')                            [1]
>>> hash(aa)                                          [2]
-3035107133505497101                                  [3]
>>> bb = ('a1', 'b2', 'c3')                           [4]
>>> hash(bb)                                          [5]
-3035107133505497101                                  [6]
>>> cc = ('a1', 'b2', 'c4')                           [7]
>>> hash(cc)                                          [8]
6618343046616662373
>>> xx = (22, 2.2e+1, 220e-1, 22.00)                  [9]
yy = []
>>> for jj in xx:yy.append(hash(jj))
...
>>> yy                                                [10]
[22, 22, 22, 22]
>>> hash(22)                                          [11]
22
>>> hash(xx)                                          [12]
6655034283120562599
```

Fig. 5.21 Python Interpreter sequence to illustrate application of the **hash** () function

assigned to **bb** in [4]. **hash**(**bb**) [5] returns the same hash value as in [3] obtained with **hash**(**aa**)—implying that **aa** and **bb** are the same entities. **cc**[7] is only marginally different from **aa** ('**c3**' is changed to '**c4**'); but its hash value [8] is conspicuously different from that of **aa**[3]. Number 22 is represented in different forms to form the **tuple xx** [9]. But all of them have the same hash value [10]— that of 22 itself [11]. This is different from the hash value of **xx** as a **tuple** [12].

All immutable objects (**number**s, **string**s, **tuple**s ...) can be hashed. Since mutable objects (**list**, **dict**, **set**), can be altered anytime, a hash value does not make sense for them; they are not hashable.

5.11 Input

The built-in function **input(pp)** facilitates interactive executions. The argument **pp** is an optional prompt. When input ('**pp**') is encountered control is transferred to the keyboard after **pp** is written/displayed on the terminal. (The system expects an input to be supplied through the keyboard). Whatever is entered through the keyboard up to the enter key, is accepted as (one line) input string and execution is resumed. The Python Interpreter sequence in Fig. 5.22 brings out typical uses.

y is assigned to **input**() in [1]—without any argument. The line—'**Maya**'— entered through the keyboard [2] is accepted and directly assigned to **y** as a string as can be seen from [3]. [4] is a more elaborate and explicit command with a prompt

```
>>> y = input()                                 [1]
Maya                                            [2]
>>> y                                           [3]
'Maya'
>>> input('What is your name please?\n')        [4]
What is your name please?                       [5]
Roshan                                          [6]
'Roshan'                                        [7]
>>> def wish():                                 [8]
...     aa = input('What is your name please? \n')
...     print('Good day to you, ' + aa)
...     return
...
>>> wish()                                      [9]
What is your name please?                       [10]
Nevan
Good day to you, Nevan
>>> import math
>>> def fx_0():                                 [11]
...     y = float(input('Give x value\n'))      [12]
...     print('sin(x): ', math.sin(y))
...     return
...
>>> fx_0()                                      [13]
Give x value                                    [14]
0.7854
sin(x):   0.7071080798594735                    [15]
>>>
```

Fig. 5.22 Illustration of simple uses of **input**() built-in function

—'What is your name please\n'. The same is displayed on the terminal [5] and system advances to the next line waiting for an input line to be fed. '**Roshan**' is fed in [6] and duly displayed [7]. **wish**() is defined as a simple function starting at [8]. It seeks an input through the prompt—'What is your name please?'. The name of a person is expected as input. 'Good day to you (name)' is returned. An execution sequence with **wish**() follows from [9].

With **math module** imported function **fx_0**() [11] displays the prompt 'Give x value' and advances to the next line. **x** can be fed as a **string** or a number; it is converted into a corresponding floating point number and assigned to **y** [12]. sin(y) is output. As an illustration **fx_0**() execution follows. ($\sin(\pi/4) \approx \sin(0.7854) \approx 0.7071080798594735$) [15].

Input() function is useful in iterative programming sequences. Typical example is an iteration where execution is interrupted and certain parameter values are altered to ensure convergence or speed up solution before resuming execution. **Input**() is also useful to debug programs at the development stage.

5.12 Exercises

1. Get **divmod**(4.3257, 1), **int**(**divmod**(4.3257, 1)[0]), and **int**(**divmod** (4.3257, 1) [1]*7). Explain the outputs.

2. With a, b as integers **divmod**(a, b) returns a **tuple** of the quotient and the remainder—both being integers. This can be used to convert integers from one base to another. With **n1** as a decimal number to be converted to base 7(say) form **n2** = **divmod**(**n1**, 7). Form **n3** = **divmod**(**n2**[0], 7). Continue the **divmod** () operations until the remainder becomes zero. Concatenate the remainder digits with **n2**[1] as the least significant digit to get the number expressed to base 7. Write program to convert a decimal integer into one of a different base.

3. With f as a decimal fraction less than one, **int**(**divmod**($f \times 7$, 1) [0]) is the most significant digit of f expressed to base 7. **divmod**($f \times 7$, 1) [1] is the rest of it. Repeat **int**(**divmod**(xx, 1)) to get the next significant digit. Write a program to convert a decimal fraction to one of different base.

4. Use the programs in the two previous exercises to convert the decimal number 7654.45678 into corresponding numbers to bases 5, 7, 9, 11. In each case continue conversion to get the most significant six digits of the fractional part. Evaluate the converted numbers and check the accuracy attained in each case (Hint: $0.435_7 = 4 \times 7^{-1} + 3 \times 7^{-2} + 5 \times 7^{-3}$).

5. *Root squaring*: Some widely used methods are available to extract roots of polynomials. With the coefficients of a polynomial being real numbers its roots are real numbers or complex numbers occurring as conjugate pairs. One of the methods of extracting the roots is by 'squaring the roots' (Mcnamee and Pan 2013). To understand the method consider the cubic polynomial with roots as a, b, and c as

$$p_1(x) = (x-a)(x-b)(x-c) = 0$$
$$= x^3 - (a+b+c)x^2 + (ab+bc+a)x - abc = 0 \quad (5.1)$$

The polynomial with all the roots with their signs changed is

$$p_2(x) = (x+a)(x+b)(x+c) \quad (5.2)$$

multiplying the two polynomials

$$p_3(x) = \left(x^2 - a^2\right)\left(x^2 - b^2\right)\left(x^2 - c^2\right) = 0$$
$$= x^6 - \left(a^2 + b^2 + c^2\right)x^4 + \left(a^2 b^2 + b^2 c^2 + c^2 a^2\right)x^2 - a^2 b^2 c^2 \quad (5.3)$$
$$= 0$$

Comparing (5.3) with (5.1) $p_3(x)$ can be seen to be a polynomial in x^2 with a^2, b^2, and c^2 as its roots. If a is real and b and c are also real or complex conjugate pairs the coefficients of $p_3(x^2)$ are all real numbers. If the roots are not known but only the coefficients of the polynomial are known as l, m, and n, we have

$$p_1(x) = x^3 - lx^2 + mx - n = 0 \text{ and}$$
$$p_2(x) = x^3 + lx^2 + mx + n = 0$$
$$p_3(x) = \left((x^3 + mx) - (lx^2 + n) \right)\left((x^3 + mx) + (lx^2 + n) \right) = 0$$
$$= x^6 + (2m - l^2)x^4 + (m^2 - 2ln)x^2 - n^2 = 0$$

This process of forming polynomials with squares of the roots of the given polynomial is continued as long as desired. With $a > b > c$, a^n becomes orders larger than b^n and c^n rapidly as n increases. If a^n is large enough to make b^n and c^n negligible compared to a^n, the coefficient of $(x^n)^2$ becomes equal to the square of the coefficient of x^n itself. This can be seen by comparing the respective coefficients of (5.1) and (5.3). A similar pattern can be observed with other coefficients also. At this stage with $(x^n - a^n)$ as a factor, the polynomial can be factorized to get $(x^{2n} - (b^n + c^n)x^n + b^n c^n)$ as the factor. Since $b^n \gg c^n$, coefficient of x^n can be taken as b^n itself. Division of coefficient of x^0 by b^n yields c^n as the third root. If the two complex roots dominate over a they can be extracted from the quadratic formed with the coefficients of x^{3n}, x^{2n}, and x^n.

With a calculator/Python try the method for a third degree polynomial. Write a program to apply the root squaring method to identify n and decide when to stop iteration to get the polynomial with x^n as its roots. Rest of the root extraction procedure is manual (not easily amenable to be programmed). Apply the method to get the roots of a few polynomials with degrees up to the 20th.

6. Two functions Ex_1 and Ex_2 have been defined in Fig. 5.23. The Python Interpretor sequence in Fig. 5.23 is obtained by running them. Explain why

```
def Ex_1():                        >>> dd = Exx.Ex_1()
    aa = []                        >>> dd(3)
    def bb(cc):                    3
        aa.append(cc)             >>> dd(3)
        return sum(aa)            6
    return bb                      >>> ee = Exx.Ex_2()
                                   >>> ee(3)
def Ex_2():                        3
    aa = 0                        >>> ee(3)
    def bb(cc):                    6
        nonlocal aa
        aa += cc
        return aa
    return bb
```

Fig. 5.23 The routines and the Python Interpreter sequence running them for Exercise 6 in Sect. 5.3

successive dd(3) and ee(3) output cumulative sums and not three itself. Delete **'nonlocal aa'** in Ex_2; try running the routine and explain the result.

7. Write a program which uses the **input**() function successively to accept a sequence of numbers and output the sum. The end of the sequence will be identified through the string 'over'.

8. *1-D random walk*: **xx** starts at zero and steps in the positive direction by unity or in the negative direction by unity. The choice of the first or the second alternative is made randomly with equal likelihood (Papoulis and Unnikrishna Pillai 2002). Write a program which will make **xx** step through 1000 consecutive steps. The span of travel of **xx** is -1000 to +1000. Get the frequency distribution of each position (that is the number of times xx took each of these values). Ideally the frequency distribution should follow binomial distribution. Compare the frequency distribution obtained with that of binomial distribution (Variance of the difference between the corresponding frequency distribution values can be an index for the comparison).

9. *Tower of Hanoi*: three vertical rods—L(Left), C (Central), and R (Right)—are given. C carries a set of n annular discs {d1, d2, d3, ... dn}stacked on it. The disc sizes (diameters) are such that size of d1 < size of d2 < size of d3 < ... < size of dn. C carries the discs in the same order as their sizes with disc d1 on top. The disc set is to be moved to the L rod with two constraints:

   a. Only one disc can be shifted at a time; but the shift can be from any rod to any other rod.
   b. A disc of larger size cannot be moved on to a disc of smaller size.

   With two discs, follow the sequence of movements: d1 → R, d2 → L, d1 → L. With three discs, follow the sequence of movements: d1 → L, d2 → R, d1 → R, d3 → L, d1 → C, d2 → L, d1 → L.
   If n is odd start with d1 → L and if it is even start with d1 → R. With n discs 2n-1 is the minimum number of moves required for the total shift. Write a (recursive) program to effect the shift.
   Use the input () function suitably and present this as an interactive game.

10. *Numerical Integration*: With y as a function of x, evaluation of the definite integral $I = \int_a^b y\,dx$ has to be done numerically if the integral is not known in closed form (e.g. error function, elliptic integral) or the functional relation cannot be expressed with known functions. The set of relations below give the integral value to different approximations for equally spaced values of x (in general the accuracy improves as the number of samples used in the expression increases), h being the spacing (Zwillinger 2003).v

$$I(\text{with a single interval} - \text{trapezoidal rule}) = \frac{h}{2}(y_0 + y_1) \qquad (5.4)$$

$$I(\text{with 2 intervals} - \text{Simpon's rule}) = \frac{h}{3}(y_0 + 4y_1 + y_2) \qquad (5.5)$$

$$I(\text{with 3 intervals} - \text{Simpon's three} - \text{eighth rule}) = \frac{3h}{8}(y_0 + 3y_1 + 3y_2 + y_3)$$

$$\tag{5.5}$$

$$I(\text{with 4 intervals} - \text{Milne's rule}) = \frac{2h}{45}(7y_0 + 32y_1 + 12y_2 + 32y_3 + 7y_4)$$

$$\tag{5.6}$$

$$I(\text{with 5 intervals}) = \frac{5h}{288}(19y_0 + 75y_1 + 50y_2 + 50y_3 + 75y_4 + 19y_5) \tag{5.7}$$

$$I(\text{with 6 intervals} - \text{Weddle's rule})$$

$$= \frac{h}{140}(41y_1 + 216y_1 + 27y_2 + 272y_3 + 27y_4 + 216y_5 + 41y_6)$$

$$\tag{5.8}$$

$$I(\text{with 7 intervals})$$

$$= \frac{7h}{17280}(751y_1 + 3577y_1 + 1323y_2 + 2989y_3 + 2989y_4 + 1323y_5 + + 3577y_6 + 751y_7)$$

$$\tag{5.9}$$

For the general case with $h = (b - a)/n$ the following (Newton-Cotes) formulae can be used:

$$I = \frac{h}{2}\left(y_a + 2\sum_{j=1}^{n-1} y_{2j} + y_b\right) \tag{5.10}$$

$$I = \frac{h}{3}\left(y_a + 2\sum_{j=1}^{(n/2)-1} y_{2j} + 4\sum_{j=1}^{(n/2)} y_{2j-1} + + y_b\right) \tag{5.11}$$

$$\leftarrow n \text{ is even}$$

Prepare routines for integration conforming to each of the relations above. Test them with values for well known functions like sin (y), exp (y), $y^{0.5}$.

11. *Numerical Differentiation*: A select set of formulae are given here (Zwillinger):
First derivative:
2-point formula:

$$y_0' = \frac{1}{h}(y_1 - y_0) \tag{5.12}$$

3-point Formula:

$$y_0' = \frac{1}{2h}(-y_{-1} - 3y_0 + 4y_1) \tag{5.13}$$

$$y_0' = \frac{1}{2h}(-y_{-1} + y_1) \tag{5.14}$$

4-point formula:

$$y_0' = \frac{1}{12h}(y_{-2} - 8y_{-1} + 8y_1 - y_2) \tag{5.15}$$

5-point formula:

$$y_0' = \frac{1}{12h}(-25y_0 + 18y_1 - 36y_2 + 16y_3 - 3y_4) \tag{5.16}$$

Second derivative:

$$y_0'' = \frac{1}{h^2}(y_{-1} - 2y_0 + y_1) \tag{5.17}$$

$$y_0'' = \frac{1}{h^2}(y_0 - 2y_1 + y_2) \tag{5.18}$$

Third derivative

$$y_0''' = \frac{1}{h^3}(y_3 - 3y_2 + 3y_1 - y_0) \tag{5.19}$$

$$y_0''' = \frac{1}{2h^3}(y_2 - 2y_1 + 2y_{-1} - y_{-2}) \tag{5.20}$$

Fourth derivative

$$y_0'''' = \frac{1}{h^4}(y_4 - 4y_3 + 6y_2 - 4y_1 + 6y_0) \tag{5.21}$$

$$y_0''' = \frac{1}{h^4}(y_2 - 4y_1 + 6y_0 - 4y_{-1} + y_{-2}) \tag{5.22}$$

Prepare routines for differentiation conforming to each of the relations above. Test them with values for well known functions like sin (y), exp (y), $y^{0.5}$.

12. A resistor and a capacitor of values R and C respectively are connected in series and a voltage V is applied to the set at time $t = 0$. The current I at any time is exp($-t/RC$) (Toro 2015). The power loss in R at any time—$p(t)$—is $i^2R(t)$. It can be expressed as a lambda function $p =$ **lambda** $R, C, t: R*\exp(-2*t/(R*C))$.

Write a program to get the power at intervals of h/RC for h in the set—{0.0, 0.1, 0.2, 0.3, 0.6, 1.0, 1.5, 2.0, 2.5, 3.0}.

13. $\int_a^b Ri^2 dt$ is the energy dissipated in R in the interval—$[a, b]$ in the above case (Toro 2015). Use the integration formulae for the general case (5.10) and (5.11) and write programs for energy dissipation in R. With $V = 1.0$, get the energy dissipated in the first five successive intervals of RC seconds each. Use $h = 0.02RC$ in each of the cases.

14. Different interpolation formulae are available to get the value of a signal from a given set of its regularly spaced samples. The Hamming window is one of them (Mitra 2013). With $g(n)$ as the given set of samples over the range—$M \le n \le +M$ the interpolated value of $g(t)$ at time t is

$$g(t) = \sum_{-M}^{+M} g(n)w(t-n) \qquad (5.23)$$

where

$$w(k) = 0.54 + 0.46cos\frac{2\pi k}{2M+1} \qquad (5.24)$$

Write a program to evaluate $g(t)$ from the $(2M + 1)$ samples.
With $f(x) = [(x - 3.0)^2 + 2.0]^{0.5}$ get samples of $f(x)$ in the range $0 \le x \le 6.0$ at regular intervals of 0.2. Use the above program for interpolation to evaluate $f(x)$ at 0.5, 1.5, 2.5, 3.5, 4.5, and 5.5. Verify by direct computation.

15. *Edge Detection*: lengths and diameters of objects are determined interposing the object edge between a laser source and detector pair and measuring the intensity of detected light at regular intervals. The scheme is as shown in Fig. 5.24 (Padmanabhan 1999). The measured values of intensity are $x_0, x_1, x_2, \ldots, x_n$ as

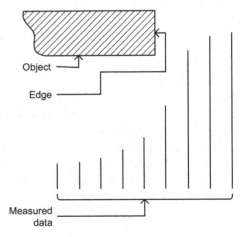

Fig. 5.24 Detection edge position using a laser source

Object

Edge

Measured data

Table 5.1 Measured values at intervals of 1 micron in the neighbourhood of the edge being detected

Displacement in microns	0	1	2	3	4	5
Value	0.0001	0.0010	0.0048	0.0183	0.0559	0.1379
Displacement in microns	6	7	8	9	10	11
Value	0.2276	0.4640	0.5360	0.7724	0.8621	0.9441
Displacement in microns	12	13	14	15	16	17
Value	0.9817	0.9952	0.9990	0.9990	0.9999	

given in Table 5.1. Determine the point where the received intensity is 50 % of the maximum and take it as the measured edge.

Write a program for this using an interpolation formula and get the value of the corresponding displacement.

An alternative is to determine the point of maximum derivative and take it as the edge. Write a program to get the derivative using a formula for derivative and determine the edge position.

References

Decoursey WJ (2003) Statistics and probability for engineering applications. Newnes (Elsevier science) Massachusetts

Gibran K (1926) Sand and foam

Mcnamee JM, Pan VY (2013) Numerical methods for roots of polynomials. Elsevier science, Massachusetts

Mitra SK (2013) Digital signal processing—A computer based approach, 4th edn. McGraw Hill, New York

Padmanabhan TR (1999) Industrial instrumentation. Springer, London

Papoulis A, Unnikrishna Pillai S (2002) Random variables and stochastic processes, 4th edn. McGraw Hill, New York

Ramalho L (2014) Fluent Python. O'Reilly Media Inc., California

Rossum Gv, Drake FL Jr (2014) The Python library reference. Python software foundation

Shyamala CK, Harini N, Padmanabhan TR (2011) Cryptography and security. Wiley India, New Delhi

Toro VD (2015) Electrical engineering fundamentals, 2nd edn. Pearson, Noida

Zhang Y (2015) An Introduction to Python and computer programming. Springer, Singapore

Zwillinger D (ed) (2003) Standard mathematical tables and formulae. Chapman & Hall/CRC, New York

Chapter 6
Additional Operations with Sequences

`tuple`, `list`, `dictionary`, and similar sequences in Python are also known as 'container Objects'. A number of methods are available for them. They are all aimed at culling out meaningful information in different ways for subsequent use. A 'method' is essentially a function with one argument. If a method '**mm**' is associated with an object '**obob**' it is called as '**obob.mm** ()'. It is equivalent to a function **mm**(**obob**) with **obob** as its argument. With these preliminaries let us examine the common methods and related operations with such container objects (Rossum and Drake 2014).

6.1 Slicing

Slicing of a sequence can be done in different ways. It is carried out using the indices of the elements in the sequence. The discussions here are with specific reference to a sequence **aa** as

aa = ['a0', 'b1', 'c2', 'd3', 'e4', 'f5', 'g6', 'h7', 'i8', 'j9', 'k10', '11'].

The details and observations are general enough and valid for any sequence. Two possible conventions of representation and use are shown in Fig. 6.1 for the sequence. One can start with index 0 at the left end and proceed as 0, 1, 2, 3, ... as indices for successive elements. Alternately start at the right end with −1 and proceed to the left with indices −1, −2, −3, ... and so on. The basic slicing structure is depicted in Fig. 6.2 along with its different options:

The most general form of usage specifies slicing as **aa**[α:β:γ] which implies a slice of **aa** starting from α and extending to β − 1; the slice is to include the elements **aa**[α], **aa**[α + γ], **aa**[α + 2 * γ], **aa**[α + 3 * γ], ... up to **aa**[β − 1] in the same order.

© Springer Nature Singapore Pte Ltd. 2016
T.R. Padmanabhan, *Programming with Python*,
DOI 10.1007/978-981-10-3277-6_6

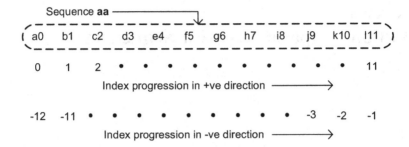

Fig. 6.1 Indexing conventions for slicing of container objects

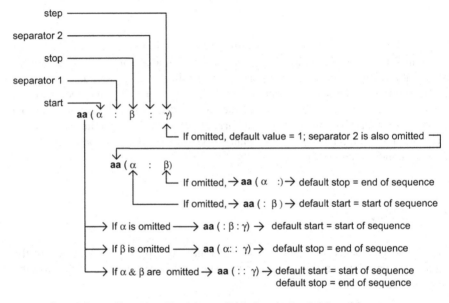

- α, β, γ can be positive or negative integers / object evaluating to integer(s).

- If $\{\alpha, \beta, \gamma\}$ combination is not logically possible, an empty list is returned.

Fig. 6.2 Slicing structure along with its options

1. If $\gamma = 1$, the slicing need be specified only as **aa**[α:β]; the second separator ':' and the γ value are omitted.

   - Further if α is also zero—that is slicing is to start at the start of **aa** itself—the slicing need be specified only as **aa**[:β]; this implies a slice of all elements in **aa** from **aa**[0] to **aa**[$\beta - 1$] in the same order.
   - In addition to γ being one, if the slicing is to continue up to the last element of **aa**, it need be specified only as **aa**[α:].

2. If $\gamma \neq 1$, both separators must be present.

   - If $\alpha = 0$, it can be omitted and slicing specified as **aa**[:β:γ].
   - If $\beta = 0$, it can be omitted and slicing specified as **aa**[α::γ].
   - If α and β are zero and the last index value of **aa** respectively, slicing is specified as **aa**[::γ].

3. α, β, and γ can be positive or negative integers/objects reducible to positive or negative integers.
4. Unrealizable $\{\alpha, \beta, \gamma\}$ sets result in an empty list being returned.

The Python interpreter sequence in Fig. 6.3 brings out the different slicing possibilities. aa in [1] has been defined as a list of elements as explained above. aa[3], aa[−2], and aa[−1] in [2] are the fourth, the last but one, and the last elements of aa. The three together has been output as a tuple. aa[3:9] as cc1 in [3] is a sliced sequence of six consecutive elements—['d3', 'e4', 'f5', 'g6', 'h7', 'i8']—the interval being the default value of one. Note that since aa[−9] is d3, aa[−9:−3] starts with it. As cc2 in [3] it represents the same sliced sequence with the negative index representation, the default step value again being one. dd1 (=aa[3:9:2]) in [4] is a list starting at aa[3] and proceeding up to aa[7] with a slicing step interval of two—['d3', 'f5', 'h7']. Similarly dd2 (=aa[−3:−9:−2]) in [4] produces a slice of aa starting at aa[−3], picking out elements at an interval of two until aa[−9]— ['j9', 'h7', 'f5']—(=[aa[−3], aa[−5], aa[−7]]. ee1 (=aa[:3]) in [5] is the slice of aa from aa[0] to aa[2]—['a0', 'b1', 'c2'] while ee2 (=aa[3:]) is the slice from aa[3] up to and including the last element of aa—['d3', 'e4', 'f5', 'g6', 'h7', 'i8', 'j9', 'k10', 'l11']. It can be seen that **aa**[:3] + **aa**[3:] is **aa** itself. aa[::2] (**ff1**) and **aa**[::−1] (**ff2**) in [6] do slicing end to end: In the former case slicing proceeds in the positive direction with a slicing interval of two; in the latter case it is in the negative direction with −1 as the slicing interval. In fact **aa**[::−1] is the reversed version of **aa**. It is the same as **aa**.reverse() discussed below. **gg1** (**aa**[2::3]) and **gg2**(a a[−2::−3]) in [7] continue slicing to the end (β being omitted). With **gg1** slicing proceeds in the positive direction and with **gg2** in the negative direction—both have three as the slicing step.

With **hh1** and **hh2** in [8] $\alpha = 0$ (implied); slicing starts at the first element and proceeds up to 7 and −7 respectively. In both cases the slicing interval is two. The list—[11, 22, 33, 44, 55, 66, 77, 88, 99]—is directly sliced in [9] at the default slicing interval of unity. The slice specified as [3:7] includes the elements—3rd, 4th, 5th, and the 6th—[44], [55], [66], [77] … [10], [11], [12] slice the string—'computer'— directly and return the respective sliced strings. [10] has $\gamma = 1$ (implied, since omitted) and returns the sliced string of four consecutive letters starting with **aa**[3]—**'pute'**. [11], and [12]—being logically unrealizable—return empty lists.

```
>>>                              >>> [11, 22, 33, 44, 55,
aa=['a0','b1','c2','d3','e4',    66, 77, 88, 99][3:7]     [9]
'f5','g6','h7','i8','j9',        [44, 55, 66, 77]
'k10', 'l11']              [1]   >>> 'computer'[3:7]      [10]
>>> bb0, bb1, bb2 = aa[3],       'pute'
aa[-1], aa[-2]             [2]   >>> aa[-3:-9:2]          [11]
>>> bb0, bb1, bb2                []
('d3', 'l11', 'k10')            >>> aa[3:9:-2]           [12]
>>> cc1, cc2 = aa[3:9], aa[-     []
9:-3]                      [3]   >>> q0 = slice(3,9,2)    [13]
>>> cc1, cc2                     >>> aa[q0]               [14]
(['d3', 'e4', 'f5', 'g6',        ['d3', 'f5', 'h7']
'h7', 'i8'], ['d3', 'e4',       >>> q1 = slice(-3, -9, -2)
'f5', 'g6', 'h7', 'i8'])                                 [15]
>>> dd1, dd2 = aa[3:9:2],        >>> aa[q1]               [16]
aa[-3:-9:-2]               [4]   ['j9', 'h7', 'f5']
>>> dd1, dd2                     >>> p0 = slice(3)        [17]
(['d3', 'f5', 'h7'], ['j9',      >>> aa[p0]               [18]
'h7', 'f5'])                     ['a0', 'b1', 'c2']
>>> ee1, ee2 = aa[:3],           >>> p1 = slice(-3)       [19]
aa[3:]                     [5]   >>> aa[p1]               [20]
>>> ee1, ee2                     ['a0', 'b1', 'c2', 'd3',
(['a0', 'b1', 'c2'], ['d3',      'e4', 'f5', 'g6', 'h7',
'e4', 'f5', 'g6', 'h7', 'i8',    'i8']
'j9', 'k10', 'l11'])            p2 = slice(3,9)          [21]
>>> ff1, ff2 = aa[::2],          >>> aa[p2]               [22]
aa[::-1]                   [6]   ['d3', 'e4', 'f5', 'g6',
>>> ff1, ff2                     'h7', 'i8']
(['a0', 'c2', 'e4', 'g6',        >>> gg = 'How are you' [23]
'i8', 'k10'], ['l11', 'k10',     >>> len(gg)
'j9', 'i8', 'h7', 'g6', 'f5',    11
'e4', 'd3', 'c2', 'b1',          >>> hh1 = gg[3:7]        [24]
'a0'])                           >>> hh1
>>> gg1, gg2 = aa[2::3], aa[-    ' are'
2::-3]                     [7]   >>> jj0, jj1, jj2, jj3 =
>>> gg1, gg2                     gg[p0], gg[p1], gg[q0],
(['c2', 'f5', 'i8', 'l11'],      gg[q1]                  [25]
['k10', 'h7', 'e4', 'b1'])       >>> jj0, jj1, jj2, jj3
>>> hh1, hh2 = aa[:7:2],         ('How', 'How are ', ' r ',
aa[:-7:2]                  [8]   'yea')
>>> hh1, hh2
(['a0', 'c2', 'e4', 'g6'],
['a0', 'c2', 'e4'])
```

Fig. 6.3 Python Interpreter sequence illustrating slicing

The arguments for slicing can be separately defined through the slice() object. Basically slice() has three forms as shown in Fig. 6.4:

1. In the simplest form **aa**(slice(β)) returns a slice of **aa** from index zero (default value) to index ($\beta - 1$).

Fig. 6.4 slice() structure
along with its options

aa(**slice**(β)) is same as **aa**[0 : β]

aa(**slice**(α, β)) is same as **aa**[α : β]

aa(**slice**(α, β, γ)) is same as **aa**[α : β: γ]

Three forms for specifying **slice**()

2. With **aa**(slice(α, β)), a slice of **aa** from index α to index (β − 1) is returned.
3. In the above two cases the slice step interval γ is unity (default value). Otherwise slice is specified fully as **aa**(slice(α, β, γ)).

   q0 in [13] in Fig. 6.3 is a slice object. With that **aa**[=**q0**] in [14] is the same as **dd1** in [4]. Similarly **aa**[**q1**] in [16] with **q1** in [15] as the slice object, is the same as **dd2** in [4]. With **p0** (=slice(3)) in [17] **aa**[p0] in [18] returns **aa** sliced up to **aa** [2], the slicing interval being the default value of unity. Similarly **aa**[**p1**] in [20] with **p1** (=**slice**(−3)) in [19] returns the sliced object extending to **aa**[−3]—['a0', 'b1', 'c2', 'd3', 'e4', 'f5', 'g6', 'h7', 'i8']—all elements from start up to **aa**[−3]. **p2** (=slice(3, 9)) in [21]—with default slice interval of unity, it has all the elements from 3rd to the 8th (inclusive). With that **aa**[**p2**] in [22] is the same as **cc1** in [3]. **gg** (='How are you') as a string of length eleven in [23] is sliced in a few ways. **hh1** (=**gg**[3:7]) in [24] returns '**are**' as the sliced string. Subsequent lines show the slicing of **gg** using the slice objects defined earlier—**p0**, **p1**, **q0**, and **q1**.

6.2 Reversing

The Python Interpreter sequence in Fig. 6.5 illustrates the use of the built-in function reversed() and the corresponding method. **a1** in [1] is a tuple of integers. reversed (a1) produces an iterator with the elements of **a1** in the reversed sequence. [2] is the corresponding list of **a1** having been reversed. **b** in [3] is a list of assorted items. **br** in [4] is the tuple formed by reversing the sequence **b**. In general reversed() can be used with any container/sequence to generate a tuple or a list of the reversed sequence. The method reverse() operates on a list. It returns the corresponding reversed sequence itself. The sequence **b** [3] is reversed by **b**.reverse() in [5] as can be seen from the new value of **b** in the following lines. **b** is restored with the subsequent **b**.reverse() in [6].

   a2 ('information') is a string; tuple (reversed (**a2**)) [7] creates a tuple of the character set of 'information' in reverse order [8]. **a2** being immutable, method reverse() is not applicable to it. However the end to end slicing in the negative direction produces a new string with the letters in 'information' appearing in the reverse order [9]. **ulta**() in [10] is the equivalent function as demonstrated through its application in [12], and [13] where **a2** ('information') is reversed and then restored.

```
>>> a1 = 1, 2, 3, 4                                              [1]
>>> list(reversed(a1))                                           [2]
[4, 3, 2, 1]
>>> b = ['Rama', 'Latha', 'Adarsh', 'Siddu', 31, 3.1]           [3]
>>> br = tuple(reversed(b))                                       [4]
>>> br
(3.1, 31, 'Siddu', 'Adarsh', 'Latha', 'Rama')
>>> b.reverse()                                                  [5]
>>> b
[3.1, 31, 'Siddu', 'Adarsh', 'Latha', 'Rama']
>>> b.reverse()                                                  [6]
>>> b
['Rama', 'Latha', 'Adarsh', 'Siddu', 31, 3.1]
>>> a2 = 'information'                                           [7]
>>> tuple(reversed(a2))                                          [8]
('n', 'o', 'i', 't', 'a', 'm', 'r', 'o', 'f', 'n', 'i')
>>> 'information'[::-1]                                          [9]
'noitamrofni'
>>> def ulta(sst):                                              [10]
...     u = ''
...     for jj in range(len(sst)-1, -1, -1):
...         u += sst[jj]
...     return u
...
>>> a0 = ulta(a2)                                               [11]
>>> a0
'noitamrofni'
>>> a3 = ulta(a0)                                               [12]
>>> a3
'information'
>>>
```

Fig. 6.5 Python Interpreter sequence illustrating reversing

6.3 Sorting

Any sequence can be sorted using sorted() function. sorted (**sq**) carries out a sorting with the sequence **sq** and returns a list. The general form of sorted() function is shown in Fig. 6.6a. key and reverse are two optional arguments as shown in the figure. The comparison operation ('<', '>') is the basis for carrying out the sorting. In the absence of both the optional arguments (key and reverse) **sq** is sorted by comparing its element directly. In case only key is present as the additional argument, it is a function of **sq** or elements of **sq** returning an item on which the comparison for sorting is carried out. Reverse is a boolean; if present it is set to true; here the comparison and sorting are done in the reverse (descending) order. The sort method shown in Fig. 6.6b has a similar structure with key and

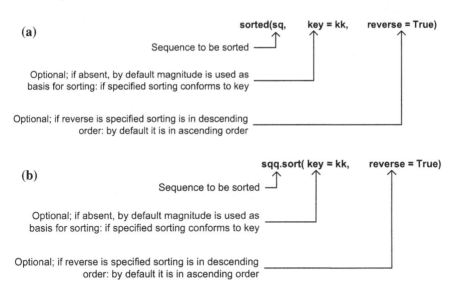

Fig. 6.6 Structure of **a** `sorted` () function and **b** `sort` () method long with their options

`reverse` having the same roles and significance. It sorts a `list` in place. For a `list` **sqq**, **sqq**.sort() returns **sqq** as a sorted list.

The Python Interpreter sequence in Fig. 6.7a illustrates the applications of sorted() method and Fig. 6.7b those of sort() function; functionally both carry out similar sorting. **ab** in [1] is a `tuple` of names; being immutable it cannot be sorted in place. But sorted(**ab**) is returned as a list as **ac** (=['**aanand**', '**arab**', '**bala**', '**ram**', '**roshan**', '**zara**']) in [2]; the sorting is in ascending order—with 'a' < 'b' < 'c' < ⋯ < 'y' < 'z'. The first, second, third, ... and c, characters in that order, are considered for the comparison in sorting. With dictionary **ad**, sorted(**ad**) returns the `list` of keys in the alphabetical order [3] (See the following section for more on this). Similar sorted `list` is returned with the key in the dictionary specified as the basis for sorting [4]. The length of the element is specified as the key for sorting in [5]. In turn '**ram**'—being of shortest length—is the first in the list and '**Roshan**' of six characters is the last one.

The module **marks1.py** has the marks of a set of students (see Fig. 5.16). **S6**, **S7**, **S8**, **S9**, and **S10** represent the students' names and their marks as respective tuples. The tuple **dta** gives the order details. **st** is a list of the five elements— **S6**, **S7**, **S8**, **S9**, **S10**. The items here have been arranged to facilitate illustration of the functions, methods, and so on. **marks1.py** has been imported ([6] in Fig. 6.7a) from the folder **demo_5** and **marks1.st** assigned to **b1** in [7]. The name of each student in each entry is the basis for sorting **b1** in [8]. The sorted list is assigned to **ai** [9]. The sorting can be seen to have been done with the names arranged alphabetically. **b1** has been sorted with the marks scored in Physics as basis for

(a)

```
>>> ab = 'arab', 'aanand', 'ram', 'bala', 'zara',
'roshan'                                                    [1]
>>> ac = sorted(ab)                                         [2]
>>> ac
['aanand', 'arab', 'bala', 'ram', 'roshan', 'zara']
>>> ad = {'arab':22, 'aanand':2, 'ram':17, 'bala':71,
'zara':33,'roshan':41}
>>> ae = sorted(ad)                                         [3]
>>> ae
['aanand', 'arab', 'bala', 'ram', 'roshan', 'zara']
>>> ag = sorted(ad, key = lambda nn:nn)                     [4]
>>> ag
['aanand', 'arab', 'bala', 'ram', 'roshan', 'zara']
>>> af = sorted(ae, key = lambda nm: len(nm))               [5]
>>> af
['ram', 'arab', 'bala', 'zara', 'aanand', 'roshan']
>>> from demo_5 import marks1                               [6]
>>> b1 = marks1.st                                          [7]
>>> ai = sorted(b1, key = lambda nk: nk[0])                 [8]
>>> ai                                                      [9]
[('Kala', 90, 86, 91, 92, 93), ('Karthik', 77, 78, 79,
80, 81), ('Karun', 85, 86, 87, 88, 89), ('Lan', 65, 86,
66, 67, 68), ('Sarani', 76, 78, 82, 83, 84)]
>>> aj = sorted(b1, key = lambda nk:nk[1])                  [10]
>>> aj                                                      [11]
[('Lan', 65, 86, 66, 67, 68), ('Sarani', 76, 78, 82, 83,
84), ('Karthik', 77, 78, 79, 80, 81), ('Karun', 85, 86,
87, 88, 89), ('Kala', 90, 86, 91, 92, 93)]
>>> ak = sorted(b1, key = lambda nk:len(nk[0]))            [12]
>>> ak                                                      [13]
[('Lan', 65, 86, 66, 67, 68), ('Kala', 90, 86, 91, 92,
93), ('Karun', 85, 86, 87, 88, 89), ('Sarani', 76, 78,
82, 83, 84), ('Karthik', 77, 78, 79, 80, 81)]
>>> al = sorted(b1, key = lambda nk:nk[3], reverse =
True)                                                       [14]
>>> al                                                      [15]
[('Kala', 90, 86, 91, 92, 93), ('Karun', 85, 86, 87, 88,
89), ('Sarani', 76, 78, 82, 83, 84), ('Karthik', 77, 78,
79, 80, 81), ('Lan', 65, 86, 66, 67, 68)]
>>> am = sorted(b1, key = lambda nk:(nk[2],nk[1]))         [16]
>>> am                                                      [17]
[('Sarani', 76, 78, 82, 83, 84), ('Karthik', 77, 78, 79,
80, 81), ('Lan', 65, 86, 66, 67, 68), ('Karun', 85, 86,
87, 88, 89), ('Kala', 90, 86, 91, 92, 93)]
>>> an = sorted(b1, key = lambda nk:(nk[2],nk[1]),
reverse = True)                                             [18]
>>> an                                                      [19]
[('Kala', 90, 86, 91, 92, 93), ('Karun', 85, 86, 87, 88,
89), ('Lan', 65, 86, 66, 67, 68), ('Karthik', 77, 78, 79,
80, 81), ('Sarani', 76, 78, 82, 83, 84)]
```

Fig. 6.7 a Python Interpreter sequence illustrating use of sorted() function **b** Python Interpreter sequence illustrating use of sort() method

(b)

```
>>> aa = [ 22, 2, 17, 71, 33, 41, 4 ]                            [1]
>>> aa.sort()                                                    [2]
>>> aa
[2, 4, 17, 22, 33, 41, 71]
>>> b1 = marks1.st                                               [3]
>>> b1.sort(key = lambda nn:nn[1])                               [4]
>>> b1                                                           [5]
[('Lan', 65, 86, 66, 67, 68), ('Sarani', 76, 78, 82, 83,
84), ('Karthik', 77, 78, 79, 80, 81), ('Karun', 85, 86,
87, 88, 89), ('Kala', 90, 86, 91, 92, 93)]
>>> b1.sort(key = lambda nn:nn[0])
>>> b1
[('Kala', 90, 86, 91, 92, 93), ('Karthik', 77, 78, 79, 80,
81), ('Karun', 85, 86, 87, 88, 89), ('Lan', 65, 86, 66,
67, 68), ('Sarani', 76, 78, 82, 83, 84)]
>>> b1.sort(key = lambda nn:len(nn[0]))
>>> b1
[('Lan', 65, 86, 66, 67, 68), ('Kala', 90, 86, 91, 92,
93), ('Karun', 85, 86, 87, 88, 89), ('Sarani', 76, 78, 82,
83, 84), ('Karthik', 77, 78, 79, 80, 81)]
>>> b1.sort(key = lambda nn:len(nn[0]), reverse = True)
>>> b1
[('Karthik', 77, 78, 79, 80, 81), ('Sarani', 76, 78, 82,
83, 84), ('Karun', 85, 86, 87, 88, 89), ('Kala', 90, 86,
91, 92, 93), ('Lan', 65, 86, 66, 67, 68)]
>>> b1.sort(key = lambda nn:(nn[2], nn[1]))
>>> b1
[('Sarani', 76, 78, 82, 83, 84), ('Karthik', 77, 78, 79,
80, 81), ('Lan', 65, 86, 66, 67, 68), ('Karun', 85, 86,
87, 88, 89), ('Kala', 90, 86, 91, 92, 93)]
>>> b1.sort(key = lambda nn:(nn[2], nn[1]), reverse =
True)
>>> b1
[('Kala', 90, 86, 91, 92, 93), ('Karun', 85, 86, 87, 88,
89), ('Lan', 65, 86, 66, 67, 68), ('Karthik', 77, 78, 79,
80, 81), ('Sarani', 76, 78, 82, 83, 84)]
```

Fig. 6.7 (continued)

comparison and returned as **aj** [10], [11]. **ak** in [13] is again the same list but sorting done with the length of the name of students as the yardstick for comparison [12]. **al** in [15] returns the list with sorting done based on the marks scored in Maths; but the sorting is done in the reverse order (91 (Kala), 87 (Karun), 82 (Sarani), 79 (Karthik), 66 (Lan)). For **am** marks in Chemistry and Physics are specified in that order [16] for sorting. If the marks scored by two or more candidates are equal, the marks in Physics has to be the basis for their comparison; with Sarani and Karthik scoring 78 in Chemistry, Sarani is ahead of Karthik in the sorted list since she gets only 76 in Physics in contrast to 77 by Karthik. Similar sorting with marks in Chemistry and Physics (in that order) as basis is done in reverse order [18] and returned [19].

The Fig. 6.7b which illustrates the use of the sort () method with sequences has **aa** in [1] as a simple list of numbers. **aa**.sort() in [2] returns **aa** in sorted form. Sorting is implicitly done in ascending order of magnitudes and **aa** is returned as the sorted list. As in the previous case the marks list has been imported (Fig. 5.16) and assigned to **b1** in [3]. The sort() function has been applied to **b1** in different ways and the respective sorted lists shown in the subsequent lines. The structure and operations of the method can be seen to be identical to their counterparts discussed with the sorted() function above.

The following are to be noted regarding all these rearrangements:

- The individual mark-lists—**S6**, **S7**, **S8**, **S9**, **S10**—remain intact since each is a (immutable) tuple.
- The key used for sorting can be specified as any desired function which returns a value/number that can be used for comparison. Being only for illustrative purpose, all the functions used here are limited to single line (lambda type) functions. If necessary the functions can be separately defined and used for specifying the key.

6.4   Operations with Sequences

A number of operators and algebraic operations with numbers involving them were discussed in Chaps. 1 and 2. The '+', '*', and comparison operations amongst them are applicable to sequences—of course with proper reinterpretation. The Python Interpreter sequence in Fig. 6.8 Illustrates the use of '+' and '*' operators. **aa** ('**Good**') in [1] is a string. **aa3** in [2] is **aa** * 3—another string with **aa**

```
>>> aa = 'Good '                              [1]
>>> aa3 = aa*3                                [2]
>>> aa3
'Good Good Good '
>>> bb = 'day'                                [3]
>>> ab = aa+bb                                [4]
>>> ab
'Good day'                                    [5]
>>> cc = [3, 5]                               [6]
>>> dd = [2, 4, 7]                            [7]
>>> cd = cc + dd                              [8]
>>> cd                                        [9]
[3, 5, 2, 4, 7]
>>> ee = ['Hello', 'How', 'are', 'you']      [10]
>>> ce = cc + ee                              [11]
>>> ce
[3, 5, 'Hello', 'How', 'are', 'you']         [12]
```

Fig. 6.8 Python Interpreter sequence illustrating use of '+' and '*' with sequences

repeated three times. **bb** ('**day**') in [3] is another string. **aa** + **bb** in [4] adds (that is concatenates) **aa** and **bb** to form a new string **ab** in [5]. **cc** and cd in [6] and [7] are two lists. **cc** + **dd** in [8] concatenates the two to form the combined list **cd** [9]. **ee** in [10] is another list of strings(words). It has been combined/concatenated with list **cc** in [6] to form the list **ce** in [11], [12]. *In fact this is characteristic of Python; built-in functions, methods, and operations are mostly generic in nature in the sense that the operation is adapted and carried out to suit the type of objects forming the arguments.*

Figure 6.9 is a Python Interpreter sequence to illustrate comparison and related operations with sequences. The method **ss**.count(**x**) counts the number of occurrences of **x** in the sequence **ss**. The number of 'o's in the sequence—'Hello how are you?'—is counted as three in [1]. [3] and the lines following use list **ff** (=[3. 2, 5, 2, 4, 7, 2]) and return the number of 3's and 2's in it. The number of occurrences of the character pair '**or**' in the whole of the string **qtt** is counted and returned in [17]. Counting of other letter sequences can be done similarly.

a, b, and **c** are tuples of numbers ([4], [5], [6])—type and size being the same for all the three. [7] is a check as to whether **a** > **b**. For the comparison here the 1st, 2nd, 3rd, … entries in individual sequences get priority in the same order. For the check **a** > **b** in [7], **a**[0] and **b**[0] are compared first. If they are not equal the comparison stops here itself. Else—as is the case here—**a**[1] and **b**[1] are compared. Here **b**[1] > **a**[1]; comparison stops with the decision **b** > **a**. In case **a**[1] = **b**[1], **a**[2] and **b**[2] will be compared. The decisions with comparison of **b** with **a** in [7] and [8], with **c** in [9], and comparison of all the three of them in [10] are carried out in this manner. **aa, bb**, and **cc** in [11], [12], and [13] are lists of strings—all of them of the same type and size. They are compared in [14], and [15]. The basis for comparison here is **a** < **b** < **c** < ⋯ < **y** < **z**. [16] compares specific elements (strings) in the lists **aa** and **cc**. Since **ac** (**aa**[2]) < **ad** (**cc**[2]) the comparison returns 'True'.

ss.index(**x**) is the simplest form of use of the method index(). It returns the index of first occurrence of **x** in the sequence **ss**. **qtt**.index('**or**') in [18] identifies the first occurrence of '**or**' in the string **qtt** (a tuple) to be at index 22. **ss**.index(**x, j**) seeks the index of the first occurrence of **x** in **ss** after the **j**th element in it. Here the search for **x** can continue up to the end of **ss**. [19] continues the search for '**or**' after the 22nd character in it and returns the index of its next occurrence as 92. The hunt for '**or**' is continued beyond in [92], its next occurrence being at index 146. The most general form for index() is **ss**.index(**x, j, k**) where the hunt for **x** in **ss** starts with index **j** and continues to **k**; of course the search stops after the first hit for **x**.

6.4.1 *Max() and Min() Functions*

The max() and min() built-in functions identify and return the maximum and minimum elements from a given set. The criteria for identifying the

```
>>> 'Hello, how are you?'.count('o')      [1]
3
>>> ff = [3, 2, 5, 2, 4, 7, 2]            [2]
>>> ff.count(3)                           [3]
1
>>> ff.count(2)
3
>>> a = 5, 10, 15, 20                     [4]
>>> b = 5, 11, 14, 1                      [5]
>>> c = 5, 10, 14, 2500                   [6]
>>> a > b                                 [7]
False
>>> a < b                                 [8]
True
>>> b > c                                 [9]
True
>>> c < a < b                             [10]
True
>>> aa = ['aa', 'ab', 'ac']              [11]
>>> bb = ['bb', 'bb', 'cc']              [12]
>>> cc = ['aa', 'ab', 'ad']              [13]
>>> aa < bb                               [14]

True
>>> aa < cc                               [15]
True
>>> aa[2] < cc[2]                         [16]
True
>>> qtt = '''What everybody echoes or in silence
passes by as true today may turn out to be falsehood
tomorrow, mere smoke of opinion, which some had
trusted for a cloud that would sprinkle fertilizing
rain on their fields'''
>>> qtt.count('or')                       [17]
3
>>> len(qtt)
209
>>> qtt.index('or')                       [18]
22
>>> qtt.index('or', 23)                   [19]
92
>>> qtt.index('or',93)                    [20]
146
>>>
```

Fig. 6.9 Python Interpreter sequence illustrating use of comparison and other operations with sequences

```
>>> aa = (2, 3, 2.5, -1.2, 0.8, -7.1)                          [1]
>>> b1, b2 = max(aa), min(aa)                                  [2]
>>> b1, b2
(3, -7.1)
>>> c1, c2 = max(aa, key = lambda x:abs(x)), min(aa, key
= lambda x:abs(x))                                            [3]
>>> c1, c2
(-7.1, 0.8)
>>> d1, d2 = max(aa, key = lambda x:1/x), min(aa, key =
lambda x:1/x)                                                 [4]
>>> d1, d2
(0.8, -1.2)
>>> max(2, 3, 2.5, -1.2, 0.8, -7.1)                            [5]
3
>>> min(2, 3, 2.5, -1.2, 0.8, -7.1, key = lambda x:1/x)
                                                              [6]
-1.2
>>> ff = 'Karthik', 'Kala', 'Karun', 'Lan', 'Sarani'  [7]
>>> f1, f2 = max(ff), min(ff)                                 [8]
>>> f1, f2
('Sarani', 'Kala')
>>> f3, f4 = max(ff, key = lambda x: len(x)), min(ff, key
= lambda x: len(x))                                          [9]
>>> f3, f4
('Karthik', 'Lan')
>>> from demo_5 import      marks1                           [10]

>>> bb = marks1.st                                          [11]
>>> e1, e2, e3 = max(bb, key = lambda x:len(x[0])),
max(bb, key = lambda x:x[0]), min(bb, key = lambda
x:x[1])                                                     [12]
>>> e1, e2, e3
(('Karthik', 77, 78, 79, 80, 81), ('Sarani', 76, 78, 82,
83, 84), ('Lan', 65, 86, 66, 67, 68))
```

Fig. 6.10 Python Interpreter sequence illustrating use of max() and min() functions

maximum/minimum value can be specified through a key. The Python Interpreter sequence in Fig. 6.10 illustrates their use. **aa** [1] is a tuple of numbers; **b1** (=max (aa)) is returned as the maximum amongst them (=3) in [2]. Similarly **b2** (in **aa**) is the minimum (at −1.2) amongst them. The maximum amongst the absolute values of the elements in **aa** is 7.1 with the key as abs(**x**) for **x**; this maximum value is assigned to **c1** in [3]. The minimum of the absolute values (=0.8) is assigned to **c2**. The reciprocals of the elements of **aa** form the basis to decide the maximum and the minimum in [4]. With this the maximum value is assigned to **d1**(=1/0.8) and minimum to **d2** (=−1/1.2). Any other criterion/metric can be used as the key to identify the min/max values. Use of max as max (2, 3, 2.5, −1.2, 0.8, −7.1) directly in [5] yields the maximum value (=3). Same holds good of the min () function as well. As an extended use the max/min criteria can be specified through a key as done in [6].

ff in [7] is a `tuple` of names. max(**ff**) is decided with the criteria **a** < **b** < **c** < ⋯ < **x** < **y** < **z** the comparison being carried out starting with the first letter. **Sarani** (=**f1**) is returned as the max—the choice being based on the first letter itself [8]. **Kala** (=**f2**) is the minimum; the selection based on the first letter will have **karthik**, **kala**, and **karun**. The second letter—being 'a' in all of them—does not change the scenario. At the third stage 'l' in **kala** (=**f2**) decides the choice.

[9] uses the length of the name—number of characters in it as the basis to decide the maximum (**f3** = **karthik**) and minimum (**f4** = **lan**). The marks-list from **demo_5** is imported [10] and assigned to **bb** in [11]. It is the same as that in Fig. 5.16. the max()/min() can be specified in different ways and extracted. [12] shows three examples. **Karthik** is the student with the longest name. His data is assigned to **e1**. Alphabetically **Sarani** comes last; her data is assigned to **e2**. The mark scored in Physics is the basis for selection of **e3**. The candidate with the lowest marks scored in physics is **lan**; his data is assigned to **e3**.

6.4.2   Additional Operations with Sequences

The Python Interpreter sequence in Fig. 6.11 illustrates the use of some additional operations with sequences. **aa** in [1] is a `list` of strings. del **aa**[3:9] in [2] deletes all the elements from **aa**[3] to **aa**[8] (inclusive) from **aa**. **aa**[2]='2C' in [3] redefines the value of **aa**[2] as can be seen from the lines following. The usage here is different from the assignment 'cc = aa[2]' where **cc** is assigned the value of **aa**[2] without altering **aa** in any way. Similarly **ab**[−1] (='7H') in [12] replaces the last element of **ab**(='h7') in [7]. The new value of **ab** is in [13]. **ab**.append(**ab1**) in [6] appends **ab1** [5] to `list` **ab** [4]—this is possible, **ab** being an iterable. The method append() appends a single element to the list; the appended element gets inserted into the `list` as its last (rightmost) element. [7] shows **ab** with **ab1** appended to it. **ab** is restored in [8] to its previous value in [4] by deleting the last element in **ab**—that is **ab1**.

ab.extend(**ab1**) in [10] enhances **ab** by appending all the elements of **ab1** to it in the same order at one go. In contrast **ab**.append(**ab1**) in [6] appends **ab1** as a single entity to **ab**.

Method append() is useful if the elements to be appended are formed one by one (as in a loop). But if the elements (more than one) to be appended are known at a stretch method extend() is a better alternative.

aa is defined afresh in [14]. del **aa**[3:9:2] in [15] deletes all elements in **aa** starting with **aa**[3] and going up to **aa**[9] at interval of 2. (start, stop, step) set is similar to that in slicing (in Sect. 6.1). The truncated **aa** in [16] is defined afresh in [17]. Elements of **an** of three elements in [18], replace three elements in **aa** through [19]. Here again the set of three elements in it—**aa**[3] to **aa**[9] at the interval of

(a)

```
>>> aa =['a0','b1','c2','d3', 'e4', 'f5', 'g6', 'h7',
'i8', 'j9', 'k10', 'l11']                                    [1]
>>> del aa[3:9]                                              [2]
>>> aa
['a0', 'b1', 'c2', 'j9', 'k10', 'l11']
>>> aa[2] = '2C'                                             [3]
>>> aa
['a0', 'b1', '2C', 'j9', 'k10', 'l11']
>>> ab = ['a0', 'b1', 'c2', 'd3', 'e4']                      [4]
>>> ab1 = ['f5', 'g6', 'h7']                                 [5]
>>> ab.append(ab1)                                           [6]
>>> ab                                                       [7]
['a0', 'b1', 'c2', 'd3', 'e4', ['f5', 'g6', 'h7']]
>>> del ab[-1]                                               [8]
>>> ab                                                       [9]
['a0', 'b1', 'c2', 'd3', 'e4']
>>> ab.extend(ab1)                                           [10]
>>> ab                                                       [11]
['a0', 'b1', 'c2', 'd3', 'e4', 'f5', 'g6', 'h7']
>>> ab[-1] = '7H'                                            [12]
>>> ab                                                       [13]
['a0', 'b1', 'c2', 'd3', 'e4', 'f5', 'g6', '7H']
>>> aa =['a0','b1','c2','d3', 'e4', 'f5', 'g6', 'h7',
'i8', 'j9', 'k10', 'l11']                                    [14]
>>> del aa[3:9:2]                                            [15]
>>> aa                                                       [16]
['a0', 'b1', 'c2', 'e4', 'g6', 'i8', 'j9', 'k10', 'l11']
>>> aa =['a0','b1','c2','d3', 'e4', 'f5', 'g6', 'h7',
'i8', 'j9', 'k10', 'l11']                                    [17]
>>> an = ['3D', '5F', '7H']                                  [18]
>>> aa[3:9:2] = an                                           [19]
>>> aa

['a0', 'b1', 'c2', '3D', 'e4', '5F', 'g6', '7H', 'i8',
'j9', 'k10', 'l11']
>>> aa = ['a0', 'b1', 'c2', 'e4', 'g6', 'i8', 'j9', 'k10',
'l11']
>>> for jj in range (len(an)):aa.insert(3+2*jj,an[jj])[20]
...
>>> aa
['a0', 'b1', 'c2', '3D', 'e4', '5F', 'g6', '7H', 'i8',
'j9', 'k10', 'l11']
>>> an.pop(1)                                                [21]
'5F'
>>> an                                                       [22]
['3D', '7H']
```

Fig. 6.11 a Python Interpreter sequence illustrating use of some methods and operations with sequences (continued in Fig.6.11b) **b** Python Interpreter sequence illustrating use of some methods and operations with sequences (continued in Fig.6.11a)

(b)

```
>>> aa =['a0','b1','c2','d3', 'e4', 'f5', 'g6', 'h7',
'i8', 'j9', 'k10', 'l11']                              [23]
>>> an = []                                            [24]
>>> for jk in range(3, 9, 2): an.append(aa.pop(jk))    [25]
...
>>> aa                                                 [26]
['a0', 'b1', 'c2', 'e4', 'f5', 'h7', 'i8', 'k10', 'l11']
>>> an                                                 [27]
['d3', 'g6', 'j9']
>>> aa =['a0','b1','c2','d3','e4','f5','g6', 'h7', 'i8',
'j9', 'k10', 'l11']                                    [28]
>>> aa.remove('d3')                                    [29]
>>> aa                                                 [30]
['a0', 'b1', 'c2', 'e4', 'f5', 'g6', 'h7', 'i8', 'j9',
'k10', 'l11']
>>> bb = [2, 3, 5, 2, 7, 1]                            [31]
>>> bb.remove(2)                                       [32]
>>> bb                                                 [33]
[3, 5, 2, 7, 1]
>>> bb.remove(2)                                       [34]
>>> bb                                                 [35]
[3, 5, 7, 1]
>>> bb.remove(2)                                       [36]
Traceback (most recent call last):
  File "<stdin>", line 1, in <module>
ValueError: list.remove(x): x not in list
```

Fig. 6.11 (continued)

two—that is **aa**[3], **aa**[5], and **aa**[7]—is replaced; '**d3**', '**f5**', and '**h7**' are replaced by '**3D**', '**5F**', and '**7H**' respectively. Needless to say, size of **an** here is to be the same as that required for the substitution.

insert(**jj**, **x**) will insert **x** at the **jj**th location in **aa**. An alternate way of inserting **an** into **aa** (done above) uses insert() in a loop [20]. But the insert operation in [19] is more elegant and compact. **an**.pop(1) in [21] pops **an**(1). With that, **an**[2] (='**7H**') in (18) takes the place of **an**[1] as can be seen from [22]. **aa** and **an** have been redefined in [23] and [24] as lists—the latter being an empty one. **an**.append (**aa**.pop(**jk**)) pops the **jk** th element in list **aa** and appends it to **an**. With that **aa**(**jk** + 1) moves to **aa**[**jk**] and number of elements in **aa** reduces by one. The popped element is appended to **an**. For **jk** = 3, 5, and 7 in succession the loop in [25] executes **an**.append (**aa**.pop(**jk**)). Table 6.1 clarifies the steps in the process. The truncated **aa** and the new **an** are in [26] and [27] respectively.

aa.remove(**x**) removes the first occurrence of element **x** from list **aa**. If **x** is not present in **aa** a '*ValueError*' is returned. The list **aa** has been restored in [28]. **aa**.remove('**d3**') in [29] removes the element '**d3**' from it as can be seen from the updated value of **aa** in [30]. **bb** is a list of integers in [31]. **bb**.remove (2) in [32] removes the first occurrence of the integer '2' from the list; the new value of **bb** is [3, 5, 2, 7, 1] as in [33]. **bb**.remove(2) in [34] removes the

Table 6.1 Execution of pop-append sequence in succession in Python Interpreter sequence in Fig. 6.11

Jk		aa	an	Elements and indices in aa after pop
	Values at start	['a0', 'b1', 'c2', 'd3', 'e4', 'f5', 'g6', 'h7', 'i8', 'j9', 'k10', 'l11']	[]	aa[3] = 'd3', aa[4] = 'e4', aa[5] = 'f5', aa[6] = 'g6', aa[7] = 'h7', aa[8] = 'i8', ...
3	After 1st pop	['a0', 'b1', 'c2', 'e4', 'f5', 'g6', 'h7', 'i8', 'j9', 'k10', 'l11']	['d3']	aa[3] = 'e4', aa[4] = 'f5', aa[5] = 'g6', aa[6] = 'h7', aa[7] = 'i8', aa[8] = 'j9', ...
5	After 2nd pop	['a0', 'b1', 'c2', 'e4', 'f5', 'h7', 'i8', 'j9', 'k10', 'l11']	['d3', 'g6']	aa[3] = 'e4', aa[4] = 'f5', aa[5] = 'h7', aa[6] = 'i8', aa[7] = 'j9', aa[8] = 'k10', ...
7	After 3rd pop	['a0', 'b1', 'c2', 'e4', 'f5','h7', 'i8', 'k10', 'l11']	['d3', 'g6', 'j9']	aa[3] = 'e4', aa[4] = 'f5', aa[5] = 'h7', aa[6] = 'i8', aa[7] = 'k10', aa[8] = 'l11', ...

remaining '2' from **bb** leaving it as [3, 5, 7, 1] in [35] without any more '2's within. Hence another bb.remove(2) in [36] returns a '*ValueError*'.

6.5 Operations with Sets

Set in Python is essentially the implementation of the set concept in mathematics. A set is a collection of well-defined, unique but unordered entities/objects. The operations/methods for sets essentially correspond to the basic set operations in mathematics.

The Python Interpreter sequence in Fig. 6.12a is intended to bring out the features of different operations with sets. A set can be formed from any collection of individual (diverse) objects. **ff** in [1] is the set formed with the elements in the list of integers—[2, 3, 5, 2, 7, 1]—as its members. **ff** in [2] has all the integers in the list without duplication. The integer '2' occurs twice in the list but only once in the set **ff**. The order of the members in the set is immaterial; hence the numbers in it—that is the members of the set—cannot be indexed; but they can be

(a)

```
>>> ff = set([2, 3, 5, 2, 7, 1])                              [1]
>>> ff                                                        [2]
{1, 2, 3, 5, 7}
>>> aa1 = ['a0', 'b1', 'c2', 'd3', 'e4', 'f5', 'g6', 'h7']
                                                              [3]
>>> aa2 = ['e4', 'f5', 'g6', 'h7', 'i8', 'j9', 'k10',
'l11']                                                        [4]
>>> aa1.extend(aa2)                                           [5]
>>> aa1                                                       [6]
['a0', 'b1', 'c2', 'd3', 'e4', 'f5', 'g6', 'h7', 'e4',
'f5', 'g6', 'h7', 'i8', 'j9', 'k10', 'l11']
>>> aa3 = ['a0', 'b1', 'c2', 'd3', 'e4', 'f5', 'g6', 'h7']
                                                              [7]
>>> as1, as2, as3 = set(aa1), set(aa2), set(aa3)              [8]
>>> as1, as2, as3                                             [9]
({'h7', 'a0', 'l11', 'k10', 'g6', 'e4', 'b1', 'd3', 'f5',
'c2', 'i8', 'j9'}, {'h7', 'l11', 'k10', 'g6', 'e4', 'f5',
'i8', 'j9'}, {'h7', 'a0', 'g6', 'e4', 'b1', 'd3', 'f5',
'c2'})
>>> aal1, aas1 = len(aa1), len(as1)                           [10]
>>> aal1, aas1                                                [11]
(16, 12)
>>> as3 = {'h7', 'a0', 'g6', 'e4', 'b1', 'd3', 'f5', 'c2'}
                                                              [12]
>>> as3.remove('b1')                                          [13]
>>> as3                                                       [14]
{'h7', 'g6', 'f5', 'a0', 'd3', 'c2', 'e4'}
>>> as3.add('b1')                                             [15]
>>> as3                                                       [16]
{'h7', 'g6', 'f5', 'a0', 'd3', 'b1', 'c2', 'e4'}
>>> as3.add('b1')                                             [17]
>>> as3
{'h7', 'g6', 'f5', 'a0', 'd3', 'b1', 'c2', 'e4'}
>>> as3.add('1B')                                             [18]
>>> as3
{'h7', 'g6', 'f5', 'a0', 'd3', 'b1', '1B', 'c2', 'e4'}
>>> as4 = as3-as1                                             [19]
>>> as4
{'1B'}                                                        [20]
>>> as1
{'h7', 'a0', 'l11', 'k10', 'g6', 'e4', 'b1', 'd3', 'f5',
'c2', 'i8', 'j9'}
>>> as5 = as1 - as3                                           [21]
>>> as5                                                       [22]
{'l11', 'k10', 'j9', 'i8'}
>>> as44 = as3.difference(as1)                                [23]
>>> as44                                                      [24]
{'1B'}
```

Fig. 6.12 a Python Interpreter sequence illustrating use of some methods and operations with sets (continued) **b** Python Interpreter sequence illustrating use of some methods and operations with sets (continued) **c** Python Interpreter sequence illustrating use of some methods and operations with sets (continued) **d** Python Interpreter sequence illustrating use of some methods and operations with sets (continued)

(b)

```
>>> as44 == as4                                          [25]
True
>>> as66, as6 = as1.intersection(as3), as1 & as3         [26]
>>> as6, as66                                            [27]
({'h7', 'a0', 'g6', 'e4', 'b1', 'd3', 'f5', 'c2'}, {'h7',
'a0', 'g6', 'e4', 'b1', 'd3', 'f5', 'c2'})
>>> as77, as7 = as1.union(as3), as1|as3                  [28]
>>> as7, as77                                            [29]
({'h7', 'a0', 'l11', 'k10', 'g6', 'e4', '1B', 'b1', 'd3',
'f5', 'c2', 'i8', 'j9'}, {'h7', 'a0', 'l11', 'k10', 'g6',
'e4', '1B', 'b1', 'd3', 'f5', 'c2', 'i8', 'j9'})
>>> as8, as88 = as1&as2&as3,
as1.intersection(as2).intersection(as3)                  [30]
>>> as8, as88                                            [31]
({'h7', 'g6', 'e4', 'f5'}, {'h7', 'g6', 'e4', 'f5'})
>>> as9, as99 = as1^as3, as1.symmetric_difference(as3)   [32]
>>> as9, as99                                            [33]
({'l11', 'k10', '1B', 'i8', 'j9'}, {'l11', 'k10', '1B',
'i8', 'j9'})
>>> st1 = 'interjection'                                  [34]
>>> st2 = 'interruption'                                  [35]
>>> st1s, st2s = set(st1), set(st2)                       [36]
>>> st1s, st2s                                            [37]
({'j', 'i', 'o', 'e', 'r', 't', 'n', 'c'}, {'p', 'i', 'o',
'e', 'r', 't', 'n','u'})
>>> au1 = as1.union(aa2)                                  [38]
>>> au1                                                   [39]
{'h7', 'a0', 'l11', 'k10', 'g6', 'e4', 'b1', 'd3', 'f5',
'c2', 'i8', 'j9'}
>>> su1 = st1s.union(st2)                                 [40]
>>> su1                                                   [41]
{'p', 'j', 'i', 'o', 'e', 'r', 't', 'n', 'u', 'c'}
>>>
su2,su3,su4=st1s.intersection(st2),st1s.difference(st2),st
1s.symmetric_difference(st2)                              [42]
>>> su2, su3, su4                                         [43]
({'i', 'o', 'e', 'r', 't', 'n'}, {'j', 'c'}, {'p', 'j',
'u', 'c'})
>>> su2.remove('r')                                       [44]
>>> su2                                                   [45]
{'i', 'o', 'e', 't', 'n'}
>>> su2.remove('x')                                       [46]
Traceback (most recent call last):
  File "<stdin>", line 1, in <module>
KeyError: 'x'                                             [47]
>>> su2.discard('x')                                      [48]
>>> su2                                                   [49]
{'i', 'o', 'e', 't', 'n'}
```

Fig. 6.12 (continued)

(c)

```
>>> su2.pop()                                              [50]
'i'
>>> su2                                                     [51]
{'o', 'e', 't', 'n'}
>>> su2.clear()                                             [52]
>>> su2                                                     [53]
set()
>>> su2 = {'o', 'e', 't', 'n'}                              [54]
>>> su2c = su2.copy()                                       [55]
>>> su2c                                                    [56]
{'t', 'n', 'o', 'e'}
>>> su2 == su2c                                             [57]
True
>>> su2 is su2c                                             [58]
False
>>> as3, alt = {'h7', 'a0', 'g6', 'e4', 'b1', 'd3', 'f5',
'c2'}, []                                                   [59]
>>> while as3:alt.append(as3.pop())                         [60]
...
>>> alt                                                     [61]
['d3', 'a0', 'f5', 'b1', 'e4', 'h7', 'c2', 'g6']
>>> as3                                                     [62]
set()
>>> as1 = {'a0', 'b1', 'c2', 'd3', 'e4', 'f5', 'g6',
'h7'}                                                       [63]
>>> as2 = {'a0', 'b1', 'c2', 'd3', 'e4', 'f5', 'g6',
'h7'}                                                       [64]
>>> as2 = {'e4', 'f5', 'g6', 'h7', 'i8', 'j9', 'k10',
'l11'}                                                      [65]
>>> as3 = {'a0', 'f5', 'c2', 'h7', 'e4', 'j9'}              [66]
>>> as1.update(as3)                                         [67]
>>> as1                                                     [68]
{'d3', 'a0', 'h7', 'f5', 'e4', 'b1', 'j9', 'c2', 'g6'}
>>> as1.intersection_update(as3)                            [69]
>>> as1                                                     [70]
{'a0', 'e4', 'j9', 'h7', 'f5', 'c2'}
>>> as1.difference_update(as3)                              [71]
>>> as1                                                     [72]
set()
>>> as1 = {'a0', 'b1', 'c2', 'd3', 'e4', 'f5', 'g6',
'h7'}                                                       [73]
>>> as1|=as3                                                [74]
```

Fig. 6.12 (continued)

counted. **aa1**, **aa2**, and **aa3** are lists of strings separately defined in [3], [4], and [7]. **aa1**.extend(**aa2**) in [5] uses the method 'extend()' to add all the elements of **aa2** to the list **aa1**. The enhanced **aa1** in [6] has 'e4', 'f5', 'g6', and 'h7' from **aa2** added to **aa1** in the same order—though they are already present in it. In fact the two 'e4's in the enhanced **aa1** are separate entities—each with its own

(d)

```
>>> as1                                                    [75]
{'d3', 'a0', 'h7', 'f5', 'e4', 'b1', 'j9', 'c2', 'g6'}
>>> as1 &= as3                                             [76]
>>> as1                                                    [77]
{'a0', 'e4', 'j9', 'h7', 'f5', 'c2'}
>>> as1 -= as3                                             [78]
>>> as1
set()
>>> as2.symmetric_difference_update(as3)
>>> as2
{'k10', 'l11', 'i8', 'a0', 'c2', 'g6'}
>>> as2 = {'a0', 'b1', 'c2', 'd3', 'e4', 'f5', 'g6', 'h7'}
>>> as2 ^ as3
{'b1', 'j9', 'g6', 'd3'}
>>> as2 = {'a0', 'b1', 'c2', 'd3', 'e4', 'f5', 'g6', 'h7'}
>>> as2 ^= as3
>>> as2
{'d3', 'j9', 'b1', 'g6'}
>>> as4, ast1 = set('interesting'), 'interposing'
>>> as4
{'s', 'n', 'g', 'r', 'e', 'i', 't'}
>>> as4.update(ast1)
>>> as4
{'s', 'n', 'g', 'p', 'r', 'e', 'i', 'o', 't'}
>>> as4 = {'s', 'n', 'g', 'r', 'e', 'i', 't'}
>>> as5 = as4.copy()
>>> as4.update(ast1)
>>> as4
{'s', 'n', 'g', 'p', 'r', 'e', 'i', 'o', 't'}
>>> as4 = as5.copy()
>>> as4.intersection_update(ast1)
>>> as4
{'s', 'n', 'g', 'r', 'e', 'i', 't'}
>>> as4.difference_update(ast1)
>>> as4
set()
>>> as4 = as5.copy()
>>> as4.symmetric_difference_update(ast1)
>>> as4
{'o', 'p'}
>>>
```

Fig. 6.12 (continued)

separate index—4 and 8 respectively; same holds good of '**f5**', '**g6**', and '**h7**' also. **as1**, **as2**, and **as3** in [8] and [9] are the sets formed from the lists **aa1**, **aa2**, and **aa3** respectively. **as1** does not have any duplicate entries—the list **aa1** has 16 elements in it whereas—the set formed from it (**as1**) has only 12 (distinct) elements in it—as can be seen from [10] and [11]. **as3**.remove('**b1**') in [13] removes the element '**b1**' from the set **as3**—as can be seen by comparing **as3** in [14] with that in [**12**]. '**b1**' has been added to **as3**—through **as3**.add('**b1**') in [15]; the restored version is in [16]. An attempt to add '**b1**' again in [17] does not alter **as3**—'**b1**' being already present in it. But **as3**.add('**1B**') in [18] adds '**1B**' as an additional element to **as3**—as can be seen from the following lines.

sets **as1** and **as3** as well as sets formed through the various possible operations are shown in the respective Venn diagrams in Fig. 6.13 (Sullivan 2008). **as4** = **as3** − **as1** as in [19] forms the set **as4** from **as3** and **as1**; as can be seen from the corresponding Venn diagram in Fig. 6.13 all the elements in **as3** which are also present in **as1** are removed. The remaining elements of **as3** form **as4**; but **as3** and **as1** remain unaltered. With this **as4** is the set of a single element '**1B**' [20]. Similarly **as1**–**as3** in [21] forms **as5** as the set of elements of **as1** left behind by removing elements common with **as3** from it. **as1**.difference (**as3**) achieves the same using the method difference() as in [23] and [24]. **as4** (=**as3** − **as1**) in [19] and **as44** (=**as3**.difference(**as1**)) in [23] produce identical sets. The Python Interpreter sequence continues in Fig. 6.12b. [25] confirms the equality of **as4** and **as44**. But **as4** and **as44** remain distinct objects.

as1 & **as3** and **as1**.intersection (**as3**) use the '&' operator and its method counterpart; both form new sets with elements common to **as1** and **as3**— assigned to **as6** and **as66** in [26]. Both are identical but distinct sets [27]. Their formation can be understood from the corresponding Venn diagram in Fig. 6.13.

as1| **as3** in [28] forms the union of **as1** and **as3** and assigns it to **as7**. **as77** = **as1**.union(**as3**) is its method based counterpart [28]. The union and intersection operations can be carried out with multiple sets as arguments as well.

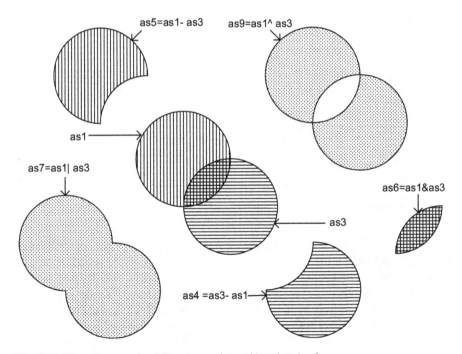

Fig. 6.13 Venn diagrams for different operations with **as1** and **as3**

[30] shows an example with the three sets **as1**, **as2**, and **as3**. **as8** and **as88** in [30] and [31] combine all the elements common to all the three of them.

With the '∧' operator, **as1** ∧ **as3** in [32] forms the set **as9** from **as1** and **as3**; **as9** in [33] has all the elements of **as1** and **as3** which are not common to **as1** and **as3**. For example 'a0' is present in **as1** as well as **as3**; it is left out of **as9**. '1B' is present only in **as3**; it is included in **as9**. Similarly 'k10' present in **as3** but not in **as1**; it is included in **as9**. **as1**.symmetric_difference(**as3**) is the method corresponding to the '∧' operation (yielding as 99).

st1 ('interjection') in [34] and **st2**('interruption') in [35] respectively are strings (see Fig. 6.12b). **st1s** and **st2 s** in [35] and [37] are the sets of integers formed out of the elements (characters) forming the strings **st1** and **st2** respectively—that—is the set of letters present in 'interjection' and is the set of letters present in 'interruption'.

With **pp** as a set and **qq**—a list, a string or any other compatible sequence −**rr** = **pp**.union(**qq**) generates the set **rr** as the union of **pp** and the elements of **qq**. Such mixed mode of forming/generating a set is possible only with the method (.union()) but not with the operator (|). Union of the elements of the set **as1** and the list **aa2** is assigned to set **au1** in [38]. **au1** so formed is in [39], [40] and [41] show the formation of a set **su1** as a union of the set **st1s** and the string **st2**. Similarly intersection, difference, and symmetric_difference methods use a set as a base argument; the second argument (as well as other arguments if present) can be sequences of other types. Examples are in [42]. Set **su2** is the set of intersection of set **st1s** and string **st2**. **su3** is the set of difference of set **st1s** and string **st2**; **su4** is the set of symmetric_difference of set **st1s** and string **st2**. [43] gives respective details.

pp.remove(**qq**) removes the element **qq** from the set **pp**. if **qq** is not present in **pp** the Python sequence rises a '*KeyErrror*'. Thus **su2**.remove('**r**') in [44] removes '**r**' as can be seen by comparing **su2** in [43] and [45]. **su2**.remove('**x**') in [46] returns a '*KeyError*' [47] since **su2** does not have '**x**' in it as a member. The method discard() is similar to the method remove(), to a certain extent. **su2**. discard('**x**') discards (removes) '**x**' from su2, if it is present. If '**x**' is not present in **su2**, no action follows as can be seen from [48] & [49].

The Python interpreter sequence continues in Fig. 6.12c. **pp**.pop() pops an element at random from **pp**. **su2**.pop() in [50] pops '**i**' from **su2** leaving it with '**o**', '**e**', '**t**', and '**n**' as its contents. **pp**.clear() clears the set **pp**. As an example **su2**.clear() in [52] clears **su2** and leaves it empty [53]. **rr** = **pp**.copy() creates **rr** as a new set—a replica of **pp** itself. **su2c** is a copy of **su2**—[55, 56]. Being copies they are identical as can be seen from [57]; but they are distinct objects [58].

For a given set **as3** [59] list(**as3**) forms a list with all the elements of **as3** being in it. The function while **as3**:**alt**.append(**as3**.pop()) in [60] achieves the same though in a roundabout manner. **alt** has been defined as an empty list beforehand [59]. 'while **as3**:**alt**.append(**as3**.pop())' pops elements at random from **as3** and appends the popped element to list alt; this continues until **as3** is empty [62].

pp.intersection(qq) has **pp** as a set and **qq** a compatible sequence and generates **rr** as the corresponding enhanced set. **pp**.intersection_update (**qq**) is a variant where the set **pp** itself is updated, its elements being only those common with **qq**. **pp** & = **qq** achieves the same with the restriction that **qq** too has to be a set. [69], [70] and [76], [77] in the Python Interpreter sequence are illustrations. Similar update variants are available with '|' ('|='), '^'('^='), and '−'('−=') as well. In all these cases the operator versions ('|=', '^=', '−=') can be used only if all the arguments on either side are sets. The respective methods are more flexible and can have the second argument as any mutable sequence. The illustrative examples for these follow from [76] onwards in the Python Interpreter sequence continued in Fig. 6.12d.

6.6   Frozensets

Any set is mutable; methods like remove(), extend(), pop() can be used with sets to add or remove elements from it. In contrast a frozenset is a 'rigid' set. Once formed it remains frozen (as with a tuple). Additional elements cannot be added to it; nor can elements be removed from it. The Python Intrpreter sequence in Fig. 6.14 illustrates its formation. **aa1** in [1] is a list of strings. '**e4**', '**f5**', '**g6**', and '**h7**' as its elements, occur twice in it. frozenset(aa1) (=**afz1**) forms a frozenset of its members and assigns it to **afz1**. **afz1** in [3] has every element as a unique one without duplication; order is not maintained either. [4] forms a set **as1** out of **aa1**. Content wise **as1** is identical to **afz1** as can be seen from [6].

The methods and operations with sets are applicable to frozensets also; the only exceptions are the update-type methods and their operator counterparts. They are not applicable to frozensets since they change the set by adding elements to it or removing elements from it. The usage being similar to that with sets, the methods/operations are not separately illustrated with frozensets.

```
>>> aa1 = ['a0', 'b1', 'c2', 'd3', 'e4', 'f5', 'g6', 'h7',
'e4', 'f5', 'g6', 'h7', 'i8', 'j9', 'k10', 'l11']       [1]
>>> afz1 = frozenset(aa1)                                   [2]
>>> afz1                                                    [3]
frozenset({'f5', 'c2', 'j9', 'd3', 'h7', 'a0', 'i8',
'l11', 'g6', 'e4', 'b1', 'k10'})
>>> as1 = set(aa1)                                          [4]
>>> as1                                                     [5]
{'f5', 'c2', 'j9', 'd3', 'h7', 'a0', 'i8', 'l11', 'g6',
'e4', 'b1', 'k10'}
>>> as1 == afz1                                             [6]
True
>>>
```

Fig. 6.14 Python Interpreter sequence illustrating formation of frozenset

6.7 Tests and Comparisons with Sets and Frozensets

A number of operations/methods are available to compare sets/frozensets with other sets/frozensets or sequences. Membership testing too can be done with them. Table 6.2 summarizes these. These can be used to initiate/execute/terminate loops.

Example 6.1 **ss** in **marks1.py** gives the details of marks obtained by a group of students in different subjects. (a) Prepare a set with the names of students. Pass marks for every subject is 60. (b) Prepare a list of students who have passed in all the subjects. (c) Prepare a list of students who have failed in at least one subject.

The Python Interpreter sequence in Fig. 6.15 produces the necessary sets. The student data has been imported and assigned to **mks** in [1]. **sm** in [2] forms the list of names of students concerned. iter(**jl**[0] for **jl** in **mks**) produces an iterator of the 0th entries (names) of the lists in **mks**. They have been combined and made into a set as **sm**. The set of names is in [3]. Empty (initial) sets of names of students who have failed in any subject (**fls**) and passed in all subjects (**pss**) are formed in [4].

For a list **jj** in **mks** **jj**[1:] is the slice of marks obtained in all the subjects by the student with name **jj**[0]. In all these subjects if the student scores pass marks his/her name is added to **pss** set in [5]. Similarly if the student scores less than 60 marks in any of the subjects, his/her name is added to the **fls** list [6]. This is done for all lists (**jjs**) in **mks**. The sets **fls** and **pss** are output in [7]. A (simpler) alternative to get the second list (once the first one is formed) is in [8]—removing all students' names who passed in all the subjects (set **pss**) from the list **sm**; this gives the list of students who did not pass in all the subjects—that is failed in at least one subject—(**fls1** in [9]) which is same as **fls** in [7].

Table 6.2 Methods related to status/comparison of sets

Sl. No	Form of operation	Remarks
1	**X** in **ss**	Returns True if **x** is in **ss**; else returns False
2	**X** not in **ss**	Returns True if **x** is not in **ss**; else returns False
3	**ss**.isdisjoint(**tt**)	Returns True if sets **ss** and **tt** have no common elements; else returns False
4	**ss**.issuperset(**tt**) **ss** > = **tt**	Returns True if every element in **tt** is an element in **ss**; else returns False
5	**ss** > **tt**	Returns True if **ss** is a proper superset of **tt**; else returns False
6	**ss**.issubset (**tt**)**ss** <= **tt**	Returns True if every element in **ss** is an element in **tt**; else returns False
7	**ss** < **tt**	Returns True if **ss** is a proper subset of **tt**; else returns False

```
>>> from demo_5 import marks1
>>> mks = marks1.ss                                         [1]
>>> sm = set(iter(jl[0] for jl in mks))                     [2]
>>> sm                                                      [3]
{'Sanjay', 'Siva', 'Nisha', 'Kishore', 'Asha'}
>>> fls, pss = set(), set()                                 [4]
>>> for jj in mks:
...     if all(jk>=60 for jk in jj[1:]):pss.add(jj[0])      [5]
...     if any(jk<60 for jk in jj[1:]):fls.add(jj[0])       [6]
...
>>> fls, pss                                                [7]
({'Siva', 'Nisha'}, {'Sanjay', 'Kishore', 'Asha'})
>>> fls1 = sm - pss                                         [8]
>>> fls1                                                    [9]
{'Siva', 'Nisha'}
>>>
```

Fig. 6.15 Python Interpreter sequence for Example 6.1

6.8 Operations with Dictionaries

The Python Interpreter sequence in Fig. 6.16 illustrates the use of different functions and methods with dictionarys. An empty dictionary **dc** is formed in [1]. **dc**['z0'] = '**ZZ0**' in [2] enters ('z0', '**ZZ0**') as a (key, value) pair into **dc**. Similarly ('y1', '**YY1**') is also added to **dc** in [3] as can be seen from [4]. With any dictionary a (key, value) pair can be added in this manner. In fact the value associated with an existing (key:value) pair can also be changed with a similar fresh assignment. The dictionary **dd** in [5] has ('b1':'**BB1**') as a (key: value) pair in it. The value is redefined as '**bb1**' in [6]. The altered **dd** is in [7]. If 'z0' in **dc** in [8] checks whether 'z0' is a key in **dc**; it being true, '**yes**' is printed out as desired. Since 'yy' is not a key in **dc** [9], a '**no**' is output. **dd**['a0'] in [10] checks for the presence of '**a0**' as a key in **dd**. If present its value (='**AA0**') is returned. Since 'aa' is not a key in **dd**, **dd**['aa'] in [11] returns a '*KeyError*'.

For the dictionary dd the method **dd**.get('c2') in [12] searches for the key '**c2**' in **dd**. It being present the associated value '**CC2**' is returned. If the key is absent as with **dd**.get(aa) in [13] the command is ignored. The same is true of the empty dictionary **ddc** in [15]: **ddc**.get('aa') in [16] is ignored. In this respect **dd**.get() is different from **dd**[]. [14] is the use of the general form of the get() method. **dd**.get('aa', bb) checks for key 'aa' in **dd**. If present the corresponding value is returned. If not the second argument specified—**bb**—is returned. In the previous case the second argument was left out; since 'aa' is not a key in **dc**, the command was ignored.

Any dictionary can be updated by adding the (key, value) pairs of another to it. [17] is a simple illustrative example. {'**f5**': '**FF5**'} as a dictionary is added to **dd**. The enhanced **dd** is in [18].

Example 6.2 Rearrange the marks in **ss** in **marks1.py** in the form of a dictionary with the students' names as the keys and the mark-sets as tuples.

The marks from **marks1.py** is assigned to **a1** [19]. An empty dictionary—**d1**—is created in [20] (initialization). Through [21] the desired dictionary is formed. For any integer **jj**, **a1**[**jj**] is the full entry in **a1** for the student concerned—**a1**[**jj**][0] is the name and the slice a1[**jj**][1:] the full set of marks. {**a1**[**jj**][0]:**a1**[**jj**] [1:]} is the dictionary for the specific student. **d1**.update( ) adds it to **d1**. This is done for every item in **a1** to form the full **d1** as in [22].

dd from Fig. 6.16 is reproduced in the Python Interpreter sequence in Fig. 6.17 [1]. The total number of entries in the dictionary **dd** can be obtained using the len() function as in [2]. The methods keys() and values() can be used directly with a dictionary to sift out the keys and values respectively as done with [3] and [4]. These values been assigned to **kk** and **vv** respectively. They can be converted to lists, sorted lists, tuples, or tuples (sorted()) as desired. If necessary the reverse option can be invoked when sorting. All these are illustrated in the lines following in the sequence.

With items(), **dd**.items() returns the dictionary items as a set of tuples—with each tuple item being a (key, value) tuple. These can be seen from [19] and [20]. If necessary this set can be converted into a tuple—[21] & [22] or a list. A (key, value) pair can be deleted from a dictionary using del. del **dd**['**d3**'] in [23] deletes ('**d3**':'**DD3**') from the dictionary **dd** as can be seen from [24]. The method dict.fromkeys('**x**', **y**) can be used to form a dictionary from the elements of a given sequence **x** (list or tuple). Every item in the dictionary so formed is assigned **y** as its value. **de** in [25] is an example where **de** is formed as a dictionary with the elements of **kkl** as the keys. Every entry in **de** is assigned the value 22 as in [26].

Example 6.3 A string **lo** is given. Get the frequencies of all the letters in **lo**.

dd.get(**x**, **y**) is a method which returns the value for the key '**x**' in the dictionary **dd**. If '**x**' is not a key in **dd y** is returned in its place. **lfq** is initialized as a blank dictionary in [1] in the Python Interpreter sequence in Fig. 6.18. For any **jj**, **lfq**[**jj**] = **z** assigns the value of **z** for the key **jj**. If **jj** is already present as a key the existing value is discarded. If **jj** is not present in **lfq**, (**jj**:**z**) pair is added to **lfq**. In [2] **lfq**[**jj**] = **lfq**.get(**jj**,0) does the following:

- If **jj** as a key is absent in **lfq**, (**jj**:**1**) becomes a new entry in **lfq**.
- If **jj** is present as a key in **lfq**, its value as an updated integer is incremented by one—that is the count of **jj** is increased by one.

In [2] this is done for every character (including white spaces) in the string **lo**. Once execution is complete **lfq** has the frequencies of all the characters in the string lo.

dictionary **dd** from Fig. 6.17 is reproduced in the Python Interpreter sequence of Fig. 6.19 in [1]. From the sequence of keys of a dictionary—**dd**.keys()—one can

```
>>> dc = {}                                                [1]
>>> dc['z0']='ZZ0'                                         [2]
>>> dc['y1']='YY1'                                         [3]
>>> dc                                                     [4]
{'z0': 'ZZ0', 'y1': 'YY1'}
>>> dd =
{'a0':'AA0','b1':'BB1','c2':'CC2','d3':'DD3','e4':'EE4'}
                                                           [5]
>>> dd['b1']='bb1'                                         [6]
>>> dd                                                     [7]
{'d3': 'DD3', 'e4': 'EE4', 'a0': 'AA0', 'b1': 'bb1',
'c2':    'CC2'}
>>> if 'z0' in dc: print('yes')                            [8]
... else:print('no')
...
yes
>>> if'yy' in dc: print('yes')                             [9]
... else:print('no')
...
no
>>> dd['a0']                                               [10]
'AA0'
>>> dd['aa']                                               [11]
Traceback (most recent call last):
  File "<stdin>", line 1, in <module>
KeyError: 'aa'
>>> dd.get('c2')                                           [12]
'CC2'
>>> dd.get('aa')                                           [13]
>>> dd.get('aa','Sorry, no aa here')                       [14]
'Sorry, no aa here'
>>> ddc= {}                                                [15]
>>> ddc.get('aa')                                          [16]
>>> dd.update({'f5':'FF5'})                                [17]
>>> dd                                                     [18]
{'a0': 'AA0', 'c2': 'CC3', 'e4': 'EE4', 'b1': 'bb1',
'f5': 'FF5', 'd3': 'DD3'}
>>> from demo_5 import marks1
>>> a1 = marks1.st                                         [19]
>>> d1 = dict()                                            [20]
>>> d1
{}
>>> for jj in
range(len(a1)):d1.update({a1[jj][0]:tuple(a1[jj][1:])})
                                                           [21]
...
>>> d1                                                     [22]
{'Sarani': (76, 78, 82, 83, 84), 'Karthik': (77, 78, 79,
80, 81), 'Kala': (90, 86, 91, 92, 93), 'Lan': (65, 86,
66, 67, 68), 'Karun': (85, 86, 87, 88, 89)}
```

Fig. 6.16 Python Interpreter sequence illustrating operations with dictionarys

```
>>> dd = {'a0':'AA0', 'b1':'BB1', 'c2':'CC3',
'd3':'DD3','e4':'EE4'}                                           [1]
>>> len(dd)                                                      [2]
5
>>> kk = dd.keys()                                               [3]
>>> vv = dd.values()                                             [4]
>>> kk, vv                                                       [5]
(dict_keys(['d3','e4','a0','b1','c2']),
dict_values(['DD3','EE4','AA0','BB1','CC3']))
>>> kkl = list(kk)                                               [6]
>>> kkl                                                          [7]
['d3', 'e4', 'a0', 'b1', 'c2']
>>> vvl = list(vv)                                               [8]
>>> vvl                                                          [9]
['DD3', 'EE4', 'AA0', 'BB1', 'CC3']
>>> kkls = sorted(kkl)                                           [10]
>>> kkls                                                         [11]
['a0', 'b1', 'c2', 'd3', 'e4']
>>> kkls1 = sorted(dd.keys())                                    [12]
>>> kkls1                                                        [13]
['a0', 'b1', 'c2', 'd3', 'e4']
>>> ktp = tuple(dd.keys())                                       [14]
>>> ktp                                                          [15]
('d3', 'e4', 'a0', 'b1', 'c2')
>>> kttp = tuple(sorted(dd.keys()))                              [16]
>>> kttp                                                         [17]
('a0', 'b1', 'c2', 'd3', 'e4')
>>> kttpr = tuple(sorted(dd.keys(), reverse = True))            [18]
>>> kttpr
('e4', 'd3', 'c2', 'b1', 'a0')
>>> dd.items()                                                   [19]
dict_items([('d3','DD3'),('e4','EE4'),('a0','AA0'),('b1',
'BB1'),('c2','CC3')])                                            [20]
>>> dtp = tuple(dd.items())                                      [21]
>>> dtp                                                          [22]
(('d3', 'DD3'), ('e4', 'EE4'), ('a0', 'AA0'), ('b1',
'BB1'), ('c2', 'CC3'))
>>> del dd['d3']                                                 [23]
>>> dd                                                           [24]
{'e4': 'EE4', 'a0': 'AA0', 'b1': 'BB1', 'c2': 'CC3'}
>>> de = dict.fromkeys(kkl, 22)                                  [25]
>>> de                                                           [26]
{'d3': 22, 'e4': 22, 'b1': 22, 'c2': 22, 'a0': 22}
```

Fig. 6.17 Python Interpreter sequence illustrating more operations with dictionaries

form an iterator. But iter(dd)—in a more compact form—does the same. [2] uses it to form **ee** as a list of keys [3]. **dd**.pop('**e4**') in [4] pops the value ('**EE4**') for the specified key ('**e4**') for the `dictionary` **dd** as in [5]. If such a key is absent in the dictionary a '*KeyError*' will be raised. However if the popping is done with **dd**.pop

```
lo = 'interjection is different from interruption'
>>> lfq = {}                                              [1]
>>> for jj in lo: lfq[jj] = lfq.get(jj,0) + 1             [2]
...
>>> for jk in lfq.items(): print(jk)
...
('i', 6)
('m', 1)
('r', 5)
('u', 1)
('f', 3)
('e', 5)
('s', 1)
('c', 1)
(' ', 4)
('d', 1)
('p', 1)
('t', 5)
('j', 1)
('o', 3)
('n', 5)
>>>
```

Fig. 6.18 Python Interpreter sequence for Example 6.3

('e4', z), the second argument (z) will be returned if 'e4' is not a key in **dd**. In the present case, after step [4] **dd** does not have ('e4':'EE4') as an item in it. Hence another attempt to pop with **dd**.pop('e4', 'sorry') in [6] returns 'sorry' [7]. **dd**.popitem() pops a (key, value) pair selected randomly from **dd**. With [8] the item ('a0': 'AA0') is returned. **dd**.popitem() is done here repeatedly until **dd** becomes empty as in [9]. Another attempt to pop an item in [10] returns 'KeyError'.

For a dictionary **d** the method **d**.setdefault('x':y) does the following:

- If 'x' is present as a key in **d**, the associated value is returned. The dictionary remains unaffected. **dd** is refreshed in [11]. **dd**.setdefault('b1') in [12] returns 'BB1' since the corresponding dictionary item is {'b1':'BB1'}. The dictionary remains untainted.
- If 'x' is not present as a key in **d**, the item {'x':y} is entered into the dictionary and the value y is returned. **dd**.setdefault ({'f5':'FF5'}) in [14] adds the item {'f5':'FF5'} into the dictionary as in [15].
- If the value 'y' is not specified in the command, that is if the command is **d**.setdefault('x') and the key 'x' is not a valid key, the item ('x':None) is entered into the dictionary—that is 'x' is entered as a key with None as the associated default value. 'g6' is not a key in **dd** as in [16]. Hence {'g6': None} is added as an additional item in the dictionary.

```
>>> dd = {'a0':'AA0', 'b1':'BB1', 'c2':'CC2',
'd3':'DD3','e4':'EE4'}                                          [1]
>>> ee = list(iter(dd))                                        [2]
>>> ee                                                         [3]
['a0', 'b1', 'e4', 'd3', 'c2']
>>> dd.pop('e4')                                               [4]
'EE4'                                                          [5]
>>> dd.pop('e4','Sorry')                                       [6]
'Sorry'                                                        [7]
>>> dd.popitem()                                               [8]
('a0', 'AA0')
>>> dd.popitem()
('b1', 'BB1')
>>> dd.popitem()
('d3', 'DD3')
>>> dd.popitem()
('c2', 'CC2')
>>> dd                                                         [9]
{}
>>> dd.popitem()                                               [10]
Traceback (most recent call last):
  File "<stdin>", line 1, in <module>
KeyError: 'popitem(): dictionary is empty'
>>> dd = {'a0':'AA0', 'b1':'BB1', 'c2':'CC2',
'd3':'DD3','e4':'EE4'}                                         [11]
>>> dd.setdefault('b1')                                       [12]
'BB1'
>>> dd                                                        [13]
{'a0': 'AA0', 'b1': 'BB1', 'e4': 'EE4', 'd3': 'DD3',
'c2': 'CC2'}
>>> dd.setdefault('f5','FF5')                                 [14]
'FF5'
>>> dd                                                        [15]
{'f5': 'FF5', 'c2': 'CC2', 'a0': 'AA0', 'b1': 'BB1',
'e4': 'EE4', 'd3': 'DD3'}
>>> dd.setdefault('g6')                                       [16]
>>> dd                                                        [17]
{'d3': 'DD3', 'a0': 'AA0', 'f5': 'FF5', 'c2': 'CC2',
'g6': None, 'e4': 'EE4', 'b1': 'BB1'}
>>>
```

Fig. 6.19 Python Interpreter sequence illustrating additional operations with dictionaries

6.9   *Arg and **Kwarg

When a statement in a Python suite accepts a sequence (like a tuple or a list) its length is normally to be known beforehand. Python offers a convenient facility to accommodate such sequences whose lengths are not known beforehand. Specifying an argument as '*a' implies that 'a' is a sequence whose length need not be fixed or known beforehand (Incidentally such arguments are mostly specified as '*arg'; but this is only a convention and not mandatory). This type of usage finds application as arguments in functions and the like. The structure and usages of such constructs are illustrated through the Python Interpreter sequence in Fig. 6.20. (1, 2, '**c**') in [1] is a `tuple`. Its first element is assigned to '**a**' and the rest are assigned to **b** as a `list` [2]. **b** is formed here using elements whose count is not known beforehand; hence **b** is a `list`. **a**, *****b** in [3] assigns the first element of the `list` [(1, 2, 3), (4, 5, 6, 7)] —namely (1, 2, 3) to **a**. The rest—the `tuple` of four integers—is assigned to **b** as a `list` [4]. [(1, 2, 3), (4, 5, 6, 7)] is a `list` of two elements. Hence **a**, *****b** in [(1, 2, 3), (4, 5, 6, 7)]:`print`(**a**, **b**) in [5] does the printing for all (both) the elements in [(1, 2, 3), (4 ,5 ,6 ,7)] sequentially. Firstly (1, 2, 3) is assigned to (**a**, *****b**) as (1), [2, 3] respectively and printed out [6]. Subsequently (4, 5, 6, 7) is split in the same manner as (4), [5, 6, 7] and again assigned to **a** and **b** and the same printed out [7].

The same sequence of elements is assigned to **a**, *****b**, and **c** in [8]. Since the sequence has only two elements—(1, 2, 3) and (4, 5, 6, 7)—they are assigned to **a** and **c** leaving an empty `list` for **b** [9].

vff() in [10] has been defined as a function (a simple illustrative example). The elements of **bb** are summed up and **bb** and this sum together is returned as a `tuple`. **vff**()—called as **vff**(*****v1**) in [11]—sums up the four numbers forming the `tuple` **v1** and returns **v1** and the sum. The list **v2** of three numbers is the argument of **vff**() in [13]; once again **v2** and the sum of the elements in it are returned. The function **vf1**(*****v3**) in [14] accepts argument **v3** as a set of numbers and returns the mean, the variance, and the argument vector itself [16]. For vectors **v1** and **v2**, **vf1**() is evaluated and returned in [17] and [18] respectively (In fact for the specific case here def **vf1**(**v3**) would have been a simpler function definition statement).

Function **dpdt**(**v1**, **v2**) in [19] has vectors **v1** and **v2** as its arguments and returns their inner product [20]. Function **ang_1**() in [21] invokes the inner product function repeatedly—to get the magnitudes of the vectors **vf** and **vd**, and their inner product. The ratio <**vc**, **vd**>/‖**vc**‖ * ‖**vd**‖ and the angle between the vectors are obtained. **ang_1**(**va**, **vb**) in [23] returns the angle between vectors **va** and **vb** as 2.300523983021863 radians. **vec_m**(*****vv**) as a function defined in [24] returns the magnitude of vector **vv**. Note that it suits **vv**s of different numbers of elements. **vec_m**() is used in [26] along with the inner product function **dpdt** to obtain the same angle.

When *****aa** is used in place of an argument in a function (or class and the like) the set of items used in its place when calling the function (or instantiating the class) are treated as though they represent a corresponding ('elastic') sequence as **aa**. ******bb** is its counterpart for a dictionary. If it is present as an argument in a function all items used in its place are treated as though they are entries (`key-value` pairs) in a `dictionary` **bb**. In the Python Interpreter sequence in Fig. 6.21 **dc1** is a `dictionary`. The function **sho_0**(**cc**) [2] prints all the `key-value` pairs of **cc** in succession—as can be seen from the function **sho_0**(**dc1**) in [3]. **sho_1**(******dd**) [4] is another function to do a similar print out. Here **dd** should comprise of pairs of the form '*key = value*'. **Sho_1**() is called in [5] with four (`key`, `value`) pairs in place of ******dd**. The desired printouts follow for all of them.

```
>>> a, *b = 1, 2, 'c'                                          [1]
>>> a, b                                                       [2]
(1, [2, 'c'])
>>> a, *b = (1, 2, 3), (4, 5, 6, 7)                            [3]
>>> a, b                                                       [4]
((1, 2, 3), [(4, 5, 6, 7)])
>>> for a, *b in [(1,2,3), (4,5,6,7)]:print(a, b)             [5]
...
1 [2, 3]                                                       [6]
4 [5, 6, 7]                                                    [7]
>>> a, *b, c = [(1,2,3), (4,5,6,7)]                            [8]
>>> a, b, c                                                    [9]
((1, 2, 3), [], (4, 5, 6, 7))
>>> v1 = (9.8, 8.7, 6.5, 5.4)
>>> def vff(*bb): return bb, sum(bb)                          [10]
...
>>> vff(*v1)                                                  [11]
((9.8, 8.7, 6.5, 5.4), 30.4)
>>> v2 = [7.4, 4.8, 6.9]                                      [12]
>>> vff(*v2)                                                  [13]
((7.4, 4.8, 6.9), 19.1)
>>> def vf1(*v3):                                             [14]
...     mn0 = sum(v3)/len(v3)                                 [15]
...     s0 = 0.0
...     for jj in v3:s0 += jj**2
...     vr0 = (s0/len(v3))-mn0**2
...     return mn0, vr0, v3                                   [16]
...
>>> vf1(*v1)                                                  [17]
(7.6, 3.0250000000000057, (9.8, 8.7, 6.5, 5.4))
>>> vf1(*v2)                                                  [18]
(6.366666666666667, 1.2688888888888883, (7.4, 4.8, 6.9))
>>> def dpdt(v1, v2):                                         [19]
...     ss = 0
...     for jj in range(len(v1)):ss += v1[jj]*v2[jj]          [20]
...     return ss
...
>>> import math
>>> ang_1 = lambda vc, vd:math.acos(dpdt(vc,
vd)/((dpdt(vc, vc)*dpdt(vd, vd))**0.5))                       [21]
>>> va, vb = (1, 2, 3, 4), (-4, -3, -2, -1)                   [22]
>>> ang_1(va, vb)                                             [23]
2.300523983021863
>>> def vec_m(*vv):                                           [24]
...     ss = 0
...     for jj in vv:ss += jj*jj                              [25]
...     return ss**0.5
...
>>> math.acos(dpdt(va, vb)/(vec_m(*va)*vec_m(*vb)))          [26]
2.300523983021863
```

Fig. 6.20 Python Interpreter sequence to illustrate usage of *arg

```
>>> dc1 = {'a0':21, 'b1':32, 'c3':43, 'd4':54}          [1]
>>> def sho_0(cc):                                       [2]
...    for mm, nn in cc.items():print("For key ", repr(mm),
"the value is", repr(nn))
...
>>> sho_0(dc1)                                           [3]
For key  'c3' the value is 43
For key  'a0' the value is 21
For key  'd4' the value is 54
For key  'b1' the value is 32
>>> def sho_1(**dd):                                     [4]
...    for mm, nn in dd.items():print("For key ", repr(mm),
"the value is", repr(nn))
...
>>> sho_1(a0=21, b1=32, c3=43, d4=54)                    [5]
For key  'c3' the value is 43
For key  'a0' the value is 21
For key  'd4' the value is 54
For key  'b1' the value is 32
>>> def sho_2(ee, *zz, **yy):                            [6]
...    print(repr(ee))                                   [7]
...    for jj in zz:print(repr(jj))                      [8]
...    for mm, nn in yy.items():print("For key ", repr(mm),
"the value is", repr(nn))                                [9]
...
>>> sho_2('ss0','rr1','pp2',67,78,a0=21, b1=32,c3=43)    [10]
'ss0'                                                    [11]
'rr1'                                                    [12]
'pp2'
67
78
For key  'c3' the value is 43                            [13]
For key  'a0' the value is 21
For key  'b1' the value is 32
```

Fig. 6.21 Python Interpreter sequence to demonstrate the usage of **kwarg

Arguments for function (or class) definitions can be a mix as in [6] for the function **Sho_2**(). They can be direct arguments, sequence members, or dictionary type members. However they should be specified and supplied in the same order. In the function here the only argument directly specified—'**ee**'—is to be printed out first [7]. It is followed by the prints of elements forming the sequence **zz** [8]. Lastly the elements of **yy**—the dictionary key-value pair type—are to be printed out [9]. **Sho_2**() is called in [10] with a set of assorted arguments. The first one— string '**ss0**'—is identified with argument **ee** in [6] and printed out [11]. The four subsequent arguments—'**rr1**', '**pp2**', (two strings) and 67, 78 (two integers)—are automatically identified forming **zz** in [6]. They are printed out in sequence from [12]. All the rest of the arguments are identified with **yy** in [6]. The prints from [13] onwards confirm this.

6.10 Exercises

1. Marks information as in Fig. 5.16 is given. Prepare a program to form the list of students who failed only in Physics. Prepare a program to get the list of students who failed in two or more subjects. Test both the programs with the data in Fig. 5.16.

2. Frequency of a letter pair occurring in a string of characters is called its 'bigram frequency'. In Example 6.3 use 'for **jk** in **lo**[:-2]' to get bigram frequencies. Prepare a program to make a dictionary of the most common ten bigram frequencies for a given string (Shyamala et al. 2011).

3. **a** and **b** are two 4-dimentional vectors. Develop a function in Python to get the dot product **a . b**. Evaluate **a . b** for **a** = [1.2,−2.3, 4.5, 6.7] and **b** = [−9.8, −8.7, 7.8, 6.5].

4. Use ***a**, ***b** and develop the function in the exercise above. Evaluate **a.b**

5. Define a Python function to get the arithmetic mean (m_a), harmonic mean (m_h), geometric mean (m_g), and weighted mean (m_w) of a set of given numbers **x** = $\{x_i\}$ (Sullivan 2008).

$$m_a = \frac{1}{n}\sum_{i=1}^{n} x_i$$

$$m_h = \left(\sum_{i=1}^{n} x_i^{-1}\right)^{-1}$$

$$m_g = \left(\prod_{i=1}^{n} x_i\right)^{1/n}$$

$$m_w = \sum_{i=1}^{n} w_i x_i \quad \text{where} \sum_{i=1}^{n} w_i = 1$$

Evaluate the means for **x** = $\{9.6, 6.7, 5.4, 3.3, 2.8, 7.2\}$ and **w** = $\{0.10, 0.16, 0.17, 0.18, 0.19, 0.20\}$.

6. The Fibbonacci sequence is a sequence of numbers satisfying the property: the ith number is $n_i = n_{i-1} + n_{i-2}$ (Sullivan 2008). Write a Python program to get n_i given n_0 and n_1.
Get all n_i up to n_{10} for the set of (n_0, n_1) values (0, 1), (−3, 4), and (1, 3).

7. *Binomial Distribution*: The coefficients of $(a + b)^n$ for $n = 1, 2, 3, \ldots$ form the "Pascal's triangle". $d_{k,n}$—the coefficient of $a^k b^{n-k}$ can be recursively expressed as

$$d_{n,k} = 1 \quad \text{if } k = 1 \text{ or } n$$
$$= d_{n-1,k} + d_{n-1,k-1} \quad \text{for all other } k.$$

$c_{n,\ k}$—the cumulative distribution coefficient can be expressed as

$$c_{n,k} = 1 \quad \text{for } k = 1$$
$$= 2n \quad \text{for } k = n$$
$$= c_{n,k-1} + c_{n-1,k} \quad \text{for all other } k.$$

Do the programs to get $d_{n,k}$ and $c_{n,k}$ recursively.

With $a = p$ and $b = 1 - p$, $d_{n,k}$ and $c_{n,k}$ above represent the binomial distribution with a mean of n_p and variance of $n_p(1 - p)$. With p = 0.5, the set represents the symmetrical distribution.

Take binomial distribution with $2^{10} = 1024$ elements. There are 11 possible values with respective probabilities. Use the program above and get the full set of probability and cumulative probability values.

8. Different (pseudo) random number generators having 'near' uniform distribution have been proposed and are in use. All of them generate x_{n-1} from x_n recursively; one conforming to ANSI C uses the relation

$$x_{n+1} = (ax_n + c) \bmod m$$

With $a = 1103515245$, $c = 12345$, and $m = 2^{31}$. The number has the range $(0, 2^{31} - 1)$. Prepare a program to generate the nth random number x_n from x_{n-1} recursively. Use the values given here for a, c, and m as default values. Use 753 as the default value for x_0. For a given d, a similar (pseudo) random number in the range $(0, d - 1)$ is $x_n \bmod d$. Modify the program to output a random number in the range $(0, d - 1)$ if a value of d is specified.

9. Let x be a random number with uniform distribution in the range $(0, 2^{n-1})$. The value of k such that $c_{n,k-1} < x < c_{n,k}$ with $c_{n,k}$ as in Exercise 7 above represents an integer conforming to binomial distribution. Combine the programs in (7) and (8) above to generate a random number with binomial distribution over a specified range.

10. $\{x_i\}$ and $\{y_i\}$ are two random sequences of length d each. The correlation function between the two is defined as

$$r(\tau) = \sum_{i=0}^{d-1-\tau} x_i y_{i-\tau}$$

for any τ (Papoulis and Unnikrishna Pillai 2002). Prepare a program to get $r(\tau)$ for τ varying from 0 to $d/10$. With $d = 1000$ get two uniformly distributed random sequences and get the $r(\tau)$ for them. When x_i and y_i are the same $r(\tau)$ is the 'autocorrelation function'. Get the autocorrelation function for both the sequences.

11. Prepare a program to show a function as a bar graph. Depict the correlation functions in Exercise 10 above as a bar graph.

12. A list of 200 students with marks in mathematics, physics, chemistry, and English is to be made available for admission to an institution with four

branches of study. Each branch admits forty students based on a rank list. The rank list for admission is to be prepared with marks in mathematics +0.5 times the sum of marks in physics and chemistry combined as the basis. Further each student has a preferred list of branches which is used for branch allotment. Use the programs in the forgoing exercises for the following.

(a) *Student list with marks*: Prepare a program to assign marks in mathematics at random in the range 80–89 conforming to binomial distribution. For this prepare an array of 1024 numbers their values being decided by the cumulative binomial distribution (0th entry has 80, 1st to 11th have entry 81st, 12th–56th have entry 82nd, ... 1023rd has entry 89). Get 200 random numbers in the range (0, 1023)—with uniform distribution—obtained with replacement. Use these as indices to allot marks from the above list.

(b) Follow the same procedure to allot marks in physics, chemistry, and English also.

(c) *Rank list*: For each student get the weighted mark as M + 0.5 * (P + C) where M, P, and C are the marks in Mathematics, Physics, and Chemistry respectively.

(d) Form a list of student data with each entry being a list with the student Serial Number (0–199), marks in Mathematics, Physics, Chemistry, English, and the weighted marks as its elements.

(e) Based on the weighted marks in (c) above, rank the students and assign ranks in descending order (student with the highest weighted marks having first rank). The rank is added as the next item in the student's list.

(f) *Branch preference list*: The list of numbers [1, 2, 3, 4] represents the four possible branches. Shuffle the list 200 times and allot to the 200 students successively; this is the branch preference list for each student. Add this list as an additional entry to the data list of each student. To shuffle a list of k numbers, with j as a random integer in the range (0, k − 1) do circular right shift of the list by j positions (This is not a good algorithm for shuffling; it suffices for the present context).

(g) *Branch allotment*: Allot branch of his/her choice to the top ranking student. Do the same to the second rank holder and so on. Continue until all the branches are full. Add the allotted branch as an additional item to each student list.

(h) *Wait list*: Have a wait-list of ten students—continuing the rank list based allotment.

(i) After allotment is over two students from each of the branches leaves the course. All these are selected randomly from the allotted sets. Continue re-allotment maintaining ranks and accommodating the eight top wait-listed students. Complete allotment. Add allotted branch as an additional item to the student data.

13. A set of n integers is given. Write programs to arrange them in ascending order—use the following algorithms (all are recursive):

(a) Form L0 as an empty list. Search the full set of integers for the smallest integer. Append the result to L0. Repeat the search with the rest of the set; continue to finish ('*Bubble sort algorithm*').

(b) Divide the set into n/2 groups of two elements each. Arrange each group in ascending order. Merge the first two groups (which are already arranged) into a single group of four elements all being in ascending order. Repeat with each pair of successive groups. Merge each pair of groups of four elements at the next stage. Continue this to completion. Two groups of n/2 elements each—already arranged in ascending order—are combined at the last stage. The merging at every stage is with two arranged sets. The procedure outlined here reduces the number of comparisons to be carried out substantially. Whenever necessary, pad up the groups with zero integers ('*Merge sort algorithm*') (Guttag 2013).

References

Guttag JV (2013) Introduction to computation and programming using Python. MIT Press, Massachusetts

Papoulis A, Unnikrishna Pillai S (2002) Random variables and stochastic processes, 4th edn. McGraw Hill, New York

Rossum Gv, Drake FL Jr (2014) (2) The Python library reference. Python software foundation

Shyamala CK, Harini N, Padmanabhan TR (2011) Cryptography and security. Wiley India, New Delhi

Sullivan M (2008) Algebra and trigonometry, 8th edn. Pearson Prentice hall, New Jersey

Chapter 7
Operations for Text Processing

Information is stored in computers as a sequence of bits—represented as a series of ones and zeroes in combinations. Same is true of digital communication as well. Printed/displayed textual information comprises of well defined character combinations in different natural languages. This gap between a binary data stream and a document/file in a visually (/audio) tangible form is bridged in two stages using well/widely accepted standards. The first stage involves a scheme of representing all possible characters as binary sequences in a conveniently usable and acceptable form. Today this is done by Unicode. The second stage involves a convenient and accepted scheme of representing a Unicode bit sequence as a byte sequence. Different Standards like UTF-8, UTF-16 and so on are available for such representation.

7.1 Unicode

Unicode (The Unicode Standard) defines a code space of 1, 114, 11 code points in the range 0–10FFFF$_h$. All characters in all languages, formatting separators, control characters, mathematical symbols, are all represented by uniquely assigned binary numbers in Unicode assigned by the Unicode consortium. A Unicode point is represented as 'U+a_h' where a_h is the hex number representing the point. Representations for most of the commonly used characters, call for the use of a maximum of 16 bits. In Unicode the characters of English language and the other (European) groups of languages are assigned separate segments in the binary sequence. This facilitates interface software development and speeds up software based conversions between the characters and their Unicode representations. The Unicode consortium also identifies characters and symbols not assigned so far, and assigns Unicode values to them. This is a continuing process.

© Springer Nature Singapore Pte Ltd. 2016
T.R. Padmanabhan, *Programming with Python*,
DOI 10.1007/978-981-10-3277-6_7

7.2 Coding

Using the Unicode number of a symbol directly in programs/files is not a practical proposition. For example the characters used for English-based items can all be represented by a 7-bit sequence—formally called the 'ASCII' scheme. It has room for 128 distinct representations. A coding scheme exploits the structured representation in Unicode to assign compact and much shorter binary values for each of the Unicode symbols. 'UTF-8' coding scheme (Original UTF-8 paper) amongst these has (almost) universal acceptance. To some extent UTF-16 scheme is also in use. Because of its widely accepted standing we restrict our discussions essentially to UTF-8 code in this book. With some legacy files other codes may have to be used. For such rare situations the relevant methods/functions in Python may be invoked.

Conversion of textual information into a corresponding bit sequence is called 'encoding'. The reverse conversion—bit sequence to text it represents—is 'decoding'. Different schemes of encoding and decoding have evolved in the last half-a-century. Out of them the ASCII scheme has turned out to be possibly the most widely used one (at least for English and other similar European languages). Different attempts at a comprehensive standardization for encoding and decoding schemes have been made. UTF-8 has possibly turned out to be the widely adapted one; incidentally UTF-8 has the ASCII as its subset which has substantially helped enhance the wide acceptance of UTF-8.

7.2.1 UTF-8

All characters can be coded in UTF-8. A basic set of 128 characters—forming the ACSII set—has a 7-bit representation. This is accommodated within a byte. This ensures backward compatibility with ASCII which has been the most widely used code so far. A file—exclusively of ASCII characters is represented as a byte sequence—each byte representing an ASCII character. The ASCII character set is given in Table 7.1 (Padmanabhan 2007). The 26 capital letters (A, B, C, ... Y, Z), the corresponding small letters (a, b, c, ... y, z), Arabic numerals (0, 1, 2, ... 9), commonly used algebraic symbols (+, −, /, *), as well as other symbols (%, $, ...) are all part of it. A number of control characters (Next Line, Tab, End of Line, Tab, End of Document, ...) are additional to these; this also includes formatting separators (comma, full stop, question marks ...). The byte value in decimal, octal, and hex form for each of the characters is given in the table.

Any Unicode character—often referred as 'Unicode point'—that can be represented in UTF-8 has a bit representation whose length can extend up to 21 bits. This possible set can be grouped into four distinct (and mutually exclusive) ranges as shown in Table 7.2. The following characterize UTF-8:

Table 7.1 ASCII character set

Ctrl	Dec	Hex	Char	Code	Dec	Hex	Char	Dec	Hex	Char	Dec	Hex	Char
^@	0	00		NUL	32	20		64	40	@	96	60	'
^A	1	01		SOH	33	21	!	65	41	A	97	61	a
^B	2	02		STX	34	22	"	66	42	B	98	62	b
^C	3	03		ETX	35	23	#	67	43	C	99	63	c
^D	4	04		EOT	36	24	$	68	44	D	100	64	d
^E	5	05		ENQ	37	25	%	69	45	E	101	65	e
^F	6	06		ACK	38	26	&	70	46	F	102	66	f
^G	7	07		BEL	39	27	'	71	47	G	103	67	g
^H	8	08		BS	40	28	(	72	48	H	104	68	h
^I	9	09		HT	41	29	)	73	49	I	105	69	i
^J	10	0A		LF	42	2A	*	74	4A	J	106	6A	j
^K	11	0B		VT	43	2B	+	75	4B	K	107	6B	k
^L	12	0C		FF	44	2C	,	76	4C	L	108	6C	l
^M	13	0D		CR	45	2D	-	77	4D	M	109	6D	m
^N	14	0E		SO	46	2E	.	78	4E	N	110	6E	n
^O	15	0F		SI	47	2F	/	79	4F	O	111	6F	o
^P	16	10		DLE	48	30	0	80	50	P	112	70	p
^Q	17	11		DC1	49	31	1	81	51	Q	113	71	q
^R	18	12		DC2	50	32	2	82	52	R	114	72	r
^S	19	13		DC3	51	33	3	83	53	S	115	73	s
^T	20	14		DG4	52	34	4	84	54	T	116	74	t
^U	21	15		NAK	53	35	5	85	55	U	117	75	u
^V	22	16		SYN	54	36	6	86	56	V	118	76	v
^W	23	17		ETB	55	37	7	87	57	w	119	77	w
^X	24	18		CAN	56	38	8	88	58	X	120	78	x
^Y	25	19		EM	57	39	9	89	59	Y	121	79	y
^Z	26	1A		SUB	58	3A	:	90	59	Z	122	7A	z
^[	27	1B		ESC	59	3B	;	91	5B	[	123	7B	{
^\	28	1C		FS	60	3C	<	92	5C	\	124	7C	|
^]	29	1D		G5	61	3D	=	93	5D	]	125	7D	}
^^	30	1E	▲	RS	62	3E	>	94	5E	^	126	7E	~
^_	31	1F	▼	US	63	3F	?	95	5F	_	127	7F	⌂

- The first set is for characters with the number of significant bits being seven or less. It has a range of 0–128 comprising of 128 characters. They are represented by a single byte each with the most significant bit being zero. Such a representation is identical to the ASCII set.
- The rest of the UTF-8 is for Unicode characters of length 8 bits or more. They are represented as 2-, 3-, or 4-byte sets depending on the number of bits in the Unicode point. If it is of 8- to 11-bits length a 2-byte representation is used. If it is of 12- to 16-bits a 3-byte representation is used. If it is of 17- or more bits in size a 4-byte representation is used.
- Unicode standard versions are updated over time—always an updated version replacing an existing one. However all updates add new characters to the

Table 7.2 Group details of unicode points and their UTF-8 representations

Sl. no.	1	2	3	4
No. of bits in code point	7	11	16	21
First code point	U+0000	U+0080	U+0800	U+10000
Last code point	U+007F	U+07FF	U+FFFF	U+1FFFF
No. of bytes in the sequence	1	2	3	4
First byte	0XXXXXXX	110XXXXX	1110XXXX	11110XXX
Second byte		10XXXXXX	10XXXXXX	10XXXXXX
Third byte			10XXXXXX	10XXXXXX
Fourth byte				10XXXXXX

existing set but do not alter the character allocation done so far (Ignore 'Korean mess'). Hence any fully debugged encoder/decoder will be always valid.

- All multi-byte representations have a leading byte and 1-, 2-, or 3-continuation bytes. All continuation bytes are of the form 10xx xxxx with b_7 and b_6 being 1 and 0 respectively.
- The leading byte has the form 110x xxxx for 2-byte representation. $b_7 b_6 b_5 = 110$ signifies the 2-byte structure. Up to 2^{11} characters can be represented with 2- and 1-byte sets together.
- 1110 xxxx is the leading byte for 3-bytes character representation. $b_7 b_6 b_5 b_4 = 1110$ signifies the 3-byte structure. Up to 2^{16} characters can be represented with 3-, 2-, and 1-byte sets together.
- 1111 0xxx is the leading byte for the 4-bytes characters—$b_7 b_6 b_5 b_4 b_3 = 1111\ 0$ signifying the 4-byte structure. Up to 2^{21} characters can be represented using all these four sets together.
- One can synchronize with any serial data stream and identify a character by examining a maximum of four consecutive bytes.

The characters in Latin languages as well as some others can be represented with the 2-byte set. It also includes characters like 'ë', 'à' (characters with diacritical marks). A substantial part of the rest of the character set can be represented by the 3-byte sets. 4-byte sets are needed only for the less common (CJK) characters, mathematical symbols, and emojis.

Example 7.1 The characters 'A', '∼', 'Δ', '←', and '√' have the Unicode values 'U+41', 'U+7e', 'U+394', 'U+2190', 'U+221a' respectively. Convert them into respective UTF-8 byte sequences.

The binary value of 41_h is 100 0001. Being a 7-bit number, its UTF-8 code is a single byte with 0 as its MSB; it is 0100 0001. Similarly the binary value of $7e_h$ is 111 1110; again being of 7-bits, the UTF-8 code is 01111110.

The binary value of 394_h is 11 1001 0100—10 bits long. From the second row in Table 7.2 one can see that its UTF-8 representation is of 2 bytes, these being 1100 1110 and 1001 0100.

The binary value of 2190_h is 10 0001 1001 0000. Being of 14-bits, the UTF-8 code is of 3 bytes (see third row in Table 7.2). These are 1110 0010, 1000 0110, and 1001 0000 respectively. Similarly the binary value of $221a_h$ is 10 0010 0001 1010—again of 14 bits; corresponding UTF-8 code is of 3 bytes—1110 0010, 1000 1000, and 1001 1010 respectively.

Example 7.2 UTF-8 byte sequences of a set of four characters are given as 0011 1100, 0011 1110, (1110 0010, 1000 1000, 1001 1110), (1110 0010, 1000 0110, 1001 0010) respectively. Obtain respective Unicode values.

The codes 0011 1100 and 0011 1110 being single bytes, the respective Unicode values are of less than 8 bits in length; they are 'U+3c', 'U+3e' respectively. (They represent '<' and '>' respectively.)

The code (1110 0010, 1000 1000, 1001 1110) is of 3 bytes; its Unicode is 'U+221e' (represents the symbol '∞'). Similarly the code (1110 0010, 1000 0110, 1001 0010) is of 3 bytes; the corresponding Unicode is 'U+2192' (represents the symbol '→').

Python as a language will be called upon to do operations on strings of characters (texts), groups of bytes (numerical), or on their combinations. A number of operations (methods, functions and the like) are available with strings and byte sequences (van Rossum and Drake 2014). Some of the latter category has already been discussed in the preceding chapter. We shall focus on the methods/functions with strings here and also on those to convert from one to another form. Input and output schemes facilitate interface with strings, byte sequences and so on. These are normally handled through print methods/functions discussed later.

7.3 Operations with `string` S

A `string` (`tuple`) in Python is an immutable sequence of Unicode characters. For a `string` **S**, **S**[i] represents the ith entity in it. The functions len(**S**), min(**S**), max(**S**), and methods **S**.index(), **S**.count() discussed in the preceding chapter are equally valid for strings also. Same is true of the slicing operation and the tests '**x** in **S**' and '**x** not in **S**'. These are not discussed here again.

The Python Interpreter Sequences in Fig. 7.1a, b illustrate the use of operations with `strings`. A set of individual sequential `strings` with separations is interpreted as a single `string`. S1[1], S2[2], S[3][5] in Fig. 7.1a are examples. 'Good' and 'morning' are two `strings` in sequence in [1]; the set is taken as a single `string` **S1**—'Good morning'—in [2]. The intervening space between 'Good' and 'morning' in [1] is ignored. Same is true of **S2** in [3] where the three `strings` —'How', 'are', and 'you' are combined into **S2** in [4]. **S1** and **S2** already defined in [2] and [4] are combined with the `string` '!' in [6]. These bring out different possibilities of forming `strings` with convenient assignment possibilities. `Strings` can be sliced to form new sub-strings as with `lists` and `tuples`. Different possibilities are illustrated from [7] to [11].

(a)

```
>>> s1 = 'Good' ' Morning'                              [1]
>>> s1                                                  [2]
'Good Morning'
>>> s2 = 'How' ' are' ' you'                            [3]
>>> s2
'How are you'                                           [4]
>>> s3 = s1 + '! ' + s2                                 [5]
>>> s3                                                  [6]
'Good Morning! How are you'
>>> s1[0]                                               [7]
'G'
>>> s1[0:1]                                             [8]
'G'                                                     [9]
>>> s1[:-1]                                             [10]
'Good Mornin'
>>> s1[2:]                                              [11]
'od Morning'
>>> s4 = 'hello how are you?'                           [12]
>>> s5 = s4.capitalize()                                [13]
>>> s5                                                  [14]
'Hello how are you?'
>>> s5.casefold()                                       [15]
'hello how are you?'
>>> s5.center(25)                                       [16]
'    Hello how are you?    '                            [17]
>>> s5.center(25,'*')                                   [18]
'****Hello how are you?***'
>>> s5.center(30,'果')                                  [19]
'果果果果果果Hello how are you?果果果果果果'
>>> s5.rjust(25)                                        [20]
'        Hello how are you?'
>>> s5.rjust(25,'@')                                    [21]
'@@@@@@@Hello how are you?'
>>> s5.ljust(25)                                        [22]
'Hello how are you?       '
>>> s5.ljust(25,'@')                                    [23]
'Hello how are you?@@@@@@@'
>>> s6 = 'One day there passed by a company of cats a wise
dog'                                                    [24]
>>> s6.count('th')                                      [25]
1
>>> s6.count(' a ')                                     [26]
2
>>> s1, s2 = 'a1b2c3', 'd 5 e 6'                        [27]
>>> s1.join(s2)                                         [28]
'da1b2c3 a1b2c35a1b2c3 a1b2c3ea1b2c3 a1b2c36'
>>> s3 = ('zZ', 'yY', 'xX')                             [29]
>>> s1.join(s3)                                         [30]
'zZa1b2c3yYa1b2c3xX'
```

Fig. 7.1 a Python Interpreter sequence illustration string operations (continued in Fig. 7.1b),
b Python Interpreter sequence illustration string operations (continued from Fig. 7.1a)

(b)

```
>>> ''.join(s3)                                      [31]
'zZyYxX'
>>> from demo_6 import twd
>>> s7 = twd.sa1                                      [32]
>>> len(s7)                                           [33]
634
>>> s7.count('th')                                    [34]
18
>>> s7.count('th', 100, 600)                          [35]
16
>>> s7.count('th', 100)                               [36]
16
```

Fig. 7.1 (continued)

SS.capitalise() returns a copy of **SS** with its leading letter capitalized. String **S4** in [12] has its leading letter 'H' capitalized to form **S5** as in [13]. **SS**. casefold() returns **SS** with all its characters converted into direct lower case form. The casefold form of a string is useful in string/phrase matching. **S5** in [14] is returned in casefold form in [15]. SS.center(**n**) centers the string **SS** in a field of **n**-wide characters leaving equally wide spaces on either side. [16] is an illustrative example.

SS.center(**nn**, 'm') is the enhanced version where **SS** is centered in a field of nn characters. The space on either side is filled with the character 'm'. 'm' can be any character. [18] and [19] are illustrative examples of such centering with added filling.

SS.rjust (**nn**, 'm') returns the string **SS** right-justified with 'm' being the total justified length of the string. The character 'm' is inserted in the blank spaces at the left. If 'm' as a character is omitted the string is returned as a right-justified one of **nn** characters with the leading spaces left unfilled. [20] and [21] are illustrative examples. Similarly **SS**.ljust(**nn**, 'm') and **SS**.ljust(**nn**) return respective left-justified strings. [22] and [23] are respective illustrative examples.

SS.count('**sb**', '**a**', '**b**') counts the number of occurrences of the defined substring—'sb'—in the string '**SS**'. The counting is done from the ath character up to the (b − 1)th character. If 'b' is left out the full string from the ath character is scanned for the count. If '**a**' is also left out counting is done for the full length of **SS**. The string **S6** is defined in [24]. [25] searches for the sub-string '**th**' in the whole of **S6** and shows there to be a single occurrence of '**th**' in it. The substrings to be searched need not be restricted to character sets; for example the count for '**a**' in [26] yields the total number of the single letter word—'**a**'—in **S6** (as two).

Concatenation of strings is direct as in [1] above; **s1**.join(**s2**) as in [28] combines the elements of string **s2** to **s1** (with **s1** and **s2** as in [27]) one by one. The result is the string '**s2**[0]**s1s2**[1]**s1s2**[2]**s1** ...'. In **s3** [29] each element

```
sa1 = '''The Wise Dog

One day there passed by a company of cats a wise dog.

And as he came near and saw that they were very intent and
heededhim not, he stopped.

Then there arose in the midst of the company a large, grave
cat and looked upon them and said, "Brethren, pray ye; and
when ye have prayed again and yet again, nothing doubting,
verily then it shall rain mice.'''

And when the dog heard this he laughed in his heart and
turned from them saying, "O blind and foolish cats, has it
not been written and have I not known and my fathers before
me, that that which raineth for prayer and faith and
supplication is not mice but bones." '''
```

Fig. 7.2 The string SA1 used in Example 7.3

itself is a string. Hence **s1**.join(**s3**) [30] is formed accordingly. ''.join(**s3**) in Fig. 7.1b [31] combines the individual elements of **s3** to form the enhanced string.

Example 7.3 A short story of Kahlil Gibran has been reproduced in Fig. 7.2 as a string—**SA1**. Count (i) the number of characters and (ii) the number of bigrams 'th' in it. (iii) Count also the number of bigrams '**th**' in the range (100, 600) in it.

SA1 is assigned to **S7** in [32] Fig. 7.1b. The number of characters in **S7** is counted as 634 with len(**S7**) [33]. The total number of the bigrams—'**th**'—in **S7** is 18 [34]. The same in the range (100, 600) is 16 [35]. The count from the 100th character up to the end is also 16 [36].

7.4 Number Representations and Conversions

In all our day-to-day dealings and transactions numbers are represented and processed in decimal form. In computers and computer-based schemes and applications numbers are represented in binary form and processed. Methods and functions available in Python do all representation and related algebra with numbers in binary form. For a convenient and compact representation numbers are more often represented in octal or hexadecimal (hex) form. But for displays, printout, and similar human related interface decimal numbers are used. Python has the flexibility to represent numbers in different ways and convert them from one form to another. These are explained and illustrated here.

7.4.1 Integers

Integers can be represented in decimal form directly. Binary, octal, and hex representations can be done in simple and well accepted formats. Illustrative details are in the Python Interpreter sequence in Fig. 7.3. **n1** [1] is the hex number 43_h. '**0x**' or '**0X**' signifies the following integer sequence to be a hex number; the integers can be from the set—{0, 1, 2, ... 8, 9, a(A), b(B), c(C), d(D), e(E), f(F)}. Small or capital letters can be used for a, b, c, d, e, and f. $0 \times 43 = 4 * 16^1 + 3 * 16^0 = 67$ (in decimal form) as can be seen from [2]. Octal numbers are represented as '**0o**' or '**0O**' followed by the number—a sequence of digits from the set—{0, 1, 2, ... 6, 7}.

```
>>> n1 = 0x43         [1]      >>> int('0xfe2', 16)          [19]
>>> n1                [2]      4066
67                             >>> 0xfe2                     [20]
>>> n2 = 0o103        [3]      4066
>>> n2                [4]      >>> l2 = []                   [21]
67                             >>> for jj in range(2,36):
>>> n3 = 0b1000011    [5]      l2.append (int('01110',jj))
>>> n3                [6]      ...
67                             >>> l2[:16]
>>> n4 = int()        [7]      [14, 39, 84, 155, 258, 399, 584,
>>> n4                [8]      819, 1110, 1463, 1884, 2379,
0                              2954, 3615, 4368, 5219]
>>> m1 = int(501)     [9]      >>> l2[16:26]
>>> m1                         [6174, 7239, 8420, 9723, 11154,
501                            12719, 14424, 16275, 18278,
>>> int(67.8901)      [10]     20439]
67                             >>> l2[26:]
>>> int('592', 36)    [11]     [22764, 25259, 27930, 30783,
6806                           33824, 37059, 40494, 44135]
>>> 2+36*(9+5*36)     [12]     >>> a1, a2, a3, a4 = 34, 0o34,
6806                           0x34, 0b1110111               [22]
>>> int('z',36)       [13]     >>> bin(a1), bin(a2), bin(a3),
35                             bin(a4)                       [23]
>>> int('zxy', 36)    [14]     ('0b100010', '0b11100',
46582                          '0b110100', '0b1110111')
>>> int('-XYZ',36)    [15]     >>> hex(a1), hex(a2), hex(a3),
-44027                         hex(a4)                       [24]
>>> 35+36*(34+33*36)           ('0x22', '0x1c', '0x34', '0x77')
                      [16]     >>> oct(a1), oct(a2), oct(a3),
44027                          oct(a4)                       [25]
>>> int('abc',30)              ('0o42', '0o34', '0o64', '0o167')
                      [17]     >>> bin(-34), oct(-0x34),
9342                           hex(-0b1110111)               [26]
>>> 12+30*(11+30*10)           ('-0b100010', '-0o64', '-0x77')
                      [18]     >>>
9342
```

Fig. 7.3 Python Interpreter sequence illustrating number representations and conversions

The octal number 0O103 in [3] is again the decimal number 67 itself [4]. '**0b**' or '**0B**' followed by a binary sequence is a binary number. 0*b*1000011 in binary form [5] is again the decimal number 67 [6].

The function int(**x**) in its simplest form accepts **x** as a number and returns its integral part as an integer. int() in [7] returns a zero [8]. int(501) in [9] returns 501 itself. int(67.8901) in [10] returns 67. The fractional part of the number is ignored and the integral part returned as an integer. However if rounding-off is to be done round() function can be used (discussed in the following section).

int(**y**, **rr**) is the general form of the int() function. Details of its use are as follows:

- If **rr** is omitted and **y** is a number, the integral part of **y** is returned as in the foregoing cases. Here the number is implicitly taken to be a decimal number.
- If **rr** is present it signifies the radix (base) of the number. It can take any value from 2 to 36. Further **y** has to be a string representing the number to the base **rr**. The characters in the string are from the set—{0, 1, 2, ... 8, 9, *a*, *b*, *c*, ... *y*, *z*} where *a*, *b*, *c*, ... *y*, *z* represent the integer values 10–35 in the same order. The letters can be capital or small versions. In addition the binary, octal, and hex strings are also acceptable.
- Negative integers have the negative sign at the left end of the string.

Lines [11]–[19] illustrate a few possible uses of int() function. In [11] 592 signifies an integer to base 36. Its decimal value is 6806 as seen from [12]. Similarly '**z**', '**zxy**', and '**XYZ**' all to base 36—are shown in the succeeding lines along with their decimal equivalent values. int('**abc**', 30) in [17] represents '**abc**' as an integer to base 30. Its equivalent decimal value is 9342. int(**0xfe2**, 16) in [19] takes **0xfe2** as a hex integer having decimal value 4066 [20].

Example 7.4 The string—'01110'—is given. Treat it as an integer to bases 2–36 and obtain respective decimal values.

I2 is formed as a null set in [21]. All the required integers are successively appended to it in the following lines. In subsequent lines **I2** is displayed in three convenient segments.

The function bin(**x**) returns the binary equivalent of **x** as a string. Here **x** can be an integer in decimal form, octal form, hex form or binary form itself as illustrated in [22]. hex(**x**) returns the hex value of integer **x** as a string. Similarly oct(**x**) returns the octal value of **x** as a string. In all these cases **x** has to be an integer but its representation can be in decimal, octal, binary, or hex form. These are illustrated in [23]–[26].

7.4.2   Floating Point Numbers

The function float(**ff**) accepts a floating point number (or an integer) **ff** as a string and returns its equivalent as a decimal value. The Python Interpreter sequences in

(a)

```
>>> f1, f2, f3, f4 = float('345.67'),
float('0.34567e3'),float('3456.7E-1'),float('-3456700e-
4')                                                        [1]
>>> f1, f2, f3, f4
(345.67, 345.67, 345.67, -345.67)
>>> g1, g2, g3, g4 = 345.67, 0.34567e3, 3456.7E-1, -
3456700e-4                                                 [2]
>>> float(g1), float(g2), float(g3), float(g4)            [3]
(345.67, 345.67, 345.67, -345.67)
>>> h = (g1, g2, g3, g4)                                   [4]
>>> list(map(float, h))                                   [5]
[345.67, 345.67, 345.67, -345.67]                         [6]
>>> j1 = h1.as_integer_ratio()                            [7]
(6081090949973279, 17592186044416)                        [8]
>>> j1[0]/j1[1]                                           [9]
345.67
>>> g4.as_integer_ratio()                                 [10]
(-6081090949973279, 17592186044416)                       [11]
>>> (2.00).is_integer()                                   [12]
True
>>> (0.20e10).is_integer()                                [13]
True
>>> (2.00e-1).is_integer()                                [14]
False
>>> nn = 67.8901                                          [15]
>>> float.hex(nn)                                         [16]
'0x1.0f8f765fd8adbp+6'                                    [17]
>>> (j1[0]/j1[1]).hex()                                   [18]
'0x1.59ab851eb851fp+8'
```

Fig. 7.4 a Python Interpreter sequence illustrating floating point number representations and conversions (continued in Fig. 7.4b), **b** Python Interpreter sequence illustrating floating point number representations and conversions (continued from Fig. 7.4a)

Fig. 7.4a, b illustrate the use of different operations related to floating point numbers. The number 345.67 (and −345.67) is represented as strings in different forms in [1] in Fig. 7.4a. float() returns the decimal value. The same set of numbers is assigned to **g1, g2, g3**, and **g4** in [2] and the float values obtained in [3]. With h = (**g1, g2, g3, g4**) as a tuple the conversion is carried out using the map() function in [5] and the result shown in [6]. A floating point number can be expressed in the rational form as a ratio of two integers using the method .as_inger_ratio(). [7] illustrates this for 345.67; the (numerator, denominator) pair is returned as a tuple in [8]. [9] confirms this by evaluating the ratio (numerator/denominator) directly; [10] does the conversion to ratio form for the negative number −345.67.

x.is_integer() tests whether x is an integer; if 'yes', 'True' is returned; else 'False' is returned; the illustrations are in [12], [13], and [14].

(b)

```
>>> hh1 = (345.67).hex()                                    [19]
>>> hh1                                                      [20]
'0x1.59ab851eb851fp+8'
>>> hh2 = float.fromhex(hh1)                                [21]
>>> hh2                                                      [22]
345.67
>>> k1 = '0x2.0fp+3'                                         [23]
>>> float.fromhex(k1)                                       [24]
16.46875                                                    [25]
>>> k3 = '0x2.0p+1'                                          [26]
>>> k4 = float.fromhex(k3)                                  [27]
>>> k4                                                      [28]
4.0
>>> float.fromhex('0xfp-1')                                 [29]
7.5
>>> round(57.654545)                                        [30]
58
>>> round(57.654545,3)                                      [31]
57.655
>>> b1 = 1.04555500000                                      [32]
>>> l2 = []                                                 [33]
>>> for jj in range(1,9):l2.append(round(b1,jj))
...
>>> l2
[1.0, 1.05, 1.046, 1.0456, 1.04556, 1.045555, 1.045555,
1.045555]                                                   [34]
>>> a1 = 1.04555000000                                      [35]
>>> l1 = []                                                 [36]
>>> for jj in range(1,9):l1.append(round(a1,jj))           [37]
...
>>> l1
[1.0, 1.05, 1.046, 1.0455, 1.04555, 1.04555, 1.04555,
1.04555]                                                    [38]
>>>
```

Fig. 7.4 (continued)

In algebra involving floating point numbers normally the numbers are present in decimal form—represented in 'int.fraction' form or in the (mantissa, exponent) form.

In Python it is also possible to represent and display a floating point hex number in (mantissa, exponent) form. Here the exponent is represented as 'pa' signifying 2^a with 'a' being the (positive/negative) exponent. With this convention a floating point decimal number **fn** can be represented in hex form using float.formhex (**fn**). The floating point decimal number 67.8901 is assigned to **nn** in [15]. It is represented in hex form as explained above using float.hex(**nn**) in [16] and [17]. The decimal number 345.67—expressed as an integer ratio in [9] (**j1**[0]/**j1**[1])—is expressed as a floating point number in hex form in [18]. It is verified through direct conversion in [19], [20] and again through reversal to decimal form in [21] and [22] (in Fig. 7.4b). **k1** in [23] is a hex number in floating point form (with binary value of 10000.01111); it is converted to decimal form through float.fromhex(**k1**) in [24] as 16.46875. Two additional examples of conversion from hex to decimal form follow from [26] to [29].

For a floating point number **x**, round(**x**) rounds **x** to the desired accuracy. With a single argument, **x** round(**x**) rounds **x** to an integer as in [30]. round (**x**, **d**) rounds **x** to a number to **d** significant digits beyond the decimal point as in [31]. The rounding off is carried out based on the actual representation of the number in memory.

Example 7.5 The numbers **b1** = 1.0455550 and **a1** = 1.045550 are represented as '1.0455550000000000121502807814977131783962249755859375 0'   and '1.045549999999999979394260662957094609737396240234375 00' respectively in the computer. Round them off to different accuracies and explain any anomaly.

list **l2** is initialized as an empty list in [33]. **b1** (=1.0455550) is rounded off to different significant digits and appended to **l2** as in [34]. In all cases the rounding is done to the nearest level as is to be expected.

A similar rounding off is done with **a1** = 1.045550 [35] and **l1** is the list of rounded numbers. [37] shows the respective values. The rounding sequence is as follows:

- 1.045549 is rounded to 1.04555.
- 1.04554 is rounded to 1.0455 and not 1.0456.
- 1.0455 is rounded to 1.046.
- 1.045 is rounded to 1.05.
- 1.04 is rounded to 1.0 and not 1.1.

7.5 More String Operations

The Python Interpreter sequence in Fig. 7.5 Illustrates some additional operations with strings. **SS**.endswith('**sb**') returns True if the string **SS** ends with the sub-sequence '**sb**'; else it returns 'False'. string **S6** in [1] ends with '**dog**'. [2] confirms this. One has the option of checking for any element in a tuple to be at the end of **SS** as illustrated by [3] and [4] with the string **S6** itself. Similar checks can be made over a selected segment of **SS** also. **SS**.endswith('**sb**', **p**, **q**) picks out the slice SS[**p**, **q**] and checks whether it ends with the sub-string '**sb**'. [5] is an illustration with **S6**. SS. startswith('**sb**', **p**, **q**) is similar to **SS**.endswith ('**sb**', **p**, **q**); it tests string **SS** for **sb** being at the start of the slice **SS** [**p**, **q**] in it. One can also test for an element in a tuple (used in place of **sb**) to be at the start of **SS** [**p**, **q**]. [5], [6], and [7] are illustrations of use of .startswith(). A select number of methods is available to check for the presence of different categories of characters in strings. **SS**.isalpha() returns 'True' if the string **SS** is non-empty

```
>>> s6 = 'One day there passed by a company of cats a wise
dog'                                                          [1]
>>> s6.endswith('dog')                                        [2]
True
>>> s6.endswith(('wise','cat', 'dog'))                        [3]
True
>>> s6.endswith(('wise','cat'))                               [4]
False
>>> a1, a2 = s6.startswith('One'),s6.startswith('day') [5]
>>> a1, a2
(True, False)
>>> a3 = s6.startswith(('One', 'day'))                        [6]
>>> a3
True
>>> s6[4:7]
'day'
>>>
a4,a5=s6.startswith('day',4,8),s6.startswith('day',0,8)[7]
>>> a4, a5
(True, False)
>>> len(s6)
52
>>> s6.endswith('wise', 0,-4)
True
>>> s6.isalnum()
False
>>> slt = []
>>> for jj in range(len(s6)):
...     if 's6[jj]'.isalpha():slt.append(s6[jj])
...
>>> slt
[]
>>> s6[0]
'O'
>>> s6[0].isalpha()
True
>>> 'hello'.isalpha()
True
>>> s6.isprintable()
True
>>> ll=['3','3.1','0.31','-0.31','1/5','-
2.0/5.0','3.0e01','-4']
>>> lm = []
>>> for jj in ll:lm.append(jj.isnumeric())
...
>>> lm
[True, False, False, False, False, False, False, False]
```

Fig. 7.5 Python Interpreter sequence illustrating additional operations with strings

Table 7.3 Methods to test `string` content: if the specified `string` is non-empty and the specified test is satisfied 'True' is returned; else 'False' is returned

isalpha()	All are alphabetic characters
isnumeric()	All are numeric characters— i.e., digits
isdecimal()	All the decimal characters—includes digit characters (0, 1, ... 9), and others defined in Unicode
isdigit()	All decimal characters and some others like ①, ②, ③, ... superscript and subscript digits, and so on as defined in unicode
isalnum	isalpha() or isdecimal() or isnumeric()
isidentifier()	Python identifier
islower()	All characters of lower case type
isprintable()	All are printable characters (excludes control, formatting characters ...)
isspace()	All are white space characters
istitle()	The string has to be a title-cased string—first letter in every word is a capital letter
isupper()	Every character in the string is in upper case
isalum()	Every character in the string satisfies one of **SS**.isalpha(), **SS**.isdecimal(), **SS**.isdigit(), or **SS**.isnumeric()
startswith ('sb', p, q)	Slice **SS[p:q]** starts with substring **sb**. One can also use a tuple in place of sb and test whether ss with an element in it
endswith('sb', p, q)	Slice **SS[p:q]** ends with substring sb. One can also use a tuple in place of **sb** and test whether **SS** ends with an element in it

and all its characters are alphabetic. Table 7.3 lists the different methods of this category with details of the checks they make. Relevant illustrative examples of usage are also shown in the sequence in Fig. 7.5.

Strings can be combined and split in different ways. Illustrative examples are in the Python Interpreter sequence in Fig. 7.6. **SS**.split() directly splits **SS** into a list of all the words in it—words in the sense of groups of characters separated by white spaces. The string **ss** in [1] is split to form the list **sp** shown in [2]. Any sequence of strings can be concatenated into one string using '**com**'.join ('sqn'). Here '**sqn**' is a sequence (like a tuple or a list). The string '**com**' is interposed between adjacent elements of '**sqn**' in forming the concatenated string. The string **sj** in [4] is formed by combining the elements of list **sp**. A white space—"—is inserted between adjacent elements in it [3]. **Sjj** in [5] is formed similarly with three white spaces between adjacent elements. **Sj** and **sjj** are again split into respective word lists in [6] using the method split() itself. Note that the intervening spaces are ignored whatever be their lengths. **Sj0** in [7] is formed by concatenating the elements of **sp** with the single character string '**$**' as the separator. With split() the argument need not be specified if white space is the separator as was done in [2]. With other separators the separator has to be specified as a string argument. **Sj0**.split('**$**') splits string **sj0** into its element treating '**$**' as the separator between adjacent elements [8]. The method .split() has two arguments in its general form—as **SS**.split('**aa**', b); here '**aa**' is the separator string and b the integer signifying that **SS** is to be split into b + 1 elements. **sp4** in

```
>>> ss = 'Hello how are you ?'                            [1]
>>> sp = ss.split()                                       [2]
>>> sp
['Hello', 'how', 'are', 'you', '?']
>>> sj = ' '.join(sp)                                     [3]
>>> sj                                                    [4]
'Hello how are you ?'
>>> sjj = '   '.join(sp)                                  [5]
>>> sjj
'Hello   how   are   you   ?'
>>> sp1, sp2 = sj.split(), sjj.split()                    [6]
>>> sp1, sp2
(['Hello','how','are','you','?'],['Hello', 'how', 'are',
'you', '?'])
>>> sj0 = '$'.join(sp)                                    [7]
>>> sj0
'Hello$how$are$you$?'
>>> sp3, sp4 = sj0.split('$'), sj0.split('$', 2)          [8]
>>> sp3, sp4                                              [9]
(['Hello', 'how', 'are', 'you', '?'], ['Hello', 'how',
'are$you$?'])                                             [10]
>>> kb = 'One may not reach the dawn save by the path of
the night'                                                [11]
>>> kbp = kb.split()                                      [12]
>>> n1 = len(kbp)                                         [13]
>>> a1 = '*'                                              [14]
>>> while n1 > 1:
...     kbb = kb.split(None, 1)                           [15]
...     kb  = a1.join(kbb)                                [16]
...     a1 = a1 + '*'                                     [17]
...     n1 -= 1                                           [18]
...
>>> kb                                                    [19]
'One*may**not***reach****the*****dawn******save*******by**
******the********path*********of**********the*********
**night'
```

Fig. 7.6 Python Interpreter sequence illustrating use of split() method with strings

[8] is formed as **sj0**.split('**$**', **2**). Two strings separated by '**$**' are extracted as '**Hello**' and '**how**'; the rest of **SS** is returned as such—as '**areyou?**'.

Example 7.6 **kb** below is a quote from 'The Madman' by Kahlil Gibran. Redo **kb** as a string with '*' separating the second word from the first, '**' separating the third from the second and so on.

kb = 'One may not reach the dawn save by the path of the night'.

kbp is the list of words in **kb** in the same order as in **kb** itself [12]. **n1** in [13] is the total number of words in **kb**. **a1** is initialized to '*' in [14]. The asterisk sequence insertions are to be done len(**kb**) − 1 times. **kb** is split into the first word and the rest as **kbb** in [15]; **a1** as the single asterisk separator inserted in between in

```
>>> ss = 'Hello how are you ?'                          [1]
>>> sr = ss.rsplit()                                    [2]
>>> sr                                                  [3]
['Hello', 'how', 'are', 'you', '?']
>>> sj0 = '&&'.join(sr)                                 [4]
>>> sj0                                                 [5]
'Hello&&how&&are&&you&&?'
>>> sr3, sr4 = sj0.rsplit('&&'), sj0.rsplit('&&',2)     [6]
>>> sr3, sr4                                            [7]
(['Hello', 'how', 'are', 'you', '?'], ['Hello&&how&&are',
'you', '?'])
>>> kb = 'One may not reach the dawn save by the path of
the night'
>>> n1, a1 = len(kb.split()), '*'                       [8]
>>> while n1 > 1:
...     kbb = kb.rsplit(None, 1)
...     kb  = a1.join(kbb)
...     a1 += '*'
...     n1 -= 1
...
>>> kb                                                  [9]
'One***********may***********not***********reach*********t
he********dawn*******save******by****the***path***of**th
e*night'
```

Fig. 7.7 Python Interpreter sequence illustrating use of variants of split() method with strings

[17] and **n1** decremented in [18]. The sequence of operations is repeated until completion. **kb** in [19] is the desired sequence.

ss.rsplit('**cc**', **d**) is the counterpart of **ss**.split('**aa**', **b**) discussed earlier. **ss** from Fig. 7.6 has been reproduced in [1] in the Python Interpreter sequence in Fig. 7.7. **ss**.rsplit() splits **ss** into words starting from the right end of **ss** [2] and assigns the resulting set of words to **sr** in [3]. The words in **sr** are joined together [4] to form the single string **sj0** in [5]. The '**&&**' pair is the separator used between adjacent words here. **sj0** is split fully into words with **sj0**.rsplit('**&&**') [6] removing the separator '**&&**'. The splitting is done here starting at the right end. **sj0**.rsplit ('**&&**', 2) splits **sj0** partially—into three parts—stripping away only the last two 'words' ('you and '?') to form the list **sr4** [7].

Example 7.7 Repeat the above exercise in Example 7.6 with '*' as separator between the last two elements of kb, '**' as the one prior to that separator and so on.

The Interpreter sequence for this is shown from [8] onwards. **kb**.rsplit (None, 1) is assigned to **kbb**. In all other respects the sequence is similar to that in Example 7.6 above. **Kb** in [9] is the desired output.

The python Interpreter sequence in Fig. 7.8a, b illustrate some additional operations with strings. **ss**.strip() in Fig. 7.8a removes all white spaces on either

(a)

```
>>> ss = '    One day there passed by a company of cats a
wise dog    '                                             [1]
>>> s6 = ss.strip()                                       [2]
>>> s6
'One day there passed by a company of cats a wise dog'
>>> s6.strip()                                            [3]
'One day there passed by a company of cats a wise dog'
>>> s6.strip('Ognd')                                      [4]
'e day there passed by a company of cats a wise do'
>>> s6.lstrip('e nOd')                                    [5]
'ay there passed by a company of cats a wise dog'
>>> s6.rstrip('a wise dog')                               [6]
'One day there passed by a company of cat'
>>> s6.replace('c', 'C')                                  [7]
'One day there passed by a Company of Cats a wise dog'
>>> s6.replace('e', 'EE', 2)                              [8]
'OnEE day thEEre passed by a company of cats a wise dog'
>>> s6.partition('company')                               [9]
('One day there passed by a ', 'company', ' of cats a
wise dog')
>>> s6.partition('Company')                               [10]
('One day there passed by a company of cats a wise dog',
'', '')
>>> ss6.rpartition('EE')                                  [11]
('OnEE day thEErEE pass', 'EE', 'd by a company of cats a
wise dog')
>>> s6.find('e ')                                         [12]
2
>>> s6.find('e ',8, 30)                                   [13]
12
>>> s6.find('e ',15)                                      [14]
47
>>> s6.find('e ',15, 45)                                  [15]
-1
>>> s6[-8:]                                               [16]
'wise dog'
>>> s6.rfind('e ', -8)                                    [17]
47
>>> s6[-45:-8]
' there passed by a company of cats a '
>>> s6.rfind('e ',-45, -8)
12
>>> s6.index('e ',15)                                     [18]
47
```

Fig. 7.8 a Python Interpreter sequence illustrating more operations with strings (continued in Fig. 7.8b), **b** Python Interpreter sequence illustrating more operations with strings (continued from Fig. 7.8a)

(b)

```
>>> s6.index('e ',15, 45)                                    [19]
Traceback (most recent call last):
  File "<stdin>", line 1, in <module>
ValueError: substring not found
>>> s6.rindex('e ',15, 45)                                   [20]
Traceback (most recent call last):
  File "<stdin>", line 1, in <module>
ValueError: substring not found
>>> s6.rindex('e ',15)                                       [21]
47
>> s6t = s6.title()                                          [22]
>>> s6t
'One Day There Passed By A Company Of Cats A Wise Dog'
>>> s6t.swapcase()                                           [23]
'oNE dAY tHERE pASSED bY a cOMPANY oF cATS a wISE dOG'
>>> s6t.lower()                                              [24]
'one day there passed by a company of cats a wise dog'
>>> s6t.upper()                                              [25]
'ONE DAY THERE PASSED BY A COMPANY OF CATS A WISE DOG'
>>> s6.zfill(70)                                             [26]
'000000000000000000One day there passed by a company of
cats a wise dog'
```

Fig. 7.8 (continued)

side of **ss** [1]. The stripped version of **ss** is s6 in [2]. In the absence of white spaces at the end, with **s6**.strip() the string remains untouched as in [3]. The generalized version of the strip method is **ss**.strip('**chr**') where '**chr**' is a set of characters to be removed. Here all combinations of the specified set in '**chr**' are removed.

ss6.strip('**Ognd**') removes '**O**' and '**n**' at the left and '**g**' at the right in [4]. Note that '**o**' at the right end—being the small letter is not removed. Hence '**d**'—precedes '**o**' and is not at the end remains untouched. **s6**.lstrip() and **s6**.rstrip() are similar to **s6**.strip(). **S6**.lstrip('**e nOd**') removes the '**e nOd**' combination at left (leading) end [5] and **s6**.rstrip('**a wise dog**') does a similar thing at the right end [6]. Again all the respective character combinations are removed in both the cases. **ss**.replace('**oo**', '**nn**', **m**) replaces the substring '**oo**' by the substring '**nn**' in the string **ss** in the first **m** occurrences of '**oo**' (**m** is an integer here). The integer **m** is optional. If replacement is sought to be done in the whole of the string '**ss**', **m** is omitted. **s6**.replace('**c**', '**C**') in [7] replaces all '**c**' in **s6** by '**C**'s. **s6**.replace('**e**', '**EE**', 2) replaces only the first two occurrences of '**e**'s in s6 by '**EE**'s [8].

ss.partition('**prt**') partitions **ss** into three segments. The first occurrence of '**prt**' in the string '**ss**' is identified; **ss** is split into one substring up to this occurrence, the substring '**prt**' itself, and the rest of **ss** as the third subset. As an illustration **s6**.partition('**company**') in [9] splits s6 into three substrings in the line following. If the specified substring '**prt**' is absent in **ss**, **ss** along with two empty substrings following it, are returned. [10] searches for '**Company**' (with a capital 'C') in **s6**. It being absent, **s6** and the two empty substrings are returned. The method .rpartition() does partitioning similarly; but here the scanning to identify the substring starts at the right end of **ss**.rpartition('**EE**') partitions **s6** as in [11].

ss.find ('**aa**', **ns**, **ne**) identifies the slice **ss[ns:ne]** in **ss**, scans it for the presence of the substring '**aa**' in it and returns the index of its first occurrence. If the integer **ne** is omitted the scanning is done in the whole of the substring **ss** from **ss[ns]** onwards. If **ns** is also omitted the whole of **ss** is scanned to identify the first occurence of '**aa**' and its location. If '**aa**' is not present in **ss** '−1' is returned as the index value. **S6**.find('**e**') [12] identifies the index of the first occurrence of '**e**' in **s6** as 2. In fact it is the location of the word ending with '**e**'. **S6**.find('**e**', 8, 30) [13] returns 12 as the index (corresponding to the word '**these**'). The next occurrence is at index 47 (corresponding to the word '**wise**') as can be seen from [14] where the full sub-sequence from **s6** is scanned. **S6**.find('**e**', 15, 45) in [15] confirms the absence of any word ending in '**e**' in this range by returning the index −1. '**e**' **in sb** scans for the presence of '**e**' in **sb** but not for its location. In this respect .find() method is more demanding; the use of the '**in**' operator suffices when it serves the purpose adequately.

ss.rfind('**aa**', **ns**, **ne**) is the counterpart of **ss**.find('**aa**', **ns**, **ne**). Here search for the sub-string '**aa**' is from the right end. Lines following [16 and 17] are illustrations for its use. Functionally **ss**.index ('**aa**', **ns**, **ne**) achieves the same purpose as **ss**.find('**aa**', **ns**, **ne**). In case the sub-string '**aa**' is not present in **ss**, a ValueError is raised. .index() differs from .find() only in this respect. A similar identity holds good for **ss**.rindex() and **ss**.rfind() as well. **s6**.index('**e**', 15) in [18] returns the index value 47. But **s6**.index('**e**', 15, 45) returns ValueError in [19] (Fig. 7.8b). **s6**.rindex('**e**', 15, 45) in [20] returns a ValueError. **S6**. rindex('', 15) returns 47 as the index in [21]. **ss**.swapcase() swaps the cases of all the letters in **ss**.

The following are additional method with strings—all illustrated through the string **s6/s6t**.

s6.title() converts the string **s6** to title form; the leading letters of all the words in it are turned into capital letters [22].

s6t.swapcase() swaps the cases of all the letters in **s6t** [23].

S6t.lower() returns a copy of **s6t** with all the characters converted to lower case [24].

s6t.uper() returns a copy of **s6t** with all the characters converted to upper case [25].

s6.zfill(70) returns a string of 70 characters as long as len(**s6**) is 70 or less. The difference between 70 and len(**s6**) is made up by filling '0' at the leading (i.e.,. left end) side [26]. If length of **s6** exceeds 70 (or the number in its place) in length, **s6** is returned without any change.

7.6 **bytes** and **bytearrays**

Computers store data as bit sequences. But even at the elementary levels of storage and processing data is treated as byte sequences. Files are more often formed, stored, and communicated in natural languages. To facilitate exchange of data between these two classes two dedicated data types—bytes and bytearrays— are available in Python. The operations dealing with these are discussed here. bytes is similar to a string with some restrictions. It is immutable and made up of only bytes. Any ASCII character—with the possibility of representation as a byte —can also be an element in it. A bytearray is the mutable counterpart of bytes; it is also made up of only bytes. Any ASCII character can also be an element in it.

When the bytes sequence is used as a whole in a program it is used as a bytes object. But if its elements are to be altered in the program it is used as a bytearray. A number of functions and methods are available to convert bytes/bytearray from one form into another. We discuss these in different groups here.

Bytes and bytearrays can be formed in different ways. The Python Interpreter sequence in Fig. 7.9a, b illustrate the methods of their formation and related operations. A set of characters can be transformed into the bytes type by preceding it with a 'b' or 'B' ([1], [2] in Fig. 7.9a). However all the characters here are constrained to be of ASCII type. ASCII characters—due to their wide use in many data/file representations/storages—enjoy this privilege. This is the simplest way of forming a bytes type string. In general any string **ss** can be represented as its equivalent bytes counterpart by encoding it. The method **ss**.encode() encodes the string **ss** directly into a bytes string. The encoding is implicitly taken to be of UTF-8 type, UTF-8 being the most widely used representation. Encoding to any specific type can be effected by specifying it through an argument. The same string ('life of zest and value') has been encoded without specifying the encoding and specifying encoding to be in UTF-8 form in [3]. The source string itself being in UTF-8 form, it remains unaltered in both cases but for the conversion to the bytes type.

A variety of encoding standards (UTF-16, UTF-32, …) can be specified as the basis to convert a given string of characters into the bytes form. Similarly a given bytes object can be converted into a string using the method bytes.decode(). If encoding is not specified UTF-8 is taken as the default type. Otherwise the encoding scheme has to be specified. **s6** in [4] in the Fig. 7.9a is a string. It is encoded into UTF-8 form and assigned to **s7** [5]. All the characters in **s6** being of the ASCII type, it remain unaltered. Subsequent decoding of **s7** using the UTF-8 format itself confirms this [7]. **s6** is encoded into UTF-16 form and assigned to **s9** [8]. In UTF-16 every Unicode point is represented as a single 2-byte long set or a pair of 2-byte long sets. With any UTF-16 string 2 bytes are added at the beginning (\xff and \xfe) signifying the direction of representation. With this **s9** has a total of 106 bytes [9] (=2 + 52 * 2); note that **s6** has 52 characters in it. **s9** is decoded with encoding specified as UTF-16 in [10] to confirm that the retrieved string is **s6** itself. Similarly s6 is encoded into UTF-32 form [11] and decoded back into **s6** itself [13] (Fig. 7.9b). UTF-32 uses a

(a)

```
l1 = b'Life of zest and verve'                           [1]
>>> type(l1)                                             [2]
<class 'bytes'>
>>> 'Life of zest and verve'.encode(),'Life of zest and
verve'.encode(encoding ='utf-8')                         [3]
(b'Life of zest and verve', b'Life of zest and verve')
>>> s6 = 'One day there passed by a company of cats a
wise dog'                                                [4]
>>> s7 = s6.encode(encoding = 'utf-8')                   [5]
>>> s7
b'One day there passed by a company of cats a wise dog'
                                                         [6]
>>> s7.decode(encoding = 'utf-8')                        [7]
'One day there passed by a company of cats a wise dog'
>>> >>> s9 = s6.encode(encoding = 'utf-16')              [8]
>>> s9
b'\xff\xfe0\x00n\x00e\x00\x00d\x00a\x00y\x00\x00t\x00h\x0
0e\x00r\x00e\x00\x00p\x00a\x00s\x00s\x00e\x00d\x00\x00b\x
00y\x00\x00a\x00\x00c\x00o\x00m\x00p\x00a\x00n\x00y\x00\x
00o\x00f\x00\x00c\x00a\x00t\x00s\x00\x00a\x00\x00w\x00i\x
00s\x00e\x00\x00d\x00o\x00g\x00'
>>> len(s6), len(s9)                                     [9]
(52, 106)
>>> s9.decode(encoding = 'utf-16')                       [10]
'One day there passed by a company of cats a wise dog'
>>> s10 = s6.encode(encoding = 'utf-32')                 [11]
>>> s10
b'\xff\xfe\x00\x000\x00\x00\x00n\x00\x00\x00e\x00\x00\x00
\x00\x00\x00d\x00\x00\x00a\x00\x00\x00y\x00\x00\x00\x00\x
00\x00t\x00\x00\x00h\x00\x00\x00e\x00\x00\x00r\x00\x00\x0
0e\x00\x00\x00\x00\x00\x00p\x00\x00\x00a\x00\x00\x00s\x00
\x00\x00s\x00\x00\x00e\x00\x00\x00d\x00\x00\x00\x00\x00\x
00b\x00\x00\x00y\x00\x00\x00\x00\x00\x00a\x00\x00\x00\x00
\x00\x00c\x00\x00\x00o\x00\x00\x00m\x00\x00\x00p\x00\x00\
x00a\x00\x00\x00n\x00\x00\x00y\x00\x00\x00\x00\x00\x00o\x
00\x00\x00f\x00\x00\x00\x00\x00\x00c\x00\x00\x00a\x00\x00
\x00t\x00\x00\x00s\x00\x00\x00 \x00\x00\x00a\x00\x00\x00
\x00\x00\x00w\x00\x00\x00i\x00\x00\x00s\x00\x00\x00e\x00\
x00\x00\x00\x00\x00d\x00\x00\x00o\x00\x00\x00g\x00\x00\x0
0'
>>> len(s10)                                             [12]
212
```

Fig. 7.9 a Python Interpreter sequence illustrating methods with bytes and bytearray (continued in Fig. 7.9b), **b** Python Interpreter sequence illustrating methods with bytes and bytearray (continued from Fig. 7.9a)

(b)

```
>>> s10.decode(encoding = 'utf-32')                         [13]
'One day there passed by a company of cats a wise dog'
>>> cc= '如果你想成为我们的赞助商或广告商'                      [14]
>>> cc8 = cc.encode(encoding = 'utf-8')                     [15]
>>> cc8                                                     [16]
b'\xe5\xa6\x82\xe6\x9e\x9c\xe4\xbd\xa0\xe6\x83\xb3\xe6\x8
8\x90\xe4\xb8\xba\xe6\x88\x91\xe4\xbb\xac\xe7\x9a\x84\xe8
\xb5\x9e\xe5\x8a\xa9\xe5\x95\x86\xe6\x88\x96\xe5\xb9\xbf\
xe5\x91\x8a\xe5\x95\x86'
>>> len(cc), len(cc8)                                       [17]
(16, 48)
>>> cc16 = cc.encode(encoding = 'utf-16')                   [18]
>>> cc16                                                    [19]
b'\xff\xfe\x82Y\x9cg`O\xf3`\x10b:N\x11b\xecN\x84v^\x8d\xa
9RFU\x16b\x7f^JTFU'
>>> cc16.decode(encoding = 'utf-16')                        [20]
'如果你想成为我们的赞助商或广告商'                              [21]
>>> cc32 =  cc.encode(encoding = 'utf-32')                  [22]
>>> cc32                                                    [23]
b'\xff\xfe\x00\x00\x82Y\x00\x00\x9cg\x00\x00`O\x00\x00\xf
3`\x00\x00\x10b\x00\x00:N\x00\x00\x11b\x00\x00\xecN\x00\x
00\x84v\x00\x00^\x8d\x00\x00\xa9R\x00\x00FU\x00\x00\x16b\
x00\x00\x7f^\x00\x00JT\x00\x00FU\x00\x00'
>>> cc32.decode(encoding = 'utf-32')                        [24]
'如果你想成为我们的赞助商或广告商'                              [25]
>>> len(cc16), len(cc32)                                    [25]
(34, 68)
>>> ce8, ce16, ce32 = 'cc[0]'.encode(encoding = 'utf-8'),
'cc[0]'.encode(encoding = 'utf-16'),
'cc[0]'.encode(encoding = 'utf-32')                         [26]
>>> ce8, ce16, ce32
(b'cc[0]', b'\xff\xfec\x00c\x00[\x000\x00]\x00',
b'\xff\xfe\x00\x00c\x00\x00\x00c\x00\x00\x00[\x00\x00\x00
0\x00\x00\x00]\x00\x00\x00')
>>> cd8, cd16, cd32 = ce8.decode(encoding = 'utf-
8'),ce16.decode(encoding = 'utf-16'),ce32.decode(encoding
= 'utf-32')                                                [27]
>>> cd8, cd16, cd32
('cc[0]', 'cc[0]', 'cc[0]')
>>> cc[0]                                                   [28]
'如'
```

Fig. 7.9 (continued)

fixed 4-byte representation for each character; additionally 4 bytes are prepended here to the lot at the beginning; with all this the encoded bytes here is s10; it is of 212 bytes (4 + 4 * 52) [12].

The encoding and decoding done with the string of Chinese characters (**cc** in [14]) bring out the generality of the encode() and decode() methods. **cc** has sixteen characters as can be seen from [17]. **cc**.encode(encoding = 'utf-8') in [15] encodes **cc** to a UTF-8-type bytes sequence [16]. Every character here has a UTF-8 representation running into 3 bytes each. Hence the encoded bytes sequence is of 48 bytes [17]. With UTF-16 every character here encodes into 2 bytes (**cc16** in [18, 19]). The bytes sequence here is 34 (2 + 2 * 16) bytes in length [25]. Similarly UTF-32 uses a four byte representation for every character to form **cc32** in [22]. [23] gives the corresponding bytes sequence; it is of sixty-eight (4 + 4 * 16) bytes [25]. The first character of **cc** (**cc**[0]) has been separately encoded into the three forms in [26] and again back to the character itself in [27].

The bytes()/bytearray() function basically returns a bytes/bytearray type sequence. A few possibilities of its formation exist. The Python Interpreter sequence in Fig. 7.10 illustrates these. **at** [1] is a string of a single Chinese character. bytes(**at**, 'UTF-8') converts it into a bytes string in the UTF-8 form; that is the UTF-8 representation of '字' is 3 bytes long. The same is assigned to **a1** in [2]. It is confirmed in [3] by encoding '字' directly. In general any string can be converted into a bytes object conforming to the desired encoding. For this the bytes() function takes two arguments—the first being the string itself and the second the encoding within single quotes (as illustrated above). In fact bytes() uses **ss**.encode() discussed earlier to do the conversion.

a1 in [2] has been slightly altered by changing its third byte (from 'x97' to 'x98') and assigned to **aa** in [4]; it is decoded in [5] into a string of a single Chinese character ('存'). The character string represented by **at** is converted into a string conforming to UTF-16 in [6]. Similarly **bb** representing the single character '存' is converted to UTF-16 form in [9].

Every character in a bytes/bytearray being a byte, some common features of representation of bytes/bytearray are noteworthy here:

- If the character has an ASCII representation the character will be used directly.
- Else the hex number will be used in the representation. However when specifying a bytes/bytearray sequence one can use either representation.
- In a sequence representing bytes/bytearray every byte value can be shown as '\xn1n2' where n1 and n2 are the MS and LS nibbles respectively.

a2—is as a bytes sequence shown in [7]; the last 2 bytes here are \x57 and \x5b represented by respective ASCII characters—'W' and '['. The first 2 bytes '\xff' and '\xfe' (related to the type of sequence representation) are outside the ASCII range and hence are retained as bytes. **aa2** defined as a bytes and displayed in the following line confirms this. Similarly **ab** in [9] has 'X' and '[' in place of their respective ASCII values.

cc in [10] is a string of Chinese characters. The UTF-8 representation of '果' **cc**[1] is **cc8** [11]; it is a three-byte sequence. The decoded value is the character '果' itself as can be seen from the line following. **cc16** in [12] is the UTF-16 value of **cc**[1] itself. In UTF-16 every character has a 2-bytes/4-bytes representation

```
>>> at = '字'                                        [1]
>>> a1 = bytes(at, 'utf-8')                          [2]
>>> a1
b'\xe5\xad\x97'
>>> at.encode()                                      [3]
b'\xe5\xad\x97'
>>> aa = b'\xe5\xad\x98'                             [4]
>>> bb = aa.decode()                                 [5]
>>> bb
'存'
>>> bytes(at, 'utf-16')                              [6]
b'\xff\xfeW['                                        [7]
>>> aa2 = b'\xff\xfe\x57\x5b'                        [8]
>>> aa2
b'\xff\xfeW['
>>> b'\xff\xfeW['.decode('utf-16')
'字'
>>> ab = bytes(bb, 'utf-16')                         [9]
>>> ab
b'\xff\xfeX['
>>> cc= '如果你想成为我们的赞助商或广告商'               [10]
>>> cc8 = bytes(cc[1],'utf-8')                       [11]
>>> cc8
b'\xe6\x9e\x9c'
>>> cc8.decode('utf-8')
'果'
>>> cc16 = bytes(cc[0],'utf-16')                     [12]
>>> cc16
b'\xff\xfe\x82Y'
>>> cc16.decode('utf-16')                            [13]
'如'
>>> cst8 = bytes(cc,'utf-8')                         [14]
>>> cst8
b'\xe5\xa6\x82\xe6\x9e\x9c\xe4\xbd\xa0\xe6\x83\xb3\xe6\x88
\x90\xe4\xb8\xba\xe6\x88\x91\xe4\xbb\xac\xe7\x9a\x84\xe8\x
b5\x9e\xe5\x8a\xa9\xe5\x95\x86\xe6\x88\x96\xe5\xb9\xbf\xe5
\x91\x8a\xe5\x95\x86'
>>> cst8.decode('utf-8')                             [15]
'如果你想成为我们的赞助商或广告商'
>>> len(cc), len(cst8)                               [16]
(16, 48)
>>> data = bytes([10, 20, 30, 40])                   [17]
>>> data
b'\n\x14\x1e('
```

Fig. 7.10 Python Interpreter sequence illustrating use of function `bytes()`

```
>>> datay = bytearray([10, 20, 30, 40])                        [1]
>>> datay
bytearray(b'\n\x14\x1e(')
>>> datay[1]= 41                                               [2]
>>> datay
bytearray(b'\n)\x1e(')                                         [3]
>>> aa = [33, 34, 35, 36, 37]                                  [4]
>>> aaby = bytearray(aa)                                       [5]
>>> aaby
bytearray(b'!"#$%')
>>> aab = bytes(aa)                                            [6]
>>> aab
b'!"#$%'
>>> bb = [222, 333, 444, 555, 666]                             [7]
>>> bby = bytearray(bb)
Traceback (most recent call last):
  File "<stdin>", line 1, in <module>
ValueError: byte must be in range(0, 256)
>>> by, ba = bytes(5), bytearray(5)                            [8]
>>> by, ba
(b'\x00\x00\x00\x00\x00',
bytearray(b'\x00\x00\x00\x00\x00'))
>>> by1, ba1 = bytes(range(48, 58, 2)),
bytearray(range(65, 91, 3))                                    [9]
>>> by1, ba1
(b'02468', bytearray(b'ADGJMPSVY'))
```

Fig. 7.11 Python Interpreter sequence illustrating use of function bytearray()

(x82Y here). The whole of **cc** is converted into UTF-8 form in [14] and decoded back in [15]. Every character here has a 3 bytes representation [16]. A sequence of integers—all in the range 0–256—can be converted into a bytes sequence using the bytes() function as in [17]. '\n' representing the 'new line' (command) has ASCII value 10_{10} and '(' has ASCII value 40_{10}.

All functions and methods pertaining to bytes above are equally true of bytearray as well, the sole difference being that the bytearray is a mutable sequence. Figure 7.11 shows use of operations similar to those with bytes in Fig. 7.10 above. As an illustrative example the array of integers **aa** (=[33, 34, 35, 36]) [4] has been converted into a bytearray using the function byteartray() in [5]. The bytes version of **aa** is obtained in [6]. Both can be seen to be composed of the same set of characters. **bb** in [7] is a sequence of integers; all of them do not have values less than 256. Hence **bb** cannot be represented as a bytes sequence or as a bytearray as can be confirmed from the following lines. **Datay** in [1] is the bytearray representation of the list [10, 20, 30, 40] itself. The second byte in it has been reassigned the value 41 in [2] and the altered bytearray is shown in [3] (In [3] ')' is the ASCII representation of 41 in b'\n) \x1e('. Data in [17] in Fig. 7.10 being immutable, cannot be altered in this manner.

The functions bytes() and bytearray() can be used directly in two more contexts. Bytes(n)/bytearray(n) with n as an integer produces a bytes/bytearray sequence of zeros the sequence length being n. This is illustrated in [8] for n = 5. bytes(range(a, b, c))/bytearray(range(a, b, c)) is a sequence of integers—a, a + c, a + 2 * c, ... a + ((b − 1 − a)//c) * c. This is converted to form a bytes/bytearray sequence. bytes(range(48, 52, 2)) produces b'0,2468' as bytes in [9]. Here {48, 50, 52, 54, 56} are the ASCII values of the numerals {0, 2, 4, 6, 8}. Similarly with ba1 in [9], {65, 68, 71, ... 89} are the ASCII values of {A, D, ... Y} respectively.

The python Interpreter sequence in Fig. 7.12 illustrates operations linking bytes objects and integers. int() converts a string or a bytes object to the corresponding integers to the base specified (see Sect. 7.4.1). [1] and [2] are additional examples of this. The string '159a' as well as the bytes object b'159a' has the decimal value 5530 (=$16^3 + 5 * 16^2 + 9 * 16^1 + 10 * 16^0$). A bytes sequence can be converted into a corresponding integer using the method int. from_bytes(). The use of its variants is illustrated from [4] to [8]. With bb as a bytes sequence int.from_bytes(bb, byteorder = 'big') converts bb into an integer taking the left most byte of bb as the MS byte. int.from_bytes(bb, byteorder = 'little') does the conversion taking bb to be the little-endian— its MS byte being taken as the right most one; both are illustrated in [4] which shows 0200h = 512_{10} and 0002h = 2_{10}. If bb is formed in the system beforehand, one can use the system byteorder itself, by specifying it as in [6]. To facilitate this, the sys module has to be imported prior to the conversion [5]. The conversions into integers so far here have implicitly taken the byte sequence to represent a positive integer. In case it is a negative integer in 2's complement form, the same may be specified through the use of a third argument as in [7] and [8]. If signed = 'False' is specified as the third argument, the bytes sequence is taken as representing a positive integer as in [7]. In [8] Signed = 'True'—as the third argument—signifying the negative integer in 2's complement form. The byte sequence—b'xfe\x00' is specified as a ('big-endian) in 2's complement form; the converted integer is at4 (=−512). If the third argument is absent the integer concerned is taken as a positive one by default as was done in [4] and [6] above.

nn.to_bytes() converts the integer nn to a corresponding byte sequence. The sequence length as the number of bytes and the type of representation as being 'big', or 'little' have to be specified as the two arguments. As an example the integer at1 (=512_{10}) is converted into a bytes sequence of both types and assigned to b1 and b2 in [9]. In both cases the number of hex characters in the sequence has been specified as four. The byte order—not being specified—is taken as 'False'; that is nn is taken as a positive number by default. If the number is a negative one represented in 2's complement form, the third argument may be specified as byteorder = 'True'. [10] illustrate both the cases. at4 (=512) and at5 (=−512) obtained earlier are reconverted into 4-byte sequences of length four characters—the number being in hex form represented as a bytes sequence. B'\xff\xff \xfe\x00' has been converted to integer (=−512) with int.from_bytes() in [11].

```
>>> ah = b'159a'                                              [1]
>>> ah1, ah2 = int(ah, 16), int('159a',16)                   [2]
>>> ah1, ah2
(5530, 5530)
>>> bb = b'\x02\x00'                                          [3]
>>>
at1,at2=int.from_bytes(bb,byteorder='big'),int.from_bytes(
bb,byteorder ='little')
>>> at1, at2                                                  [4]
(512, 2)
>>> import sys                                                [5]
>>> at3 = int.from_bytes(bb,byteorder=sys.byteorder)         [6]
>>> at3
2
>>> at4 = int.from_bytes(bb, byteorder = 'big', signed =
'False')                                                      [7]
>>> at4
512
>>> at5 = int.from_bytes(b'\xfe\x00',byteorder = 'big',
signed = 'True')                                              [8]
>>> at5
-512
>>> b1,b2 = at1.to_bytes(4, byteorder='big'),
at1.to_bytes(4, byteorder= 'little')                          [9]
>>> b1, b2
(b'\x00\x00\x02\x00', b'\x00\x02\x00\x00')
>>> b3, b4 = at4.to_bytes(4, byteorder='big', signed =
'False'), at5.to_bytes(4, byteorder='big', signed =
'True')                                                       [10]
>>> b3, b4
(b'\x00\x00\x02\x00', b'\xff\xff\xfe\x00')
>>> int.from_bytes(b'\xff\xff\xfe\x00', byteorder='big',
signed = 'True')                                              [11]
-512
>>> bytes.fromhex('1e1f2021222324252627')                    [12]
b'\x1e\x1f !"#$%&\''
>>> bytes.fromhex('303132333a3b3c')                          [13]
b'0123:;<'
>>> bytes.fromhex('7a7b7c7d7e7f808182')
b'z{|}~\x7f\x80\x81\x82'
>>> list(b'z{|}~\x7f\x80\x81\x82')                            [14]
[122, 123, 124, 125, 126, 127, 128, 129, 130]
```

Fig. 7.12 Python Interpreter sequence illustrating methods linking bytes objects and integers

Number representations in computer work are often in hex form. A method of conversion of integers in hex form directly into byte sequences is available as bytes.hex(nn) where nn is a hex number represented as a string. [10], [11], and [12] are illustrations of its use. The number is made up of hex integer pairs in a sequence. Each pair is identified as a character in forming the bytes sequence. As a

```
>>> c1,c2,c3,c4,c5 =
chr(0x41),chr(0x37e),chr(0x7e),chr(0x2190),chr(0x221a)
                                                          [1]
>>> c1, c2, c3, c4, c5
('A', ';', '~', '←', '√')
>>> chr(x03b4)                                            [2]
Traceback (most recent call last):
  File "<stdin>", line 1, in <module>
NameError: name 'x03b4' is not defined
>>> d1, d2, d3, d4, d5 = ord('A'), ord(';'), ord('~'),
ord('←'), ord('√')                                        [3]
>>> d1, d2, d3, d4, d5
(65, 894, 126, 8592, 8730)
>>> cc1, cc2, cc3, cc4, cc5 = '\u0041', '\u037e',
'\u007e','\u2190', '\u221a'                               [4]
>>> cc1, cc2, cc3, cc4, cc5
('A', ';', '~', '←', '√')
>>> c01, c02, c03, c04, c05 = '\U00000041', '\U0000037e',
'\U0000007e','\U00002190','\U0000221a'                    [5]
>>> c01, c02, c03, c04, c05
('A', ';', '~', '←', '√')
>>> g1, g2 = '\N{GREEK CAPITAL LETTER OMEGA}', '\N{GREEK
SMALL LETTER BETA}'                                       [6]
>>> g1, g2
('Ω', 'β')
```

Fig. 7.13 Python Interpreter sequence illustrating methods with Unicode

check the bytes sequence formed in [12] is converted back to a list in [13]. Note that {122, 123, 124, ... 130} are the decimal equivalents of the hex number set {7a, 7a, 7c, 82}.

A few simple functions/methods are available to convert characters into respective Unicode numbers and vice versa. The Python Interpreter sequence in Fig. 7.13 illustrates their use. The function chr(**nn**) treats **nn** as the Unicode representation of a character and returns the corresponding character. [1] shows a few examples. The Unicode values of a set of characters are converted into respective characters and assigned to **c1**, **c2**, ... **c5**. The integer x03b4 does not represent any valid Unicode character; hence chr(x0b4) in [2] returns an error. The function ord('**cc**') converts the character string—'**cc**'—into the corresponding integer. Here '**cc**' has to be a single Unicode character. The character set {'A', ';', '~', '←', '√'} is converted back to the corresponding set of integers in [3]. The integer values are output in decimal form here.

The escape sequence '**upqrs**' with **pqrs** as a hex number of four hex characters (a 16-bit number) is treated as a Unicode character. The Unicode set used in [1] is reproduced in [4] with this representation. Similarly a Unicode character can be represented as '\\U**pqrstuvw**' with a capital 'U' preceding eight hex characters (a 32-bit number). [5] illustrates this for the same set of characters as considered

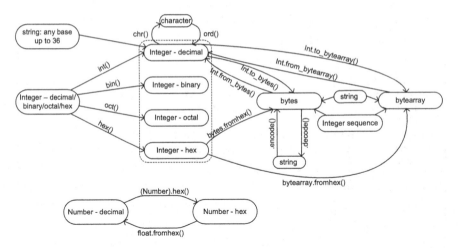

Fig. 7.14 A compact representation of the conversion possibilities between numbers and sequences in Python

above. '\N{**name**} also can be used to represent Unicode characters. Here '**name**' is the name for the character in the Unicode database. [6] is an illustration for the character pair ('Ω', 'ß').

A number of functions and methods for conversions amongst numbers, strings, bytes and so on have been discussed. The scheme shown in Fig. 7.14 is a compact representation of all these together.

7.7   Other Operations with Sequences

The functions/methods applicable to `tuples` and `strings` are equally applicable to `bytes`. Similarly the functions and methods with lists are applicable to bytearrays. These are not discussed again here.

7.8   `string` Module

With the ASCII character set as basis a few character sets have been defined in the module `string`. They can be of use in text processing; the `string` can be downloaded and any set within accessed as `string.xx`. The details are summarized in Table 7.4.

Table 7.4 Constants defined in the `string` module

Item	Contents
ascii_lowercase	'abcdefghijklmnopqrstuvwxyz'
ascii_uppercase	'ABCDEFGHIJKLMNOPQRSTUVWXYZ'
ascii_letters	ASCII_lowercase + ASCII_uppercase
Digits	'0123456789'
Hexdigits	'0123456789abcdefABCDEF'
Octdigits	'01234567'
Punctuation	Punctuation character set
Whitespace	Space, tab, linefeed, return, formfeed, and vertical tab
Printable	Digits, ascii_letters, punctuation, and d whitespace

7.9 Exercises

1. The `string` **SS** = 'Holidays' is given. Center it filling it with four numbers of '*' on either side followed by five numbers of '@'.
2. The `string` **SS** = 'Holidays' is given. Center it filling it with ten numbers of '*@' on left side and an equal numbers of '@*' on the right.
3. The `string` **SS** = 'Holidays' is given. Center it filling it with ten numbers of '*' on left side and five numbers of '@' followed by six numbers of '^' on the right.
4. Round off the numbers considered in Example 7.5 to 12 decimal places. Let **N12** be such a rounded number. Obtain **N11** from it by rounding to 11 decimal places. Similarly obtain **N10** from **N11**, **N9** from **N10** and so on. Do this for both the numbers and explain any anomaly.
   In classical cryptography encryption, decryption, and cryptanalysis are all done using simple algebra with characters and their numerical representations. The following exercises relate to classical cryptography (Shyamala et al. 2011).
5. Take a long enough text material (about 10,000 characters). If all the white spaces in it (coma, full stop, colon, question mark, blank space, and c) are removed and all characters in capital letters are converted to small letters, we will be left with a continuous sequence of small letters. Such a sequence is called a 'plain text' in cryptography parlance. With some effort a plain text can be converted back to (almost) the original text we started with. Write a program to prepare a plain text and convert the text we started with to plain text.
6. Obtain the frequencies of all the 26 letters in the above plain text through a program for it.
7. The letter pairs 'th', 'ht', 'in', 'on', 'gh', ... occur more commonly in normal English text. These are called 'bigrams'. Write a program to get the frequencies of all the bigrams and retain the data for the most frequent 20 of them. Get the most frequent 20 bigrams for the above plain text.

8. A letter set of three like 'ght', 'ion', 'the' is called a 'trigram'. Write a program to get the frequencies of all the trigrams and retain the data for the most frequent 20 of them. Get the most frequent 20 trigrams for the above plain text.

9. The normalized letter frequencies form the probabilities of occurrence of the respective letters. With p_i as the probability of occurrence of the ith letter, $\sum p_i^2$ is called 'the Index of Coincidence (IC)'. The IC values for general texts in different languages are known. For English texts IC = 0.0655; in contrast for a completely random text it has the value of 0.0385. Write a program to get the IC value and get it for the given text.

   Armed with the letter frequencies, knowledge of the dominant bigrams and trigrams, and the IC values one should be able to do cryptanalysis of most of the common conventional ciphers.

10. The 'Substitution Cipher' uses a look-up table (LUT) to substitute every letter in the plain text with the one in the LUT to generate the cipher text. Write a program to generate the cipher text from the plain text using the LUT. Use it to get the cipher text for the given plain text.

11. A cipher text obtained using the Substitution Cipher is given. One can get its letter frequencies, compare with those of English text, and identify the substitution used for the most common letters like 'e', 's', 't' etc. Similarly one can identify the substitution used for the letters with the least frequencies like 'z', 'q', 'x', etc. Still some indecision remains. The most common bigrams and trigrams can be identified and compared. With these the substitution used for many of the letters can be identified. Armed with these and our familiarity with common English words (eng?ish → english, re?ain → remain ...) additional identification can be done. Identifying the plain text in this manner constitutes 'Cryptanalysis'. Obtain the cipher text with a substitution cipher. Do cryptanalysis and retrieve the plain text (With readily available programs and cipher text of about 300 letters the exercise may take a few hours of effort for completion).

12. With 'a', 'b', 'c', ... 'z' represented by 1, 2, 3, ..., 26, the Affine Cipher uses the relation $y = (ax + b) \% 26$ to substitute the letter represented by integer x by the letter represented by integer y. a and b are integers (the two together forms the encryption/decryption 'key') with the constraint on a that its only common factor with 26 is one. Write a program to get the cipher text for a given plain text with Affine Cipher (for given a and b values).

13. Affine Cipher is a special case of a Substitution Cipher. For a given cipher text one can obtain the letter frequencies; by comparison with the known frequencies of common texts a few most dominant letters can be identified. By substitution in the equation $y = ax + b$ the same can be confirmed. Do cryptanalysis of the crypto text in Exercise (12) above.

14. With $a = 1$, the Affine Cipher becomes a 'Shift Cipher'. 'Vigenere Cipher' is a generalized version of the 'Shift Cipher'. It uses a set of m key values—{b_1, b_2, ... b_m}. The plain text is split into successive blocks of m letters each (normally m will be a single digit integer). The first letter of each block is shifted by b_1,

the second by b_2, and so on up to the mth letter (by b_m). Do this successively for all the blocks. This completes encryption. Prepare a program to do encryption conforming to Vigenere Cipher. Get the cipher text for the given plain text.

15. Cryptanalysis of Vigenere Cipher is a more challenging affair. One has to identify the value of m first and then the set $\{b_1, b_2, \ldots b_m\}$. The IC concept can be used to identify the m value. With c_i as the ith letter in the cipher text, the sub-sequence of letters—$\{c_1, c_{1+m}, c_{1+2m}, \ldots\}$—forms a Shift Cipher type crypto-text with b_1 as the shift. It will have the characteristics of a normal text; its IC value will be close to that of plain text (=0.0655). Same is true of the other $(m - 1)$ sub-sequences also. With different values of m (2, 3, 4, ...), form the sub-sets $\{c_1, c_{1+m}, c_{1+2m}, \ldots\}$. Get the character frequencies and the IC values. The m-value which yields the IC closest to 0.0655 is the correct one. The procedure can be repeated with successive sub-sequences to confirm the m-value. Once the m-value is identified, with each of the m separate sub-sequences the procedure in Exercise (13) above can be used to get the set—$\{b_1, b_2, \ldots b_m\}$. With the m value and the full set $\{b_1, b_2, \ldots b_m\}$ known the plain text can be recovered. For the cipher text in the last exercise, do cryptanalysis and retrieve the plain text (With all the programs available cryptanalysis and plain text retrieval may take a few hours).

16. *Huffman Coding*: One of the earliest schemes of lossless data compression was proposed by Huffman (Forouzan 2013). We shall go through a simplified version of the scheme. A data transmission scheme uses a set of four symbols {a, b, c, d} with probabilities of occurrence {0.45, 0.3, 0.15, 0.1} respectively. The Huffman scheme for the set follows:

The symbols are arranged in descending order of probabilities. The most probable symbol is assigned the code value 0—a single bit. For the rest the first bit is taken as 1. The second most probable symbol is assigned the second bit value—0 and its code is 10. For the rest the second bit is assigned the value 1; a third bit is also assigned to them with values of 0 for the more probable one and value of 1 for the less probable one respectively (see Fig. 7.15).

Fig. 7.15 Huffman coding scheme for the example in Exercise 7.16

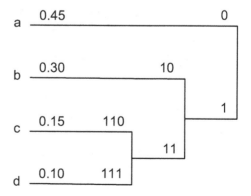

The average number of bits per symbol is $0.45 \times 1 + 0.3 \times 2 + 0.15 \times 3 + 0.1 \times 3 = 1.8$—a conspicuous gain over the value of 2 with brute force encoding.

The general algorithm for assigning codes is as follows:

a. Arrange the symbols in descending order of probabilities of occurrence. The last symbol is the least probable one. Each symbol is assigned a node.
b. Combine the least two probable symbols into one node having the combined probability value.
c. If the number of nodes left is one the 'coding tree' is complete. Else go to step (a).

Assign bit value—0 (code value = 0)—to the top node. Subsequent bit values and code values are assigned as in Fig. 7.15.

Decoding the received bit sequence into symbols, proceeds in the reverse sequence. With each succeeding bit identify the branches and nodes until a symbol is identified. Once this is done start all over again for identification of the next symbol.

a. Write a Python program to assign code values to the given set of symbols, knowing their probabilities.
b. Write a Python program to produce the bit sequence given the message symbol sequence.
c. Write a Python program to decode the encoded bit sequence and produce the message symbol sequence.
d. A notepad file is given. It is made up of ASCII characters. Prepare the table of symbols and their probabilities.
e. For the file in (d) above do coding and decoding.

17. Arithmetic coding is an efficient scheme of lossless compression of data (Forouzn). Operation of a simplified form of arithmetic coding is explained here through an example.

A message sequence is made up of the four symbols 'A', 'B', 'C', and 'D'. An additional symbol 'E' is used as the last one to indicate the end of the message sequence. The probability of occurrence of each symbol is specified beforehand. Table 7.5 gives the assigned probability values. Symbol 'E' is assigned the (nominal very low) probability of 0.05 arbitrarily. The table also has the list of cumulative probability ranges. The encoding process is explained here with reference to the message sequence 'BCDDDBE'. Figure 7.14 depicts the procedure.

Table 7.5 The symbols, their probability values, and the cumulative probability values for the Example in Exercise 7.17

Symbol	A	B	C	D	E
Probability	0.1	0.3	0.2	0.35	0.05
Cumulative probability range	0.0–0.1	0.1–0.4	0.4–0.6	0.6–0.95	0.95–1.0

The symbol sequence is identified by its probability and the probability value forms the basis to decide the code to be assigned to it. The first symbol 'B' is assigned the probability range 0.1–0.4 (P_1Q_1) as shown in the first line in the figure.

The second symbol 'C' has the absolute probability range 0.4–0.6. Hence the first and the second symbols together is assigned the absolute probability range within the (P_1Q_1) band as $0.1 + (0.4 - 0.1) \times 0.4$ to $0.1 + (0.4 - 0.1) \times 0.6$—that is 0.22–0.28—shown blown up in the second line. This range is represented by (P_2Q_2) in line 2 in the figure.

The third symbol 'A' has the absolute probability range 0.0–0.1. Hence the sequence 'BCA' is assigned the probability range $0.22–0.22 + (0.28 - 0.22) \times 0.1$—that is 0.22–0.226—shown blown up in the third line. This range is represented by (P_3Q_3) in line 3 in the figure.

Proceeding successively in the same vein the probability range formation for the full sequence—'BCADDBE'—is shown in the figure. Finally the sequence has the specific probability range 0.225142975–0.225154 assigned to it. The corresponding binary range is **0.001110011010001011110000 101001010001100111** to **0.0011100110100011101100010010101010010000101** any binary value within this range can be used to uniquely represent this sequence. Specifically 0.001110011010001 suffices here since this part is common for the full range. The additional bits are discarded since they do not add any additional information of interest to us here.

The code for the sequence—'BCADDBE'—is generated from the binary value of the probability for it. It involves two changes:

a. Truncate the number of bits at a point where the value has crossed the point P7 in Fig. 7.16 signifying that the next symbol in the sequence is 'E' itself —that is the sequence has ended (this has been done above).
b. Ignore the '0.' part of the probability and use only the rest of the bit sequence. '0.' is superfluous and does not add any information to the sequence.

Any source sequence of characters from the set in Table 7.5 can be encoded in the same manner. The encoding algorithm is summarized as follows:

a. Start with the table of probabilities and cumulative probabilities.
b. Identify the probability range of (P_1Q_1) for the first character.
c. Let the probability range for ($P_{i-1}Q_{i-1}$) be $D_{is} \sim D_{ie}$ where 's' and 'e' signify the Start and End of the range.
d. The jth character in the table has the absolute cumulative probability range (C_{j-1}, C_j).
e. For all i from 2 onwards up to the last character (nth) in the source sequence, do the following recursively:

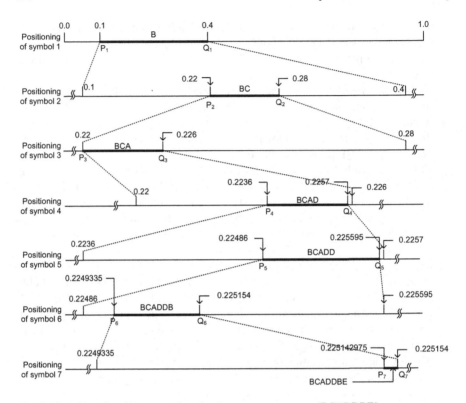

Fig. 7.16 Arithmetic coding procedure for the message sequence 'BCADDBE'

f. Let S_i be the ith character in the sequence. We have the recursive relations for D_{is} and D_{ie} as $D_{is} = D_{i-1,s} + (D_{i-1,e} - D_{i-1,s}) C_{si-1}$ and $D_{ie} = D_{i-1,s} + (D_{i-1,e} - D_{i-1,s}) C_{si}$. Update the probability range for the character sequence up to and inclusive of S_i using these.

g. With a total of n characters in the sequence $(D_{ns} \sim D_{ne})$ is the probability range representing the last character ('E'). Truncate it such that the truncated value lies within $(D_{ns} \sim D_{ne})$ range. Remove the '0.' part of the probability value of the truncated number to get the code for the sequence.

h. Successive characters in the source sequence affect only the trailing bits of the probability being evaluated. Hence the leading bits of the coded sequence can be progressively taken out from the left end and added to code as soon as they stabilize in value.

The decoder algorithm is as follows:

a. Prefix the received sequence with '0.' to form the cumulative probability p_c of the sequence.

b. Identify the $(P_1 \, Q_1)$ segment where p_c lies. Identify the first symbol S_1.

c. Subtract the cumulative probability D_{1s} represented by P_1 from p_c to form $(p_c - D_{1s})$.

d. Continue the procedure for encoding recursively in the reverse order until the end of message symbol 'E' is identified. This completes decoding/decompression.

Prepare programs for encoding and decoding conforming to the above procedures. Test them with typical sequences.

18. Use the `random.choice()` method from the `math` module and generate sequences of 10, 20, and 30 characters. Use these to test the above two programs.

19. As long as the models used for encoding and decoding are identical the basic procedure for arithmetic coding can be modified/simplified/made more optimal/efficient in different ways. A few such modifications are suggested below which can be tried:

a. The source sequence can be split into sub-sequences of fixed lengths (say 100 characters each). With this the need for the end of sequence character —'E'—can be eliminated. The last sub-sequence can be appended with known dummy characters to make up its length.

b. Instead of 'E' a known small sequence of characters (a rarely occurring combination) can be used to signify the end of sequence.

c. The probability table can be updated at regular intervals using the information from the sequence itself. This makes the scheme more optimal.

d. A ternary sequence can be used in place of the binary sequence; this may be better suited for transmission schemes which use three voltage levels $(+V, 0, -V)$ for signaling.

e. One adaptation of arithmetic coding uses the following procedure:
Obtain the frequencies of all the characters in the source file. With n characters in the source file prepare a table of n entries for the character set, the characters being arranged in the descending order of their frequencies—the most frequent character being in the first row. Here each code value is $\lceil \log_2 n \rceil$ bits long. For the most frequent 15 characters use 0_h, 1_h, 2_h, ... E_h as the code values leaving out F_h. For all the rest use a different coding table starting with 0_h. Assign code values afresh for the second lot prefixing each value with F. Thus the full code comprises of two coding tables—one for the most common 15 characters (each of 4 bits) and the other for the rest (all starting with F). The encoding table is prefixed to the coded sequence. The encoding is efficient only if the latter set has conspicuously low probabilities.

f. An adaptation of arithmetic coding works directly on the binary sequence to be encoded. The source file is split into 12-bits blocks. The frequencies of all the 2^{12} possible blocks are obtained. They are arranged in descending order and code values assigned as in (e) above.

20. On the lines discussed in Exercises 2–4 in Chap. 5, write a program to convert a number in a given base to one in another base. The function int (**a**, base = **b**) has to be used in a functional loop for this. The base here can be any integer up to 36. Convert a number from one base to another and do the reverse to verify the correctness.

References

Forouzan B (2013) Data communications and networking, 5th edn. McGraw Hill, New York

Original UTF-8 paper. (http://doc.cat-v.org/plan_9/4th_edition/papers/utf)

Padmanabhan TR (2007) Introduction to microcontrollers and their applications. Alpha Science International Ltd, Oxford

Shyamala CK, Harini N, Padmanabhan TR (2011) Cryptography and security. Wiley India, New Delhi

The Unicode Standard: A Technical—Introduction. (http://www.unicode.org/standard/principles. html)

van Rossum G, Drake FL Jr (2014) The Python library reference. Python Software Foundation

Chapter 8
Operations with Files

Information in different forms is stored in files and retrieved from them. A number of file related operations are available in Python (van Rossum and Drake 2014); their details and use are discussed here.

8.1 Printing

Information can be displayed on the monitor or written into files using the print() function. The Python Interpreter sequence in Fig. 8.1 illustrates the use of comparatively simpler forms of print() function. A number or a sequence of numbers —like (**nn**, **mm**) in different forms of representation—can be displayed directly on the monitor using print() as can be seen from [1]; the same is true of any item which can be printed/output directly. a is assigned the result of 3.0 * 2 and b is computed as a/2.0 in the following line. Both are displayed using print(a, b) in [3]. print() function without any argument returns a blank [4]. {**a1**, **a2**, **a3**, **a4**} is a set of strings [5]. print(a1) in [6] prints out the string a1 directly. A more general form of the print() function is print(**e1**, **e2**, **e3**, ... , sep = '**fg**', end = '**hj**'). Three sets of arguments are present here.

- **e1**, **e2**, **e3**, ... , is a comma separated set of entities which can be printed directly. These can be numbers and strings/or their combinations which can be printed directly.
- The second argument is specified as sep = '**fg**'; '**fg**' has to be a string. It is used as the separator between **e1** and **e2**, **e2** and **e3**, and so on in the printout. If this argument is absent, **e1**, **e2**, **e3**, ... are printed out without any separator between any two of these.
- The third argument—end = '**gh**' has '**gh**' as a string. The print() is executed here with '**gh**' forming the end part of the printout. If '**gh**' is absent, by default the Interpreter advances to the next line after executing the printout.

© Springer Nature Singapore Pte Ltd. 2016
T.R. Padmanabhan, *Programming with Python*,
DOI 10.1007/978-981-10-3277-6_8

```
>>> print(3, 3.3, 3.3e-1, 0x3b, 0o46)                    [1]
3 3.3 0.33 59 38
>>> a = 3.0**2                                           [2]
>>> b = a/2.0
>>> print(a, b)                                          [3]
9.0 4.5
>>> print()                                              [4]

>>> a1 = 'The sun is ever ready'                         [5]
>>> a2 = 'To dispel the darkness of night'
>>> a3 = 'With the golden rays of dawn'
>>> a4 = 'To herald Day afresh'
>>> print(a1)                                            [6]
The sun is ever ready
>>> print(a1, a2, sep = ',')                             [7]
The sun is ever ready,To dispel the darkness of night
>>> a0 = ('aa', 'bb', 'cc', 'dd')                        [8]
>>> print(a0)
('aa', 'bb', 'cc', 'dd')
>>> for i in a0:print(i, end= ',')                       [9]
...
aa,bb,cc,dd,>>>
>>> print(*a0, sep = ', ')                               [10]
aa, bb, cc, dd
>>> print(a1,end = '\n')                                 [11]
The sun is ever ready
>>> print(a1, a2, sep = '\n')                            [12]
The sun is ever ready
To dispel the darkness of night
>>> print(a1, a2, a3, a4, sep = '\n', end = '!\n')       [13]
The sun is ever ready
To dispel the darkness of night
With the golden rays of dawn
To herald Day afresh!
>>> print(*a0, sep = '\t')                               [14]
aa      bb      cc      dd
>>> for i in a0:print(i, sep = '\v')                     [15]
...
aa
bb
cc
dd
>>> for i in a0:print(i, end= '\v')                      [16]
...
aa
  bb
    cc
      dd
        >>>
```

Fig. 8.1 Python Interpreter sequence illustrating print()—simpler versions

a1 and **a2** are printed out in [7] with the sep being specified as ',' **a0** in [8] is a tuple of strings. It is directly printed out in [8] as print(**a0**). The elements of **a0** are successively printed out in a loop in [9]. Each print execution ends with a comma. [10] is a more elegant realization of the same. The sequence—'\n' (the backslash followed by 'n')—signifies a new line (as in ASCII set). Its use in [11] implies that at the end of printing 'a', advance to a new line. The output can be seen in the following line (Execution of [11] is in no way different from that of [6] above, since in the absence of 'end' specification, Interpreter advances to the next line by default). Python—like other computer languages—uses a number of such escape sequences in strings; each such sequence is a single character with an implied significance. The Escape sequences and their respective meanings are listed in Table 8.1. [12] prints out **a1** and **a2**, as **a1** followed by **a2** in a new line (In contrast both are on the same line in [7]). [13] specifies **a1**, **a2**, **a3**, and **a4** to be printed out on successive lines. Further '!' mark is to be printed out at the end of **a4**; then the interpreter advances to the new line.

Successive elements of **a0** are printed out in [14]. A tab (as '\t') separates the successive arguments output from **a0**. print() execution ends with a tab as can be seen from the output. '\v' is the vertical tab. With the loop in [15] the interpreter prints out every element of **a0** followed by the next after a vertical tab; that is after printing out every item the interpreter advances after a vertical tab. In contrast with [16] every printout ends with a vertical tab. The subtle difference between the two is noteworthy.

The print() variety possible continues with Fig. 8.2. **b0** in [1] has the single quote—"'"—as part of the string. The double quotes at either end impart the string status to the sequence. [2] prints out the string; the single quote is retained here. The same holds good of **b1** in [3] and with print(**b1**) in the following line; all the (three) single quotes are part of the string here. **b2** in [4] has backslash ('\') as part of the string. With the printout of **b2** in [5] '\n' is misinterpreted as an escape character as can be seen from the output in the two lines following. The backslash

Table 8.1 Escape sequences used/recognized in strings

Escape sequence	Meaning
\n	New line
\\	Backslash (\)
\'	Single quote (')
\"	Double quote (")
\t	ASCII Horizontal Tab (TAB)
\v	ASCII Vertical Tab (VT)
\ooo	Character with octal value ooo
\xhh	Character with hex value hh
\N{name}	Character named name in the Unicode database
\uxxxx	Character with 16-bit hex value xxxx
\Uxxxxxxxx	Character with 32-bit hex value xxxxxxxx

```
>>> b0 = "The Sun:'Never do I shirk dawn!'"              [1]
>>> print(b0)                                            [2]
The Sun:'Never do I shirk dawn!'
>>> b1 = " 'The Sun:'never do I shirk dawn!' "           [3]
>>> print(b1)
 'The Sun:'never do I shirk dawn!'
>>> b2 = "The Sun:\never do I shirk dawn!"               [4]
>>> print(b2)                                            [5]
The Sun:
ever do I shirk dawn!
>>> b3 = "The Sun:\\never do I shirk dawn!"              [6]
>>> print(b3)                                            [7]
The Sun:\never do I shirk dawn!
>>> cc1,cc2,cc3,cc4,cc5
='\u0041','\u037e','\u007e','\u2190','\u221a'            [8]
>>> print(cc1, cc2, cc3, cc4, cc5, sep = '*')            [9]
A*;*~*←*√
>>> c0 = '\u0050*\u0051*\u0052'                          [10]
>>> c0                                                   [11]
'P*Q*R'
>>> len(c0)                                              [12]
5
>>> print(c0)                                            [13]
P*Q*R
```

Fig. 8.2 Python Interpreter sequence illustrating print()—simpler versions (continued)

pair—'\\' with **b3** in [6]—is an escape sequence; it avoids the wrong interpretation of '\n' as the 'newline' character [7].

The Unicode values of a set of characters are assigned to **cc1** to **cc5** in [8]. In fact these are from Fig. 7.11. The set has been printed out with '*' as the separator in [9]. Here '\u' is the escape character as can be confirmed from the output. With U+0050, U+0051, U+0052 being the Unicode values of 'P', 'Q', and 'R' respectively the string **c0** in [10] is 'P * Q * R' as can be seen from [11]. len(**c0**) in [12] returns 5—the string being made up of the sequence of these five characters. Print(**c0**) outputs 'P * Q * R' treating \U as the escape character signifying the Unicode representation [13].

8.2   String Formatting

Simple and unsophisticated use of the print() function was demonstrated in the foregoing section. Present versions of Python (>3) facilitate convenient formatting of entities to form strings. These strings may be added/stored in appropriate databases or printed as outputs. Thus formatting and printing become delinked; it adds a level of flexibility to program execution. The string is formed from a tuple of items.

Basically the different elements in the string represent the information to be formatted. They are all linked together and suitably padded with additional literal text (if necessary) to form the formatted string. Two versions of the formatting scheme are available. The version described first here is comparatively rigid; it is essentially an earlier version (from C) retained for continuity. The second one is more comprehensive and flexible; it is the one recommended to be used.

8.2.1   Formatting—Version I

Details of formatting in the first version are summarized in Fig. 8.3. The scheme is characterized by the following:

1. The `string` has as many replacement fields as the number of entities in the `tuple`. The replacement fields appear in the same order as the entities in the tuple.
2. The modulo operator '%' signifies the start of each replacement field.
3. The '%' character is followed by four optional components and a final mandatory character signifying the type of conversion to be carried out. This conversion character can be one from Table 8.2.
4. The first optional component is a mapping key. It is present only if the items to be put in the replacement fields are specified through a `dictionary` instead of a tuple.
5. An optional flag modifies the structure/orientation of the entity. The possible flag types and their effects are given in Table 8.3.
6. An integer specifying the width/number of spaces to be allocated in the string to the entity forms the next component.

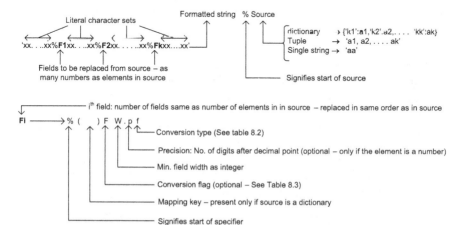

Fig. 8.3 Details of string formation for printing—Version I

Table 8.2 Conversion characters for the first version of string formatting

Conversion	Meaning
'd'	Signed integer decimal
'i'	Signed integer decimal
'o'	Signed octal value
'x'	Signed hexadecimal (lowercase)
'X'	Signed hexadecimal (uppercase)
'e'	Floating point exponential format (lowercase)
'E'	Floating point exponential format (uppercase)
'f'	Floating point decimal format
'F'	Floating point decimal format
'g'	Floating point format—uses lowercase exponential format if exponent is less than 4 or not less than precision, decimal format otherwise
'G'	Floating point format—uses uppercase exponential format if exponent is less than 4 or not less than precision, decimal format otherwise
'c'	Single character (accepts integer or single character string)
'r'	String (converts any Python object using repr())
's'	String (converts any Python object using str())
'a'	String (converts any Python object using ascii())
'%'	No argument is converted, results in a '%'character in the result

Table 8.3 Conversion flags for the first version of string formatting

Flag	Meaning
'#'	Value conversion will use alternate form
'0'	Conversion will be zero padded for numeric values
'−'	Converted value is left adjusted (overrides the '0' conversion if both are given)
' '	(a space) A blank should be left before a positive number (or empty string) produced by a signed conversion
'+'	A sign character ('+' or '−') will precede the conversion (overrides a "space" flag)

7. A dot—'.'—followed by an integer signifying the desired precision in the presentation is the next component. This and the two previous components implicitly assume the `tuple` entity to be a number.
8. A modulus character—'%'—at the end of the `string` being formed precedes the object to be formatted.
9. In case the formatting is for a single item, it can be present as such. There is no need of presenting it as a (single element) `tuple`.
10. If the field width/precision is specified through an asterisk mark—'*'—the concerned numerical value has to be available as an integer in the `tuple`; position-wise it is prior to the entity concerned.

A number of formatting examples is given in the illustrative Python Interpreter sequence in Fig. 8.4. **aa** is assigned the numerical value of −3.21 in [1]. Being a

```
>>> aa = -3.21                                              [1]
>>> print('n=%6.2f'% aa)                                    [2]
n= -3.21
>>> az = (3, -3.2104, -321.04, 321.04, -3210.401)           [3]
>>> while True:
...     print('%#8.2f'%az[0])                               [4]
...     print('%08.2f'%az[1])                               [5]
...     print('% 8.2f'%az[2])                               [6]
...     print('%-8.2f'%az[3])                               [7]
...     print('%8.2e'%az[4])                                [8]
...     break
...
    3.00                                                    [4a]
-0003.21                                                    [5a]
 -321.04                                                    [6a]
321.04                                                      [7a]
-3.21e+03                                                   [8a]
>>> rm = {'Name':'Roshan', 'Subject': 'Maths', 'Marks':
100}                                                        [9]
>>> print('%(Name)s gets in %(Subject) s %(Marks)4d out of
100' %rm)       [10]
Roshan gets in Maths  100 out of 100                        [10a]
>>> ab = 91                                                 [11]
>>> while True:
...     print('Hex value of ab is %8x'%ab)                 [12]
...     print('Explicit Hex value of ab is %#8x'%ab)       [13]
...     print('Octal value of ab is %8o'%ab)               [14]
...     print('Explicit Octal value of ab is %#8o'%ab)     [15]
...     break
...
Hex value of ab is        5b                                [12a]
Explicit Hex value of ab is      0x5b                       [13a]
Octal value of ab is       133                              [14a]
Explicit Octal value of ab is     0o133                     [15a]
>>> z1 = ('h',123)                                          [16]
>>> 'cc = %c, nn = %c' %z1                                  [17]
'cc = h, nn = {'
>>> z0 = 42.109                                             [18]
>>> '%*.2f'%(8,z0)                                          [19]
'   42.11'
>>> '%8.*f'%(2,z0)                                          [20]
'   42.11'
>>> '%*.*f'%(8, 2, z0)                                      21]
'   42.11'
```

Fig. 8.4 Python Interpreter sequence illustrating string formatting conforming to Version 1

single item it is directly fitted into the string and output [2]. The width specified as six is for the whole number representation—inclusive of the sign and the decimal point. **az** in [3] is a tuple of numbers selected to bring out the flexibility possible in formatting. The numbers are printed out to different format specifications in the following lines. The flag—'#'—in [4] demands output in decimal form [4a] even though the number (**az**[0] = 3) is an integer. With proper formatting specified the numbers for [4], [5], and [6] are output [4a], [5a], and [6a] properly aligned. The same is not true of the next two outputs. The flag—'0'—in [5] and [5a] ensures 0 padding to the left of the number in lieu of blank spaces. The blank space used as a flag in [6] is a space provision for a sign (as '−' if the number is negative). The flag —'−'—in [7] and [7a] results in left adjusted output. The output uses the floating point exponent in [8] and [8a] due to the use of the conversion character—'e'. **rm** in [9] is a dictionary of three entries—two strings followed by an integer. The string—'**Roshan gets in Maths 100 out of 100**' [10a]—is formed from it and output. The keys—'**Name**' and '**subject**'—are replaced by the respective string s ('**Rohan**' and '**Maths**') and the third key—'**Marks**'—replaced by the corresponding integer—100. The integer value—91—is assigned to **ab** in [11] and output in different formats in succeeding lines—that is hex and octal values with and without respective prefixes (0x and 0O respectively). **z1** in [16] is a tuple of two elements—a single character string ('**h**') and an integer (123). With U+123 as the Unicode of a character ('{') a string is formed in [17] with the single character format. With '*' as the width allocated for the entity in [19] the width value is specified (as 8) in the tuple that follows. Similarly the asterisk in [20] signifies the precision desired. Its value is specified as two in the tuple. In [21] the width as well as the precision is specified in the tuple itself. In all these cases the assignments to the asterisks have to precede the concerned element value in the same order.

8.2.2   Formatting—Version II

The second version of formatting combines items from a set of specified entities/objects to form a formatted string. The entities can be numbers, strings, tuples, lists, dictionarys or their mix. They can be present in the formatted string *in toto* or in specified/selected parts rearranged in a desired order. The formatting structure is shown in Fig. 8.5. The following regarding the formatting are noteworthy here:

In general the formatted string—strg in strg.format(....) —is composed of literal character sets and 'replacement fields' in a sequence. Each replacement field is enclosed within curly brackets as { }. It specifies an item to be identified from the arguments specified within the method strg.format(...) and how the same is to be structured and merged into the formatted string. The specification is broadly composed of three parts each being optional:

1. The field name is an integer (from 0 onwards) which stands for the serial number of the entity from which the information is to be taken. If the data/information is within the entity its location/identifier may be specified after

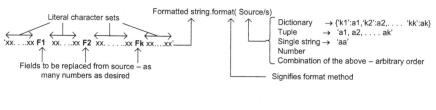

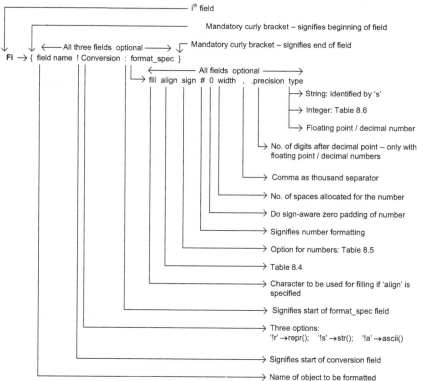

Fig. 8.5 Details of string formation for printing—Version II

a dot—'.'—(in case the entity is a dictionary item, the field name is the key of the entity concerned). If the replacement fields are specified in the same order as the sequence of entities within the brackets, the serial number can be omitted; the interpreter will assume them to be 0, 1, 2, ... and so on, in the same order.

2. The character—'!'—identifies the conversion field, if the same is present. Three forms of conversions—specified as '!s', '!r', and '!a' are possible. With **ee** as the specified item, these return str(**ee**), repr(**ee**), and ascii(**ee**) respectively.

3. The character ':' specifies the format specification if the same is present. The format specification here is again composed of a number of optional fields:

Table 8.4 Alignment options—formatting Version II

Option	Meaning
'<'	Forces field to be left-aligned within available space (default for most objects)
'>'	Forces field to be right-aligned within available space (default for numbers)
'='	Forces padding to be placed after sign (if any) but before digits—used for printing fields in the form '+000000120'—only for numeric types
'^'	Forces field to be centered within available space

a. The item may be specified as a number, a character, or a string.
b. The width—in the width field—is an integer specifying the number of spaces allocated to the item. If the same is omitted the Interpreter will automatically allot the minimum space width demanded of the item. If the actual width is less than what is allocated, the additional spaces will be filled as specified in the fields—'fill and align'.
c. 'fill' represents any character which can be used to fill the free space.
d. 'align' symbol is present only if the filling is called for. There are four possibilities as shown in Table 8.4.
e. The option—'#'—signifies that the item being formatted is a number. Further the number type offers flexibility in terms of additional fields:

    i. The sign field has three options as given in Table 8.5.
    ii. In case the number is an integer the representations possible are as given in Table 8.6. Note that the 'c' option implicitly assumes the given integer to be the Unicode value of the character concerned.
    iii. The options available for the floating point numbers are in Table 8.7. Here 'width' represents the total width (as the number of spaces) allocated for the number inclusive of the sign and the decimal point.

The illustrative examples formatted conforming to Version I in Fig. 8.4 are formatted conforming to Version II and presented in the Python Interpreter sequence in Fig. 8.6. The print out of numbers in **az** [1], the sequence formed from the dictionary **rm** [2] and the different representations of the number **ab** [3] can be seen to be the same as their counterparts in Fig. 8.4. **z1** [4] is a tuple of two elements—a single character string—'**h**'—and the integer—123 (with ASCII value '{ '). It has been formatted in [5] with 0[0] and 0[1] specifying the arguments in replacement field. Here **z1** is a single entity being formatted. In [6]—'**h**' and 123 —are two successive entities being formatted—identified through indices 0 and 1 respectively. [7] uses the starred version of **z1** the entities being identified again through indices 0 and 1 respectively.

Table 8.5 Sign options—formatting Version II

Option	Meaning
'+'	Indicates that a sign should be used for both positive as well as negative numbers
'−'	Indicates that a sign should be used only for negative numbers (default behavior)
Space	Indicates that a leading space should be used on positive numbers, and a minus sign on negative numbers

Table 8.6 Details of integer presentation types—formatting Version II

Type	Meaning
'b'	Binary format—outputs number in base 2.
'c'	Character—converts integer to corresponding Unicode character before printing
'd'	Decimal Integer—outputs number in base 10
'o'	Octal format—outputs number in base 8
'x'	Hex format—outputs number in base 16, using lower-case letters for digits above 9
'X'	Hex format—outputs number in base 16, using upper-case letters for digits above 9
'n'	Number—same as 'd', except that current locale setting is used to insert appropriate number separator characters
None	Same as 'd'

Table 8.7 Details of floating point number presentation types—formatting Version II

Type	Meaning
'e'	Exponent notation—prints number in scientific notation using letter 'e' to indicate exponent; default precision is 6
'E'	Exponent notation—uses upper case 'E' as separator character; otherwise same as 'e'
'f'	Fixed point—displays number in fixed-point form; default precision is −6
'F'	Fixed point—same as 'f', but converts *nan* to NAN and *inf* to INF
'g'	General format—for a given precision p ≥ 1, this rounds number to p significant digits and then formats result in either fixed-point format or in scientific notation, depending on its magnitude. The precise rules are as follows: suppose that the result formatted with presentation type 'e' and precision p − 1 would have exponent **exp**. Then if −4 ≤ **exp** < p, the number is formatted with presentation type 'f' and precision p − 1 − **exp**. Otherwise, the number is formatted with presentation type 'e' and precision p − 1. In both cases insignificant trailing zeros are removed from the significant, and the decimal point is also removed if there are no remaining digits following it. Positive and negative infinity, positive and negative zero, and nans, are formatted as inf, −inf, 0, −0 and nan respectively, regardless of the precision. A precision of 0 is treated as equivalent to a precision of 1. The default precision is 6
'G'	General format. Same as 'g' except switches to 'E' if the number gets too large. The representations of infinity and NAN are uppercased, too
'n'	Number—same as 'g', except that current locale setting is used to insert appropriate number separator characters
'%'	Percentage—multiplies number by 100 and displays in fixed ('f') format, followed by a percent sign
None	Similar to 'g', except that fixed-point notation, when used, has at least one digit past the decimal point. The default precision is as high as needed to represent the particular value. The overall effect is to match the output of str() as altered by other format modifiers

The formatting examples in Fig. 8.7 illustrate the variety and flexibility possible when formatting with Version II. The set of simple strings in the list **az** [1] are directly formatted into a string in [2]. The desired replacement order being the same as in **az**, the index values are not specified. **ay** in [3] is a dictionary of four items. They are formatted into a string [4] by specifying the keys in the

```
>>> az = (3, -3.2104, -321.04, 321.04, -3210.401)        [1]
>>> while True:
...     print('{0[0]:#8.2f}'.format(az))
...     print('{0[1]:=#08.2f}'.format(az))
...     print('{0[2]: #08.2f}'.format(az))
...     print('{0[3]:-#8.2f}'.format(az))
...     print('{0[4]:#8.2e}'.format(az))
...     break
...
    3.00
-0003.21
-0321.04
  321.04
-3.21e+03
>>> rm = {'Name':'Roshan', 'Subject': 'Maths', 'Marks':
100}                                                       [2]
>>> print('{0[Name]} gets in {0[Subject]} {0[Marks]} out
of 100'.format(rm))
Roshan gets in Maths 100 out of 100
>>> ab = 91                                                [3]
>>> while True:
...     print('Hex value of ab is {0:8x}'.format(ab))
...     print('Explicit Hex value of ab is
{0:#8x}'.format(ab))
...     print('Octal value of ab is {0:8o}'.format(ab))
...     print('Explicit Octal value of ab is
{0:#8o}'.format(ab))
...     break
...
Hex value of ab is       5b
Explicit Hex value of ab is      0x5b
Octal value of ab is      133
Explicit Octal value of ab is     0o133
>>> z1 = ('h',123)                                         [4]
>>> 'cc = {0[0]}, nn = {0[1]:c}'.format(z1)                [5]
'cc = h, nn = {'
>>> 'cc = {0}, nn = {1:c}'.format('h',123)                 [6]
'cc = h, nn = {'
>>> 'cc = {0}, nn = {1:c}'.format(*z1)                     [7]
'cc = h, nn = {'
>>>
```

Fig. 8.6 Python Interpreter sequence illustrating string formatting conforming to Version II—the examples are the same as those in the sequence in Fig. 8.4

respective replacement fields. In [5] and [6] a dictionary of a single item is specified in different forms but the (intended) formatting is the same. The string 'Uma' is specified through its **key** in [7] in the replacement field. Two arguments —both dictionarys—are present in [8]; but only one item from the second dictionary is sought by the formatted string. Four different types of entities are

```
>>> az = ['aa', 'bb', 'cc', 'dd']                              [1]
>>> 'This is a sequence:{} & {} * {} ^ {}'.format(*az) [2]
'This is a sequence:aa & bb * cc ^ dd'
>>> ay = {'k1': 'p1','k2': 'q1','k3': 'r1','k4': 's1'} [3]
>>> 'This too is a sequence: {k1} ** {k2} ** {k3} **
{k4}'.format(**ay)                                             [4]
'This too is a sequence: p1 ** q1 ** r1 ** s1'
>>> 'My name is {0[nn]}'.format(dict(nn='Pad'))              [5]
'My name is Pad'
>>> 'My name is {0[nn]}'.format({'nn':'Pad'})               [6]
'My name is Pad'
>>> 'My name is {0[nm]}'.format({'nn':'Pad','nm':'Uma'})[7]
'My name is Uma'
>>> 'My name is {1[aa]}'.format({'nn':'Pad', 'nm':'Uma'},
{'ab':'Ravi','aa':'Chandra'})                                [8]
'My name is Chandra'
>>> it1 = 34                                                  [9]
>>> it2 = (43.5, 'Swapnam')                                  [10]
>>> it3 = [34.98, it1/it2[0], 'Sat', 'Amritam']             [11]
>>> it4 = {'r1':'Ganga', 'r2':'Yamuna', 'r3':'Krishna',
'r4':'Sindhu'}                                               [12]
>>> ss1 =
'aa:{0},bb:{2[1]},cc:{2[2]},dd:{3[r3]}'.format(it1,it2,it3,
it4)                                                          [13]
>>> ss1
'aa : 34, bb : 0.7816091954022989, cc : Sat, dd : Krishna'
>>> import math                                              [14]
>>> print(math.pi)                                           [15]
3.141592653589793
>>> 'v1 = {0}, v2 = {0!s}, v3 = {0!r}'.format(math.pi) [16]
'v1 = 3.141592653589793, v2 = 3.141592653589793, v3 =
3.141592653589793'
>>> 'A value of pi is: {0.pi!s}; but a workable appx. value
is: {0.pi:8.5f}'.format(math)                                [17]
'A value of pi is: 3.141592653589793; but a workable appx.
value is:  3.14159'
>>> from demo_5 import marks1                                [18]
>>> while True:                                              [19]
...     print(*marks1.dtb, sep = '\t')
...     for jj in marks1.ss:print(*jj, sep = '\t')
...     break
...
Name   Phy.  Chem. Math. Mechn. Engl.                         [20]
Kishor 75    66    91    87     76
Sanjay 81    62    95    91     62
Siva   41    51    45    39     52
Asha   88    78    97    83     72
Nisha  50    61    68    40     81
```

Fig. 8.7 Python Interpreter sequence illustrating the variety and flexibility in formatting possible with Version II

formed in [9], [10], [11], and [12]—a number, a string of two different types of items, a list of different types of items including one involving computation of an algebraic expression and the last one being a dictionary. All these form arguments for forming **ss1**—the formatted string in [13]. The replacement fields to form **ss1** are also in different orders.

The math module is imported [14] and the value of π directly printed out in [15]. **v1**, **v2**, and **v3** in the formatted string in [16] represent π in three different ways—all giving identical results. The field width specified for π in [17]—5 digits —gives a corresponding approximate value of π. pi (π) has been defined as a number in the math module (see 'math.__dict__'); hence it is accessed as math. pi here.

Example 8.1 Marks earned by a set of students in different subjects are given as a set of strings in '**demo_5.marks**1' (see Fig. 5.16). The subject names and the student names are also given there. Output the data as a well arranged formatted table.

The program to present the information is in the suite from [19]. The output is presented in the lines starting with [20]. The table is properly formatted (spaces uniformly set out and aligned) since the length of every entity in the table is equal to/less than the default tab size (8). If the length of any quantity exceeds this tab size, the program has to be suitably changed.

8.3   Files and Related Operations

Modules (see Sect. 4.2) serve as platforms to store python code and functions in conveniently organized form. When required, they can be retrieved and used through 'importing'. Data as a number sequence or as bland text can be stored as 'files'. In the Python environment, a file is a string or a bytes object stored in a specified location. A set of associated methods provides access to the file to use specified and selected parts from it or modify it in desired ways. We shall study these in some detail here.

8.3.1   String/Text Files

'*String files*' are made up of characters—encoded in UTF-8 form unless specified otherwise; they are also called '*text files*' (In contrast bytes files are sequences of bytes). The function open() is used to open a file. It may be opening of an existing file or a new file to be used for storage. [1] in the Python Interpreter sequence in Fig. 8.8 opens a file—with file name '**ft**'; **d1** = open('**ft**', 'w') is the command to open this file. **ft** has been opened here in 'write' mode—'w' signifies this—in the current directory. **d1** represents the opened file object. Since no such file exists in

```
>>> d1 = open('ft', 'w')                              [1]
>>> s1 = 'Let us make a fresh start'                  [2]
>>> d1.write(s1)                                      [3]
25                                                    [4]
>>> d1.close()                                        [5]
>>> d2 = open('ft', 'r')                              [6]
>>> d2.read()                                         [7]
'Let us make a fresh start'
>>> d2.read()                                         [8]
' '
>>> d2.close()                                        [9]
>>> d3 = open('/home/trp/Documents/fta', 'w')        [10]
>>> e1 = ('a1', 'b2', 'c3', 'd4')                    [11]
>>> for jj in e1:d3.write(jj)                        [12]
...
2
2
2
2
>>> d3.close()                                       [13]
>>> d3 = open('/home/trp/Documents/ftb','w')         [14]
>>> for jj in e1:d3.write(jj + '\n')                 [15]
...
3
3
3
3
>>> d3.close()                                       [16]
>>> d4 = open('/home/trp/Documents/fta', 'r')        [17]
>>> mm = d4.read()                                   [18]
>>> mm                                               [19]
'a1b2c3d4'
>>> d4.close()                                       [20]
>>> with open('/home/trp/Documents/ftb','r') as d5:mn =
d5.read()                                            [21]
...
>>> d5.closed                                        [22]
True
>>> mn                                               [23]
'a1\nb2\nc3\nd4\n'
```

Fig. 8.8 Python Interpreter sequence illustrating file related operations

the current directory, '**ft**' has been opened as a new file. As mentioned earlier all items written into the file represented by '**ft**' together will be stored as a string/bytes object. **s1** in [2] is a single string. **d1**.write(**s1**) in [3] writes **s1** as a text in the file (through **d1**). write() is the method used to do the writing. The write() command on execution returns the total number of bytes written into the file. Here it is 25 as seen from [4]. Once opened in this manner as many

(a)   **(b)**

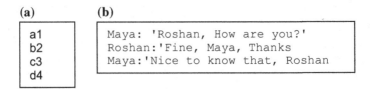

Fig. 8.9 Content of files—ftb (**a**) and fmr (**b**)—after each is written and closed

characters/character sequences as desired can be written into the file. When the desired writing is complete the file can be closed with **d1**.close() as in [5]. Whenever a file is opened for writing or other related operations it should be closed with the method close() to free up the system resources committed to the opened file. The file **ft** is opened again in [6] but this time it is in 'read' mode as the second argument—'r'—signifies. **d3**.read() in [7] uses the 'read' method to read the contents of **ft**. Another read in [8] returns an empty string since the content of **ft** has already been read in [7] itself. **d2**.close() in [9] is the formal closing of **ft** to avoid the file being left open as well as to free the resources used by **ft** when **ft** was in the open state. A new file—'**fta**'—has been opened in [10] with **d3** representing the open file here. The file path has been specified with open() itself—mandatory when the file opened is in another directory (and not the current one). **fta** has been opened in the directory—'Documents'. **e1** is a tuple of strings [11]. They are all written in the same sequence into **fta** in [12]. Since each string here—'**a1**', '**b2**', '**c3**', and '**d4**'—is of two characters, each write() returns '2' on completion of writing. The resulting full content of **fta** is a single string of eight characters —'**a1b2c3d4**'. The same can be seen from [17] to [20] where **fta** is opened again —this time in read mode specifying the path [17]. The contents are read [18], displayed [19], and the file is closed [20]. Another file—**ftb**—is opened in [14] with its path specified. The elements of **e1** are written into it in [15] in four separate and successive lines. Here each write() comprises of three characters—two being the string and the third the new line character—'\n'. When **ftb** is closed after this write sequence, its content is a sequence of four lines (**a1, b2, c3, d4**); all these four lines together make up the file content. The file content has been reproduced in Fig. 8.9a; nevertheless it still remains a single string—'**a1\nb2\nc3\nd4\n**'.

When file operations are desired to be done in a clear sequence use of the 'with' keyword makes it elegant. The file is automatically closed as part of the sequence obviating the need for a separate 'close()' command. **ftb** is opened in [21] in this manner for reading and its contents—as a string—is assigned to **mn** and **ftb** closed; [22] confirms this. **mn**—a single string of four lines—(as explained earlier) is shown in [23]. [21] constitutes a single operation; multiple commands also can be executed in the same manner within a single suite.

Additional methods with files and the flexibility they offer are brought out through the Python Interpreter sequence in Fig. 8.10. **h1** in [1] represents a new file —**fmr**—opened in the current directory in the 'write' mode. Three strings are written in succession into the file—[2], [3], [4]—and the file is closed. Each of the

```
>>> h1 = open('fmr', 'w')[1]
>>> h1.write("Maya: 'Roshan,
How are you?'" +'\n')      [2]
29
>>> h1.write("Roshan:'Fine,
Maya, Thanks" +'\n')       [3]
27
>>> h1.write("Maya:'Nice to
know that, Roshan" +'\n')[4]
32
>>> h1.close()            [5]
>>> h2 = open('fmr', 'r')[6]
>>> h3 = open('faa', 'w')[7]
>>> while True:           [8]
...     mm = h2.readline()[9]
...     if mm :h3.write(mm)
                         [10]
...     else:break        [11]
...
29
27
32
>>> h2.close()
>>> h3.close()
>>> with open('faa', 'r') as
h4:h4.read()              [12]
...
"Maya: 'Roshan, How are
you?'\nRoshan:'Fine, Maya,
Thanks\nMaya:'Nice to know
that, Roshan\n"
>>> h5 =open('faa','r') [13]
```

```
>>> while True:           [14]
...     mm = h5.readline()
...     if mm :print(mm)
...     else:break
...
Maya: 'Roshan, How are you?'

Roshan:'Fine, Maya, Thanks

Maya:'Nice to know that,
Roshan

>>> h5.seek(0)            [15]
0
>>> while True:           [16]
...     mm = h5.readline()
...     if mm :print(mm, end
='')
...     else:break
...
Maya: 'Roshan, How are you?'
                         [17]
Roshan:'Fine, Maya, Thanks
Maya:'Nice to know that,
Roshan
>>> h5.close()            [18]
>>> h5 =open('faa','r') [19]
>>> h5.readline()         [20]
"Maya: 'Roshan, How are
you?'\n"
>>> h5.tell()             [21]
29
>>> h5.close()            [22]
>>>
```

Fig. 8.10 Python Interpreter sequence illustrating additional file related operations

three strings ends with a newline and the file contents at that stage look as in Fig. 8.9b. However (in the Python environment) the file itself is a single string comprising of these lines. **fmr** is opened (as **h2**) in the read mode in [6] and another file—**faa**—again in the same directory—is opened in write mode [7] as **h3**. The suite of statements from [8] reads **fmr** line by line and writes it to **faa**. readline() reads one line of the opened file and advances the file pointer to the start of the following line. After all the lines are read from **faa**, **mm** = h2.readline() returns an empty string. This terminates the loop. From the number of characters written successively (29, 27, and 32) one can see that all the three lines in **fmr** have been written into **faa**. Following this **h2** and **h3** are closed. **faa** has been opened again in [12], its contents read, and **faa** closed after completion of the read operation. The

Table 8.8 Details of mode options available with write() function

Character	Meaning
'r'	Open for reading (default)
'w'	Open for writing—existing file content is erased
'x'	Open for exclusive creation, failing if the file already exists
'a'	Open for writing, appending to the end of the file
'b'	Binary mode
't'	Text mode (default)
'+'	Open a disk file for updating (reading and writing)

whole file can be seen to be a single string composed of the three succeeding lines. **faa** is opened again in [13] in read mode. It is read line by line and each line printed on the terminal. The print(**mm**) function has a newline ending by default; this explains the additional blank line after every line has been printed out.

With **aa** as a file opened in read mode the method **aa**.seek(**nn**) transfers the file pointer to the nnth location. Thus with **h5**.seek(0) in [15] **h5** seeks the 0th character in **faa**—that is the start of the file itself. The sequence from [16] again reads **faa** line by line and prints out the same on the terminal. The print (**mm**, end '=') specifies a blank as end of the line which removes the default blank line which was inserted earlier by default. The printout line by line of **faa** from [17] onwards confirms this. **faa** is closed in [18] and again opened in [19]. One line of this is read in [20]; at this stage **h5** points to the beginning of next line (29) since the first line of 29 characters occupying positions 0–28 has been read. The method **h5**.tell() in [21] returns the current position of the opened file **h5** (in number of bytes from the beginning of **h5**).

The open() function offers more flexibility than explained so far:

- If mode is not specified the file is opened in 'read—text' mode.
- The mode options available are summarized in Table 8.8 (r, w, a, b, t, +). Opening in default mode, mode = 'r', or mode = 'rt'—all these imply the same. In all these cases the file is opened in 'text read' mode.
- The default encoding for the text file is UTF-8. However to write/read other files the encoding may be specified as encoding = 'UTF-16' and the like when opening the file.
- When a file is opened in 'a' mode, items written are appended to the file content.
- When opened in 'r+' mode one can read the file content as well as update it. However the updating here has to be done with care; it may be done at the beginning or overwritten depending upon the operations prior to the writing.
- Whenever an existing file is opened in 'w' mode, the entire contents are erased and writing done afresh.
- With 'w + b' as mode the file is opened in 'write' mode for bytes write. With an existing file the contents are cleared and the file opened afresh.
- 'r + b' mode opens the file for access for 'read/write' in bytes form.

(a)

```
>>> e1 = ('a1', 'b2', 'c3', 'd4')                        [1]
>>> p1 = open('ftz', 'w')                                [2]
>>> for jj in e1:p1.write(jj + '\n')
...
3
3
3
3
>>> p1.close()
>>> p2 = open('ftz','r+')                                [3]
>>> p2.readline()                                        [4]
'a1\n'
>>> p2.write('e5')                                       [5]
2
>>> p2.close()
>>> with open('ftz','r') as p3:p3.read()                 [6]
...
'a1\nb2\nc3\nd4\ne5'
>>> p4 = open('ftz','r+')                                [7]
>>> p4.write('f6')
2
>>> p4.seek(0)                                           [8]
0
>>> p4.read()                                            [9]
'f6\nb2\nc3\nd4\ne5'
>>> p4.write('g7')
2
>>> p4.seek(0)                                           [10]
0
>>> p4.read()                                            [11]
'f6\nb2\nc3\nd4\ne5g7'
>>> p4.close()
>>> with open('ftz','w') as p5:                          [12]
...     for jj in e1:p5.write(jj + '\n')
...
3
3
3
3
```

Fig. 8.11 a Python Interpreter sequence illustrating file access variations (continued in Fig. 8.11b) **b** Python Interpreter sequence illustrating file access variations (continued from Fig. 8.11(a))

(b)

```
>>> with open('ftz','a') as p6:p6.write('Aa\n')        [13]
...
3
>>> p6.close()
>>> with open('ftz','r') as p7: p7.read()              [14]
...
'a1\nb2\nc3\nd4\nAa\n'
>>> dd = b'Dhruva as a star is an eternal symbol of HOPE'
                                                       [15]
>>> ee = b'\x65\x66\x67\x68'                           [16]
>>> with open('fty', 'w+b') as q1:                     [17]
...     q1.write(dd)
...     q1.write(b'\n')
...     q1.write(ee)
...
45
1
4
>>> q2 = open('fty', 'r+b')                            [18]
>>> q2.read()
b'Dhruva as a star is an eternal symbol of HOPE\nefgh'
>>> q2.seek(0)                                         [19]
0
>>> q2.readline()                                      [20]
b'Dhruva as a star is an eternal symbol of HOPE\n'
>>> q2.readline()                                      [21]
b'efgh'
>>> q2.close()
>>> d1 = open('Rubiayat')                              [22]
>>> while True:                                        [23]
...     mm = d1.readline()
...     if mm == '3\n':break
...
>>> for jj in range(5):d1.readline()                   [24]
...
'\n'
'And, as the Cock crew, those who stood before\n'
'The Tavern shouted--"Open then the Door!\n'
'"You know how little while we have to stay,\n'
'"And, once departed, may return no more."\n'
>>> d1.close()
```

Fig. 8.11 (continued)

The Python Interpreter sequence in Fig. 8.11 show additional illustrations of file access variations. The string elements of tuple **e1** [1] are written into a file **ftz** in the current Directory [2]. **ftz** is again opened in [3] for reading and updating—in 'r+' mode. After the first line is read in [4] the string '**e5**' is written into **ftz** [5] and

ftz closed. 'e5' can be seen to be appended at the end of the file as the read contents reveal in [6]. The file is again opened in 'r+' mode [7] and the string 'f6' written into it. A fresh read of the file [9] shows that 'f6' has been added at the beginning of the file. The updating done can be seen to depend on the previous accesses after the file has been opened. Again writing the string 'g7' into **ftz** and reading the file content [11] confirms this. tuple 'e1' has been written afresh into the file **ftz** [12]. Subsequently **ftz** has been opened for appending—mode 'a' [13] and string 'aA' appended to it. The appending can be seen to be done at the end of the file [14] as expected.

 dd [15] and 'ee' [16] are two byte objects. A new file **fty** has been opened for writing bytes (mode—'w + b') [17]. **dd** and **ee** are written into it in successive lines; when read, the file content is output as a single file object [18]. A fresh line by line reading of **fty** (starting at the beginning of the file) shows the file content as bytes—and written in two successive lines [19], [20], [21].

Example 8.2 '**Rubiayat**' is a string file (a few couplets from 'Rubiayat' by Omar Khayyam) in the current directory. The couplets are entered in it with the Serial Number as the title. Print out the third couplet.

 '**Rubiayat**' is opened in read mode in [22]. Successive lines are read using the method—readline() in a loop to identify the third couplet [23]. The loop is terminated as soon as '3' is read in a line. The subsequent four lines—read with readline() in a following loop are printed out [24] ('**d1**.close()' has been omitted in the listing).

8.4   Exercises

1. Prepare a python program to print out the 'pyramid of integers' as in Fig. 8.12. Save it in a file, read it back and reproduce it.
2. In Fig. 8.12 replace every integer by its 9's complement (nine minus the integer) and get a new pyramid of integers.
3. In the pyramid in Fig. 8.12 replace every integer by S % 10 where S is the sum of all the integers to the left in the same row.
4. Prepare a program to replace an integer in the range (0, 25) by a corresponding alphabetic character. Use this to prepare a pyramid of alphabetic characters as in Fig. 8.13.
5. Replace every character in Fig. 8.13 by the next one; replace 'Z' by 'A'.
6. The Gregorian calendar has the following features:

Fig. 8.12 Pyramid of integers

```
              9
             989
            98789
           9876789
            . . . .
          98 . . 0 . . .89
```

Fig. 8.13 Pyramid of
alphabetic characters

```
              A
             AB
           ABCBA
          ABCDCBA
           . . . .
         AB . . Z. . .BA
```

- If a year is divisible by 400 it is not a leap year.
- All years divisible by four—barring the above set—are leap years.
- A leap year has 366 days. All other years have 365 days.
- Since 365 % 7 = 1, if a day is a Monday the same day in the succeeding year is a Tuesday in a non-leap year.
  With the above data as basis prepare a program to find out the weekday of any given date (Start from any day—say today—for which the date and weekday are known). Test it with the known dates:

7. Prepare a program to get the date and the weekday of a day d days behind/ahead of today; test it for d = 100, 1000, −1000, −1000.
8. Prepare a program to get the number of days elapsed from 01/01/2000 up to the specified date. Get these for the dates 01/03/2003 and 03/03/2004.
9. Prepare a program to express an integer in Roman numerals. Convert 1357 and 963 into Roman numerals. The rules to express an integer in Roman numerals:

   a. M, D, C, L, X, V, and I represent 1000, 500, 100, 50, 10, 5 and 1 respectively.
   b. If the number to be converted—N—exceeds 1000, the representation starts with M. If 500 < N < 1000, the number starts with a D and so on.
   c. As long as M, D, C, L, X, V, and I appear in the same order—not necessarily all of them—the number value is the algebraic sum of the respective integral values. Thus   MM = 2000,   MMDCCLXXVIII = 2000 + 500 + 200 + 50 + 20 + 5 + 3 = 2778.
   d. Only I, X, C, and M can be repeated in this manner in the number representation.
   e. A single I, X, or C (representing 1, 10, or 100) can precede a symbol of the next larger value—V, X, L, C, D, or M; it signifies a corresponding negative integer. Thus IV = 5 − 1 = 4, IX = 10 − 1 = 9, CXLV = 100 − 10 + 50 + 5 = 145, MMCMLXIV = 3000 − 100 + 50 + 10 − 1 + 5 = 2964.

Note that in any number D, L, and V (500, 50, and 5) can appear only once. Others—M, C, X, and I can appear in a number only a maximum of three times. The rules followed for conversion have different variants; but what is given here suffices for us.

10. Prepare a program to convert an integer expressed in Roman numerals to an equivalent one in decimal form. Convert MMMDXCIV and DCCXXXIV into corresponding decimal form.

Reference

van Rossum G, Drake FL Jr (2014) The Python library reference, Python software foundation

Chapter 9
Application Modules

The Python Standard Library has a set of application modules with a possible wide spectrum of users (van Rossum and Drake 2014). These are of interest here.

9.1 `random` Module

The `random` module in Python provides a variety of options that go with random variables, random processes and their uses. As with random number generators in computer based systems a pseudo random number generator is at the base of the module; its period (in number of bits) being orders larger than the size of numbers and sequences used, the operations are essentially random. The method `random.random()` returns a (53-bit) floating point number in the range [0.0, 1.0)—the number being a random selection based on a uniform distribution over the range (see [2] in Fig. 9.1). All other methods/functions are based on this basic selection. The basic methods available are the following: Their use is illustrated with the Python Interpreter sequence in Fig. 9.1.

- A random seed **nn** initializes the generator to a seed integer **nn**. All subsequent calls to different methods use this initialized generator as the basis; the result is a deterministic sequence. Results of any random number based simulation/study can be reproduced later by setting the seed to this number. This can be used to confirm repeatability. Another application is to satisfy the need of using a common (random data based) database for different simulations. The seed is set to 253 in [3]. A set of random numbers—**b1**, **b2**, and **c1** are generated following this [4], [5].
- `random.getrandbits(`**bb**`)` yields a sequence of **bb** random bits. The sequence is returned as an integer [6] and [7].

© Springer Nature Singapore Pte Ltd. 2016
T.R. Padmanabhan, *Programming with Python*,
DOI 10.1007/978-981-10-3277-6_9

```
>>> import random                                              [1]
>>> a1, a2 = random.random(), random.random()                 [2]
>>> a1, a2
(0.9498945651083229, 0.8683184526154862)
>>> random.seed(253)                                           [3]
>>> b1, b2 =  random.random(), random.random()                [4]
>>> b1, b2
(0.5381932447267871, 0.381638895027388)
>>> c1 = random.random()                                       [5]
>>> c1
0.8657010059498668
>>> random.getrandbits(24)                                     [6]
10945737
>>> bin(11585575)
'0b101100001100100000100111'                                  [7]
>>> random.seed(253)                                           [8]
>>> bb1, bb2 = random.random(), random.random()               [9]
>>> bb1, bb2
(0.5381932447267871, 0.381638895027388)
>>> cc1 = random.random()                                      [10]
>>> cc1
0.8657010059498668
>>> random.getrandbits(24)                                     [11]
10945737
*      *      *      *      *      *      *      *      *
>>> import random
>>> random.seed(253) #new session
>>> b10, b20 = random.random(), random.random()               [12]
>>> b10, b20                                                   [13]
(0.5381932447267871, 0.381638895027388)
>>> c10 = random.random()                                      [14]
>>> c10
0.8657010059498668
>>> random.getrandbits(24)                                     [15]
10945737
>>> as1 = ('aa', 'bb', 'cc')                                   [16]
>>> random.seed(as1)                                           [17]
>>> for kk in range(4):print (random.random(), end = ', ')
...                                                            [18]
0.791859970310408, 0.37548758581805664,
0.5826090061124767, 0.46081059752309517,
>>> random.seed(as1)                                           [19]
>>> for kk in range(4):print (random.random(), end = ', ')
...                                                            [20]
0.791859970310408, 0.37548758581805664,
0.5826090061124767, 0.46081059752309517,
```

Fig. 9.1 Python Interpreter sequence to illustrate the features of the random module

- The seed for the random generator is reset to the earlier value (=253) in [8] and the command sequence repeated. One can see that **bb1**, **bb2**, and **cc1** obtained here [9], [10] have the same values as **b1**, **b2**, and **c1** obtained earlier. The `random.getrandbits`(24) that follows in [11] returns the same 24-bit set as obtained earlier [6].
- A fresh Python session is started (after closing the above one) and random imported again. The seed is set to the value (=253) [12] used in the foregoing session. The previous command sequence is repeated. **b10**, **b20**, and **c10** obtained here [13], [14] have the same values as **b1**, **b2**, and **c1** in the last session. Same holds good of `random.getrandbits`() in [15] as well.
- When the seed is specified as an integer it is directly used as the seed for the pseudo random generator. Alternately it can be a `string`, `bytes`, or `bytearray`. In all these cases the equivalent binary string is used as the seed for the pseudo random generator. If the seed is not specified the current system time is taken as the seed. The `tuple` **as1** in [16] is taken as the seed in [17]. A set of four random numbers in the interval [0.0, 1.0) is generated in [18]. The seed value is restored in [19] and a further set of four random numbers is generated in [20]; these can be seen to be repetitions of the set obtained earlier.
- `random.choice`(**aa1**) returns a randomly selected element from the sequence **aa1**. **aa1** remains unaltered. **aa1** can be a `list`, `bytes`, `tuple` and so on. In the Python Interpreter sequence in Fig. 9.2 **aa1** is a list of `tuples`. A random element is selected from it as '**hh**' and the `tuple` '**hh**' is returned in [2]. In the line following a similar random selection is done successively three more times (in turn '**dd**', '**bb**', and '**cc**' are returned).
- `random.sample`(**aa1**, **k**) uses **aa1** as a base; a sample of **k** elements from **aa1** is selected at random and returned. In [3] a sample of three elements is returned ('**aa**', '**cc**', '**hh**') since **k** = 3. The original set aa1 remains undisturbed. Further the samples are selected independently and randomly. Hence the sample set can be subdivided further (if necessary) and used as independent sample sets.
- `random.shuffle`(**AA**) shuffles the sequence **AA** randomly in place. **aa1** has been assigned to **bb** in [4] and bb shuffled in [5]. The shuffled sequence can be compared to the original one [1].
- `random.randrange`(a, b, c) uses a sequence—{a, $a + c$, $a + 2 * c$, ... $c * ((b - a - 1)//c)$} and returns a randomly selected element from it. `random.randrange`(5, 2000, 15) returns 13115 in [6]. (13115 − 5)//15 = 874; thus the 874th element is selected at random and returned. If c is left out an integer in the range (a, b) is selected randomly and returned. If only b is specified, an integer less than b is returned. [7] is an illustration.
- `random.randint`(a, b) returns a randomly selected integer between a and b (inclusive). [8] is an illustration. This is an alias for `random.randrange`(a, $b + 1$). These essentially do `random.choice`(a, $b + 1$, c)—in the sense that it

```
>>> import random
>>> aa1 = ['aa', 'bb', 'cc', 'dd', 'ee', 'ff', 'gg',
'hh','ii']                                                      [1]
>>> random.choice(aa1)
'hh'                                                            [2]
>>> random.choice(aa1),
random.choice(aa1),random.choice(aa1)
('dd', 'bb', 'cc')
>>> random.sample(aa1, 3)                                       [3]
['aa', 'cc', 'hh']
>>> bb = aa1                                                    [4]
>>> random.shuffle(bb)                                          [5]
>>> bb
['ff', 'aa', 'hh', 'ii', 'cc', 'gg', 'bb', 'dd', 'ee']
>>> random.randrange(5, 20000, 15)                             [6]
13115
>>> random.randrange(20000)                                    [7]
6438
>>> random.randint(5, 20000)                                   [8]
19040
>>> random.uniform(31.423, 2.5749)                             [9]
28.457518611990324
>>> t1 = random.getstate()                                     [10]
>>> type(t1)
<class 'tuple'>
>>> random.choice(aa1)                                         [11]
'ee'
>>> random.uniform(97.3257, 1.297548)                          [12]
15.883851475768225
>>> random.setstate(t1)                                        [13]
>>> random.choice(aa1)                                         [14]
'ee'
>>> random.uniform(97.3257, 1.297548)                          [15]
15.883851475768225
>>> import os
>>> os.urandom(11)                                             [16]
b'_1\x81[\xfd?\xce\xd2\xfao\x86'
>>> os.urandom(11)
b'\xc7\x0fqZ{\xbdv\x0e\xfd\xfep'                               [17]
```

Fig. 9.2 Python Interpreter sequence to illustrate the additional features of the random module

is equivalent to generating a sequence with range $(a, b + 1, c)$ and making a random choice from it.

- random.uniform(**n1**, **n2**) returns a randomly selected floating point number. The selection is based on a uniform continuous distribution in the closed interval [**n1**, **n2**]. Thus random.uniform (31.423, 2.5749) in [9] returns the number 28.457518611990324.

- random.getstate() captures and returns the current state of the (pseudo random) generator which is at the base of the random module. **t1** in [10] represents the full state as an object. random.setstate (**t1**) sets the state of the generator to t1 as done in [13]. Hence a previously captured internal state is restored here and the generator functioning continues from that state.
- Recapturing and restoration as above facilitates rerun of any random sequences used earlier. [14] returns a random choice from aa1. It is followed in [15] by a random selection of a floating point number in the interval (97.3257, 1.297548) assuming uniform and continuous distribution. The returned quantities—the string '**ee**' and the number 15.883851475768225—can be seen to be reproductions of [11] and [12] respectively obtained earlier following the same sequence.
- Assigning a seed with randseed() starts the pseudo random generator afresh with the seed. In contrast rand.setstate() restores a frozen state in the pseudo random generator and continues there from.
- **Random number for cryptographic applications**: The built-in module random generates a pseudo random number—it is fully deterministic in the sense that the full sequence of numbers generated can be reproduced by reusing the seed/through random.setstate() as was explained earlier. Hence the random numbers generated here are not recommended for cryptographic applications. The OS module can be used to generate a byte sequence of desirable number of bytes; this uses an OS-specific random source to generate the sequence. [16] and [17] are examples of two 11-byte sequences generated in this manner. Random numbers returned by os.urandom() are not predictable; hence they are suitable for use in cryptographic applications.

9.1.1 Distribution Functions

A set of commonly used distribution functions in single variables is available in the random module. The parameter values are input into the module and random.**p**(**a**, **b**, ...) returns a random number conforming to the specified distribution function **p** (). **a**, **b**, ... are the arguments specifying the distribution. As an example random. gauss(3.0, 2.0) signifies a Gaussian distribution function with mean value 3.0 and variance 2.0. A call to this function returns a number conforming to Gaussian distribution.

gss(**aa**, **bb**) in Fig. 9.3 is a function (in module **dst_aa**.py) which return a list of 1000 random numbers conforming to the Gaussian distribution. **aa** and **bb** (both to be specified) are the mean and sigma values to be used for the distribution. The numbers are obtained through repeated calls to random.gauss(**aa**, **bb**). The program also returns a bar graph representation of the number frequencies in

```
def  gss(aa, bb):
    "returns 1000 random numbers conforming to
Gaussian distribution, their frequencies, & histogram
plot - aa & bb are mean and sigma respectively; "
    xd, gg = [], [0]*20
    for jj in range(1000):
        x = random.gauss(aa, bb)
        xd.append(x)
        xx = int(3.0*(x - aa)//bb)
        if xx < -9: gg[0] += 1
        elif xx > 8: gg[19] += 1
        else: gg[xx+10] += 1
    mx = max(gg)
    for kk in gg:print('*'*(20*kk//mx))
    return xd, gg
```

Fig. 9.3 Listing of a Python function using Gaussian distribution: A bar graph of number frequencies is made and a list of random numbers returned

Fig. 9.4 Bar graph obtained by calling and executing the Python function in Fig. 9.3

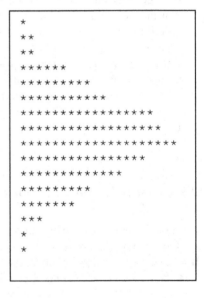

the range (mean ±3σ); it is reproduced in Fig. 9.4. Each bar represents the frequency of numbers in the interval (6σ/20).

The distribution functions supported through the random module along with the parameters to specify the functions (Krishnan 2006; Zwillinger 2003) are given in Table 9.1.

Table 9.1 Details of the distribution functions available in the `random` module in Python. In each case the function (when called) returns a number n conforming to the specified distribution

Type of distribution	Calling function	Details of parameter(s)	Range of n
Uniform	uniform (a, b)		$[a, b]$
Triangular	triangular (a, c, b)	c is the mode. Default values of a, c, b are 0, $(a + b)/2$, 1	$[a, b]$
Beta	Betavariate (α, β)	α and β—both are greater than 0	$[0, 1]$
Exponential	expovariate (a)	a^{-1} is the mean	$[0, \infty)$ if $a > 0$ and $[0, -\infty)$ if $a < 0$
Gammavariate	gammavariate (α, β)	α and β—both are greater than 0	$(0, \infty)$
Gaussian	gauss(μ, σ)	μ is the mean and σ the standard deviation	$(-\infty, \infty)$
Log normal	Lognomvariate (μ, σ)	$\sigma > 0$	$[0, \infty]$
Normal distribution	normalvariate (μ, σ)	μ is the mean and σ the standard deviation	$[-\infty, \infty]$
Von Mises	Vonmisesvariate (μ, κ)	μ is the mean angle and κ the concentration parameter	$\mu \pm \pi$
Pareto	Paretovariate (a)	a is the shape parameter	$(0, 1]$
Weibull	Weibullvariate (α, β)	α and β are the scale and shape parameters	$(0, \infty]$

9.2   statistics Module

The **statistics** module offers the facility to extract the key statistical information for the given sample set. The sample values have to be real numbers. They need not be ordered. The semantics of the methods are given in Table 9.2. The function **stsc (aa)** (in module **dst_aa**.py) reproduced in Fig. 9.5 accepts a sequence of numbers as input; it returns statistical information compiled using the statistics module, as a dictionary. The sequence of 1000 random numbers (conforming to Gaussian distribution) obtained earlier is used as input to **stsc**() and the statistical information extracted presented as a dictionary in Fig. 9.6. For a sufficiently large sample set the mean and median values should be 3.0—the mean value used to generate the sample set; the variance should be 4.0, since $\sigma = 2.0$ for the generated sample set.

Table 9.2 Quantities that can be calculated using statistics module. **dd** is the numerical input data presented as a sequence (`list`, `tuple` and c)

Quantity	Calling function	Returned quantity
Mean	mean(**dd**)	Arithmetic mean
Median	median(**dd**)	Median (middle) value—need not be an element of dd
Median low	median_low(**dd**)	If len(**dd**) is odd both return the median value; if `len`
Median high	median_high (**dd**)	(**dd**) is even, median low and median high return the lower and the higher of the median values
Median grouped	median_grouped (**dd**)	50th percentile of **dd**
Mode	mode(**dd**)	Most common element in dd (only if it is unique)
Standard deviation	pstdev(**dd** [, μ])	Standard deviation of the population: if μ is given, it is taken as the mean; else it is computed and used
Population variance	Pvariance (**dd** [, μ])	Population variance: if μ is given, it is taken as the mean; else it is computed and used
Sample standard deviation	stdev(**dd** [, $\bar{x}$])	Standard deviation of the sample: if $\bar{x}$ is given, it is taken as the mean; else it is computed and used. With sample set, this is preferred to pstdev()
Sample variance	variance (**dd** [, $\bar{x}$])	Variance of the sample: if $\bar{x}$ is given, it is taken as the mean; else it is computed and used. With sample set, this is preferred to pvariance()

```
def stsc(aa):
    "Collection of statistical information for the sample
set -- aa"
    dm = {}
    dm['mean'] = statistics.mean(aa)
    dm['median'] = statistics.median(aa)
    dm['median_low'] = statistics.median_low(aa)
    dm['median_high'] = statistics.median_high(aa)
    dm['median_grouped'] = statistics.median_grouped(aa)
    dm['pstdev'] = statistics.pstdev(aa)
    dm['pvariance'] = statistics.pvariance(aa)
    dm['stdev'] = statistics.stdev(aa)
    dm['variance'] =statistics.variance(aa)
```

Fig. 9.5 Python function to list out the statistical information extracted from a given data sequence

```
{'mean': 3.028618804120159, 'median_low':
3.0320745925400603, 'median_grouped': 2.5325557618709977,
'median': 3.032315177205529, 'variance': 4.028059120629807,
'pvariance': 4.024031061509177, 'stdev':
2.0070025213312035, 'median_high': 3.0325557618709977,
'pstdev': 2.0059987690697065}
```

Fig. 9.6 Statistical information extracted from the data set obtained by executing the routine in Fig. 9.3

9.3   Array Module

The array module allows a set of compact mutable sequences to be represented and accessed efficiently. Three types of sequence elements are possible here—characters, integers, and floating point numbers. Being restricted in scope of representation each element and hence the array itself occupies less memory space (as compared with a mutable sequence like list); access and execution involving them are also faster especially when the sequence concerned is large in size (like image files). Operations involving such arrays are illustrated here through the Python Interpreter sequence in Fig. 9.7.

Module array is imported in [1] in Fig. 9.7a. The basic array is formed by invoking the method array as array.array('**a**', **bb**). The character '**a**' here specifies the array being initialized. Possible '**a**' values with the associated type details are given in Table 9.3. The array formed can be one of the three types explained below:

- **bb** is a bytes, or bytearray type of object. The array is specified as type 'B' or 'b'. In either case the characters of **bb** are converted into corresponding integers to form the array elements. With 'B' as type all the characters are treated as positive integers with range 0–256. The sequence **c1** [2] (type bytes) is converted to **c2** an array of integers in [3] as seen from the lines following. The first element in **c1**—'9'—as an ASCII character has the integer value of 57 which is the first element of the array **c2**; similarly with all the other elements. **bb1** in [4] is formed as a bytearray from the string of hex characters—'2211 abcd effe aabb ccdd cddc'. **bb2** is formed as an array of corresponding positive integers in [5]. **c2n** in [6] is an array of signed integers formed from the bytes sequence **c1** itself. However all elements of the array **c2n** happen to be positive integers. **bb3** [7] is formed as an array of signed integers from **bb1**. In both these cases the array type is specified as 'b' and each character is converted into a signed integer in the range ±127. Comparing with **bb2** one can see that the integers greater than 127 in array **bb2** are represented as corresponding negative integers. In all the cases here every array element is of a single byte type.
- **a1** [8] is a list of floating point numbers. An array of floating point numbers **a3** is formed through array.array('f', **a1**). Every element in the array **a3** is four bytes long. **a2** formed from **a1** in [10] is also an array of floating point numbers. But every element in the array here is of double precision category represented by an 8-byte set.
- As a third alternative a sequence of integers—positive or negative—can be the source to be converted into an array. b1 in [11] is such a sequence (a list) of signed integers. **b2** in [12] is formed as an array of signed integers (with **b1** as the basis) through array.array('i', **b1**). The elements of the array here can be of 2 or 4 bytes depending on the machine. Similar other integer sequences can be formed with the first argument of the method array.array specified as 'I', 'h', 'H', 'l', 'L', 'q', or 'Q'. 'q' and 'Q' signify 8-bytes long integers. In such cases the integers concerned can be 4-bytes or 8-bytes long depending on the system.

(a)

```
>>> import array                                              [1]
>>> c1 = b'98765abcde'                                        [2]
>>> type(c1)
<class 'bytes'>
>>> c2 = array.array('B', c1)                                 [3]
>>> c2
array('B', [57, 56, 55, 54, 53, 97, 98, 99, 100, 101])
>>> bb1 = bytearray.fromhex('2211 abcd effe aabb ccdd
cddc')                                                        [4]
>>> bb1
bytearray(b'"\x11\xab\xcd\xef\xfe\xaa\xbb\xcc\xdd\xcd\xdc'
)
>>> bb2 = array.array('B', bb1)                               [5]
>>> bb2
array('B', [34, 17, 171, 205, 239, 254, 170, 187, 204,
221, 205, 220])
>>> c2n = array.array('b', c1)                                [6]
>>> c2n
array('b', [57, 56, 55, 54, 53, 97, 98, 99, 100, 101])
>>> bb3 = array.array('b', bb1)                               [7]
>>> bb3
array('b', [34, 17, -85, -51, -17, -2, -86, -69, -52, -35,
-51, -36])
>>> a1 = [1.2, 22.3, 3.4, 4.5, 5.6]                           [8]
>>> a3 = array.array('f', a1)                                 [9]
>>> a3
array('f', [1.2000000476837158, 22.299999237060547,
3.4000000953674316, 4.5, 5.599999904632568])
>>> a2 = array.array('d', a1)                                 [10]
>>> a2
array('d', [1.2, 22.3, 3.4, 4.5, 5.6])
>>> b1 = [2, -3, 44, -55, 678, 8901, -87654]                  [11]
>>> b2 = array.array('i', b1)                                 [12]
>>> b2
array('i', [2, -3, 44, -55, 678, 8901, -87654])
>>> b2[:3]                                                    [13]
array('i', [2, -3, 44])
>>> b2.buffer_info()                                          [14]
(35327984, 7)
>>> a2.itemsize, b2.itemsize                                  [15]
(8, 4)
>>> b2.byteswap()                                             [16]
>>> b2
array('i', [33554432, -33554433, 738197504, -905969665, -
1509818368, -987627520, -1700135169])
>>> b3 = array.array('q', [2, -3, 44, -55, 678, 8901, -
87654])                                                       [17]
>>> b3
array('q', [2, -3, 44, -55, 678, 8901, -87654])
```

Fig. 9.7 a Python Interpreter sequence to illustrate array formations (continued in Fig. 9.7b) **b** Python Interpreter sequence to illustrate array formations (continued in Fig. 9.7c) **c** Python Interpreter sequence to illustrate array formations (continued from Fig. 9.7b)

(b)

```
>>> b3.byteswap()                                              [18]
>>> b3
array('q', [144115188075855872, -144115188075855873,
3170534137668829184, -3891110078048108545, -
6484620513460092928, -4241827899029585920, -
7302024945339465729])
>>> bb3 = array.array('l',b1)                                  [19]
>>> bb3
array('l', [2, -3, 44, -55, 678, 8901, -87654])
>>> bb3.itemsize                                               [20]
8
>>> bb3.byteswap()                                             [21]
>>> bb3
array('l', [144115188075855872, -144115188075855873,
3170534137668829184, -3891110078048108545, -
6484620513460092928, -4241827899029585920, -
7302024945339465729])
>>> c2n.append(-107)                                           [22]

>>> c2n
array('b', [57, 56, 55, 54, 53, 97, 98, 99, 100, 101, -
107])
>>> c2nn = array.array('b', b'f')                              [23]
>>> c2nn
array('b', [102])
>>> cc2 = c2n +c2nn                                            [24]
>>> cc2
array('b', [57, 56, 55, 54, 53, 97, 98, 99, 100, 101, -
107, 102])
>>> cc2.reverse()                                              [25]
>>> cc2
array('b', [102, -107, 101, 100, 99, 98, 97, 53, 54, 55,
56, 57])
>>> cc2.extend(c2nn)                                           [26]
>>> cc2
array('b', [102, -107, 101, 100, 99, 98, 97, 53, 54, 55,
56, 57, 102])
>>> br1 = bytes([20, 61, 102, 143, 184, 225])                 [27]
>>> br1
b'\x14=f\x8f\xb8\xe1'
>>> br2 = bytearray([254, 215, 186, 147, 108, 69, 30])        [28]
>>> br2
bytearray(b'\xfe\xd7\xba\x931E\x1e')
>>> c2nn.frombytes(br1)                                        [29]
>>> c2nn                                                       [30]
array('b', [102, 20, 61, 102, -113, -72, -31])
>>> c2nn.frombytes(br2)                                        [31]
>>> c2nn                                                       [32]
array('b', [102, 20, 61, 102, -113, -72, -31, -2, -41, -
70, -109, 108, 69, 30])
```

Fig. 9.7 (continued)

(c)

```
>>> c2nn.tobytes()                                                [33]
b'f\x14=f\x8f\xb8\xe1\xfe\xd7\xba\x931E\x1e'
>>> c2nn.tostring()                                               [34]
b'f\x14=f\x8f\xb8\xe1\xfe\xd7\xba\x931E\x1e'
>>> b0 = c2nn.tolist()                                            [35]
>>> b0                                                            [36]
[102, 20, 61, 102, -113, -72, -31, -2, -41, -70, -109,
108, 69, 30]
>>> b1 = [34, 17, -85, -51, -17, -2, -86, -69, -52, -35, -
51, -36]                                                          [37]
>>> for kk in b1:c2nn.append(kk)                                  [38]
...
>>> c2nn
array('b', [102, 20, 61, 102, -113, -72, -31, -2, -41, -
70, -109, 108, 69, 30, 34, 17, -85, -51, -17, -2, -86, -
69, -52, -35, -51, -36])
>>> c2nn.count(-2)                                                [39]
2
>>> c2nn.index(-51)                                               [40]
17
>>> c2nn.insert(17, 102)                                          [41]
>>> c2nn
array('b', [102, 20, 61, 102, -113, -72, -31, -2, -41, -
70, -109, 108, 69, 30, 34, 17, -85, 102, -51, -17, -2, -
86, -69, -52, -35, -51, -36])
>>> c2nn.pop(17)                                                  [42]
102
>>> c2nn                                                          [43]
array('b', [102, 20, 61, 102, -113, -72, -31, -2, -41, -
70, -109, 108, 69, 30, 34, 17, -85, -51, -17, -2, -86, -
69, -52, -35, -51, -36])
>>> len(c2nn)
26
>>> cn = array.array('b')                                         [44]
>>> for kk in range(26):cn.append(c2nn.pop())                     [45]
...
>>> cn
array('b', [-36, -51, -35, -52, -69, -86, -2, -17, -51, -
85, 17, 34, 30, 69, 108, -109, -70, -41, -2, -31, -72, -
113, 102, 61, 20, 102])
>>> c2nn                                                          [46]
array('b')
>>> cn.index(-2)                                                  [47]
6
>>> cn.remove(-2)                                                 [48]
>>> cn.index(-2)                                                  [49]
17
```

Fig. 9.7 (continued)

Table 9.3 Characters used to define `arrays` and their significance: all except 'u' (already obsolete) signify numbers

Type code	C type	Minimum size in bytes
'b'	Signed char	1
'B'	Unsigned char	1
'u'	Py_UNICODE	2
'h'	Signed short	2
'H'	Unsigned short	2
'i'	Signed int	2
'I'	Unsigned int	2
'l'	Signed long	4
'L'	Unsigned long	4
'q'	Signed long	8
'Q'	Unsigned long	8
'f'	Float	4
'd'	Double	8

The sequence operations like slicing, indexing, concatenation can be used with `array`. A number of other methods are also available with `arrays`. b2[:3] in [13] in Fig. 9.7a forms a slice of the first three elements of `array` **b2** formed earlier. The method **b2**.`buffer_info`() returns a `tuple` of two items [14] comprising of the memory address of **b2** and the number of elements in **b2**. The method `itemsize`() returns the size of the elements of the concerned `array` in number of bytes. **a2**.`itemsize` and **b2**.`itemsize` [15] return 4 and 8 as the respective values.

`byteswap`() swaps the bytes of the array concerned. Such swapping may be called for with serial interface protocols which use the alternate byte sequence representation. **b2**.`byteswap`() in [16] swaps the bytes of the elements of array **b2**. With a 4-bytes representation of integer 2, **b2**[0] (=00 00 00 02h) when swapped becomes 33,554,432 (=02 00 00 00 = 2^{25}); similarly with the other swapped elements. The array **b3** in [17] is formed with the `list` **b1** [11] used to form **b2** in [12]; hence its elemental values are the same as those with **b2**. But here every element is of 8-byte type. [18] in Fig. 9.7b forms its swapped version (for example with the first element, 2^{57} = 144,115,188,075,855,872). **bb3** [19] has 'l' as its index for its formation. It is again an `array` of signed integers each being 8-bytes long [20]—the same as **b3** having index 'q' for its formation in [17] above. In turn the swapped version of **bb3** [21] is identical to the swapped version of **b3** itself. **c2n** in [6] formed earlier in Fig. 9.7a is an array of signed single byte integers formed from corresponding characters. The `append`() method is used in [22] in Fig. 9.7b to append −107 to **c2n**. The single character b'**f**' is converted to a corresponding array **c2nn** (=102) in [23]. Subsequently **c2n** and **c2nn** are combined in [24] to form a single bytes type single integer array **cc2**.

The method `reverse`() reverses the sequence in the array in place. **cc2**.`reverse`() in [25] is an example of its application. **cc2**.`extend(c2nn)` in [26] extends the array by combining **c2nn** with it. `append`() appends an integer (a single element) to the array. extend() extends the array to another array of the same type; extend() is the same as doing a set of successive append() operations in a loop.

Conversion from an array to a list, bytes, string are possible through methods dedicated for the same namely: tolist(), tobytes(), and tosrtring() respectively. Similarly fromlist(), frombytes() and fromstring() can be used to extend arrays by appending the set of elements from the respective sequences. **br1** in [27] and **br2** in [28] are bytes and bytearray type sequences. **c2nn**.frombytes(**br1**) [29] appends the full set of elements from bytes **br1** to **c2nn** [30]. **c2nn**.frombytes(**br2**) [31] extends **c2nn** further by appending all elements of the bytearray **br2** to it [32]. **c2nn**.tobytes() [33] (Fig. 9.7b) returns the bytes sequence of elements of c2nn. Similarly **c2nn**. tostring() [34] and **c2nn**.tolist() [35] return respective string and list sequences. The latter in [36] is assigned to **b0**.

b1 [37] is an array of single byte signed integers; its elements are appended to **c2nn** in the same sequence [38]. As mentioned earlier this needs the elements of **b1** to be of the same type as those of **c2nn**. **c2nn**.count(−2) [39] returns the number of occurrences of −2 in **c2nn**. **c2nn**.index(−51) [40] returns the index of the first occurrence of −51 in **c2nn**. **c2nn**.insert(17, 102) [41] inserts 102 at the indexed location (17th) of **c2nn**. The new value of **c2nn** accessed in the following line confirms this.

c2nn.pop(17) in [42] pops the 17th element of **c2nn**. The last inserted element 102 is popped out of **c2nn** here. **c2nn** is accessed and again output in [43] which confirms this. As an exercise **cn** is initialized as an empty array in [44]. Elements of **c2nn** are popped out successively and appended to **cn** [45]. **cn** is the reversed version of **c2nn** and **c2nn** is left as an empty array [46].

cn.index(−2) [47] returns the index of first occurrence of −2 in **cn**. **cn**. remove(−2) [48] removes −2 at its first occurence in **cn**. The subsequent **cn**. index(−2) in [49] confirms this by showing the index position of first occurrence of −2 as 17 in the new **cn**. Files—being binary or bytes type of sequences—can be converted to arrays and vice versa. The Python Interpreter sequence in Fig. 9.8 illustrates use of the relevant methods. File '**ft**' is opened in [1] and its content assigned to **ds1**[2] and the file closed. An empty array **gg1** (type 'B'—unsigned single byte character) is formed [3]. **gg1**.fromstring (**ds1**) in [4] fills up **gg1** with the sequence of unsigned integers representing string **ds1**. The methods tostring() and fromstring() are retained for compatibility with older versions of Python; these will be discontinued in later versions. tobytes() and frombytes() may be used instead.

[5] returns the length of **gg1** as well as **ds1** as 25 and 25 showing that the full string **ds1** has been converted to form **gg1**. typecode returns the character used to create the array. **gg1**.typecode in [6] returns the character representing the elements of array **gg1**. array. typecodes [7] returns the full character set possible to form arrays. The returned set conforms to the set of characters in Table 9.3.

```
>>> d2 = open('ft','r')                                    [1]
>>> ds1 = d2.read()
>>> ds1                                                    [2]
'Let us make a fresh start'
>>> d2.close()
>>> gg1 = array.array('B')                                 [3]
>>> gg1
array('B')
>>> gg1.fromstring(ds1)                                    [4]
>>> gg1
array('B', [76, 101, 116, 32, 117, 115, 32, 109, 97, 107,
101, 32, 97, 32, 102, 114, 101, 115, 104, 32, 115, 116,
97, 114, 116])
>>> len(gg1), len(ds1)                                     [5]
(25, 25)
>>> gg1.typecode                                           [6]
'B'
>>> array.typecodes                                        [7]
'bBuhHiIlLqQfd'
>>> with open('fty', 'r+b') as d1:d1.read()               [8]
...
b'Dhruva is a symbol of eternal HOPE\n\n'
>>> gg3 = b'A light that leads \n'                         [9]
>>> ga3 = array.array('B', gg3)                           [10]
>>> d1 = open('fty','a+b')                                [11]
>>> ga3.tofile(d1)                                        [12]
>>> d1.close()
>>> with open('fty', 'r+b') as d1:d1.read()               [13]
...
b'Dhruva is a symbol of eternal HOPE\n\nA light that leads
\n'
>>> d2 = open('fty', 'r+b')
>>> gg2 = array.array('B')                                [14]
>>> gg2.fromfile(d2, 35)                                  [15]
>>> d2.close()
>>> gg2
array('B', [68, 104, 114, 117, 118, 97, 32, 105, 115, 32,
97, 32, 115, 121, 109, 98, 111, 108, 32, 111, 102, 32,
101, 116, 101, 114, 110, 97, 108, 32, 104, 111, 112, 101,
32, 72, 79, 80, 69, 10])
>>> gg2.tostring()                                        [16]
b'Dhruva is a symbol of eternal HOPE\n'
>>>
```

Fig. 9.8 Python Interpreter sequence illustrating data transfer between array and file

Transfer of data between arrays and files is facilitated by methods `tofile()` and `fromfile()`. File 'fty' has '**Dhruva** is a symbol of eternal hope' as its content [8]. **gg3** in [9] is a bytes type sequence (**b** 'A light that leads'). **ga3** [10] is an `array` formed from **gg3**. **fty** is opened [11] in the 'append' mode, **ga3** written to it [12], and **fty** closed. Here **ga3**.`tofile(d1)` writes **ga3** to the open file represented by **d1**. **fty** is read afresh in [13] and its contents displayed. **gg2** is declared as a new (empty) `array` [14] and content of file **fty** transferred to it as an `array` [15]. Subsequently **gg2** is converted to a string [16] through **gg2**.`tostring()`. **gg2**. `fromfile(`**d2**, 35) in [15] fills the array **gg2** with 35 characters from the open file represented by **d2**. In general **gf**.`fromfile(`**f0**, **n**) accesses the open file **f0**, gets *n* characters and fills the array **gf** with it. The type of reading, writing, and appending are decided here by the mode selected to open the file concerned.

9.4 bisect Module

Some applications require mutable sequences (like `lists`, `arrays`) to be sorted or changed by additions/deletions frequently. Doing these through dedicated sorting algorithms/routines can be a tedious affair especially if the sequence concerned is large in size. The bisect module has a compact set of methods tailored for this purpose. Their use is illustrated through the Python interpreter sequence in Fig. 9.9.

The module `bisect` is imported. A sorted list of 10 random integers in the range (0–1000) is prepared as **ll** [1]. **ll1** is another list of random integers (again in the same range 0–1000) [2]. **ll1** is not sorted. The method `bisect.bisect_left` (**ll**, **ll1**[0]) [3] accepts two arguments: **ll** a sorted mutable sequence (`list`) and **ll1**[0] an integer (an element of the same type as those in **ll**). The position where **ll1**[0] can fit into **ll** is returned; but **ll** itself remains unaffected. In effect **ll1**[0] bisects **ll** into two parts the one on the left with all the elements being less than **ll1** [0] and the one on the right with all the elements being greater than **ll1**[0]. If **ll** has an element equal to **ll1**[0] the bisection point is taken as to its left. `bisect.` `bisect()` and `bisect.bisect_right()` are similar to `bisect.bi-` `sect_left()` in operation. But both these show the bisection after the existing entry in case the two are equal. `bisect.bisect(`**ll**, **ll1**[2]) [4] and `bisect.` `bisect_right(`**ll**, **ll1**[2]) [5] illustrate their applications. The methods `bisect.` `insort_left()`, `bisect.insort()`, and `bisect.insort_right()` take two arguments—a sorted mutable sequence being the first and an item of the same type as the elements of the sequence being the second. All of them insert the second argument into the sorted sequence retaining the sorting. Their use is illustrated in [6], [7], and [8] respectively. The updated list is also shown in each case. In all the three cases the first argument is the sorted mutable sequence and the second one the element to be inserted.

`bisect.insort_left(`**ll**, **ll1**[6], `lo` = 1, `hi` = 6) as in [9] is the use of the method in the generalized version. The segment of **ll** between the specified `lo` and `hi` values is in focus here for the insertion of **ll1**[6]. Incidentally **ll1**[6] (=398) [9]

```
>>> import bisect, random
>>> ll = []
>>> for kk in range(10):ll.append(random.randrange(1000))
...
>>> ll
[4, 635, 993, 846, 410, 153, 970, 460, 26, 256]
>>> lls = ll.sort()                                              [1]
>>> ll
[4, 26, 153, 256, 410, 460, 635, 846, 970, 993]
>>> lll = []
>>> for kk in
range(10):lll.append(random.randrange(1000))
...
>>> lll                                                          [2]
[576, 488, 858, 225, 941, 532, 398, 474, 151, 640]
>>> bisect.bisect_left(ll, lll[0])                               [3]
6
>>> bisect.bisect(ll, lll[1])                                    [4]
6
>>> bisect.bisect_right(ll, lll[2])                              [5]
8
>>> bisect.insort(ll, lll[3])                                    [6]
>>> ll
[4, 26, 153, 225, 256, 410, 460, 635, 846, 970, 993]
>>> bisect.insort_right(ll, lll[4])                              [7]
>>> ll
[4, 26, 153, 225, 256, 410, 460, 635, 846, 941, 970, 993]
>>> bisect.insort_left(ll, lll[5])                               [8]
>>> ll
[4, 26, 153, 225, 256, 410, 460, 532, 635, 846, 941, 970,
993]
>>> bisect.insort_left(ll, lll[6], lo = 1, hi = 6)              [9]
>>> ll
[4, 26, 153, 225, 256, 398, 410, 460, 532, 635, 846, 941,
970, 993]
>>> bisect.insort_left(ll, lll[7], lo = 2, hi = 5)             [10]
>>> ll
[4, 26, 153, 225, 256, 474, 398, 410, 460, 532, 635, 846,
941, 970, 993]
>>> la = ['RAM', 'KISHORE', 'ANAND', 'ZARA', 'MAYA',
'ROSHAN']                                                       [11]
>>> la.sort()                                                   [12]
>>> la
['ANAND', 'KISHORE', 'MAYA', 'RAM', 'ROSHAN', 'ZARA']

>>> bisect.insort(la, 'DHARA')                                  [13]
>>> la
['ANAND', 'DHARA', 'KISHORE', 'MAYA', 'RAM', 'ROSHAN',
'ZARA']
```

Fig. 9.9 Python Interpreter sequence illustrating the methods with bisect module

fits snugly in the index range (1–6) of **ll**—that is between 256 and 410. However **ll1**[7] (=474) in the following line [10] is larger than the largest element **ll**[4] in the specified range **ll**[2:5]. Hence it is fitted as the next element in 11. The segment **ll**[2]–**ll**[5] remains sorted but not the whole of ll. The sorting range can be specified through the lower (lo) and the higher (hi) limits with the other methods of bisect as well.

la in [11] is a list of names. It has been sorted in [12]. A new name '**Dhara**' has been inserted into the list in [13]. The methods in bisect can be used similarly with any mutable sequence in Python that can be sorted using Python's data structure.

9.5   heapq Module

In Python the 'heapq' module pertains to a class of mutable sequences where the individual elements are arranged in a binary tree fashion. The value of every parent node in the binary tree is greater than the values of its two daughter nodes. More specifically $v[k] \geq v[2 * k + 1]$ and $v[k] \geq v[2 * k + 2]$ where $v[k]$ is the value at the kth node for all k values. Often such an organized entity is called a '*heap*'. The methods available with the heapq module do operations conforming to these inequalities. As such in a heapq $v[0]$ is always the smallest element. If it is popped out the smaller one between $v[1]$ and $v[2]$ takes its place (being the new smallest element); in turn the rest of the heap is automatically updated in a similar fashion.

The Python Interpreter sequence in Fig. 9.10 facilitates understanding of the facilities with heapq. heapq is imported in [1] in Fig. 9.10a. **lb** is formed as a list [3] of integers 0–15. The way it is presented 1b is a sorted list. heapq.heapify (**lb**) [4] executes the method .heapify() with **lb**; it rearranges the elements of **lb** as a heap. Incidentally **lb** being a sorted list, it is already a heap. **lb** as a heap is depicted in the binary tree form in Fig. 9.11. Here the serial number of each node in shown within brackets beside the integer value at the node. heapq.heappop(**lb**) in [5] pops and returns the smallest element of the heap **lb**. The heap is updated automatically. The updated heap is shown in Fig. 9.12a in binary tree form. The updation process can be understood by comparing the heap here with that in Fig. 9.11. The nodes in Fig. 9.12a where the values are changed, are identified in block letters; the dotted arrow in each case shows the sequence of changes in the content of the nodes.

The values at the two daughter nodes of node 0-N1 and N2-1 and 2—are compared and 1 (being the smaller of the two) occupies node N0. N2 and its branches beneath remain untouched. Node 1 (N1) is filled by one of its daughters— (N3 and N4) (having values 3 and 4); 3 (from N3) being the smaller value occupies

(a)

```
>>> import heapq                                          [1]
>>> lb = []                                               [2]
>>> for gg in range (16):lb.append(gg)
...
>>> lb
[0, 1, 2, 3, 4, 5, 6, 7, 8, 9, 10, 11, 12, 13, 14, 15]
                                                          [3]
>>> heapq.heapify(lb)                                     [4]
>>> lb
[0, 1, 2, 3, 4, 5, 6, 7, 8, 9, 10, 11, 12, 13, 14, 15]
>>> heapq.heappop(lb), lb                                 [5]
(0, [1, 3, 2, 7, 4, 5, 6, 15, 8, 9, 10, 11, 12, 13, 14])
>>> heapq.heappop(lb), lb                                 [6]
(1, [2, 3, 5, 7, 4, 11, 6, 15, 8, 9, 10, 14, 12, 13])
>>> heapq.heappop(lb), lb                                 [7]
(2, [3, 4, 5, 7, 9, 11, 6, 15, 8, 13, 10, 14, 12])
>>> heapq.heappop(lb), lb                                 [8]
(3, [4, 7, 5, 8, 9, 11, 6, 15, 12, 13, 10, 14])
>>> heapq.heappop(lb), lb                                 [9]
(4, [5, 7, 6, 8, 9, 11, 14, 15, 12, 13, 10])
>>> heapq.heappop(lb), lb                                 [10]
(5, [6, 7, 10, 8, 9, 11, 14, 15, 12, 13])
>>> heapq.heappop(lb), lb                                 [11]
(6, [7, 8, 10, 12, 9, 11, 14, 15, 13])
>>> heapq.heappop(lb), lb                                 [12]
(7, [8, 9, 10, 12, 13, 11, 14, 15])
>>> heapq.heappop(lb), lb                                 [13]
(8, [9, 12, 10, 15, 13, 11, 14])
>>> heapq.heappop(lb), lb                                 [14]
(9, [10, 12, 11, 15, 13, 14])
>>> heapq.heappop(lb), lb                                 [15]
(10, [11, 12, 14, 15, 13])
>>> heapq.heappop(lb), lb                                 [16]
(11, [12, 13, 14, 15])
>>> heapq.heappop(lb), lb                                 [17]
(12, [13, 15, 14])
>>> heapq.heappop(lb), lb                                 [18]
(13, [14, 15])
>>> import random                                         [19]
>>> gg1 = []
>>> random.seed(2)
>>> for kk in range(16):gg1.append(random.randint(0,
1000))                                                    [20]
...
>>>
```

Fig. 9.10 **a** Python Interpreter sequence illustrating the methods with heapq module (continued in Fig. 9.10b) **b** Python Interpreter sequence illustrating the methods with heapq module (continued from Fig. 9.10a)

(b)

```
>>> gg1
[978, 883, 970, 869, 57, 93, 86, 369, 855, 173, 753, 828,
685, 874, 315, 257]
>>> hp1 = []                                                    [21]
>>> for kk in gg1:
...     heapq.heappush(hp1, kk)
...     print(hp1)
...
[978]
[883, 978]
[883, 978, 970]
[869, 883, 970, 978]
[57, 869, 970, 978, 883]
[57, 869, 93, 978, 883, 970]
[57, 869, 86, 978, 883, 970, 93]
[57, 369, 86, 869, 883, 970, 93, 978]
[57, 369, 86, 855, 883, 970, 93, 978, 869]
[57, 173, 86, 855, 369, 970, 93, 978, 869, 883]
[57, 173, 86, 855, 369, 970, 93, 978, 869, 883, 753]
[57, 173, 86, 855, 369, 828, 93, 978, 869, 883, 753, 970]
[57, 173, 86, 855, 369, 685, 93, 978, 869, 883, 753, 970,
828]
[57, 173, 86, 855, 369, 685, 93, 978, 869, 883, 753, 970,
828, 874]
[57, 173, 86, 855, 369, 685, 93, 978, 869, 883, 753, 970,
828, 874, 315]
[57, 173, 86, 257, 369, 685, 93, 855, 869, 883, 753, 970,
828, 874, 315, 978]
>>>
```

Fig. 9.10 (continued)

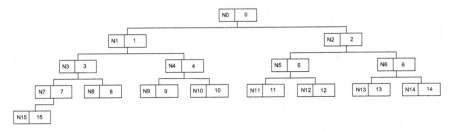

Fig. 9.11 Heap of integers in the range 0–15 showing the nodes and their respective contents: with each node Ni on the left is the *i*th node and the integer on the *right* is its content

N1. Node 4 and its daughter branches remain untouched. In the same vein N3 is filled by the value 7 from its daughter node N7. Similarly 15 occupies node N7. Node N15 being empty, gets deleted.

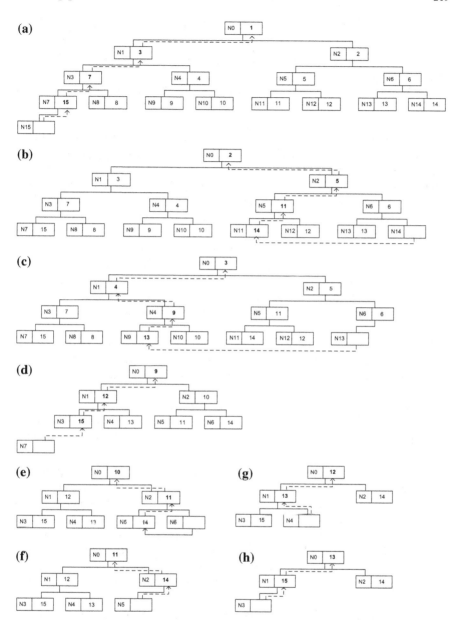

Fig. 9.12 Status of the heapq in Fig. 9.11 after successive pops: in each case the arrows in dotted lines show the movement of the node contents conforming to the heapq algorithm. Figs. (a)–(c) show the status after popping 0, 1, and 2 respectively. Figs. (d)–(h) show the status after popping integers 8–12

The resulting heap has 14 elements in it with 1 at node N0 being the smallest element. Note that the heap is no longer in sorted order though it still conforms to the basic rule of heap—any parent node holding value lower than those in its two daughter nodes.

The heap **lb** is continually popped in [6]–[18]. The heaps at some of the selected stages are shown in Fig. 9.12. In every case the changed values are identified in bold form.

With **aa** in a heap and **bb**—an entity of the same type as the elements of **aa**, the method heapq.heappush(**aa**, **bb**) pushes **bb** into the heap **aa**. **gg1** [20] is a set of random numbers (integers) in the range (0–1000). Heap **hp1** [21] (in Fig. 9.10b) is formed by successively pushing elements from **gg1** into heap **hp1**—done by the **for** loop. Formation of the heap and migration of elements node to node conform to the basic heap rule mentioned earlier: $v[k] \geq v[2 * k + 1]$ and $v[k] \geq v[2 * k + 2]$ for all k values.

Different methods available with heap are illustrated in the Python Interpreter sequence in Fig. 9.13. **la** [2] in Fig. 9.13a is a list of random numbers. **lb** [2] is another similar list of random numbers which have been reset as a heap. heap. heapreplace(**lb**, **la**[0]) [3] pops the smallest item from **lb**(=31) and pushes **la**[0] (881) into the heap lb. The updated **lb** has 881 taking up the position due to it in the heap.

lc[5] is a new heap formed from **la** with all its elements except **la**[0]. heapq. merge(**aa**, **bb**, **cc**) is to merge the heaps **aa**, **bb**, and **cc** into a single heap and returns the corresponding iterable. There is no constraint on the number of arguments for the method .merge(). List (heap.merge(**lb**, **lc**)) [6] merges heaps **lb** and **lc** and returns the combined heap as a list **ld**.

heapq.heappushpop() combines the push followed by pop into a single method. heapq.heappushpop(**lb**, 222) [7] pushes 222 into **lb** and pops its smallest element—65.

heapq.heapreplace(**aa**, **bb**) removes the smallest item from heap **aa** and pushes **bb** into it. The subtle difference between heapreplace() and heap-pushpop() is to be clearly understood. In heappushpop() the incoming item is pushed into the heap and then the popping done. heapreplace() does the same in the reverse order. **a1** as a list of integers in [8] is converted into a heap in [9]. heapq.heapreplace(**a1**, 12) [10] pops out a1[0] (=15) and then inserts 12 into **a1**. The resulting **a1** is in [11]. heapq.heappushpop(**a1**, 11) in [12] pushes 11 into the heap. It—being the smallest element in the heap—is popped out. The heap in effect remains the same [13].

Two methods are available to extract a desired number of smallest and largest values from a heap. heapq.nlargest(4, **ld**) [14] returns the largest four elements of ld as a list. Similarly heapq.nsmallest(4, **ld**) returns the smallest four elements of **ld** as a list ([15] in Fig. 9.13b). These methods are recommended only for small values of n. Sorting the queue and slicing may be more attractive for larger values.

In general the methods in heap may be applied to any list of elements whose values can be compared in Python. An example is considered here by way of

(a)

```
>>> import heapq, random                                    [1]
>>> random.seed(3)
>>> la, lb = [], []
>>> for kk  in range (12):
...     la.append(random.randint(0,  1000))
...     lb.append(random.randint(0,  1000))
...
>>> heapq.heapify(lb)
>>> la, lb                                                  [2]
([881, 237, 155, 948, 399, 15, 795, 163, 980, 43, 798,
843], [31, 154, 65, 535, 308, 687, 888, 776, 605, 650,
759, 886])
>>> heapq.heapreplace(lb, la[0])                            [3]
31
>>> lb
[65, 154, 687, 535, 308, 881, 888, 776, 605, 650, 759,
886]
>>> lc = la[1:]                                             [4]
>>> heapq.heapify(lc)                                       [5]
>>> lc
[15, 43, 163, 237, 155, 795, 948, 980, 399, 798, 843]
>>> ld = list(heapq.merge(lb, lc))                          [6]
>>> ld
[15, 43, 65, 154, 163, 237, 155, 687, 535, 308, 795, 881,
888, 776, 605, 650, 759, 886, 948, 980, 399, 798, 843]
>>> lb, lc
([65, 154, 687, 535, 308, 881, 888, 776, 605, 650, 759,
886], [15, 43, 163, 237, 155, 795, 948, 980, 399, 798,
843])
>>> heapq.heappushpop(lb, 222)                              [7]
65
a1 = [881, 237, 155, 948, 399, 15, 795]                     [8]
>>> heapq.heapify(a1)                                       [9]
>>> a1
[15, 237, 155, 948, 399, 881, 795]

>>> heapq.heapreplace(a1, 12)                               [10]
15
>>> a1                                                      [11]
[12, 237, 155, 948, 399, 881, 795]
>>> heapq.heappushpop(a1, 11)                               [12]
11
>>> a1                                                      [13]
[12, 237, 155, 948, 399, 881, 795]
>>> heapq.nlargest(4, ld)                                   [14]
[980, 948, 888, 886]
```

Fig. 9.13 **a** Python Interpreter sequence illustrating methods with heapq (continued in Fig. 9.13b) **b** Python Interpreter sequence illustrating methods with heapq (continued from Fig. 9.13a)

(b)

```
>>> heapq.nsmallest(4, ld)                                    [15]
[15, 43, 65, 154]
>>>
medals=[(2,'Silver'),(3,'Bronze'),(1,'Gold'),(5,'Next_tria
l'),(4, 'Certificate')]                                       [16]
>>> medals[0] < medals[1]                                     [17]
True
>>> hp = []                                                   [18]
>>> for kk in medals:heapq.heappush(hp, kk)                  [19]
...
>>> heapq.heappop(hp)
(1, 'Gold')
>>> heapq.heappop(hp)
(2, 'Silver')
>>> medals
                                    [20]
[(2, 'Silver'), (3, 'Bronze'), (1, 'Gold'), (5,
'Next_trial'), (4, 'Certificate')]
>>>
```

Fig. 9.13 (continued)

illustration. **medals** in [16] is a set of tuples—each of two elements—a number and a string. The elements of **medals** can be compared as illustrated in [17]. Elements of **medals** have been used to form the heap hp [18, 19] as the two subsequent heapq.heappop(hp) operations show. **medals** remains unaffected [20].

The following observations are in order here:

- Use of heap becomes attractive (compared with the use of a sorted list) when the list is frequently updated and the element having the smallest value called up. Sets of time-stamped tasks calling for prioritizing (using different selection criteria if necessary) are examples. Schedulers are also of this category.
- Any sorted list is a heap but the reverse is not true.

9.6 Exercises

1. Obtain sets of 1000 numbers conforming to each of the distributions in Table 9.1. The parameter values suggested are given in Table 9.4.
   Obtain the frequency distribution in each case with 20 equally spaced intervals. All the numbers beyond a reasonably chosen upper/lower limit(s) may be clubbed together in a single interval.
   In each, extract the statistical information listed in Table 9.2.

Table 9.4 Data for Exercise 1

Distribution	Parameter values
uniform(a, b)	a = 2.0, b = 6.0
triangular(a, c, b)	a = 2.0, b = 6.0
Betavariate(α, ß)	α = 2.0, ß = 5.0
expovariate(a)	Mean = 0.8
gammavariate(α, ß)	α = 5.0, ß = 1.0
gauss(μ, σ)	μ = 1.0, σ = 2.0
Lognomvariate(μ, σ)	μ = 1.0, σ = 2.0
normalvariate(μ, σ)	μ = 1.0, σ = 2.0
Vonmisesvariate(μ, κ)	μ = π, κ = 2.0
Paretovariate(a)	a = 2.0
Weibullvariate(α, ß)	α = 1.0, ß = 5.0

2. A few sentences are reproduced below and assigned to 'SS'. Get the set of words in them. Form a list, a sorted list and a heapq of the set.
SS = "The copper tube lines that carried pneumatic supply and signals were as common in the industry as the electric power supply conduits. With the advent of electronic schemes all these have become things of the past. Quantities which were ignored (gas concentration) and those perceived as not measurable (high temperature) have catapulted and fallen prey to sensors".

3. Form **aa** as a list of 16 random numbers in the range [0.0, 1), all rounded to four digits. Form **bb** as a sorted list from **aa**. Form cc as a heap from **aa**—do these manually.
Continuously pop **bb** and cc. Observe how the list and the heap change.

4. An eatery offers four types of dishes—**d**[0], **d**[1], **d**[2], and **d**[3]. A set of 40 customers line up to buy the dishes. Each customer has his own order of preferences for the dishes. Initially the customers queue up in front of the dish counters—ten at each counter. The sale and queue progress take place at intervals 1, 2, 3, ... set by a counter **Ct**. When **Ct** = 1, the first set of sales takes place; when **Ct** = 2, the second set of sales takes place, and so on. Whenever **Ct** advances a maximum of four customers is allowed to change Queue (customers always observe the status of remaining stock and take decisions accordingly). The change is allowed in the order—last person in the queues for **d**[0], **d**[1], **d**[2], and **d**[3]; the last but one person in the queues for **d**[0], **d**[1], **d**[2], and **d**[3]; and so on.
Assign the dish preferences randomly for the 40 customers—have it as a tuple of numbers for each customer.
Do the necessary program and carry out the following:
Select the persons randomly and fill the four queues initially.
Track the progress of sales, queue movement, and the movement of people.
Give the queue status when one of the items is completely sold off, and when two of them are completely sold off. Identify the people who did maximum number of 'queue jumping' and show their 'queue jumping' history.

5. Write a program to generate test marks data for a class of 30 students in six subjects each in a particular Semester. The subjects are '**b1**', '**b2**', '**b3**', '**b4**', '**b5**', and '**b6**'. The student names are '**s1**', '**s2**', '**s3**', ..., and '**s30**'. In each subject the mark is assigned randomly confirming to Gaussian distribution with a given mean and sigma value set. For the six subjects take these set values as {(70, 15), (60, 12), (75, 8), (65, 11), (75, 9), (70, 14)} respectively. Write a program and generate the marks data for all the students in all the subjects; in each case have the mark score correct to one decimal digit. Store the data in a dictionary with the student's name being the key and the marks obtained forming a corresponding array of six entries each as the value. Use these as the base data to test the programs in the following exercises:

   a. Ten percent of the students fail in each subject. For each subject identify the pass mark.
   b. For each subject get the average mark of the students who have passed.
   c. The students who have passed are to be given grades—'A', 'B', and 'C'— the number getting these grades being in the ratio—1:3:2. The top one sixth of the students who have passed (the integer closest to that) is to be given 'A' grade; the next three sixth (integer closest to that) is to be given 'B' grade. The rest are given 'C' grade. Assign the grades in all the subjects for all the students who have passed. For each student assign the grades tuple of six entries—each entry being 'A', 'B', 'C', or 'F' ('F' signifies failure).
   d. Students who have failed in more than two subjects are to repeat the Semester.
   e. The student who gets maximum number of 'A's is the first rank holder. If this number is more than one use the sum of marks in all the subjects to decide the first rank.

   Write a Python program to do all the above and complete the exercise. All the computed data is to be made available in the form of a dictionary with student's name as the key, marks in all the subjects forming another tuple, 'First rank', 'Repeat semester', or 'semester completed' being an additional entry. All these together as a list should form the value against the key.

6. The annual rainfall in the **n** districts of a state is given for 10 consecutive years. The following data is to be generated:

   a. The annual average rainfall for the state.
   b. If the rainfall in a district exceeds the state average for three consecutive years the district is termed 'rain-fed'.
   c. If the rainfall in a district is below the state average for three consecutive years the district is termed 'rain-deficient'.
   d. If the rainfall in a district for the last 3 years is within $m \pm 0.2\sigma$ – m being the average rainfall for that district in the last 10 years and σ^2 its variance— predict the coming year's rainfall as **p** mm with a 'good confidence level'. In all other districts predict the coming year's rainfall as the last year's itself without an attached confidence level tag.

Write a Python program for all the above computations.

Generate test data with a mean of 600 mm annual rainfall and sigma of 25 mm for six districts for all the 10 years. Run the program for this case and get the results.

7. Let $\{y_0, y_1, y_2, \ldots y_n\}$ be the samples of a function $y(x)$ for x in the interval $a \leq x \leq b$, the samples being at equally spaced intervals of $h = (b - a)/n$. Formulae to different approximations are available to compute the area A bounded by the x-axis between $x = a$, $a = b$ and the curve $y(x)$. Two of the simpler one are given below (Zwillinger 2003):

Trapezoidal Rule:

$$A = (y_0 + 2y_1 + 2y_2 + \cdots 2y_n + y_n)h/2$$

Simpson's Rule:

$$A = (y_0 + 4y_1 + 2y_2 + \cdots 4y_n + y_n)h/3$$

Prepare a program to compute the area using (a) Trapezoidal rule and (b) Simpson's rule.

$\frac{x^2}{p^2} + \frac{y^2}{q^2} = 1$ is the equation of an ellipse in the x–y Plane; its part in the first quadrant is shown in Fig. 9.14. Find the area enclosed by the axes and the ellipse in the first quadrant (shaded area) for $p = 4$ and $q = 3$. Do it for 100 and 1000 as the values of n. The actual area is $\pi pq/4$. Find the percentage error in both the cases.

8. The Monte Carlo method offers a radically different approach to get the area (Guttag 2013). Obtain a sufficiently large number of random points within the area enclosed by $x = a$, $x = b$, $y = 0$, and $y = y_m$ where y_m is the maximum

Fig. 9.14 The first quadrant part of an ellipse

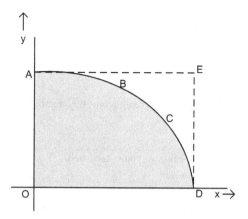

value of y within the interval $[a, b]$ of x (i.e., the rectangle enclosed by the vertical lines at a and b and the horizontal lines at 0 and y_m). If f is the fraction of the points lying within the area of interest $f(b - a)y_m$ is the desired area. The random point (x, y) can be obtained with x as a random number in the interval $[a, b]$ with uniform distribution and y as another random number in the interval $[0, y_m]$ again with uniform distribution. Write a program to get the area using the Monte Carlo method. Estimate the area of the ellipse segment shown in Fig. 9.14; do it with 10,000 and 1,00,000 number of random points. Find the percentage error in both the cases.

9. With $p = q = 1$ in (7) above the ellipse reduces to a circle with unit radius. The area shown in Fig. 9.14 for this case is $\pi/4$. Use this to estimate the value of π; do this with 10,000 and 1,00,000 number of random points. Find the percentage error in both the cases.

10. Ram makes a request to Shyam: Can you please lend me one thousand rupees?

   (a) Shyam's answer has five possible values with probabilities as given in Table 9.5. The answer is to be decided using a random number in the range $\{1, 100\}$ with uniform distribution; if the number is in the range $\{1, 15\}$ the decision is 'A' and so on.

   (b) The decision matrix in Table 9.6 is to be used to decide the answer. Use a random number in the range $\{1, 10\}$ to decide Shyam's mood—he is in good mood if the number is six or less; else he is in bad mood.
   Write programs to generate the answers and test them.

Table 9.5 Shyam's reply probability matrix for Case a

Answer	Percentage probability of answer
A: Yes, I shall give you immediately	15
B: No I am sorry	10
C: Yes, it depend on when you can repay me	30
D: Yes, provided you back it up with a surety	20
E: Yes, give me 12% annual interest	25

Table 9.6 Shyam's reply probability matrix for Case b

Answer	Percentage probability of answer	
	Good mood: 60%	Bad mood: 40%
A: Yes, I shall give you immediately	50	8
B: No I am sorry	8	50
C: Yes, it depend on when you can repay me	15	12
D: Yes, provided you back it up with a surety	12	15
E: Yes, give me 12% annual interest	15	15

11. Sandeep has a farm of 110 coconut trees. The trees are planted in ten rows—the odd rows having eleven trees and the even ones having nine trees. The co-ordinates of the trees in the first row are (0, 0), (0, 2), (0, 4), ..., and (0, 10); the co-ordinates of the trees in the second row are (1, 1), (1, 3), (1, 5), ..., and (0, 9); similarly with other rows. He has assessed the quality of the trees with values one, two, and three assigned to them—based on their age, health, and type of fruit. 35, 35, and 40 numbers of trees have values assigned one, two, and three respectively. He wants to partition the farm into three parts of equal values or at least nearest to that and give to his three sons.

   (a) Select trees randomly and assign quality values one, two, and three to each conforming to the constraint given above.
   (b) The partition is to be done with vertical parting lines. Decide their positions such that the value differences amongst the three partitions are the minimum.
   (c) Do partitions with two parallel lines of unit slope each conforming to the condition in (b) above.
   (d) With diagonally opposite corners of the plot as centres draw circular arcs and do the partition again conforming to the condition in (b) above.

12. *Her Majesty's Judgement*: The Queen in 'Alice in Wonderland' watches the game of Crochet. She doles out judgments at random—'*Cut off his head*', '*Cut off her head*'. We have a more sophisticated queen here lording over a population of 1000. At regular intervals she picks out anyone of her subjects randomly and declares him/ her the accused. The accused is doled out a judgment —selected randomly from a set of four. Implement the scheme and help out the computer savvy queen for the first ten judgments.

13. *Selective Institutional Admissions*: '*Thou shalt obey the rules of the land*', said the Lord of the Land. The Land has two ('disciplined and devoted to The Lord') communities—the '*Elite* (E)' and the '*Committed* (C)'—with 70 and 30% of the population. The Land has a sacred Institution and there is a mad rush for admissions. Every year for the fifty seats in the institution, 10,000 belonging to both the communities apply—all being equally eligible. '*The admissions shalt be proportional and equal injustice be done to all*', had decreed the Lord. The wise elders of both the communities (C and E) evolved the admission procedure as follows:

   The 6,000 applications from the E community be numbered E[0], E[1], E[2], ..., and E[5999]; similarly the 4000 applications of the C community be numbered C[0], C[1], C[2], ..., and C[3999]. Have a basket of 100 balls—70 marked 'E' and the remaining 30 marked 'C'. Pick a ball at random from the basket; if it is marked 'E', pick out a random number from the 6000 E-set and assign a seat to that applicant. Do these 50 times to complete admissions. (The random pickings from the applicants set is to be without replacement.)

14. *Matrix multiplication:* A and B are matrices of sizes $n \times m$ and $m \times n$ respectively. Their product C is a matrix of size $n \times n$ with element c_{ij} given by

$$c_{ij} = \sum_{k=1}^{m} a_{ik}b_{kj}$$

Write a program to get the product of two matrices and test it with specific data generated with matrices of random numbers. Use **arrays** to represent vectors and matrices of numbers.

15. *Solution of matrix equation:* The matrix equation $Ax = b$ with A being an $n \times n$ matrix, and b an n-dimensional vector can be solved for the n unknowns —x—by different methods. '*Gauss Elimination*' is one of the popular methods of solution (Kreyszig 2006). The method is presented as an algorithm here: Form the augmented matrix C of size $n \times (n + 1)$ where

$C_{ij} = a_{ij}$ for all i and $j = 1$ to n
$\quad = b_j$ for all i and $j = n + 1$

For $j = 1$ to $n - 1$
$\quad$ For $k = j + 1$ to n

$$d_{kj} = \frac{c_{kj}}{c_{jj}}$$

$\quad$ For $m = j + 1$ to $n + 1$

$$c_{km} = c_{km} - d_{kj}a_{jm}$$

$$x_n = \frac{c_{n,n+1}}{c_{n,n}}$$

For $j = n - 1$ to 1

$$x_j = \frac{1}{c_{jj}}\left(c_{j,n+1} - \sum_{k=j+1}^{n} a_{j,k}x_k\right)$$

The vector $[x_j]$ forms the solution. Use `arrays` to represent vectors and matrices of numbers.

16. Form the tuple **SS** = 'all quality inner garments'—(display in a shop window) Get the collection of words in **SS**, jumble them, and form different combinations of phrases through a program.

References

Guttag JV (2013) Introduction to computation and programming using Python. MIT Press

Kreyszig E (2006) Advanced engineering mathematics, 9th edn. Wiley, New Jersey

Krishnan V (2006) Probability and random processes. Wiley, New Jersey

van Rossum G, Drake FL Jr (2014) The Python library reference. Python Software Foundation

Zwillinger D (ed) (2003) Standard mathematical tables and formulae. Chapman & Hall/CRC, New York

Chapter 10
Classes and Objects

Various types of data/information representation and operations involving them have been dealt with so far. With a good grasp of all these, one is in a position to develop programs and use them to get desired output and information. Such programs are useful to do intensive numerical work, format/rearrange text based information, and so on. Such programming is called '*functional programming*'. In functional programming a number of functions are executed in a linear sequence with appropriate (conditional) branching.

The functional programming approach becomes tedious and often unwieldy for many of the ambitious and comprehensive computational applications of today. The following are typical of such situations:

- A university with a number of faculties, members of the faculty, programs offered, students, administration, and the like.
- A manufacturing organization with its stake holders and their respective interests, operational entities like financing, materials management, 'Works' carrying out manufacturing, quality assurance, packing and dispatch, marketing, warehousing, and distribution.
- Train control in Railways: trains with different routes and schedules, co-ordination with different sections, management of unexpected delays and emergencies.
- Organizing and running an e-business—its access and update, its security, servicing customers, warehouse management, website and its management.
- Live streaming of a cricket/soccer match: streaming from multiple video cameras, playback in slow motion, extract meaningful information, and display the same, co-ordinate ad displays.

In situations like the above a functional programming approach will be quite demanding in terms of programming and debugging efforts. Each application above is of a 'class'—wherever the application is, it fits into a common pattern. The program calls for the use of different types of modules and their coordinated functioning. A program developed for one instance—a framework—can fit for all

© Springer Nature Singapore Pte Ltd. 2016
T.R. Padmanabhan, *Programming with Python*,
DOI 10.1007/978-981-10-3277-6_10

cases. The framework program will have various sub-programs—all properly defined and interconnected. Once developed and debugged the program can be used repeatedly by suitably changing the interface. The concepts of *class* and *object* in Python (as well as in other languages like C++, Java) are aimed at facilitating development of such large programs.

10.1   Objects

In Python any entity which has a name (identity) assigned to it is an 'object' (van Rossum and Drake 2014). It can be an integer, a number (real or complex), a list, a string, a function, and so on. There is no restriction on it. Further one does not have to formally declare the type of entity before assignment. Python does it and adapts itself on the fly—transparent to the user. Every object in Python has its own id (Identity)—a number representing its address in the memory. Consider the Python Interpreter sequence in Fig. 10.1 which brings out the basic characteristics of objects. With the assignment **a** = 3 in [1] Python understands **a** to be an integer and assigns the numerical value 3 to it. These are evident from [2] and [3] respectively. Further the id (**a**) in [4] signifies its specific identification (address) in memory. **b** = **a** in [5] declares **b** as another quantity identical to **a**. In Python **b** is essentially another tag/name for the given quantity (object) with id (8978848). In other words '**a**' and '**b**' are two different name tags for the same entity. [6] clarifies this. '**b**' is assigned a different value in [7] and it acquires a different identity—it has become a different object (though of the same type). [7], [8], and [9] confirm this. '**b**' is assigned the numerical value 3.0 in [10]. '**b**' is no longer an integer. It is a different object with a different identity [11]. However '**a**' remains the integer object committed earlier. '**c**' in [12] is a list of assorted items. With **d** = **c** in [13] d is another name tag for this list object. **d**[2] = 4 + 3*j* in [14] changes an element in the list. The change is reflected in **c** as well. **c** and **d** have the same identity [15] and they point to the same object. The list **d** has been given a fresh assignment in [16]— a tuple of two items in it. **d** is now a different (type of) object—as can be verified from the ids of **c** and **d** [17].

10.2   Classes

A class is a user defined prototype of an object. The features, versatility, and flexibility of classes are brought out progressively here. Appropriate illustrative examples are interspersed at each stage. The listing of a simple class—**Teacher**— is reproduced in Fig. 10.2a. It is in the module—school.py. We would like to build up a more comprehensive class for a school here; the present one is a step in this direction.

```
>>> a = 3                                                  [1]
>>> type(a)                                                [2]
<class 'int'>
>>> a                                                      [3]
3
>>> id(a)                                                  [4]
8978848
>>> b = a                                                  [5]
>>> id(b)                                                  [6]
8978848
>>> b = 5                                                  [7]
>>> a, id(a)                                               [8]
(3, 8978848)
>>> id(b)                                                  [9]
8978912
>>> b = 3.0                                                [10]
>>> id(b)                                                  [11]
140381507170688
>>> c = [2, 5.0, 3-4j, 'cc']                               [12]
>>> d = c                                                  [13]
>>> d[2] = 4+3j                                            [14]
>>> c, d
([2, 5.0, (4+3j), 'cc'], [2, 5.0, (4+3j), 'cc'])
>>> id(c), id(d)                                           [15]
(140381505950728, 140381505950728)
>>> d = (9.0, b*b)                                         [16]
>>> id(c), id(d)                                           [17]
(140381505950728, 140381505950600)
>>>
```

Fig. 10.1 Python Interpreter sequence to bring out the basic features of objects

A class definition—like Teacher—typically comprises of the following:

- 'Class Teacher:' is the first statement of the definition [1]. The full definition follows this in an indented suite of statements that follow. Here **Teacher** is the name of the class. It is customary to capitalize a class name and we have conformed to this.
- The first statement in the suite is a string—normally describing briefly the scope of the class [2]. This string can be accessed as '**Teacher**.__doc__'; in general the access is through ClassName.__doc__.
- The rest of the suite of statements within the class definition is of two types:
  - Statements where variables are defined and assigned values. **tchn** = 0 in [3] is an example. **tchn** is a class variable (with a zero value assigned). A class, in general, may have nil, one or more such class variables.

(a)

```
class Teacher:                                        [1]
  "Teacher information"                               [2]
  tchn = 0                                            [3]
  def __init__(self, nm, ag):                         [4]
      self.name = nm                                  [5]
      self.age = ag                                   [6]
      print('New teacher with name: {} & of age:
{}'.format(self.name, self.age))
      Teacher.tchn += 1                               [7]

  def  Th_cnt(self):                                  [8]
      "Give number of teachers on roll"
      if Teacher.tchn > 1:print('{} Teachers are on the
rolls'.format(Teacher.tchn))
      elif Teacher.tchn == 1:print('There is only one
teacher on the rolls')
      else: print('There is no teacher on the rolls')
```

(b)

```
>>> import school
>>> t1 = school.Teacher('Rakesh', 31)                [9]
New teacher with name: Rakesh & of age: 31
>>> t2 = school.Teacher('Ramya', 24)                 [10]
New teacher with name: Ramya & of age: 24
>>> t3 = school.Teacher('Shyama', 32)                [11]
New teacher with name: Shyama & of age: 32
>>> t4 = school.Teacher('Harini', 35)                [12]
New teacher with name: Harini & of age: 35
>>> t1.tchn                                          [13]
4
>>> t1.tchn, t2.tchn, t3.tchn, t4.tchn               [14]
(4, 4, 4, 4)
>>> id(t1.tchn),id(t2.tchn),id(t3.tchn),id(t4.tchn)  [15]
(8978880, 8978880, 8978880, 8978880)
>>> t1.tchn = 5                                      [16]
>>> id(t1.tchn),id(t2.tchn),id(t3.tchn),id(t4.tchn)  [17]
(8978912, 8978880, 8978880, 8978880)
>>> t4.age                                           [18]
35
>>> t4.age = 36                                      [19]
>>> t4.age
36
>>> t1.Th_cnt()                                      [20]
4 Teachers are on the rolls
```

Fig. 10.2 **a** Definition of Teacher as a class **b** details of instantiation of class Teacher

- A number of functions which are valid and used within the class are also defined within the suite. Each such function is a 'method' belonging to the class.

A class is said to 'encapsulate' the data and methods applicable to it. The variables and methods belonging to a class are its 'attributes'. They are accessed using the 'dot' convention.

- The method defined as __init__(self. **nm**, **ag**) [4] is a special method of the class. It initializes the object created. In the specific case here it has three arguments. nm, and ag are the arguments specified/supplied at the time of the object formation. 'self' is a dummy argument. It represents the object itself. Although any name can be used to signify this, self is the widely used (and accepted) name for it. The '__init__()' method definition can occur anywhere within the class definition; but it is customary to keep it as the first method in line with its uniqueness/significance.
- With **Teacher** .__init__() defines two variables—self.**name** and self.**age**—and assigns values to them as **nm** [5] and **ag** [6]. Then the name and the type of the object are printed out. Following this the teacher count (**tchn**) is incremented by one [7].
- The class **Teacher** has one more method defined within it—**th_cnt**(self) [8]. If called, the method prints out the number of Teachers in a convenient format.
  complex, list, tuple, dict, & c are all available classes in Python representing built-in data types. A user defined class creates a new data type—a customer-defined data type which can be used along with the available ones.

10.2.1   Instantiation

Different objects conforming to the class Teacher can be formed by direct assignment. The module school has been imported in Fig. 10.2b. The assignment t1 = **School.Teacher**('**Rakesh**', 31) in [9] results in the formation of an object **t1** conforming to the class '**Teacher**'. The arguments here—their type, number and order have to be the same as used in the __init__() method defined within the class definition discussed above. **t1** is referred as an 'instance' of class **Teacher** and the process of its formation is 'instantiation'. The __init__() method is automatically executed as part of the instantiation. Whenever a class is invoked to create an instance, the arguments given are passed on to the __init__() method in it. The method (in the specific case here) has four executable statements; referring to the class definition of **Teacher** in Fig. 10.2a their execution results in the following:

- [5] results in a new variable **t1.name** being generated and the string —'**Rakesh**'—being assigned to it. Here **t1** automatically take the place of self.

- In line with [6] another variable **t1.age** is generated and **ag** (the integer value = 31) is assigned to it. Here again **t1** takes the place of self.
- A string involving **t1.name** and **t1.age** is formed and printed out; the line following [9] in the figure confirms this.
- **Teacher.tchn** is incremented in [7]. This has two ramifications: Access and assignment of variable **Teacher.tchn** implies that a class variable is accessed and incremented. Further **t1** being an instance of the class **Teacher**, the variable appears as **t1.tchn** and automatically it is incremented.

Three additional objects of class **Teacher**—**t2**, **t3**, and **t4**—are formed in [10], [11], and [12] respectively—all similar to **t1**; each has an assigned name and age respectively. **t1**, **t2**, **t3**, and **t4**—the objects conforming to the same class—**Teacher** —are additional instances of the class **Teacher**. All the four objects—**t1**, **t2**, **t3**, and **t4**—formed here are identical in structure and properties—characterized by the variables and methods associated with them. All conform to the class **Teacher**.

t1.tchn in [13] is a variable (again an object) and represents the value of **tchn** of the instance **t1**. It has been accessed in [13] and it can be seen to have the value 4 —being the total count of the objects of class **Teacher** at this stage. The values of **t1.tchn**, **t2.tchn**, **t3.tchn**, and **t4.tchn** are accessed and reproduced [14]. **tchn** is a class variable. Whenever a new instance of **Teacher** is created, it is accessed within __init__() through **Teacher** and **tchn** updated. As such **t1.tchn**, **t2. tchn**, **t3.tchn**, and **t4.tchn** are different names for the same object. This is evident from [15] where the respective ids (=8978880) are accessed and displayed. **t1.tchn** alone is accessed separately and its value changed in [16]. It has become a different variable as can be seen by comparing its new id (=8978912) with those of **t2.tchn**, **t3.tchn**, and **t4.tchn** (=8978880) as done in [17]. **t4.name** and **t4.age** are two attributes specific to the instance **t4**. **t4.age** has been accessed [18] and changed from 35—assigned during instantiation—to 36 [19]. It confirms that the instance variables can be accessed and changed anytime (as is with the common class attribute/variable **.tchn**) provided the proper syntax is stuck to.

Teacher has one more method defined within it—**th_cnt**() [8]. It takes self as its only argument and outputs a statement showing the number of objects of class **Teacher**. **t1.th_cnt**() in [20] executes this method and displays the total number of teachers on the role. In general any method defined in a class has self as its first argument; it stands for the instance on which it is called to operate.

Student is another class defined within the module school; its listing is reproduced in Fig. 10.3a. It is similar to the teacher class. It has three attributes: the class attribute **stdn**, the method __init()__, and a second method—**st_cnt**(). Four students have been instantiated as **s1**, **s2**, **s3**, and **s4** (in [2], [3], [4], and [5]) in Fig. 10.3b. The student count has been accessed subsequently—as **s1.stdn** in [6]—and confirmed as 4. The instance method—**s1.St_cnt**() prints the current value of the number of students on the rolls in a specified format. It has been accessed and displayed in [7].

As mentioned earlier the variables and method definitions within a class are known as 'attributes' of the class. (In Python any quantity bb accessible as **aa.bb** is

(a)

```
class Student:                                          [1]
  "Student information"
  stdn = 0
  def __init__(self, nm, ag):
    self.name = nm
    self.age = ag
    print('New Student with name: {} & of age:
{}'.format(self.name, self.age))                        [2]
      Student.stdn += 1
  def St_cnt(self):                                     [3]

    "Give number of students on roll"
    if Student.stdn > 1:print('{} students are on the
rolls'.format(Student.stdn))
    elif Student.stdn == 1:print('There is only one
student on the rolls')
    else: print('There is no student on the rolls')
```

(b)

```
>>> from demo_9 import school                           [1]
>>> s1 = school.Student('Maria', 18)                    [2]
New Student with name: Maria & of age: 18
>>> s2 = school.Student('Adarsh', 19)                   [3]
New Student with name: Adarsh & of age: 19
>>> s3 = school.Student(' Rana', 17)                    [4]
New Student with name: Rana & of age: 17
>>> s4 = school.Student('Latha', 20)                    [5]
New Student with name: Latha & of age: 20
>>> s1.stdn                                             [6]
4
>>> s1.St_cnt()                                         [7]
4 students are on the rolls
>>> school.Teacher.__doc__                              [8]
'Teacher information'
>>> school.Teacher.__name__                             [9]
'Teacher'
>>> school.Student.__name__
        [10]
' Student'
>>> t1.__dict__
      [11]
{'tchn': 5, 'name': 'Rakesh', 'age': 31}
>>> t1.__class__
      [12]
<class 'demo_9.school.Teacher'>
```

Fig. 10.3 **a** Definition of Student as a class **b** Details of instantiation of class Student

an attribute of **aa**.) Variables **stdn** and tchn are attributes of the classes **Student** and **Teacher** respectively. The methods **st_cnt** and **th_cnt** in **Student** and **Teacher** respectively are also attributes of the respective classes. **t1**.**name** and **t1**. **age** are assigned within the instance of **t1**. They are attributes of instance **t1**; same is true of **t2.name**, **t2.age**, **t3.name**, **t3.age**, **t4.name**, and **t4.age** also.

The attributes mentioned above are 'acquired' by the class or instance concerned by virtue of the class definition. Apart from these every class has a set of built-in attributes which store the basic information regarding the class. These are all of the 'read only' type and cannot be altered during access. All these have the form __xx__. As mentioned earlier __doc__ returns the 'docstring' (acronym for 'Document string') of the class if it is present. Thus **School.Teacher**.__doc__ in [8] returns the string—'Teacher information' which is the docstring of the class **Teacher** ([2] in Fig. 10.2). .__name__ returns the name of the class as in [9] and [10]. The attributes of an instance and their values are stored as a dictionary within. The same can be accessed to know the status of the instance. t1.__dict__ in [11] returns all the attributes of t1 and the respective assigned values. .__class__ returns the source information of the class to which the instance belongs [12]. A few more built-in attributes are available; they are discussed later.

A user-defined variable within a class whose name starts with two or more underscores has a special status in Python. It is 'protected'—in the sense that it cannot be accessed from outside for reading or modification. The class **Pupil** in the module school is reproduced in Fig. 10.4; it is similar to the class Student. An instance of **Pupil** has a tag associated with it (in addition to the name and age). It is .**__rating** [2]. It is assigned a value as part of initialization; but **__rating** is not visible outside. The **__rating** is 20 if the **Pupil**'s name is '**Sandhya**', else it is 10 (one way of rating pupils!). Two instances of class **Pupil** (**p1** and p2) have been created in the Python Interpreter sequence in Fig. 10.4 [4] and [5]. **Renu** [4] is assigned a rating of 10 while **Sandhya** [5] is assigned a rating of 20 as can be seen from [6] and [7]. Attempt to access **p1**.**__rating** in [8] returns an attribute error confirming its inaccessibility. **p1**.**__dict__** in [9] returns a dictionary with all the attributes of p1 and their assigned values. **p1**.**__rating** does not appear here stressing its inaccessibility.

The method .__str__() returns a printable string [3]. In the specific case here it is a formatted string giving out the name and the roll number of the **Pupil**. print (**p2**) directly prints out the string [10]. This is a convenient way of providing any key information about the instance. **p1.mm** = 80 (marks obtained by **Renu** in Maths) in [11] introduces a new attribute exclusively for the instance **p1** and assigns the value 80 for it. **mm** as an attribute has been added exclusively to **p1** but not to any other instance of the class **Pupil**. In turn **p1**.__dict__ is also updated (transparent to the user). The same is confirmed from the following line where **p1**. __dict__ has been accessed again and shown [12].

```
class Pupil:                                                 [1]
    'Pupil information'
    pln = 0
    def  __init__(self, nm, ag):
        self.name = nm
        self.age = ag
        if nm == 'Sathya':self.__rating = 20               [2]
        else:self.__rating = 10
        Pupil.pln += 1
    def  info(self):
        print('New entrant:{} of age:{} rated
{}'.format(self.name, self.age, self.__rating))
    def  Pl_cnt(self):
        "Give number of pupils on roll"
        if Pupil.pln > 1:print('{} pupils are on the
rolls'.format(Pupil.pln))
        elif Pupil.pln == 1:print('There is only one pupil
on the rolls')
        else: print('There is no pupil on the rolls')
    def __str__(self): return '{} is the {}th pupil in the
school'.format(self.name,Pupil.pln)                        [3]
>>> from demo_9 import school

>>> p1 = school.Pupil('Renu', 28)                          [4]
>>> p2 = school.Pupil('Sathya', 29)                        [5]
>>> p1.info()                                              [6]
New entrant:Renu of age:28 rated 10
>>> p2.info()                                              [7]
New entrant:Sathya of age:29 rated 20
>>> p1.__rating                                            [8]
Traceback (most recent call last):
  File "<stdin>", line 1, in <module>
AttributeError: 'Pupil' object has no attribute '__rating'
>>> p1.__dict__                                            [9]
{'name': 'Renu', 'age': 28, '_Pupil__rating': 10}
>>> print(p2)                                              10]
Sathya is the 2th pupil in the school
>>> p1.mm = 80                                             [11]
>>> p1.__dict__                                            [12]
{'age': 28, 'name': 'Renu', 'mm': 80, '_Pupil__rating':
10}
```

Fig. 10.4 Python Interpreter sequence to illustrate the special status of instance variables with two leading underscores in their names

10.3   Functions with Attributes

A set of functions available with objects relate to their attributes directly. getattr (**O**, '**n**') returns the value of attribute '**n**' of the object **O**. Here **O** can be an instance of a class. Figure 10.5 is a continuation of the Python Interpreter sequence in

Fig. 10.5 Python Interpreter sequence to illustrate the use of attribute related functions

```
>>> getattr(p1,'age')                        [1]
28
>>> setattr(p1,'branch', 'EEE')              [2]
>>> p1.branch                                [3]
'EEE'
>>> hasattr(p1, 'branch')                    [4]
True
>>> hasattr(p2,'branch')                      [5]
False
>>> delattr(p1, 'branch')                     [6]
>>> hasattr(p1, 'branch')                     [7]
False
class Guru:                                   [8]
        'Salute the Guru'
        pass
>>> school.Guru.__doc__                       [9]
'Salute the Guru'
>>> g1 = school.Guru()                        [10]
>>> g1.name = 'Uma'                           [11]
>>> g2 = school.Guru()                        [12]
>>> hasattr(g1, 'name')                       [13]
True
>>> hasattr(g2, 'name')                       [14]
False
>>> g2.name = 'Rama'                          [15]
>>> hasattr(g2, 'name')                       [16]
True
```

Fig. 10.4. getattr(**p1**, '**age**') [1] returns the value of **p1.age**. In fact getattr (**p1**, '**age**') is essentially an alternative for **p1.age**. setattr(**O**, '**n**', **v**) sets the value of attribute **O.n** to **v** if **n** is already an attribute of **O**. If '**n**' is not an existing attribute of **O**, such a new attribute will be created and **v** assigned as its value. setattr(**p1**, '**branch**', '**EEE**') [2] adds the attribute '**branch**' to the object **p1** and assigns the value '**EEE**' (string) to it. The same is confirmed in [3] which outputs **p1.branch**. hasattr(**O**, '**n**') checks for the presence of attribute '**n**' for the object **O**. True or False is returned depending on whether the attribute is present or not. The query hasattr(**p1**, '**branch**') [4] returns 'True' confirming the presence of such an attribute. But **p2** does not possess this attribute as can be seen from [5]. delattr(**p1**, '**branch**') in [6] deletes the specified attribute for the instance **p1**. A fresh query hasattr(**p1**, '**branch**') in [7] returns 'False' confirming this.

All the above four attribute related functions allow attributes to be created, modified, or deleted as the case may be, for the selected object (instance of the class here). Other instances of the class remain untouched.

10.4   **pass** : **Place Holder**

pass statement in Python does not signify any operation. It is a place holder when a statement is mandatory but no code need be executed. It is useful to assign attributes to class instances dynamically. **Guru** in **school** (reproduced in Fig. 10.5) is a class without any executable code in it [8]. **school.Guru.__doc__** [9] returns the docstring of **Guru**. **g1** in [10] is an instance of **Guru**. A new attribute **g1.name** is created and 'Uma' (string) assigned to it [11]. **g2** is another instance of **Guru** [12]. [13] shows that name is an attribute of **g1** but **g2** is not endowed with this attribute [14]. However a subsequent allocation of a name to **g2** [15] is confirmed in [16]. This emphasizes the possibility of dynamic creation and enhancement of individual instances of a class.

Two additional examples for classes are considered here to stress the variety possible. The module 'padha' has a class—**Mishram**—defined in it (Fig. 10.6). It accepts two arguments—**xx**, **yy**,—evaluates an assorted set of functions involving them, and assigns the results to a tuple. From the nature of the functions here one can see that both the arguments are to be numbers; the set—**x**, **y** (=0.2, 4.2)—has been taken as the argument set [1] in the Python Interpreter sequence in Fig. 10.7 and a1 is instantiated as an object of class **Mishram** [2]. [3] confirms this. **a1.xy** has been output in [4];

The instance **a2** of **Mishram** in [5] has complex numbers as arguments. In turn elements of **a2.xy** in [6] are also complex. As with all operators, functions & c., in Python, the type of argument need not be specified separately. But the need to use argument types consistent with the operations remains.

padha.Mishram1 (Fig. 10.6) is another class with two string arguments—**xx**, **yy**—as inputs. It prints out a string involving two objects (**x1** and **x2**). **x1** is a concatenated string; **x2** is the 'greater' of the two strings (Vide Sect. 6.3). **a3** in Fig. 10.7 is an instance of **Padha.Mishram** [8] with 'VidyaLavanya' and

```
class Mishram:
    "return assorted functions"
    def __init__(self, xx, yy):
        self.xy = (xx*xx, 1.0/xx, xx/yy, xx+yy)

class Mishram1:
    "Play with strings"
    def __init__(self, xx, yy):
        self.x1 = xx + '--' + yy
        self.x2 = xx if xx > yy else yy
    def opt(self):
        print ('The combined string is: ', self.x1, ':
The boss is:', self.x2)
```

Fig. 10.6 Definitions of two classes to illustrate the varieties possible in the methods

```
>>> x1, y1 = 2.0, 4.2                                              [1]
>>> a1 = padha.mishram(x1, y1)                                     [2]
>>> a1
<demo_10.padha.mishram object at 0x7f6aa8ce5080>                   [3]
>>> a1.xy                                                          [4]
(4.0, 0.5, 0.47619047619047616, 6.2)
>>> a2 = padha.mishram(1+2j, 2.0-3j)                               [5]
>>> a2.xy                                                          [6]
((-3+4j), (0.2-0.4j), (-
0.30769230769230776+0.5384615384615384j), (3-1j))
>>> s1, s2 = 'Vidhya Lavanya', 'Salija'                            [7]
>>> a3 = padha.mishram1(s1, s2)                                    [8]
>>> a3.opt()                                                       [9]
The combined string is:  Vidhya Lavanya--Salija :   The
boss is: Vidhya Lavanya
```

Fig. 10.7 Python Interpreter sequence to illustrate use of classes in Fig. 10.5

'**Salija**' as the arguments. The printed output is in [9] ('**VidyaLavanya**' becomes the boss thanks to the fact that 'V..' > 'S..').

10.5   Overloading

When a class is defined in Python it is possible to define methods within it where any of the basic operations can be reinterpreted to suit the local environment. Conceptually the redefined role of the operator constitutes an emulation of the operator to suit the local environment. Such a redefinition of the operator function is known as '*overloading*' in Object Oriented Programming parlance.

A set of routines and interpreter sequences are considered here to illustrate the overloading of the operators. The examples are often contrived in nature—done more to illustrate the overloading aspect.

The class **vng** [1] in Fig. 10.8 accepts a vector as an argument and returns a vector—with all the component values negated (signs changed). def__neg__(self) in [2] achieves this by negating the individual elements successively and forming a new vector. **v1** in the Python Interpreter sequence in Fig. 10.9 has been defined as a vector with four components—the component values being given as respective numbers. **v1n** (Fig. 10.9) in [2] is an instance of **vng**—'-**vng**' in [3] outputs the negated vector. The '-' operator—preceding '**v1n**' here signifies the overloaded role of '-'.

Use of '__neg__' in [2] (Fig. 10.8) signifies the overloading of the operator. In a similar manner __abs__, __complex__, and __int__ stand for overloading of the functions—abs(), complex(), and int() respectively.

```
class vng:                                              [1]
    "Return the negative of a vector"
    def __init__(self, xx):
        self.xa = xx
    def __neg__(self):                                  [2]
        yy = []
        for hh in self.xa: yy.append(-hh)
        return yy
class vng_n:                                            [3]
    "Return the norm of a vector - sum of abs. values of
components"
    def __init__(self, xx):
        self.xa = xx
    def __abs__(self):                                  [4]
        yy = []
        for hh in self.xa: yy.append(abs(hh))
        return sum(yy)
class vng_x:                                            [5]
    "Return the bytes pair as a complex number"
    def __init__(self, xx):
        self.xa = xx
    def __complex__(self):                              [6]
        return complex(int(self.xa[0], base = 16),
int(self.xa[1], base = 16))
class vng_i:                                            [7]
    "Return the integer equivalent of the bytes in
specified base"
    def __init__(self, xx):
        self.xa = xx
    def __int__(self):                                  [8]
        return int(self.xa[0], base = self.xa[1])
```

Fig. 10.8 Overloading examples (single argument)

Vng_n [3] (Fig. 10.8) has been defined to give $\sum_i |x_i|$ as the output (l^1 norm in vectors). **v1am** ([4] in Fig. 10.9) is an instance of class **vng_n**. abs(**v1am**) $(1.2 + 2.3 + 3 + 4 + 5.7 = 16.2)$ [5] gives the value of the norm. **vng_x** [5] in Fig. 10.8 accepts two numbers as bytes objects, converts them into respective integers to base 16 [6] and returns a complex number with these as its real and imaginary parts. **v2** ([6] in Fig. 10.9) is a pair of bytes (171, 205) objects. **V2_x** [7] is an instance of **vng_x(v2)**. complex(**v2_x**) [8] returns the corresponding complex number.

The class **vng_i** [7] in Fig. 10.8 accepts a bytes object and an integer (range 0–35) as a tuple argument and returns the bytes object as an integer to the base of the integer—the second element of the tuple [8]. **v3** [9] in Fig. 10.9 is a tuple —bytes object (b'**tmf01**') and an integer (=30) combined. **v3_i** is an instance of **vng_i** with **v3** as its argument. int(**v3_i**) [10] is the corresponding integer value. Its value is confirmed by direct evaluation in [11].

```
>>> from demo_10 import padha_b
>>> v1 = (1.2, -2.3, -3, 4, 5.7)                              [1]
>>> v1n = padha_b.vng(v1)                                     [2]
>>> -v1n                                                      [3]
[-1.2, 2.3, 3, -4, -5.7]
>>> v1am = padha_b.vng_n(v1)                                  [4]
>>> abs(v1am)                                                 [5]
16.2
>>> v2 = (b'ab', b'cd')                                       [6]
>>> v2_x = padha_b.vng_x(v2)                                  [7]
>>> complex(v2_x)                                             [8]
(171+205j)
>>> v3 = (b'tmf01', 30)                                       [9]
>>> v3_i = padha_b.vng_i(v3)
>>> int(v3_i)                                                 [10]
24097501
>>> 29*(30**4)+22*(30**3)+15*(30**2)+1                        [11]
24097501
>>> v4 = ((b'mna1', 25), (b'obc7', 25))                       [12]
>>> v4_x = complex(int(padha_b.vng_i(v4[0])),
int(padha_b.vng_i(v4[1])))                                   [13]
>>> v4_x                                                      [14]
(358376+382182j)
>>> complex(int(v4[0][0], v4[0][1]),int(v4[1][0],
v4[1][1])) [15]
(358376+382182j)
```

Fig. 10.9 Python Interpreter sequence to illustrate overloading with classes in Python (Single argument)

v4([12] in Fig. 10.9) is a tuple of two bytes-type integers. Each set has been converted into a corresponding integer by instantiation in [13]; the pair has been again converted into a corresponding complex number [14]. Confirmation the conversion has been done in [15] directly using int() function itself.

The overloading discussed thus far pertains to operands with single arguments. Similar overloading is possible with operands involving multiple arguments also. A set of examples are considered to illustrate their use. The program—**vct2**—and the relevant Python Interpreter sequence are in Figs. 10.10 and 10.11 respectively. Class **vc2** in Fig. 10.10 [1] accepts arguments—**x1**, **x2**, and **x3**—a set of three numbers being components of a vector. They are assigned to components **c1**, **c2**, and **c3**. __add__(self, ott) is defined as a method which accepts two such vectors—self and ott (signifies 'other') as arguments [2] and the set of three sums is returned as vector. These two tasks together constitutes the __add__()

```
class vct2:                                                    [1]
   "Vector operations - overloading operators"
   def __init__(self, x1, x2, x3):self.c1, self.c2, self.c3
= x1, x2, x3
   def __add__(self, ott):                                     [2]
      return (self.c1+ott.c1, self.c2+ott.c2,
self.c3+ott.c3)
   def __mul__(self, ott):                                     [3]
      return  self.c1*ott.c1 + self.c2*ott.c2 +
self.c3*ott.c3
   def __sub__(self, ott):                                     [4]
      return (self.c1-ott.c1, self.c2-ott.c2, self.c3-
ott.c3)
   def __truediv__(self, ott):                                 [5]
      return (self.c1/ott.c1, self.c2/ott.c2,
self.c3/ott.c3)
   def __floordiv__(self, ott):                                [6]
      return (self.c1//ott.c1, self.c2//ott.c2,
self.c3//ott.c3)
   def __mod__(self, ott):                                     [7]
      return (self.c1%ott.c1, self.c2%ott.c2,
self.c3%ott.c3)
   def __divmod__(self, ott):                                  [8]
      return (divmod(self.c1,ott.c1),
divmod(self.c2,ott.c2), divmod(self.c3,ott.c3))
   def __pow__(self, ott):                                     [9]
      return (pow(self.c1,ott.c1), pow(self.c2,ott.c2),
pow(self.c3,ott.c3))
```

Fig. 10.10 Overloading examples (multiple arguments)

method within **vct2**. In the Python Interpreter sequence in Fig. 10.11 **dd** (3.3, −4.4, 1.1) [1] and **ee** (−2.3, 3.1, 4.3) [2] represent two such vectors. **ff = dd + ee** in [3] signifies vector addition as defined in __add__. The sum vector (1.0, −1.3000000000000003, 5.4) is returned as [3].

Multiplication, substraction, true-division, floor division, mod operation, and power are successively defined in a similar manner as __mul__, __sub__, __truediv__, __floor__, __mod__, and __pow__ respectively in **vct2**. They correspond to '*', '−', '/', '//', '%', and '**' respectively. The operations **dd * ee**, **dd − ee**, **ee/ff**, **ee//ff**, **ee%ff**, and **gg ** hh** have been carried out conforming to these (Fig. 10.11). The vector components of **ee, ff, gg**, and **hh** have been taken as integers here. (**gg ** hh** in 'vector form' as defined here does not make sense—the same has been done here more as an exercise to highlight the overloading of the pow() operator).

Methods of the form '**__XYZ__**' are predefined in Python ('*special methods*'). In a class being created, any of these special methods can be defined to suit the context. Conversely one need not define a new method like '**__XYZ__**' but use one

```
>>> dd = padha_c.vct2(3.3, -4.4, 1.1)              [1]
>>> ee = padha_c.vct2(-2.3, 3.1, 4.3)              [2]
>>> ff = dd + ee                                   [3]
>>> ff
(1.0, -1.300000000000003, 5.4)
>>> hh = dd*ee                                      [4]
>>> hh
-16.5
>>> cc = padha_c.vct2(9.8, 8.7, -6.5)              [5]
>>> dd = padha_c.vct2(1.3, -2.4, -6.4)             [6]
>>> cc - dd                                         [7]
(8.5, 11.1, -0.09999999999999964)
>>> cc/dd                                           [8]
(7.538461538461538, -3.625, 1.015625)
>>> ee = padha_c.vct2(-22, 33, 44)                 [9]
>>> ff = padha_c.vct2(7, 9, 11)                    [10]
>>> ee/ff                                           [11]
(-3.142857142857143, 3.6666666666666665, 4.0)
>>> ee//ff                                          [12]
(-4, 3, 4)
>>> ee%ff                                           [13]
(6, 6, 0)
>>> divmod(ee,ff)                                   [14]
((-4, 6), (3, 6), (4, 0))
>>> gg = padha_c.vct2(7, 8, 9)                     [15]
>>> hh = padha_c.vct2(4, 3, 2)                     [16]
>>> gg**hh                                          [17]
(2401, 512, 81)
```

Fig. 10.11 Python Interpreter sequence to illustrate overloading with classes in Python (Two arguments)

available with necessary definition. All the 'overloading' examples discussed above are of this category.

10.5.1   Overloading in Basic Python

The concepts of classes, their instances, and objects are all basic to Python. Assignments like **x** = 4, **y** = x^2, **z** = 'sat', **zz** = '**Gamaya**' automatically take **x**, **y**, **z** as objects. All operations which make sense and are valid are interpreted suitably. The following (typical) operations and their interpretations are to be viewed in this light.

$$\mathbf{xx} = x * x$$
$$\mathbf{x2} = x + 2$$
$$\mathbf{xy} = 4 + y \left(= 4 + x^2 = 20\right)$$
$$\mathbf{xsx} = z * 4 = \mathbf{SatSatSatSat}$$
$$\mathbf{xpzz} = \text{`Sat} + \text{''} + \text{`Gamaya'} \left(= \mathbf{Sat\,Gamaya}\right)$$

Python automatically adapts and interprets operations '+', '*', and the like to suit the context (overloading when necessary). But attempts to use the operators as below (subtracting, dividing, or multiplying strings) do not make sense. Hence they are not valid (in Python) either.

$$\mathbf{zmzz} = z - zz$$
$$\mathbf{zdzz} = z/zz$$
$$\mathbf{xsz} = 4 * z$$
$$\mathbf{xdzz} = x/zz$$

10.6 Inheritance

Inheritance is an important and useful feature that goes with classes. It pertains to a class ('child') having another class as an argument ('parent'); the child class implicitly inherits the attributes of the parent class. This obviates the need for redefining/assigning values for these attributes.

The listing of class **Admn_a (Student)** is reproduced in Fig. 10.12. It defines a class **Admn_a**. **Admn_a** has the class **Student** (listed in Fig. 10.3) as its sole argument. Such a class definition inherently implies that **Admn_a** inherits class **Student**. With this the attributes of **Student**—variables as well as methods— become accessible from within Admn_a. The suite of class **Admn_a** in Fig. 10.12 (from module school) and the related Python Interpreter sequence in Fig. 10.13 bring out the key features of giving shape to inheritance and using them. **Admn_a** has been set to keep track of details of **Student** instances and the branches of study allotted to them. '*Administrator of school*' is the docstring of **Admn_a**. **rgstr1** carries the basic Student branch registration details in a dictionary form. '**CE**', '**EE**', and '**ME**' are the three designated branches. keys and the associated values as integers represent the number of students with each specific branch allotted. For a student in a base class (also known as 'parent class', 'super class') **Admn_a** is a derived class (also known as 'child class', 'subclass'). def__init__(self, **nm1**, **ag1**, **branch1**) [3] relates to the single argument class—**Student** which is input to class **Admn_a**. The first two arguments—**nm1**, **ag1**—are assigned to the (instantiated) **Student** as **name** and **age** in [4]. The third argument—**branch1**—is allotted as the third argument of (instantiated) Student [5]. Such assignment to a base class in

```
class Admn_a(Student):                                   [1]
        'Administrator of school'
        rgstr1 = {'CE': 0, 'EE': 0, 'ME': 0}             [2]
        def __init__(self, nm1, ag1, branch1):           [3]
            Student.__init__(self, nm1, ag1)             [4]
            self.brn = branch1                           [5]
            Admn_a.rgstr1[self.brn] = Admn_a.rgstr1
[self.brn] +1                                            [6]
        def __str__(self):                               [7]
            return "{} branch has {} students after {}'s
registration".format(self.brn, Admn_a.rgstr1 [self.brn],
self.name)
```

Fig. 10.12 Listing of class **admn_a**

```
>>> st1 = school.Admn_a('Adarsh', 21, 'ME')            [1]
New Student with name: Adarsh & of age: 21             [2]
>>> print(st1)                                          [3]
ME branch has 1 students after Adarsh's registration
>>> st1.St_cnt()                                        [4]
There is only one student on the rolls
>>> st2 = school.Admn_a('Thiru', 18, 'ME')             [5]
New Student with name: Thiru & of age: 18              [6]
>>> print(st2)                                          [7]
ME branch has 2 students after Thiru's registration
>>> st2.St_cnt()                                        [8]
2 students are on the rolls
>>> import imp
>>> imp.reload(school)                                  [9]
<module 'demo_10.school' from '/home/trp/demo_10/school.py'>
>>> st3 = school.Admn_a('Priya', 17, 'EE')            [10]
New Student with name: Priya & of age: 17
>>> print(st3)                                         [11]
EE branch has 1 students after Priya's registration
>>> st4 = school.Student('Durga', 16)                 [12]
New Student with name: Durga & of age: 16
>>> print(st4)                                         [13]
Durga of age 16 has registered as a student
>>>
```

Fig. 10.13 Python Interpreter sequence related to Fig. 10.12

addition to what was done within Student itself is possible with derived classes. With this a Student (base class) instantiated through **Admn_a** (derived class) has all the three specified attributes attached to it. The register carrying details of branch allotted (**rgstr1**) is updated with the branch allocation in [6]. Details of the updated branch alone are returned [7] as a string.

School has been imported; as mentioned earlier classes **Student** and **Admn_a** are in it. **st1** is formed as an instance of **Admn_a** [1] in Fig. 10.13. One student instance—'**Adarsh** of 21 years—has been allocated '**ME**' branch through the in-stantiation. Instantiation of the child class **Admin_a** automatically implies instantiation of a corresponding student class. [2] confirms this. It is the result of execution of print('New Student with name: Adarsh & of age 21) from the class **Student** ([2] in Fig. 10.3a). From [3] (execution of print(st1)) one can see that ME number has been updated to 1 with Adarsh's registration. **st1**.**st_cnt**() in [4] returns the student count from **Student** ([3] in Fig. 10.3a).

st2 [5] represents registration of a second student (**Thiru** of 18 years again with '**ME**' as branch) on the same lines as **st1**. Once again 'New student with name: **Thiru** & **age** 18' [6] is output from **Student**. 'print(**st2**)' [7] outputs the updated status of **rgstn1** in **Admn_a**. **st2**.**st_cnt**() [8] has been culled out from **Student** instantiation—**st2**.

The example considered here brings out the key features of inheritance as follows:

- The parent class inherited by the child class is specified as an argument in the definition of the child. In general a child class definition can have a number of parent classes as arguments.
- The __init__() method ([3] in Fig. 10.12) in the child assigns all the neces-sary arguments to the parents through suitable assignments within it (through self ... type statements).
- The child can modify the structure of the parent introducing additional attributes through the assignments within it. However such additional attributes are applicable only for the instantiation done through the child. Further the instantiation of a child obviates the need to instantiate its parent separately.

The class student is altered by adding the method __str__() to it. (The enhanced version of Student is reproduced in Fig. 10.14.) The updated version of school is reloaded in [9] (Fig. 10.13). A new student '**Priya**' is instantiated through **Admin_a** in [10]. print(**st3**) in [11] prints the string returned for **st3** as defined in **Admin_a**. Its (different) definition in **Student** is overridden here by the child '**Admin_a**'. '**Durga**' is registered as a student by instantiating student directly as st4 in [12]. print(**st4**) prints the string st4 as in the new class definition for student. The overriding is not applicable here. In fact __init__() as done in **Admin_a** overrides the __init__() in the present (student) with the addition of a new attribute self.**brn** [5] (Fig. 10.12). In general such overriding allows any method in a parent to be differently implemented by a child.

10.6.1 Multiple Inheritances

Multiple inheritances have many dimensions and raise many issues. We shall get into these in depth through a series of examples.

```
class Student:
  "Student information"
  stdn = 0
  def __init__(self, nm, ag):
    self.name = nm
    self.age = ag
    print('New Student with name: {} & of age:
{}'.format(self.name, self.age))
    Student.stdn += 1

  def St_cnt(self):
    "Give number of students on roll"
    if Student.stdn > 1:print('{} students are on the
rolls'.format(Student.stdn))
    elif Student.stdn == 1:print('There is only one
student on the rolls')
    else: print('There is no student on the rolls')
#__str__() newly added
  def __str__(self):
    return "{} of age {} has registered as a
student".format(self.name, self.age)
```

Fig. 10.14 class **Student** enhanced by adding method __str__() to it

Admin_c in Fig. 10.15 is a version different from **Admin_a** considered above; the **administrator** has become more comprehensive here by taking care of both— **Student** and **Teacher**. It accepts the two classes—**Student** as well as **Teacher** —defined earlier. The listing and scope of **Admin_c** are fairly simple. It is to be instantiated with four arguments—two (name and age) for student and two (name and age) for teacher. The __init__() method [2] directly assigns these to teacher [3] and student [4] respectively. **Admin_c** as a class has been instantiated in Fig. 10.16 as **sstt**. Execution of the parent methods—(**Student** and **Teacher**)— results in the printouts [3] and [4]. Declaration of the child class and the argument assignments are clear and straightforward here. These can be directly extended to cases with more number of parents. As long as the arguments used in the instantiation are properly assigned there is no muddling or confusion.

The class **Admin_b** reproduced in Fig. 10.15 is a modified version of **Admin_c**. It has **Student** and **Teacher** as its two parent classes. Each accepts three arguments —**name**, **age**, and **branch** respectively. The **name** and **age** are assigned to attributes of the respective parent classes. The **branch** (string) is used to update the respective registers—**rgstrt** [6] and **rgstrs** [7] maintained as dicts. Their updation [11] and [12] as well as the __str__ [13] require the branches to be assigned in the local __init__ itself [8] (We tolerate wrong grammatical sentence here to avoid 'if, elif' etc., cluttering the suite). This needs all the six arguments to be appropriately assigned locally as in [8]. The concerned statements are more lengthy and cumbersome; such assignments were not warranted in **Admin_c** since all the four arguments were directly passed on to the respective __init__ methods. **Admin_b** has been

```
class Admn_c(Student, Teacher):                      [1]
    'Administrator of school_c'
    def __init__(self, nms, ags, nmt, agt):          [2]
        Teacher.__init__(self, nmt, agt)             [3]
        Student.__init__(self, nms, ags)             [4]

class Admn_b(Student, Teacher):                      [5]
    'Administrator of school_b'
    rgstrS = {'CE': 0, 'EE': 0, 'ME': 0}             [6]
    rgstrT = {'CE': 0, 'EE': 0, 'ME': 0}             [7]
    def __init__(self,nmt,agt,brt,nms,ags,brs):      [8]

self.nt,self.at,self.bt,self.ns,self.as1,self.bs=nmt,agt,br
t,nms,ags, brs
        Student.__init__(self, self.ns, self.as1)    [9]
        Teacher.__init__(self, self.nt, self.at)     [10]
        Admn_b.rgstrS[self.bs] += 1                  [11]
        Admn_b.rgstrT[self.bt] += 1                  [12]
    def __str__(self):                               [13]
#       return Teacher.__str__(self) + ';' +
Student.__str__(self)
        return "{} branch has {} students after {}'s
registration & {} branch has {} Teachers after {}'s
registration ".format(self.bs,Admn_b.rgstrS[self.bs],
self.ns, self.bt, Admn_b.rgstrT [self.bt], self.nt)
```

Fig. 10.15 classes **Admn_c** and **Admn_b**

instantiated [4] in Fig. 10.16 as **stte**; the printouts with parent implementations (**Student** and **Teacher**) are in [6] and [7]. The __str__() in **Admin_b** has been output in [8]. The updated status of **rgstrt** and **rgstrt** can be seen here. Once again the definitions and assignments can be seen to be straightforward and applicable to cases with more than one parent class as long as the structure of the classes remains similar.

```
>>> from demo_10 import school                       [1]
>>> sstt = school.Admn_c('Adarsh', 17,'Thilagam', 32) [2]
New teacher with name: Thilagam & of age: 32         [3]
New Student with name: Adarsh & of age: 17           [4]
>>> stte = school.Admn_b('Thilagam', 32,'EE', 'Adarsh',
17, 'ME')                                            [5]
New Student with name: Adarsh & of age: 17           [6]
New teacher with name: Thilagam & of age: 32         [7]
>>> print(stte)                                      [8]
ME branch has 1 students after Adarsh's registration & EE
branch has 1 Teachers after Thilagam's registration
>>>
```

Fig. 10.16 Python Interpreter sequence related to Fig. 10.14

10.7 super()

The multiple inheritance procedure as illustrated in the foregoing section is relatively inflexible. The built-in function super() facilitates multiple inheritance implementations in different ways and with flexibility. Basically super() returns a proxy object to delegate control to a parent or sibling class depending on the context.

Let us consider a few illustrative examples to understand super(). The examples deal with a 'cacophony of Gods' clamoring for attention. Class **AA** [1] in Fig. 10.17a has the method **sat**() defined in it [2]. **pa** is an instance of AA [3] and **pa**.**sat**() [4] prints out '**AA** is the God' as expected. The absence of any argument in **AA** obviates the need for __init__() in the prescribed format; this form of class definition does not make any difference (as is explained presently). Class **CA(AA)** has been defined as a child class [5] with class **AA** as its parent. The method **sat**() has been defined in **CA**. 'CC is the true God' is to be printed out and control transferred to the method in the parent **AA**. super.**sat**() [7] implies this. Class **CA** is initiated as **pac** in [8]. Execution of **pac**.**sat**() [9] shows the chained execution of **sat** where control is transferred from child **CA** to parent **AA** due to the presence of super.**sat**() [7] in the child class. The chaining here is generic in nature. **AA** does not explicitly appear in the super.**sat**() statement.

Class **BB** [10] is similar to class (**AA**). It carries the **sat**() method; in addition it has super.**sat**() [11] within it. If **sat**() is executed in an instantiation of class **BB**, '**BB** is the real God' will be printed and control transferred to the next 'class in line' due to the super.**sat**() [11]. In the absence of any argument in **BB**, it does not offer any scope for direct instantiation. Class **CC(BB)** [12] is defined on the same lines as class **CA(AA)** above. After instantiation if **sat**() is executed '**CC** is the True God' will be printed out and control transferred to the parent **BB** due to the presence of super.**sat**() [14] in it as pointed out earlier. However the presence of super.**sat**() [11] in **BB** leaves execution incomplete. A direct instantiation of **CC** is not feasible. Consider class **DD(CC, AA)** [15] with the two parent classes; it has its own super.**sat**() [17] in its **sat**() definition [16]. **DD** has been instantiated as **pp** in [18]. Execution of **pp**.**sat**() in [19] results in the chain printouts in the lines following. Through the super.**sat**() sequence execution proceeds as **DD** → **CC** → **BB** → **AA**. The transfer **BB** to **AA** is due to the presence of **AA** as the next parent in the definition of **DD**. super() effects transfer and the chained execution following the logic.—'*start at left end* → *proceed first vertically as long as specified* → *step ahead horizontally to the right* → *vertically as long as specified* → *step ahead horizontally to the right* → ··· ' up to the logical end. The transfer proceeds as indicated in Fig. 10.18. This is the '*Method Resolution Order* (mro)' followed for the transfer chain. The mro is available as a built-in read-only attribute within the class definition. The mro for **DD** can be obtained as **DD**.__mro__ [20]. It conforms to the execution order.

By way of variety the above sequence of classes have been redefined as **Aa**[21], **Bb**[22], **Cc**[24], and **Dd**[26] in Fig. 10.17b. But in each of these cases the method

(a)

```
>>> class AA():                                              [1]
...     def sat(self): print('AA is the God')                [2]
...
>>> pa = AA()                                                [3]
>>> pa.sat()                                                 [4]
AA is the God
>>> class CA(AA):                                            [5]
...     def sat(self):                                       [6]
...         print('CC is the true God')
...         super().sat()                                    [7]
...
>>> pac = CA()                                               [8]
>>> pac.sat()                                                [9]
CC is the true God
AA is the God
>>> class BB():                                              [10]
...     def sat(self):
...         print('BB is the real God')
...         super().sat()                                    [11]
...
>>> class CC(BB):                                            [12]
...     def sat(self):                                       [13]
...         print('CC is the true God')
...         super().sat()                                    [14]
...
>>> class DD(CC, AA):                                        [15]
...     def sat(self):                                       [16]
...         print('DD is the supreme God')
...         super().sat()                                    [17]
...
>>> pp = DD()                                                [18]
>>> pp.sat()                                                 [19]
DD is the supreme God
CC is the true God
BB is the real God
AA is the God
>>> DD.__mro__                                               [20]
(<class '__main__.DD'>, <class '__main__.CC'>, <class
'__main__.BB'>, <class '__main__.AA'>, <class 'object'>)
```

Fig. 10.17 a Python Interpreter illustrating the basic ideas of function super() (continued in Fig. 10.17b) **b** Python Interpreter illustrating the basic ideas of function super() (continued from Fig. 10.17a)

sat() has super() preceding the print() [23], [25], [27]. As a result the control is transferred from **Dd** to **Cc** to **Bb** to **Aa**. After the print out in **Aa** control reverts to **Bb** and **sat**() execution is continued and completed there; similarly from Bb

(b)

```
>>> class Aa():                                                    [21]
...     def sat(self): print('Aa is the God')
...
>>> class Bb():                                                    [22]
...      def sat(self):                                            [23]
...        super().sat()
...        print('Bb is the real God')
...
>>> class Cc(Bb):                                                  [24]
...     def sat(self):                                             [25]
...        super().sat()
...        print('Cc is the true God')
...
>>> class Dd(Cc, Aa):                                              [26]
...      def sat(self):                                            [27]
...        super().sat()
...        print('Dd is the supreme God')
...
>>> pd = Dd()                                                      [28]
>>> pd.sat()                                                       [29]
Aa is the God
Bb is the real God
Cc is the true God
Dd is the supreme God
>>>
```

Fig. 10.17 (continued)

Fig. 10.18 Depiction of inheritance chaining with classes for the example in Fig. 10.16: Depending on the number and type of parents the *vertical* → *horizontal* → *vertical* → *horizontal* → . . type of chained transfer continues as much as necessary

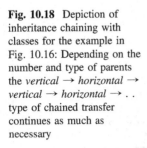
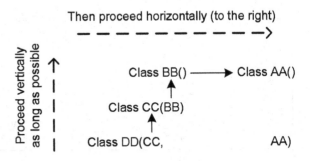

control reverts to **Cc** and then to **Dd** for task completion. **Dd** is instantiated as **pd** [28]. **pd.sat**() [29] output conforms to the sequence explained.

The examples considered above bring out the following features of the use of super() in chained execution:

- All source classes carry the super() statement.
- All recipient classes except the last one which need not effect a transfer, continue with the transfer through the super statement.

- To ensure proper identification and chaining of the method, super() statement in all the clauses concerned/involved carry the same signature—here it is 'super.**sat**()'.
- The mro gives the sequence followed for inheritance.
- The mro being a clear structure different involved inheritance structures can be used with parent and child classes. In all the cases the mro provides the unique and clear inheritance path.
- The fact that the signature used in the inheritance chain is the same makes room for accommodating parents whose scope can be changed/defined later.

The Python Interpreter sequence in Fig. 10.19 is the same set of classes (**A1**, **B1**, **C1**, and **D1**) used in place of **AA**, **BB**, **CC**, and **DD** earlier) defined more elaborately. All of them have the __init__ method defined. The super.__init__() in each case establishes the general inheritance chain. But the methods **sat**() remain

```
>>> class A1():
...     def __init__(self):super().__init__()
...     def sat(self): print('A1 is the God')
...
>>> class B1():
...     def __init__(self):super().__init__()
...     def sat(self):
...         print('B1 is the real God')
...         super().sat()
...
>>> class C1(B1):
...     def __init__(self):super().__init__()
...     def sat(self):
...         print('C1 is the true God')
...         super().sat()
...
>>> class D1(C1, A1):
...     def __init__(self):super().__init__()
...     def sat(self):
...         print('D1 is the supreme God')
...         super().sat()
...
>>> dd = D1()
>>> dd.sat()
D1 is the supreme God
C1 is the true God
B1 is the real God
A1 is the God
>>>
```

Fig. 10.19 A Python Interpreter sequence illustrating some aspects of multiple inheritance

```
>>> class A2():                                          [1]
...     def __init__(self):super().__init__()
...     def sat(self): print('A2 is the God')            [2]
...     def asat(self):pass                              [3]
...
>>> class B2():                                          [4]
...     def __init__(self):super().__init__()
...     def asat(self):                                  [5]
...       print('B2 is the real Fake God')
...       super().asat()
...
>>> class C2(B2):                                        [6]
...     def __init__(self):super().__init__()
...     def sat(self):                                   [7]
...         print('C2 is the true God')
...         super().sat()
...
>>> class D2(C2, A2):                                    [8]
...     def __init__(self):super().__init__()
...     def sat(self):                                   [9]
...       print('D2 is the supreme God')
...       super().sat()
...     def asat(self):                                  [10]
...       print('D2 is the supreme Fake God')
...       super().asat()
...
>>> dd = D2()                                            [11]
>>> dd.sat()                                             [12]
D2 is the supreme God
C2 is the true God
A2 is the God
>>> dd.asat()                                            [13]
D2 is the supreme Fake God
B2 is the real Fake God
>>>
```

Fig. 10.20 A Python Interpreter sequence illustrating the variety possible with multiple inheritance

the same. The instantiation as **dd** and execution of **dd.sat**() yields the same results as earlier. However the linkage through __init__() shows the path for generalization for cases with multiple parents and more than one method—inherited in different ways.

The Python Interpreter sequence in Fig. 10.20 has a set of classes (**A2**, **B2**, **C2**, and **D2**) with two methods—**sat**() and **asat**()—linked in different ways. The structure and linking of the classes is similar to the case considered above. **dd** [11] is an instance of **D2**. The mro for **dd** is similar to that in Fig. 10.17 [20]—reproduced below:

(<class '__main__.**D2**'>, <class '__main__.**C2**'>, <class '__main__. **B2**'>, <class '__main__.**A2**'>, <class 'object'>).

The method **sat**() in **D2** [9] continues through **C2** [7] and **B2** to **A2** [2]. **dd.sat**() [12] outputs the chained execution of **sat**() conforming to mro. Since **sat**() is not defined in **B2** it is bypassed and search continued to **A2** [2]. Similarly **dd**.**asat**() [11], [5], [3] bypasses **C2** since it is not defined in **C2**. The logical execution of **dd**. **asat**() continues up to (and terminates in) **A2**. The presence of def **saat** (self):pass [3] in **A2** ensures its completion. **A2** has no executable statement in its **asat**(). If def **asat**(self).pass is omitted in **A2** the chained execution of **asat**() conforming to mro cannot be completed. The example brings out two more aspects of super().

- The class chain should provide for logical completion of the execution of the chained methods.
- If an intermediate class in the mro chain does not have a chained function defined in it, the same will be bypassed in the execution chain.

We revisit the example with **Admn**(**Student**, **Teacher**) with the use of super() function. The module **School_c** with the classes **Student**, **Teacher**, and **Admn_sp**(**Student**, **Teacher**) is reproduced in Fig. 10.21. All the three classes have been curtailed in scope to focus only on inheritance where the parents are to be supplied arguments in the desired order. When **Admn_sp**(**Student**, **Teacher**) [12] is instantiated, the required argument set is supplied the arguments in the desired order. def__init__(self, **brs**, **brt**, *Arg) [13] accepts **brs** and **brt** (Student branch and Teacher branch) and assigns them to self.**bs** and self.**bt** [14]; the rest of the arguments supplied are passed on to the next in line in the mro through super().__init__(*Arg) [15]. Thus due to def__init__(self, **nms**, **ags**, *Arg) [2], Student [1] accepts the next two arguments as **nms** and **ags** (name and age of the Student respectively); they are assigned to self.**name** [3] and self. **age** [4] (of the student) respectively. Once again the rest of the arguments are passed on to the next in the mro through super().__init__(*Arg) [7]. Teacher (next in the mro) accepts the rest of the arguments as **nmt** and **agt** [10] (name and age of the **Teacher** respectively). This completes the __init__ chain. def __str__(self) [16] in class **Admn_sp**() passes control to the def __str__(self) [8] in Student. Super.__str__() [17] ensures this. The Super.__str__() in Student [9] in turn passes control to the def __str__(self) [11] in **Teacher**. The string formed here is concatenated with string in **Student** (self.**stt**); the combined string [9] is returned through the sibling class **Admn_sp** [17].

Additionally the method **nunt**(self) [18] in class **Admn_sp** returns details of the new entrants to the **School** as a string.

School_c has been imported in [1] in the Python Interpreter sequence in Fig. 10.22. The child class **Admn_sp**() has been instantiated as **sta** in [2]. The number of arguments, their types, and their sequence match the requirements conforming to the mro (**Admn_sp** → **Student** → **Teacher**). The outputs in [3] and [4] are the printouts demanded at instantiation of **Student** and **Teacher** respectively. Details of the new entrants as the string **sta.nunt**() are in [5]. The string returned by instantiation of **sta** is in [6].

```
class Student:                                              [1]
  "Student information"
  stdn = 0
  def __init__(self, nms, ags, *Arg):                      [2]
    self.name = nms                                         [3]
    self.age = ags                                          [4]
    Student.stdn += 1
    print('New Student with name: {} & of age:
{}'.format(self.name, self.age))                            [5]
    self.stt ="{} of age {} has registered as a student;
".format(self.name,self.age)                                [6]
    super().__init__(*Arg)                                  [7]
  def __str__(self):                                        [8]
    return self.stt + super().__str__()                     [9]

class Teacher:                                              [10]
  "Teacher information"
  tchn = 0
  def __init__(self, nmt, agt):

    self.name = nmt

    self.age = agt
    Teacher.tchn += 1
    print('New teacher with name: {} & of age:
{}'.format(self.name, self.age))
  def __str__(self):                                        [11]
    return "{} of age {} has registered as a
teacher".format(self.name, self.age)

class Admn_sp(Student, Teacher):                            [12]
  'Administrator of school_b'
  rgstrS = {'CE': 0, 'EE': 0, 'ME': 0}
  rgstrT = {'CE': 0, 'EE': 0, 'ME': 0}
  def __init__(self, brs, brt, *Arg):                       [13]
    self.bs, self.bt = brs, brt                             [14]
    Admn_sp.rgstrS[self.bs] += 1
    Admn_sp.rgstrT[self.bt] += 1
    super().__init__(*Arg)                                  [15]
  def __str__(self):                                        [16]
    return super().__str__()                                [17]
  def nunt(self):                                           [18]
    return "The Number of students in {} branch is {}  &
The Number of Teachers in {} branch is {}
".format(self.bs,Admn_sp.rgstrS[self.bs], self.bt,
Admn_sp.rgstrT [self.bt])
```

Fig. 10.21 A modified version of the **school** module

```
>>> from demo_10 import School_c                          [1]
>>> sta = School_c.Admn_sp('EE', 'ME', 'Adarsh',
17,'Thilagam', 32)                                        [2]
New Student with name: Adarsh & of age: 17                [3]
New teacher with name: Thilagam & of age: 32              [4]
>>> sta.nunt()                                            [5]
'The Number of students in EE branch is 1  & The Number of
Teachers in ME branch is 1 '
>>> print(sta)                                            [6]
Adarsh of age 17 has registered as a student; Thilagam of
age 32 has registered as a teacher
```

Fig. 10.22 The Python Interpreter sequence instantiating the **School** in Fig. 10.20

In all cases the *mro is central to the linking of arguments, methods & c.* Two additional observations on the use of super () are in order here:

- The number, sequence, and types of arguments used in instantiation should match the requirements.
- As many (diverse) parents as required for the inheritance scheme can be accommodated in the chain.

10.8 Execution from Command Line

The discussions and illustrations of Python program execution have been carried out so far in the interactive mode. Python functions as an interpreted language wherein each statement is executed and the system returns the prompt in the next line of input. Alternately readymade scripts—whole programs—can be run directly without opening Python per se. This mode and its salient features are illustrated here.

term_tst_a.py is a simple Python module reproduced in Fig. 10.23. **aa** and **bb** are assigned values [1] and their ratio printed out [2]. Further a function **prd(a1, b1)** with two arguments **a1** and **b1** is defined [3]; it prints out the **a1** × **b1** product.

```
'Demonstration of difference between importing & direct
running_A'
aa, bb = 2.1, 3.2                                         [1]
print('aa/bb = ', aa/bb)                                  [2]
def prd (a1, b1):                                         [3]
    print ('Product of {}*{} = {}'.format(a1, b1, a1*b1))
    return
```

Fig. 10.23 A program to illustrate command line execution

```
trp@trp-Veriton-Series:~$ python3.5 term_tst_a.py          [1]
aa/bb =  0.65625                                           [2]
trp@trp-Veriton-Series:~$ python3.5                        [3]
Python 3.5.0 (default, Nov  3 2015, 20:42:24)
[GCC 4.8.4] on linux
Type "help", "copyright", "credits" or "license" for more
information.
>>> import term_tst_a                                     [4]
aa/bb =  0.65625                                          [5]
>>> a0, b0 = 2.1, 3.2                                     [6]
>>> term_tst_a.prd(a0, b0)                                [7]
Product of 2.1*3.2 = 6.720000000000001
>>> #Exit Python                                          [8]

trp@trp-Veriton-Series:~$ python3.5 term_tst.py          [9]
Sum of aa & bb =  5.300000000000001                      [10]
trp@trp-Veriton-Series:~$ python3.5                      [11]
Python 3.5.0 (default, Nov  3 2015, 20:42:24)
[GCC 4.8.4] on linux
Type "help", "copyright", "credits" or "license" for more
information.
>>> import term_tst                                      [12]
Difference of aa & bb =  -1.1                            [13]
>>> a0, b0 = 2.1, 3.2                                    [14]
>>> term_tst.prd(a0, b0)                                 [15]
Product of 2.1*3.2 = 6.720000000000001
>>> if __name__ == '__main__':                           [16]
...     import math                                      [17]
...     a1, b1 = 2.1, 3.2                                [18]
...     c1 = a1**2 + b1**2
...     d = math.sin(c1**0.5)
...     print('d = ', d)                                 [19]
...
d =  -0.6334000576166239                                 [20]
>>>
```

Fig. 10.24 Execution of Program in Fig. 10.23 in command line as well as in interpreter mode after opening python environment

In the sequence in Fig. 10.24 the terminal is opened as indicated by the '$' prompt in the first line. 'python3.5 term_tst_a.py' is the command [1] to run the above module directly. The module is run; all the statements—those at the zero indent level—are executed. aa, bb = 2.1, 3,2 assignments are made and the print ('aa/bb = 'aa/bb) executed as seen from [2]. Further the function prd(a1, b1) is defined (though not used). All these are done here without Python being opened for continuous execution or importing the module term_tst_a.py. Subsequently Python is opened in [3] and the same module—term_tst_a—imported in [4]. Once again aa, bb = 2.1, 3.2 assignments followed by the print('aa/bb = 'aa/bb) take place.

```
'Demonstration of difference between importing & direct
running'
aa, bb = 2.1, 3.2                                          [1]

if __name__ == '__main__':                                 [2]
    print('Sum of aa & bb = ', aa + bb)                    [3]
else: print('Difference of aa & bb = ', aa - bb)           [4]

def prd (a1, b1):                                          [5]
    print ('Product of {}*{} = {}'.format(a1, b1, a1*b1))
    return
```

Fig. 10.25 A routine to demonstrate the use of '__main__' to identify and use the execution environment

Since prd(a1, b1) has been defined, calling it with arguments a0 and b0 (=2.1 and 3.2 respectively) as 'term_tst_a.prd(a0, b0)' leads to its execution [7].

term_tst.py in Fig. 10.25 is another routine done to illustrate a different dimension of the command line execution. As had been mentioned earlier every entity in Python—like function, module, class, and the like has a name associated with it. It appears in its __dict__ as an attribute. Further during execution the active execution environment is identified by assigning the name '__main__'. The module **term_tst.py** brings out a possible use of this. The compound statement starting with [2] in it has two parts. If the module is invoked for execution directly "__name == '__main__'" is true. **aa + bb** is printed out [3]; else (that is when the module is imported by another program), the clause in [4] (print('Difference of **aa & bb** = ', **aa − bb**)) is executed. The Python environment is closed and the terminal started afresh in [8] in Fig. 10.24. term_tst.py is executed directly from the open terminal [9].

if __name__ == '__main__': in [2] (Fig. 10.25) being True, the main clause following (print('Sum of aa & bb = ', **aa + bb**)), is executed here as can be seen in [10] in Fig. 10.24. Following this python3.5 is again opened in [11] and in the Python environment module **term_tst** imported [12] (Note the need to retain '**.py**' extension for direct execution but not for importing). [13] is the output resulting from the execution of the 'zero indent level' statements. Reverting to Fig. 10.25 the **term_tst**' is not the execution environment. Hence the 'else:print('Difference of aa and bb = ', **aa − bb**)" is executed [4]. [13] in Fig. 10.24 confirms this. Further the function **prd**() is defined as in [5] in Fig. 10.25; calling it as **term_tst.prd(a0, b0)** [15] (in Fig. 10.25) with arguments (**a0** = 2.1 and **b0** = 3.2) results in its due execution [16].

[17] is an illustration of another use of "if __name == '__main__'". Since the program execution environment is assigned the name '__main__' the set of executable statements following [17] are parsed and the set executed only when you come out as in [20]. In contrast normally each of the statements here [18] to [19] would have been executed one after another in the interpreter mode.

```
trp@trp-Veriton-Series:~$ python3.5 -c "print('Maya
complemented Nevan:You look smart today too')"          [1]
Maya complemented Nevan:You look smart today too
trp@trp-Veriton-Series:~$ python3.5 -c "a, b = 2.1, 4.2; c
= b/a; print(c)"                                         [2]
2.0
trp@trp-Veriton-Series:~$ python3.5 -m term_tst_a        [3]
aa/bb =  0.65625
```

Fig. 10.26 Illustration of command line execution with options

The flexibility offered by the possibility of steering execution through the 'if __name__ == '__main__' ' clause can be used judiciously to suit the environment. Testing a program segment during development is a typical example. A separate segment of program under "if __name__ == '__main__'" can be included for this. When the module is imported by another program this test (dormant) segment will be ignored.

The command line execution of Python code has a set of options associated with it. Use of two of them is illustrated in Fig. 10.26. (Others are of use mainly in parsing, debugging, &c and are not discussed here.) The option -c implies that the script following is a code segment to be executed directly. [1] is simple illustration of this with single line print out. [2] is a more detailed one where a set of Python statements are bunched together to form the executable script. The semicolon ';' is the separator between adjacent statements.

The option '-m' signifies that *the name of the module to be executed follows*. As an illustrative example the module '**term_ts**t' (listing in Fig. 10.23) has been executed in [3]. Note that the module name is specified here without the '.py' extension.

10.9   Exercises

1. *Materials Management*: Efficient sourcing of all items required for the production in a manufacturing organization is the task of a Materials Manager. Let us understand the role through a tangible example—that of manufacture of an electric fan. Insulated wire, stampings, insulating varnish, fins, capacitor, connecting wires (harness), paint, and hardware items like shaft and casing castings —these are the major items to be sourced. The manager's tasks are the following:
   Have an idea of production schedule as weekly production rate.
   Ensure timely availability of all materials for uninterrupted production. For each item he should have at last two vendors (to prevent supplier monopoly).

He should not stock too many numbers of an item; it can lead to inefficient use of working capital. But he has to match supply to production rate. This is to be done for each item to minimize blocking of working capital.

Do vender development when situation demands.

Have a clear index of performance and try to optimize it continuously.

Have a provision to update index of performance regularly/when required.

Develop a program for materials management. Materials manager, items in stock, item_used can possibly be the classes. Each item can be an instance of the class item_used. Define inputs to classes and class functions. Identify inheritance sequences and incorporate all these in the program.

2. Evolve a simulation scheme to test and validate the above Materials Management software.
3. Identify the tasks to be carried out in running a (neighbourhood) grocery store. Define classes, attributes, and inheritance suitably and do a program to run the store. Test it with simulated data.
4. Allotting grades to students using the marks scored in different subjects, ranking of students, carrying out student admissions, and staffing have been dealt with in some detail through examples and exercises in the previous chapters. Combine these with the Class structure using **Student**, **Teacher**, and **Admin** discussed in the present chapter. Formulate a university management system to manage admissions and grading.
5. The 'cacophony of Gods' (Sect. 10.7) has different claimants to godhead vying with each other to establish authority. The following is another situation with possibilities of misleading communication.

Akbar has often been said to be the Greatest Emperor. The cultural diversity he accommodated in his palace is widely acclaimed. Akbar's harem of 163 wives of different religious backgrounds adds colour to this.

Akbar's successor 'Rabka'—did not like this. He ordered all 'Akbar' to be replaced by 'Rabka' vis-a-vis harem ownership. He declared 'Akbar was a brute'.

'Rabka's successor—'Barka'—wanted his name to take the coveted place. He wanted 'Rabka' also to be declared a brute.

Structure a scheme with suitably defined classes and show how different historians will depict the situation. Historians devoted to Akbar, Rabka, and Barka and another one looking at history with a detached perspective can be considered here.

6. The following is another situation replete with interesting possibilities of wrong communication.

Some communities consider the word 'wife' to be too personal to be used in pleasantries/conversations. They use 'family' in its place; others use 'home front' instead. A brief question/answer session is here:

(a) Ram: How is your wife?
(b) Raghu: My wife is fine. My wife is my home front and she runs the family.
(c) Replace 'wife' with 'family' in (a) above.
(d) Replace 'wife' with 'home front' in (a) above.

The 'Vastu-guru' wanted the home front to be shifted to the backyard and the present home front to be the waste dump.

Madame 'Women_libber' ordered all 'home front' to be replaced by 'sweetheart'.

Bring out possible question/answer sessions between Ram and Raghu considering different alternatives like Ram not being aware of Raghu carrying out the Vastu-guru's suggestion, Ram obeying Madam Women-libber (Raghu being ignorant of it) and so on. Define separate classes for each of the activities—Ram's query, Raghu's answer, Vastu-guru's service, and Madam Women-libber's dictum. Tie them up suitably in a parent–child scheme.

Reference

van Rossum G, Drake FL Jr (2014) The Python library reference. Python Software Foundation

Chapter 11
Time Related Operations

Some files/documents require a time-stamp to be included in them. Various calendar related actions are demanded by some databases. Performance comparison of different programs demands the time taken for execution to be estimated. Three time related modules—time, datetime, and calendar—are available in Python to facilitate all these (van Rossum and Drake 2014).

11.1 Time Standards

The time related modules in Python have provision to express and convert time/time intervals involving two common time Standards—UTC (ITU 2002) and ISO 8601. Both of these are briefly discussed here to facilitate understanding of the relevant provisions in Python.

The Coordinated Universal Time (acronym UTC) is the Standard which defines times, time zones, and relates them. UTC is a refined version of the GMT; it uses the atomic clock as the basis. The proleptic Gregorian calendar is the basis for UTC. 00.00 h on the first of January 1970 at 0° longitude—called the '*epoch*'—is taken as the starting point for time as well as calendar. Each year is of 365 days (366 days in leap years), each day is of 24 h, each hour is of 60 min, and each minute is of 60 s. The time is adjusted by a maximum of one second at irregular intervals (agreed by the competent International community) to account for the slowing down of Earth. The Standard times in different countries are all tied to the UTC time with offsets ranging from −12 h to +14 h in intervals of 30 min (occasionally 15 min). Network protocols, World Wide Web Standards, and the like use the UTC system as the basis.

ISO 8601 specifies formats for representing time, date, and related information. This is recommended for information exchange. The time related modules/classes in Python have the provision to accommodate these in different contexts. The salient features of the representation are discussed here.

© Springer Nature Singapore Pte Ltd. 2016
T.R. Padmanabhan, *Programming with Python*,
DOI 10.1007/978-981-10-3277-6_11

- Date representation uses the proleptic Gregorian calendar as the basis.
- Time representation uses the 24-h scheme. Time can be represented as UTC or local time or an appropriate combination. Time and Date can be represented separately individually or in a combined form.
- All the representations start with the largest temporal quantity first (year for Date, and Hour for time) at left.

Possible Date-Time representations are summarized in Fig. 11.1 for the specific Date—25th February 2016 at Time 13 h 53.5 min in India. The same also can be compactly represented as 20160225T1353.5. Corresponding UTC time and

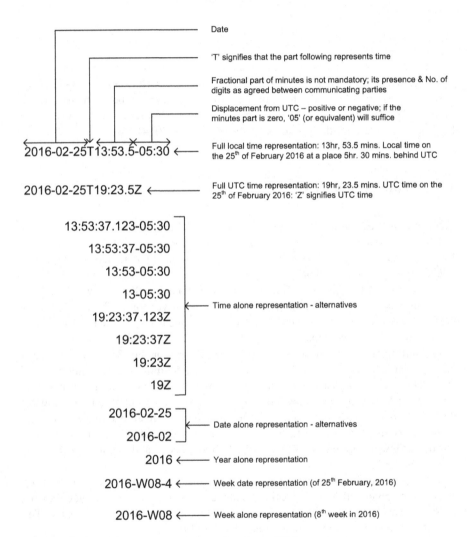

Fig. 11.1 Date and time representations conforming to UTC

Fig. 11.2 Time interval representation conforming to UTC

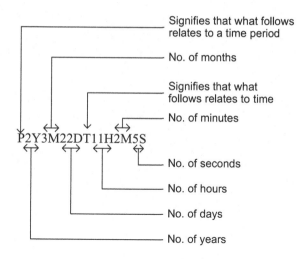

different truncated versions of Date/Time representation are also shown in the figure. The corresponding format for time interval (period) is shown is Fig. 11.2 for the specific period of 2-years, 3-months, 22-days, 11-h, 2-min, and 5-s. The corresponding compact form is P00020322T110205.

11.2 `time` Module

The module `time` is imported in the Python Interpreter sequence in Fig. 11.3. With **t1** = time.time() in [1] t1 is the total time elapsed since epoch. It is in seconds in floating point mode with 1 μs precision. time.gmtime(t1) converts **t1** into a format in terms of year, month, day, hours, minutes, and seconds (items 0–5 in the same order) [2]. It also includes the day of the week (with Monday being assigned 0) and the serial number of the day in the year (items 6 and 7). The last field is the change for daylight change whenever it is implemented. The indices, their significance, and range are summarized in Table 11.1. The timezone flag = 0, in the absence of daylight saving time in the zone. This is referred as the 'struct_-time' representation. struct_time is a tuple of nine fields and any of these can be accessed by proper indexing [3]. time.gmtime() without any arguments returns the current UTC time in the same 9-field format [4]. time.localtime(t1) converts **t1** into the 9-field format—as local time. The difference between time.gmtime(**t1**) and time.localtime(**t1**) is to be clearly understood. In the specific case here the local time is 5 h 30 min ahead of UTC which accounts for the difference between the two.

time.strftime(format, string) [5] accepts the 9-field time (**struct_time**) as a **tuple** and returns the corresponding time in a specified 'compact format'. The formatting details confirm to those in Table 11.2. Methods are available to convert time amongst these three formats (seconds from epoch, **struct_time**, and the compact format). These are summarized in Table 11.3. Their uses are illustrated in the Python Interpreter sequence in Fig. 11.3. In all these cases the time argument

```
>>> import time, calendar
>>> t1 = time.time()                                          [1]
>>> t1
1455891360.1407747
>>> tg = time.gmtime(t1)                                      [2]
>>> tg
time.struct_time(tm_year=2016, tm_mon=2, tm_mday=19,
tm_hour=14, tm_min=16, tm_sec=0, tm_wday=4, tm_yday=50,
tm_isdst=0)
>>> tg[3]                                                     [3]
14
>>> time.gmtime()                                            [4]
time.struct_time(tm_year=2016, tm_mon=2, tm_mday=19,
tm_hour=14, tm_min=17, tm_sec=12, tm_wday=4, tm_yday=50,
tm_isdst=0)
>>> time.localtime(t1)
time.struct_time(tm_year=2016, tm_mon=2, tm_mday=19,
tm_hour=19, tm_min=46, tm_sec=0, tm_wday=4, tm_yday=50,
tm_isdst=0)
>>> time.strftime("%a, %d %b %Y %H:%M:%S - Good time it
is!'",tg)                                                    [5]
"Fri, 19 Feb 2016 14:16:00 - Good time it is!'"
>>> time.ctime(t1)                                           [6]
'Fri Feb 19 19:46:00 2016'
>>> tdb = time.strptime("26  September 1949", "%d %B %Y")
                                                             [7]
>>> tdb
time.struct_time(tm_year=1949, tm_mon=9, tm_mday=26,
tm_hour=0, tm_min=0, tm_sec=0, tm_wday=0, tm_yday=269,
tm_isdst=-1)
>>> time.asctime(tg)                                         [8]
'Fri Feb 19 14:16:00 2016'
>>> t3 = time.mktime(tdb)                                    [9]
>>> t3
-639552600.0
>>> t2 = calendar.timegm(tdb)                               [10]
>>> t2
-639532800
>>> t2-t3
19800.0
>>> time.timezone                                           [11]
-19800
>>> divmod(time.timezone,3600),(time.timezone%3600)/60[12]
((-6, 1800), 30.0)
>>> time.tzname                                             [13]
('IST', 'IST')
```

Fig. 11.3 Python Interpreter sequence illustrating the use of features in the time module

Table 11.1 Details of the nine attribute of the time tuple

Index	Attribute	Values
0	tm_year	(e.g.: 2016)
1	tm_mon	range [1, 12]
2	tm_mday	range [1, 31]
3	tm_hour	range [0, 23]
4	tm_min	range [0, 59]
5	tm_sec	range [0, 61][a]
6	tm_wday	range [0, 6], 0 is for Monday
7	tm_yday range	[1, 366]
8	tm_isdst	0, 1 or −1[b]

[a]normal range is [0, 59]; 60 is for timestamps involving 'leap seconds'; 61 is for historical reasons

[b]tm_isdst flag signifies whether the time zone uses a separate daylight saving time; if yes, the flag is set to 1 else it is reset (=0). −1 is used as the flag for daylight saving time in mktime()

can be input in the desired format. In its absence the current time is used as the default argument.

time.ctime(**aa**) accepts an argument **aa**—representing a time span from the epoch the unit of time being in seconds. It is converted into a string in local time and returned as can be seen from [6]. The time **t1** in [1] is converted and displayed here. The string is in the form shown in Fig. 11.4. This as a string is converted into time. struct_time form (of 9 or less fields) by time.strptime (string, time) [7]. time.asctime(**tg**) converts struct_time that **tg** represents, to the format in Fig. 11.4 [8]. time.asctime() without an argument, returns the current time represented by time.localtime() in the same format. time.mktime() takes the 9-field struct_time as argument and returns the corresponding epoch time in seconds [9]. calendar.timegm(**t1**) (this is from the module calendar; calendar has been imported here for the specific purpose of invoking this method. Calendar has been discussed separately later) accepts the 0-field struct_time as argument, treats it as gmtime() and returns the corresponding UTC time in seconds [10]. time.mktime(**tdb**) treats **tdb** as the local time tuple while calendar.timegm(**tdb**) treats it as the UTC time tuple. For Coimbatore (India) the difference is −19 800 s showing the local time to be 5.30 h ahead of UTC. In fact the attribute time.timezone returns the difference between UTC time and local time. The timezone is the offset of local time with respect to UTC. The offset to the West is taken as positive. For India it is negative and 5.30 h head of UTC [11]. time.tzname is the name of the time zone as a tuple. The first of these is the DST (Daylight Saving Time) and the second one the local DST time zone. The latter may be ignored if not specified. It is not applicable for India; the time zone name for Indian time is 'IST (Indian Standard Time)' [13].

The attributes time.monotonic(), time.perf_counter(), and time. process_time() represent the system time with clear differences—all of them

Table 11.2 Formatting details for time representation

Type specifier	Meaning	Examples
"%a"	Weekday name (abbreviated)	Sun, Mon, ..., Sat
"%A"	Weekday name (full)	Sunday, Monday, ... Saturday
"%w"	Weekday (number) ·	0, 1, ... 6
"%d"	Day of the month	01, 02, 09, 10, 11, ... 31
"%b"	Name of the month (abbreviated)	Jan, Feb, ... Dec
"%B"	Name of the month (full)	January, February, ...
"%m"	Month (decimal number)	01, 02, ... 09, 10, 11, 12
"%y"	Year (without century)	00, 01, 02, ...
"%Y"	Year (four digit)	0001, 0002, ... 2016, ... 9998, 9999
"%H"	Hour (24-h clock)	01, 02, ... 10, 11, ... 23
"%p"	AM/PM	AM/PM
"%M"	Minutes	00, 01, 02, ... , 59
"%S"	Seconds	00, 01, 02, ..., 59
"%f"	Microseconds	000000, 000001, ... 999999
"%z"	UTC offset (+HHMM/−HHMM)	(empty), +0230, −0230
"%Z"	Time zone name	(empty), UTC, IST, EST
"%j"	Day of the year	001, 002, ... 365, 366
"%U"[a] "%W"[b]	Week number of the year	00, 01, ... 52, 53
"%c"	Appropriate date and time representation	'Fri Feb 19 14:16:00 2016'
"%x"	Appropriate date representation	02/19/2016
"%X"	Appropriate time representation	14:16:00
"%%"	A literal "%" character	−

[a]00 signifies the week of days before 1st Sunday of the year
[b]00 signifies the week of days before 1st Monday of the year

representing time as floating point numbers correct to different precision levels. None of these is related to the epoch or the Gregorian calendar. All are derived from the processor from its basic clock.

time.monotonic() is monotonic clock to the highest precision possible (1 ns here). It is not affected by system clock updates. time.perf_counter() is similar to time.monotonic() but follows system clock updates. time.process_time() represents the time the processor spends on the specific process concerned. It is not affected by the idling time of the processor. All these three quantities represent relative time values. Their absolute value is not significant; only relative differences count here. time.sleep(**n**) suspends execution of the Python processor for *n* seconds. The set of times in [1] in Fig. 11.5 bring out the subtle differences in the three attributes. time.monotonic(), time.perf_counter(),

Table 11.3 Time and date conversion possibilities with `time` module

Method	Arguments	Returned quantity
.gmtime()	Nil	Local time in 9-field format
	Epoch time in seconds—t_e	t_e as UTC time—9-field format
.localtime()	Nil	Local time in 9-field format
	Time in seconds—t_s	T_s as local time—9-field format
.strftime()	Format, 9-field string	Date-time string in specified format
.strptime()	String, format	Time in 9-field format
.asctime()	Nil	Local time in specified format
	Time as 9-field string	time in specified format
.ctime()	Nil	Current time returned in specified format
	Epoch time in seconds—t_e	Local time returned in specified format
.mktime()	Time as 9-field string	Epoch time in seconds
Calendar.timegm()	Time as 9-field string	

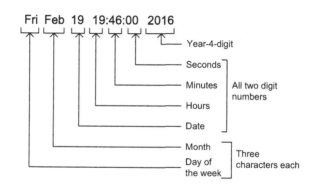

Fig. 11.4 Representation of time and date in Python in the string format

and `time.process_time()` are obtained; after an idle time (`time.sleep(5)` of 5 s) all the three are again sought (Their respective values after the 5 s sleep period). The `perf_counter()` value is marginally larger than the `time.monotonic()` value. The increase represents the processor processing time (~1.5 μs). Their values after the execution of the command line are again only marginally greater than 5 s [2]. These increases again represent the respective processing times. In fact the absolute value here 10909.75 s (3 h 0 min 9 s) represents the time after the PC was turned on. `time.process_time()` values are quite small. They represent the time spent by the processor for the task. Note that the 5 s sleep time does not affect this value. `.perf_counter()` signifies a system wide time. `.process_time()` signifies the time for the specific process. Of course their difference matters when more than one process is running on the system. Both these

```
>>> import time
>>> tt = time.monotonic(),time.perf_counter(),
time.process_time(), time.sleep(5),
time.monotonic(),time.perf_counter(),time.process_time() [1]
>>> tt
(10804.752875891, 10804.752877337, 0.026679803000000002,
None, 10809.757923513, 10809.757924931, 0.026719506)
>>> tt[4]-tt[0], tt[5]-tt[1], tt[6]-tt[2]                    [2]
(5.0050476220003475, 5.005047594000644, 3.970299999999857e-
05)
>>> def aabb(a,b):                                          [3]
...     'illustrate difference between time.perf_counter(),
time.process_time()'
...     t1a, t2a = time.perf_counter(), time.process_time()
                                                            [4]
...     jj, kk = 0, 0
...     while jj < a:
...       while kk < b:kk += 1
...       kk = 0
...       jj += 1
...     time.sleep(1)                                       [5]
...     t1b, t2b = time.perf_counter(), time.process_time()
                                                            [6]
...     return  t1a, t1b, t2a, t2b                          [7]
...
>>> cc = aabb(1000, 1000)                                   [8]
>>> cc
(11155.423874185, 11156.489652546, 0.029701717000000002,
0.094428805)
>>> cc[1]-cc[0], cc[3]-cc[2]                                [9]
(1.0657783610004117, 0.064727088)
>>> cd = aabb(500, 1000)                                    [10]
>>> cd
(11234.591541786, 11235.628423382, 0.095591875,
0.131425346)
>>> cd[1]-cd[0], cd[3]-cd[2]                                [11]
(1.036881596000967, 0.03583347099999999)
>>>
```

Fig. 11.5 Python Interpreter sequence illustrating the use of features in the `time` module

can be used to ascertain and compare the time of execution of different routines. The function **aabb(a, b)** [3] is to illustrate such an application. The arguments **a** and **b** here are integers. **kk** is repeatedly incremented from 0 to **b** − 1, **a** times. This defines the function. Its time of execution should be **a** * **b** times the time to increment. Overheads will increase it marginally. **t1a** and **t2a** are the values of time.perf_counter() and time.process_time() at the start of execution of **aabb()** [4]; **t1b** and **t2b** are their respective values at the end [6]. All these four quantities are returned by the function [7]. After execution of the main routine, the time.sleep(1) [5] adds an additional idling second to the function. aabb() is

```
>>> tstrg = ('clock', 'monotonic', 'perf_counter',
'process_time', 'time')                              [1]
>>> for jj in
range(len(tstrg)):time.get_clock_info(tstrg[jj])
...
namespace(adjustable=False, implementation='clock()',
monotonic=True, resolution=1e-06)
namespace(adjustable=False,
implementation='clock_gettime(CLOCK_MONOTONIC)',
monotonic=True, resolution=1e-09)
namespace(adjustable=False,
implementation='clock_gettime(CLOCK_MONOTONIC)',
monotonic=True, resolution=1e-09)
namespace(adjustable=False,
implementation='clock_gettime(CLOCK_PROCESS_CPUTIME_ID)',
monotonic=True, resolution=1e-09)
namespace(adjustable=True,
implementation='clock_gettime(CLOCK_REALTIME)',
monotonic=False, resolution=1e-09)
>>> time.altzone                                     [2]
-19800
>>>
```

Fig. 11.6 Python Interpreter sequence displaying details of times in time module (continued from Fig. 11.14)

called with a = 1000 and b = 1000 and the returned tuple (of four numbers) assigned to cc[8]. **cc**[3]–**cc**[2] is the increase in the processing time representing the execution duration. **cc**[1]–cc[0] is essentially 1 s more than the specific process time represented by **cc**[3]–**cc**[2]. The program mainly involves 10^6 increments to a number. With 64 727 088 ns (**cc**[1]–**cc**[0]) as execution time, each increment takes 65 ns (apprx.). The basic speed of the processor is 3 Ghz (33 ns as basic clock time). The incrementing requires two processor clock periods for execution. The routine is executed again with a = 500 and b = 1000. The corresponding execution time (to do 500 000 increments) is 35 833 471 ns (apprx.)—half of the time for the last case as is to be expected.

process_time() can be used to compare the speed of performance of different algorithms. When multiple processes are involved the process_time() and perfo_counter() can be put to similar use at a different level.

The implementation details of individual clocks in the time module can be obtained by invoking the method time.get_clock_info('name_of_clock'). The details for the five clocks discussed earlier are obtained and displayed in the Python Interpreter sequence in Fig. 11.6 [1]. time.altzone stands for the offset (in seconds) of the local time from the UTC time. India—where this PC is run—is ahead of UTC by 5 h 30 min. Correspondingly time.altzone is −19 800 in India [2].

11.3 `datetime` Module

The `datetime` module has a set of classes and constants (attributes) defined in it. These are useful to define specific dates, times, time intervals and the like. They facilitate working with different instances of time, their relations and so on. The classes `date`, `time`, `datetime`, and `timedelta` are classes defined in `datetime`; each has methods defined within it which follows a pattern. We shall illustrate these and see how they are all closely related. The Python Interpreter sequence in Fig. 11.7 has the class date (within the module datetime) in focus. Date (1990, 11, 22) in [1] represents a specific date (22nd Nov 1990) assigned to **d1**. The three arguments of date are the year (four digits), month (two digits) and date (two digits) respectively. `date.today()` assigned to **d2** [2] represents the corresponding data for today (the day this sequence was prepared).

`date.timetuple(d1)` and `date.timetuple(d2)` in [3] return the respective 9-field `tuple`s of time instant discussed earlier (`time.struct_time`). The hour, minute, and seconds values are set to zero here—date being the concern. The three items in date can be accessed and changed separately using year, month, and day as the respective keys. As an example the year in **d1** is changed to 1992 and the changed date assigned to **d3** in [4]. `date.timetuple[d3]` is in [5]. **d3**.`toor-dinal` [6] returns the number of days elapsed from the start of the proleptic Gregorian calendar up to the day of **d3**. (727 524: 2015 × 365 = 735 475. The disparity 727 524–735 475 is due to the corrections to the calendar implemented at the time of adoption of the calendar and also on other occasions). `date.fro-mordinal(727 524)` [7] converts the number back to the date we started with. The date corresponding to any time from epoch in seconds (such as one returned by `time.time()`) can be retrieved using `time.fromtimestamp()`. With **t1** in [8] as argument the corresponding date is retrieved in [9]. The residual hours etc., are ignored here.

d3.`weekday()` [10] returns the weekday that **d3** represents. Here Monday is taken as 0 and Saturday as 6. However **d3**.`isoweekday()` represents the day with Monday as 1 and Sunday as 7 (in line with the ISO Standard). This explains the difference between the two integers (6 and 7) returned.

A week in the ISO calendar starts on a Monday. If the first of January in a year is on a Friday, Saturday, or Sunday the first week of the year starts on the Monday following; else it starts on the Monday preceding. The first of January is on a Monday in 1990, Tuesday in 1991, Wednesday in 1992 and Friday in 1993 [11] and [12]. **dd1**.`isocalendar()` [13] returns a 3-`tuple` with year, week number, and weekday as its three elements. All these three quantities conform to the ISO Calendar. January 1st of 1992 being a Friday it is shown as being in the 53rd week (of year 1991). In the other three cases January 1st is on Monday, Tuesday, and Wednesday and it is in the first week of the year. **d3**.`isoformat()` and **d3**.`__str__()` [14] also return the date information in **d3** but to a different format as YYYY-MM-DD. **d3**.`ctime()` [15] returns `time.ctime()` corresponding to **d3**.`timetuple()`. In fact it is equivalent to `time.ctime(time.mktime`

```
>>> from datetime import date
>>> d1 = date(1990, 11, 22)                                 [1]
>>> d2 = date.today()                                       [2]
>>> date.timetuple(d1), date.timetuple(d2)                  [3]
(time.struct_time(tm_year=1990, tm_mon=11, tm_mday=22,
tm_hour=0, tm_min=0, tm_sec=0, tm_wday=3, tm_yday=326,
tm_isdst=-1), time.struct_time(tm_year=2016, tm_mon=2,
tm_mday=23, tm_hour=0, tm_min=0, tm_sec=0, tm_wday=1,
tm_yday=54, tm_isdst=-1))
>>> d3 = d1.replace(year=1992)                              [4]
>>> date.timetuple(d3)                                      [5]
time.struct_time(tm_year=1992, tm_mon=11, tm_mday=22,
tm_hour=0, tm_min=0, tm_sec=0, tm_wday=6, tm_yday=327,
tm_isdst=-1)
>>> d3.toordinal()                                          [6]
727524
>>> date.fromordinal(727524)                                [7]
datetime.date(1992, 11, 22)
>>> t1 = 1455891360.1407747                                 [8]
>>> date.fromtimestamp(t1)                                  [9]
datetime.date(2016, 2, 19)
>>> d3.weekday(), d3.isoweekday()                           [10]
(6, 7)
>>>
dd1,dd2,dd3,dd4=date(1990,1,1),date(1991,1,1),date(1992,1,
1),date(1993,1,1)                                           [11]
>>> dd1.weekday(), dd2.weekday(), dd3.weekday(),
dd4.weekday()                                               [12]
(0, 1, 2, 4)
>>> dd1.isocalendar(),
dd2.isocalendar(),dd3.isocalendar(),dd4.isocalendar()
((1990, 1, 1), (1991, 1, 2), (1992, 1, 3), (1992, 53, 5))
                                                            [13]
>>> d3.isocalendar(), d3.isoformat(), d3.__str__()          [14]
((1992, 47, 7), '1992-11-22', '1992-11-22')
>>> d3.ctime()                                              [15]
'Sun Nov 22 00:00:00 1992'
>>> d3.strftime("%d %B %Y"), d3.__format__("%d %B %Y")[16]
('22 November 1992', '22 November 1992')
>>> date.min, date.max, date.resolution                    [17]
(datetime.date(1, 1, 1), datetime.date(9999, 12, 31),
datetime.timedelta(1))
```

Fig. 11.7 Python Interpreter sequence illustrating the use of features in the datetime module

(**d3**.timetuple()). The date information can be converted into the date-month-year format with strftime() and .__format__(). Both return the date information to the same format here [16].

date.min and date.max represent the earliest and the last date which can be accommodated in the date class. They are 1-1-1 and 12-31-9999 respectively [15]. date.resolution is the smallest interval possible. It is one day [17].

11.3.1   *time Objects*

The datetime module has a class time defined in it (not to be confused with the time module discussed at the beginning of the chapter). All arguments within it implicitly use the local time as the basis—unless separately specified (see Sect. 11.3.4). The methods provided here and the arguments used are all in line with similar ones in the date class in the foregoing section.

The object time can be defined with values for hour, minute, second, microsecond, (and time zone if specified) as its arguments; they are in the same order as here with value of hour at the left end. All these are optional. If anyone of this set is left out the rest are specified as in a dict with hour, minute, second, and microsecond as the respective keys. Two aspects of any instance of time are noteworthy:

- The default values for all the arguments are zero; hence only the non-zero values need be specified.
- If the order is maintained the time instance can be compactly set in terms of numbers alone without resorting to the dict format. Thus time(2), time(2, 3), time(2, 3, 4), and time(2, 3, 4, 567 899) are all time objects representing times of (2 h), (2 h 3 min), (2 h 3 min 4 s), and (2 h 3 min 4 s 567 899 µs.) respectively.

In the Python Interpreter sequence in Fig. 11.8 **t1** in [2] has been specified with hour, minute, second, and microsecond being 11, 12, 13, and 145 678 respectively, in the same order. The respective keys are not given since the order is maintained. **tm** in [3] has been specified as a time of 12 min. Since all arguments following minutes are zero they are not displayed here. The rest of the quantities are understood to be zero. **tm** value in the following lines confirms this. A time object like **t1** can be edited and specific arguments in it changed using the method re-place(). **t3** in [4] has been redefined in this manner. **tt**.isoformat() returns a string representing the value of the time object **tt**. The string confirms to ISO 8601 format as 'HH:MM:SS:mmmmmm'. The values of **t1**, **tm** and **t3** are returned as a tuple in [5]. The method .__str__() in [6] is functionally the same as the method isoformat(). **tt**.strftime() returns the time object **tt** as a string. Its format is specified as an argument string. The formatting details conform to Table 11.2. **t1** is displayed in this manner in [7]. .__format__() is functionally equivalent to strftime(). .dst() returns the DST value if specified. In India where this PC is run DST is none. Hence **t1**.dst() and tz.dst() in [9] return (None, None) as a tuple.

```
>>> from datetime import  time                            [1]
>>> t1 = time(11, 12, 13, 145678)                         [2]
>>> tm = time(minute = 12)                                [3]
>>> tm
datetime.time(0, 12)
t3 = t1.replace(hour = 10, second = 14)                   [4]
>>> t1.isoformat(),tm.isoformat(), t3.isoformat()         [5]
('11:12:13.145678', '00:12:00', '10:12:14.145678')

>>> t1.__str__()                                          [6]
'11:12:13.145678'
>>> t1.strftime("%H:%M:%S")                               [7]
'11:12:13'
>>> t1.__format__("%H:%M:%S")                             [8]
'11:12:13'
>>> t1.dst(), t3.dst()                                    [9]
(None, None)
>>> time.min, time.max, time.resolution                   [10]
(datetime.time(0, 0), datetime.time(23, 59, 59, 999999),
datetime.timedelta(0, 0, 1))
>>>
```

Fig. 11.8 Features of time class in the datetime module

time.min and time.max are the respective minimum and maximum time values that can be specified. They are (0, 0) and (23, 59, 59, 999 999) respectively as can be seen from [10].

11.3.2 *datetime Objects*

The date class pertains to dates and related methods. They have the Gregorian Calendar as the basis. The time class pertains to the time instances and intervals with 24 h 60 min 60 s for a day (any changes to the day by the addition of one second done when necessary to account for the slowing down of Earth is not considered). The datetime class offers methods which are meaningful combinations of their counterparts in date and time. Similarly the objects on offer here are meaningful combinations of their counterparts in date and time. The Python Interpreter sequence in Fig. 11.9 brings out the salient features of datetime. datetime is imported from datetime module [1]. datetime.now() [2] returns the current local date and time together as a tuple. Essentially it represents the time since epoch as a tuple. It has the year, the month, day of the month, hour, minute, second, and microsecond as its elements. datetime.today() also has the same items on offer. But depending on the platform now() may offer relatively better precision. datetime.utcnow() too represents the time since epoch but as a tuple conforming to the UTC. [2] returns all these three quantities. The differences are only

in microseconds (57 and 15 respectively) being the delay in the sequential executions. Barring this difference, now() and today() are the same. utcnow()—being
UTC-based—is behind these by 5 h, 30 min. Any time since epoch can be

(a)

```
>>> from datetime import datetime                          [1]
>>> n2, d2, nu = datetime.now(), datetime.today(),
datetime.utcnow()                                          [2]
>>> n2, d2, nu
(datetime.datetime(2016, 3, 9, 19, 58, 50, 473443),
datetime.datetime(2016, 3, 9, 19, 58, 50, 473500),
datetime.datetime(2016, 3, 9, 14, 28, 50, 473515))
>>> dt1 = datetime(1990, 11, 22, 11, 12, 13, 145678)  [3]
>>> dt1.timetuple()                                        [4]
time.struct_time(tm_year=1990, tm_mon=11, tm_mday=22,
tm_hour=11, tm_min=12, tm_sec=13, tm_wday=3, tm_yday=326,
tm_isdst=-1)
>>> dt1.utctimetuple()                                     [5]
time.struct_time(tm_year=1990, tm_mon=11, tm_mday=22,
tm_hour=11, tm_min=12, tm_sec=13, tm_wday=3, tm_yday=326,
tm_isdst=0)
>>> dt2 = dt1.replace(month = 9, minute = 33)          [6]
>>> dt2
datetime.datetime(1990, 9, 22, 11, 33, 13, 145678)
>>> dt1.toordinal()                                        [7]
726793
>>> dr = datetime.fromordinal(726793)                      [8]
>>> dr
datetime.datetime(1990, 11, 22, 0, 0)
>>> from datetime import date, time                        [9]
>>> d1, t1 = date(1990, 11, 22), time(11, 12, 13, 145678)
                                                          [10]
>>> datetime.combine(d1, t1)                              [11]
datetime.datetime(1990, 11, 22, 11, 12, 13, 145678)
>>> datetime.date(dt1), datetime.time(dt1)               [12]
(datetime.date(1990, 11, 22), datetime.time(11, 12, 13,
145678))
>>> dt1.weekday(), dt1.isoweekday(), dt1.isocalendar(),
dt1.isoformat()                                          [13]
(3, 4, (1990, 47, 4), '1990-11-22T11:12:13.145678')
>>> dt1.isoformat('&')
'1990-11-22&11:12:13.145678'
>>> dt1.__str__()                                        [14]
'1990-11-22 11:12:13.145678'
>>> ds = datetime.strptime("Tue Mar 8 21:22:23 2016", "%a
%b %d %H:%M:%S %Y")                                      [15]
>>> ds
datetime.datetime(2016, 3, 8, 21, 22, 23)
```

Fig. 11.9 a Python Interpreter sequence illustrating the use of features in the datetime class
(continued in Fig. 11.9b). **b** Python Interpreter sequence illustrating the use of features in the
datetime class (continued from Fig. 11.9a)

(b)

```
>>> dt1.__format__("%a %b %d %H:%M:%S %Y")                [16]
'Thu Nov 22 11:12:13 1990'
>>> dt1.ctime()                                           [17]
'Thu Nov 22 11:12:13 1990'
>>> t1 = 1455891360.1407747                               [18]
>>> dp = datetime.fromtimestamp(t1)                       [19]
>>> dp
datetime.datetime(2016, 2, 19, 19, 46, 0, 140774)
>>> dup = datetime.utcfromtimestamp(t1)                   [20]
>>> dup
datetime.datetime(2016, 2, 19, 14, 16, 0, 140774)
>>> dt1.timestamp()                                       [21]
659252533.145678
>>> datetime.min, datetime.max, datetime.resolution       [22]
(datetime.datetime(1, 1, 1, 0, 0),
datetime.datetime(9999, 12, 31, 23, 59, 59, 999999),
datetime.timedelta(0, 0, 1))
>>>
```

Fig. 11.9 (continued)

represented as a datetime object—**dt1** in [3] is an example. The tuple here has the same fields as explained above. Any of them can be accessed through indexing or respective keys—as year, month, day, minute, second, or microsecond respectively. dt1.timetuple() returns **dt1** as a 9-field tuple as time.struct_time() [4]. tm_yday here signifies the serial number of the day concerned from January 1 of the year. dt1.utctimetuple [5] represents the same time as a tuple with UTC time as the basis.

Any element or selected combinations of elements in a datetime object like **dt1** can be redefined using their respective keys. Formation of **dt2** from **dt1** in [6] is an example. Here the month and minute alone have been redefined. **dt2** is accessed and displayed in the following line.

dt1. toordinal in [7] converts the date in the datetime object represented by **dt1** into the corresponding ordinal conforming to the Gregorian calendar. The reverse conversion—from ordinal to the corresponding datetime object is achieved using the method datetime.fromordinal(). Same is illustrated in [8] (where 726 793 obtained earlier is converted back to the corresponding datetime object); the hour, minute, second, and microsecond value are set to zero here.

A date object conforming to the date class and a time object conforming to the time class (the date and time classes described earlier) can be elegantly combined into a single a single datetime class. The same has been done in [10] and [11]. date and time have been imported from datetime module [9]. **d1** and **t1** are specific date and time objects [10] conforming to these. They have been combined in [11] to form the single datetime object which has all the respective elements in it in a single tuple. **d1** as a datetime object can be split into its

corresponding date and time components through datetime.date(**dt1**) and
datetime.time(**dt1**) respectively as in [12]. **dt1**.weekday() [13] returns the
serial weekday with Monday represented as 0. **dt1**.isoweekday() represents the
same conforming to the ISO (where 1 represents Monday).

dt1.isocalendar returns a tuple of three quantities from **dt1**; the year, the
week number, and the weekday—in the same order—are its elements [13]. All the
three of them conform to the ISO. **dt1**.isoformat in [13] returns a string. It
represents the date and time (as in **dt1**) in the ISO8601 format as YYYY-MM-DD
THH:mm:ss.mmmmmm (see Fig. 11.1). If the microsecond field is zero it will be
automatically left out of the string. Here T signifies the start of the time part of
dt1. It is inserted by default. Any desired character can be specified in its place.
Thus **dt1**.isoformat('&') will return the same string as '1990-11-22 &
11:12:13.145 678' as can be seen from the lines following.

dt1.__str__() [14] returns the same string as **dt1**.isoformat() itself.
datetime.strptime('str', format) accepts any date and time data and forms a
datetime object with it. The data has to be supplied as a string ('str' here) and its
format ('format' here) specified. ('str', format) in the same order forms the argument set. The format specification details are as in Table 11.2. [15] is an illustration
of its use to form the datetime object **ds**. **dt1**.__format__(format) returns **dt1**
itself as a formatted string [16] (Fig. 1.9b)—the reverse of what datetime.
strptime() does. **dt1**.ctime() also returns a string representing the date and
time of **dt1**. The formatting details conform to Table 11.2. This is in a specified
format [17]—same as with time.ctime() in [6] in Fig. 11.3. The format for **dt1**.
ctime() is fixed whereas that for **dt1**.__format__(format) has to be defined.

datetime.fromtimestamp(**t1**) [19] takes the argument **t1** as the time in
seconds from epoch [18] and returns the corresponding datetime object (Here **t1** is
taken as the epoch-based time at the location concerned (local time).
Correspondingly datetime.utctimestamp(**t1**) returns the time **t1** as the
datetime object with UTC as the basis [20]. **dt1**.timestamp() returns the
datetime object dt1 as the corresponding time from epoch in seconds [21]—a
floating point number similar to time.time() in [1] in Fig. 11.3.

datetime.min and datetime.max [22] represent the smallest and largest
values possible for datetime. datetime.resoluion [22] is the smallest possible
difference between two datetime values—1 µs.

These three quantities (their values) are in line with their counterparts—date.
min, date.max, and time.resolution in time class.

11.3.3 Time Intervals

The class timedelta in the module datetime facilitates formation of objects
representing time intervals. These can be used with objects of time() and date()
classes; their attributes also can be altered as desired. Instances of class time delta
represent time intervals. The time interval can be defined in terms of weeks, days,

```
>>> from datetime import timedelta                          [1]
>>> td1 = timedelta(weeks = 1, days = 2, hours = 3,
minutes = 4)                                                [2]
>>> td1
datetime.timedelta(9, 11040)
>>> td2 = timedelta(9, 11040)                               [3]
>>> td2
datetime.timedelta(9, 11040)
>>> td3
=timedelta(days=2,hours=3,minutes=4,seconds=5,milliseconds
=6,microseconds=7)                                          [4]
>>> td3
datetime.timedelta(2, 11045, 6007)
>>> td4=timedelta(days=-2,hours=3,minutes=-4seconds=-
5,milliseconds=-6,microseconds=7)                           [5]
>>> td4
datetime.timedelta(-2, 10554, 994007)
>>> td1.total_seconds()                                     [6]
788640.0
>>>
```

Fig. 11.10 Python Interpreter sequence illustrating the use of features in the timedelta class

hours, minutes, seconds, milliseconds, and microseconds. These can be used as keys to specify respective component values. When specified through the key in this manner, the order need not be maintained (any order is acceptable). All of them need not be necessarily specified. Those absent are taken as zero by default. Python stores the interval in terms of corresponding days, seconds, and microseconds and any necessary conversion is done internally—transparent to the user. The python Interpreter sequence in Fig. 11.10 pertains to timedelta and its attributes. timedelta is imported from datetime in [1]. **td1** in [2] is such a typical time interval specified. **td1** is converted and returned as datetime.timedelta (9, 11 040) in the following lines. **td2** in [3] is spelt out directly in terms of days and seconds without the keys. **td2** is returned as such in the following lines. The three arguments—days, seconds, and microseconds—can be specified in this compact manner in the same order. **td3** in [4] is a time interval specified with a precision of 1 µs. The argument values for timedelta can be positive or negative. **td4** [5] is a time interval some of its arguments being negative numbers. The corresponding stored value is returned in the following line.

$3 \text{ h} - 4 \text{ min} - 5 \text{ s} - 6 \text{ ms} + 7 \text{ µs} = (3 \times 3600 - 4 \times 60 - 6) \text{ s} + (1000\ 007 - 600) \text{ µs} = 10\ 554 \text{ s} + 994\ 007 \text{ µs}.$

Thus **td4** is stored as the tuple: (−2, 10 554, 994 007).

td1.total_seconds() returns the total interval value as seconds. [6] is an illustration.

The values of individual arguments in a timedelta object should be such that the time interval specified is within the range that can be supported by the data structure involving the three arguments—days, seconds, and microseconds. This implies the following constraints on the arguments specified.

timedelta.min: timedelta (−999 999 999) (=10^{10} − 1)

timedelta.max: timedelta(days = 999 999 999, hours = 23, minutes = 59, seconds = 59, microseconds = 999 999) (1010 days − 1 μs).

11.3.4 tzinfo

time and datetime objects discussed so far relate to the place of origin at the formation time. Taking specific examples datetime.now() as **n2** in [2] in Fig. 11.9 represents the time instant: 19 h, 58 min, 50.473443 s on the 9th of March 2016 in India, since the PC/system is operated in India. But the tuple that **n2** represents does not carry any information regarding the origin of the object **n2**. **n2** could as well have been a corresponding time instant in Bangladesh 30 min before (since Bangladesh Standard Time is 30 min ahead of India). Such an object in Python is called a 'naïve object'. Similarly nu (datetime.utcnow()) in [2] in Fig. 11.9 represents the time instant 72 μs (473 515–473 443) behind n2. But the representation here is 5 h 30 min. behind that of n2 since it has UTC as its reference. **nn** too is a naïve object. This is true of all the datetime/time related objects discussed so far. All these are naïve objects in the 'Pythonic' sense. None of them carry any information regarding their origin. Python has the provision to incorporate the source-related information also into the time concerned. Time instants and objects with such source information incorporated within them are called 'aware objects'. Extracting a naïve object from an aware object and clamping a naive object into a corresponding aware object are also possible. The tzinfo class in the datetime module serves these purposes.

tzinfo is an abstract base class which cannot be instantiated. It has three methods defined in it. These together represent the full time source information:

- A convenient name that can be assigned to the time concerned—like IST (Indian Standard Time). It is called the 'tzname'.
- The time offset from UTC: it can have a value in minutes representing a timedelta in the range—±1439(24 × 60 − 1).
- The daylight saving time (DST) adjustment value in minutes (east of UTC is implied): DST value may normally extend up to 1 h. If it is zero DST is taken as None.

A typical implementation of tzinfo is shown in Fig. 11.11. It is designated '**desitime**' [2]. utcoffset is the method which returns the offset from UTC. It is 5 h 30 min here. tzname() returns a name given to the specific time zone. It is '**Bhatta_time**' (Courtesy 'Arya Bhatta'). dst() returns the DST value as None (since IST does not have a Daylight saving component in it). **desitime** is assigned to **dz1** in [3]. Its use to form aware objects has been illustrated using

(a)

```
>>> from datetime import tzinfo, datetime, timedelta [1]
>>> class desitime(tzinfo):                          [2]
...     def utcoffset(self, dt0):return timedelta(hours =
5, minutes = 30)
...     def tzname(self, dt0):return 'Bhatta_time'
...     def dst(self, dt): return timedelta(0)
...
>>> dz1 = desitime()                                 [3]
>>> ddnz, ddnu, ddnn = datetime.now(tz =
dz1),datetime.utcnow(), datetime.now()               [4]
>>> ddnz, ddnu, ddnn                                 [5]
(datetime.datetime(2016, 3, 11, 8, 8, 34, 75061,
tzinfo=<__main__.desitime object at 0x7efd18070da0>),
datetime.datetime(2016, 3, 11, 2, 38, 34, 75102),
datetime.datetime(2016, 3, 11, 8, 8, 34, 75105))
>>> ddnz.tzinfo, ddnu.tzinfo, ddnn.tzinfo            [6]
(<__main__.desitime object at 0x7efd18070da0>, None,
None)
>>> ddnz.utcoffset(), ddnz.tzname(), ddnz.dst()      [7]
(datetime.timedelta(0, 19800), 'Bhatta_time',
datetime.timedelta(0))
>>> class bdeshtime(tzinfo):                         [8]
...     def utcoffset(self, dt0):return timedelta(hours =
6)
...     def tzname(self, dt0):return 'Bdeshtime'
...     def dst(self, dt0): return timedelta(0)
...
>>> dzb = bdeshtime(tzinfo)                          [9]
>>> ddne = ddnz.astimezone(tz = dzb)                 [10]
>>> ddne                                             [11]
datetime.datetime(2016, 3, 11, 8, 38, 34, 75061,
tzinfo=<__main__.bdeshtime object at 0x7f11877d5fd0>)
```

Fig. 11.11 a Python Interpreter sequence illustrating the use of features in the tzinfo class (continued in Fig. 11.11b). **b** Python Interpreter sequence illustrating the use of features in the tzinfo class (continued in Fig. 11.11a)

datetime.now() [4]. datetime.now(tz = **dz1**) in [4] is assigned to **ddnz**. tz having been assigned to **dz1**, **ddnz** carries the information regarding the time zone of its formation; it is an aware object. datetime.now() as **ddnn** in [4] has tz as None by default. It remains naïve. Barring this difference **ddnz** and **ddnn** are the same (of course making allowance for the 75 105–75 061 = 44 µs processor delay in the formation of **ddnn**). datetime.utcnow() as **ddnu** [4] represents the same instant with reference to UTC. It can be seen to be 5 h 30 min behind **ddnz** and **ddnn** (allowing for the disparity of a few µs as mentioned earlier). Implicitly **ddnu** has tz as None and remains naïve. **ddnz**, **ddnu** and **ddnn**—all the three of them have been

(b)

```
>>> ddne.utcoffset(), ddne.tzname(), ddne.dst()          [12]
(datetime.timedelta(0, 21600), 'Bdeshtime',
datetime.timedelta(0))
>>> ddn0 = ddnz.replace(tzinfo = None)
>>> ddn0
datetime.datetime(2016, 3, 11, 8, 8, 34, 75061)          [13]
>>> from datetime import time                            [14]
>>> dtz = time(7, 38, 34, 75061, tzinfo = dz1)           [15]
>>> dtz
datetime.time(7, 38, 34, 75061, tzinfo=<__main__.desitime
object at 0x7f11877d5da0>)
>>> dtz.utcoffset(), dtz.dst(), dtz.tzname()
(datetime.timedelta(0, 19800), datetime.timedelta(0),
'Bhatta_time')                                           [16]
>>> dtz.isoformat()                                      [17]
'07:38:34.075061+05:30'
>>> dtzb = dtz.replace(tzinfo = dzb)
>>> dtzb
datetime.time(7, 38, 34, 75061, tzinfo=<__main__.bdeshtime
object at 0x7f11877d5fd0>)
>>> dtzb.isoformat()                                     [18]
'07:38:34.075061+06:00'
>>>
```

Fig. 11.11 (continued)

accessed and their values shown in [5]. The `tz` information for all the three objects has been reproduced in [6]. **ddnu**.`tzinfo` and **ddnn**.`tzinfo` remain `None` and **ddnz**. `tzinfo` returns its address [7]. The three attributes of **ddnz**.`tzinfo` accessed as **ddnz**.utcoffset, **ddnz**.tzname, and **ddnz**.dst [7] are the values assigned in [2] and [3] earlier.

The `datetime` represented by an aware object like **ddnz** can be changed to another (in a different `timezone`) through the use of its `tzinfo`. `.astimezone()` can be used for this with the new `timezone` information as argument. A new `tzinfo` set has been defined as **bdesh**(`tzinfo`) in [8]. It is assigned to **dzb** in [9]. **ddne** [10] is formed as a new datetime object [11] representing the same time instant as **ddnz** itself. But it has been expressed as 'Bangladesh time'. **ddne** too is an aware object. Its time zone components are in [12]—as defined for **dzb** in [9].

ddnz.`replace` (`tzinfo = None`) 'erases' `tzinfo` (the time zone information) in **ddnz** and converts it into a naïve object; it is assigned to **ddno**. Value of **ddno** in [13] confirms this.

The time objects discussed in Sect. 11.3.1 are all naïve—the default `tz` value was `None` for all of them. A naïve time too can be converted into a corresponding aware time by tagging the associated `tzinfo` into it. `time` has been imported in [14] from the `datetime` module. **dtz** has been defined as an aware time with `tzinfo = dz1` [15]. It represents the time—7 h 38 min 34.75061 s as '**Bhatta_time**'—confirmed in

[16]. **dtz** being an aware time, **tdz**.isoformat [17] displays the time conforming to the ISO format. By way of an exercise **dtz**.replace(tzinfo = **dzb**) changes the tzinfo in **dtz** and assigns the new time to **dtzb**. **dtzb** is an aware object with 'Bdesh_time' as basis. The same is displayed in ISO format in [18].

11.3.5 Algebra with Time Objects

Objects of the type date, datetime and timedelta can be combined meaningfully to form other objects. The combination operations are of the add, subtract, multiply, and divide types. The operation should be meaningful and dimensionally correct (for example a floating point number cannot be added to a timedelta object but a multiplication of a timedelta by a number is like scaling and is acceptable). The basic operations possible are illustrated here.

The Python Interpreter sequence in Fig. 11.12 is concerned with time intervals represented by timedelta type objects. timedelta has been imported from module datetime. **td1** and **td3** have been defined as two time intervals [2], [3]. **td4** and **td5** are two objects formed as **td1** + **td3** and **td1** − **td3** [4]. Their values in the following lines represent these intervals in days, seconds, and microseconds.

```
>>> from datetime import timedelta                        [1]
>>> td1 = timedelta(weeks = 1, days = 2, hours = 3,
minutes = 4)                                              [2]
>>> td3 = timedelta(days=2, hours=3, minutes=4, seconds=5,
milliseconds=6, microseconds=7)                           [3]
>>> td4, td5, td6, td7 = td1+td3, td3-td1, td3*3, td1*2.71
                                                          [4]
>>> td4, td5, td6, td7
(datetime.timedelta(11, 22085, 6007), datetime.timedelta(-
7, 5, 6007), datetime.timedelta(6, 33135, 18021),
datetime.timedelta(24, 63614, 400000))
>>> tf0, tf1, ff1, ii1 = td1/3.24, td3/2, td3/td1,
td1//td3                                                  [5]
>>> tf0, tf1, ff1, ii1
(datetime.timedelta(2, 70607, 407407),
datetime.timedelta(1, 5522, 503004), 0.23311651197884967,
4)
>>> td3, tt0 = td1%td3, divmod(td1, td3)                  [6]
>>> td3, tt0
(datetime.timedelta(0, 53259, 975972), (4,
datetime.timedelta(0, 53259, 975972)))
>>> abs(td1), str(td1), repr(td1)                         [7]
(datetime.timedelta(9, 11040), '9 days, 3:04:00',
'datetime.timedelta(9, 11040)')
>>>
```

Fig. 11.12 Python Interpreter sequence illustrating the algebraic features with timedelta class

The timedelta objects can be multiplied by integers or floating point numbers—positive or negative. The result is also a timedelta object. If necessary it will be rounded to microseconds. If the result is outside the permissible range an error will be returned. As illustration **td3** * 3 and **td1** * 2.71 are formed and assigned to **td6** and **td7** in [4]. Their values are in the following lines. timedelta value can be divided by a number (integer or floating point)—positive or negative. The result is also a timedelta object. **tf0** (=**td1**/3.24) and **tf1** (=**td3**/2) in [5] are illustrative examples. **td1** and **td3** being of the same type **td3**/**td1** [5] is a number (representing **td3** as a fraction of **td1**). Similarly **td1**//**td3**—being the floor of the ratio—is an integer (=4 in [5]). It signifies that **td1** is more than **td3** by four (but not five) times. **td1**%**td3** is the residue of the division. It is a time interval object [6]. divmod(**td1**, **td3**) combines the floor division and the residue operations and returns the result as a string of two elements—an integer and a timedelta object [6]. abs(**td1**) returns a positive timedelta its duration being the same as that of **td1** [7]. repr(**td1**) returns the time interval represented by **td1** as string. str(**td1**) returns **td1** as a string in a specified format [7]. repr(**td1**) and str(**td1**) essentially constitute executions of the functions repr() and str() respectively.

td3 has been defined as a timedelta object in [2] in Fig. 11.13. **dt1** [3] and **dt2** [4] are datetime objects—both being naïve. A timedelta object can be added to/subtracted from a datetime object. The result is another datetime object. **dt3** and **dt4** are datetime objects defined in this manner as **dt1** + **td3** and

```
>>> from datetime import timedelta, datetime, date    [1]
>>> td3 = timedelta(days=2, hours=3, minutes=4,
seconds=5, milliseconds=6, microseconds=7)
                                                      [2]
>>> dt1 = datetime(1990, 11, 22, 11, 12, 13, 145678)  [3]
>>> dt2 = datetime(1993, 12, 23, 18, 17, 16, 987654)  [4]
>>> dt3, dt4 = dt1+td3, dt2-td3                        [5]
>>> dt3, dt4
(datetime.datetime(1990, 11, 24, 14, 16, 18, 151685),
datetime.datetime(1993, 12, 21, 15, 13, 11, 981647))
>>> td0 = dt3 - dt2                                    [6]
>>> td0
datetime.timedelta(-1126, 71941, 164031)
>>> dt2 > dt1                                          [7]
True
>>> d1, d2 = date(1990, 11, 22),date(1993, 12, 23)    [8]
>>> d1-d2, d1+td3, d2-td0                              [9]
(datetime.timedelta(-1127), datetime.date(1990, 11, 24),
datetime.date(1997, 1, 22))
>>> d1 > d2                                            [10]
False
>>>
```

Fig. 11.13 Python Interpreter sequence illustrating the algebraic features with timedelta and datetime classes

dt2 − **td3** in [5]. Their values are accessed and shown in the following lines in the figure.

The difference between two datetime objects represents a time interval—it is a timedelta object. **dt3** − **dt2** is formed as a timedelta object in [6] and its value accessed and shown in the following line. Any two datetime objects can be compared since they are of the same type. The comparison operators can be used here with proper reinterpretation. **dt2** [4] of year 1993 is larger than **dt1** [3] of year 1990; hence **dt2** > **dt1** in [7] returns True implying **dt2** succeeds **dt1**. Other comparison operations also can be used in a similar manner.

The algebra relating datetimes between themselves and datetime with timedeltas are applicable to dates as well. When dates and timedeltas are combined only the date component of timedelta is significant. The time components (seconds, and microseconds) if present are ignored. **d1** and **d2** in [8] are two date objects. **d1** + **td3** [9] adds the years, months, and days of **td3** to the corresponding elements of date **dt1** to form a new date (incidentally only two days are to be added to dt1 to form the new date). Similarly **d2** − **td0** is a new date preceding **d2**. **d1** − **d2** [9] represents a time interval; it is automatically returned as a timedelta object.

Comparison operators can be used with dates. A date succeeding another is interpreted as the larger one; in this sense **d1** > **d2** is False [10]. Other comparisons can be done similarly.

11.4 Calendars

Calendar related operations are in focus in the calendar module. Calendars in different formats can be produced and printed using the classes and methods here. Date linked operations also can be done. The functions here use the datetime module for various operations (this need not concern us directly here since using the classes in calendar does not need a separate 'import of datetime' to be done). The calendar for any specific year can be set up in different ways. The months, weeks, and days in it can be accessed for any necessary operation. The selected calendar can be formatted or printed in desired formats. The Python Interpreter sequence in Fig. 11.14 illustrates the calendar related operations and their applications. The calendar module has been imported in [1]. The class calendar. TextCalendar(firstweekday = 0) instantiates a plain text calendar [2]. By default the week is taken as starting on a Monday. If necessary it can be set to any other day by assigning the proper integer value to firstweekday (for example firstweekday = 6 implies a week starting on Sunday). **cdr1** in [2] defines a text calendar with Monday (default value) as the first day of the week. The method cdr. prmonth (2016, 3, w = 4) prints the calendar for the third month of year 2016 in a specific tabular form as in the following lines. Here 'March 2016' is centered and displayed at the top. The week days—in their short form are in the following row. Each subsequent row represents a week. The week can be seen to start with a

```
>>> import calendar                                           [1]
>>> cdr1 = calendar.TextCalendar()                            [2]
>>> cdr1.prmonth(2016, 3, w = 4)                              [3]
              March 2016
  Mon  Tue  Wed  Thu  Fri  Sat  Sun
         1    2    3    4    5    6
    7    8    9   10   11   12   13
   14   15   16   17   18   19   20
   21   22   23   24   25   26   27
   28   29   30   31
>>> cdr1.formatmonth(2016, 3, w = 4)                          [4]
'         March 2016\nMon  Tue  Wed  Thu  Fri  Sat
 Sun\n    1    2    3    4    5    6\n   7    8    9   10
  11   12   13\n 14   15   16   17   18   19   20\n 21   22
  23   24   25   26   27\n 28   29   30   31\n'

>>> cdr2 = calendar.TextCalendar(firstweekday = 6)            [5]
>>> cdr2.pryear(2016, m = 2)                                  [6]
```
Reproduced separately in Figure 11.15
```
>>> cfr2016 = cdr2.formatyear(2016)                           [7]
>>> len(cfr2016)                                              [8]
2056
>>> cfr2016[:180]                                             [9]
'                              2016\n\n        January
 February                   March\nSu Mo Tu We Th Fr Sa
 Su Mo Tu We Th Fr Sa       Su Mo Tu We Th Fr Sa\n  '
>>> cfr2016[180:252]                                          [10]
'              1  2          1  2  3  4  5  6
  1  2  3  4  5\n  '
>>> cc1 = calendar.Calendar(firstweekday = 2)                 [11]
>>> ccliw = cc1.monthdayscalendar(2016, 3)                    [12]
>>> ccliw[:2]                                                 [13]
[[0, 0, 0, 0, 0, 0, 1], [2, 3, 4, 5, 6, 7, 8]]
```

Fig. 11.14 Python Interpreter sequence illustrating the features of calendar module

Monday; 'w = 4' specifies the width allocated for each day in the display to be equal to four. The default value is the minimal one–two per date with one intervening space. If necessary a specified number of blank lines can be added between rows by (by assigning the number to l). l = 0 by default implies no blank line between the rows of a week.

cdr1.formatmonth(2016, 3, w = 4) [4] returns the calendar data for March 2016 as a formatted string. In fact this is the formatted string counterpart of the printed information above.

cdr2 [5] has been defined as another text calendar with weeks beginning on Sundays. **cdr2**.pryear(2016, m = 2) prints the entire calendar for the year 2016 in a specified format. The same is shown separately in Fig. 11.15 (only the part pertaining to January–August). **cdr2**.pryear(y, w = 2, l = 1, c = 6, m = 3) is the general form for it. Values given are the default values for the arguments for the

```
                                        2016

                 January                              February
         Su Mo Tu We Th Fr Sa                 Su Mo Tu We Th Fr Sa
                           1  2                   1  2  3  4  5  6
          3  4  5  6  7  8  9                  7  8  9 10 11 12 13
         10 11 12 13 14 15 16                 14 15 16 17 18 19 20
         17 18 19 20 21 22 23                 21 22 23 24 25 26 27
         24 25 26 27 28 29 30                 28 29
         31

                  March                                April
         Su Mo Tu We Th Fr Sa                 Su Mo Tu We Th Fr Sa
             1  2  3  4  5                                    1  2
          6  7  8  9 10 11 12                  3  4  5  6  7  8  9
         13 14 15 16 17 18 19                 10 11 12 13 14 15 16
         20 21 22 23 24 25 26                 17 18 19 20 21 22 23
         27 28 29 30 31                       24 25 26 27 28 29 30

                   May                                  June
         Su Mo Tu We Th Fr Sa                 Su Mo Tu We Th Fr Sa
          1  2  3  4  5  6  7                           1  2  3  4
          8  9 10 11 12 13 14                  5  6  7  8  9 10 11
         15 16 17 18 19 20 21                 12 13 14 15 16 17 18
         22 23 24 25 26 27 28                 19 20 21 22 23 24 25
         29 30 31                             26 27 28 29 30

                  July                                August
         Su Mo Tu We Th Fr Sa                 Su Mo Tu We Th Fr Sa
                           1  2                   1  2  3  4  5  6
          3  4  5  6  7  8  9                  7  8  9 10 11 12 13
         10 11 12 13 14 15 16                 14 15 16 17 18 19 20
         17 18 19 20 21 22 23                 21 22 23 24 25 26 27
         24 25 26 27 28 29 30                 28 29 30 31
         31
```

Fig. 11.15 The calendar returned by executing 'cdr2.pryear(2016, m = 2)' in Fig. 11.14: only the part January–August is shown

year 'y'. 'w' is the width allocated for each date, 'l' is the number of lines per row, 'm' is the number of months in each row. The entire calendar of 12 months is split into groups of 'm' months and displayed as blocks of 'm' months in each row. 'c' is the spacing between adjacent months.

cdr2.formatyear(2016) returns the full calendar for 2016 as a formatted string [7]. The formatting details are identical to the pryear() method discussed above. The string (**cfr2016**) is of length 2056 characters [8]. The characters representing the first few lines of the calendar are accessed and reproduced in [9] and [10]. The formatting details can be related to the calendar in Fig. 11.15 above. When a calendar is defined by default a week is taken as starting on a Monday; this is true of **cdr1** in [1] and the following few executable statements in the figure. **cdr2** in [5] has the first day of the week defined as Sunday (with firstweekday); any other day can be defined as the first day of the week in the same manner. **cc1** [11] has the first day defined as Wednesday (firstweekday = 2).

A set of methods are available which return the calendar for a chosen year as a list. The ways in which the date, weekday, and the month are included in the list differ. **cc1**.monthdayscalendar(2016, 3) returns the calendar for the month of March in 2016 [12] as a list(**cc1iw**); here the week starts on a Wednesday. The calendar is arranged into weeks, every week starting on a Wednesday and ending on the following Tuesday. The dates are arranged accordingly. 1st March 2016 being a Tuesday the set of dates for the first week forms the list [0, 0, 0, 0, 0, 0, 0, 1]. For the second week it continues as [2, 3, 4, 5, 6, 7, 8]. This can be seen from **cc1iw**[:2] accessed and reproduced in [13].

The Python Interpreter sequence in Fig. 11.14 is continued in Fig. 11.16. **cc** in [14] is a calendar starting on a Sunday as earlier. **cciw** in [15] is the calendar for March 2016—similar to **cc1** in [11]. With the week starting on a Sunday (and 1st March falling on a Tuesday) the first 2 weeks look as follows (reproduced from **cciw** [:2] in [16]): [[0 0 1 2 3 4 5] [6 7 8 9 10 11 12]].

cc.monthdays2calendar(2016, 3) (=**ccmc**) [17] returns the calendar for the month of March 2016 as a list; it is again arranged week wise. [18] accesses the data for the first two weeks. The data for each day is a tuple of two numbers—the date and the day of the week respectively.

cc.monthdatescalendar(2016, 3) [19] returns the datetime.date() objects for the dates of the month concerned (March) as the object **ccmt**. These are also arranged week wise. The first week starting on a Sunday is represented by datetime.date(2016, 2, 28)—the 28th of February 2016 on a Sunday. **ccmt** [:2] [20] accesses the list of datetime.date objects for the first two weeks—starting with 28th of February (Sunday 2016) and ending with 12th March 2016.

cc.yeardatescalendar(2016) (=**ccyd** [21]) returns the full year's calendar as a list of datetime.date objects. The list is segmented into groups of three months each (default value—can be changed if desired). The data for each group is again arranged month wise and that for each month week wise (similar to.pryear () in [6] in Fig. 11.14). The week starts on the set day—Sunday here. [22] Accesses the 0th group of the calendar (months of January, February, and March)—the 0th month in it (January) and the first 3 weeks of this month (as **ccyd** [0][0][3]).

cc.yeardays2calendar(2016) (=**ccy2**) returns the similar calendar as a list for the year 2016 itself [23]. Here every day is represented as a tuple of date and weekday (similar to **ccmc** [18]). **ccy2** [0][0][3] in [24] shows the segment of the calendar for the first three weeks; these tuples represent the same set of datetime.date objects as in [22] above.

cc.yeardayscalendar(2016) (=**ccyt**) in [25] returns the full year's calen-dar arranged in the same form (default groups of three months each, each group of

```
>>> cc = calendar.Calendar(firstweekday = 6)              [14]
>>> cciw = cc.monthdayscalendar(2016, 3)                  [15]
>>> cciw[:2]                                               [16]
[[0, 0, 1, 2, 3, 4, 5], [6, 7, 8, 9, 10, 11, 12]]
>>> ccmc = cc.monthdays2calendar(2016, 3)                 [17]
>>> ccmc[:2]                                               [18]
[[(0, 6), (0, 0), (1, 1), (2, 2), (3, 3), (4, 4), (5, 5)],
 [(6, 6), (7, 0), (8, 1), (9, 2), (10, 3), (11, 4), (12,
5)]]
>>> ccmt = cc.monthdatescalendar(2016, 3)                 [19]
>>> ccmt[:2]                                               [20]
[[datetime.date(2016, 2, 28), datetime.date(2016, 2, 29),
datetime.date(2016, 3, 1), datetime.date(2016, 3, 2),
datetime.date(2016, 3, 3), datetime.date(2016, 3, 4),
datetime.date(2016, 3, 5)], [datetime.date(2016, 3, 6),
datetime.date(2016, 3, 7), datetime.date(2016, 3, 8),
datetime.date(2016, 3, 9), datetime.date(2016, 3, 10),
datetime.date(2016, 3, 11), datetime.date(2016, 3, 12)]]
>>> ccyd = cc.yeardatescalendar(2016)                     [21]
>>> ccyd[0][0][:3]                                        [22]
[[datetime.date(2015, 12, 27), datetime.date(2015, 12,
28), datetime.date(2015, 12, 29), datetime.date(2015, 12,
30), datetime.date(2015, 12, 31), datetime.date(2016, 1,
1), datetime.date(2016, 1, 2)], [datetime.date(2016, 1,
3), datetime.date(2016, 1, 4), datetime.date(2016, 1, 5),
datetime.date(2016, 1, 6), datetime.date(2016, 1, 7),
datetime.date(2016, 1, 8), datetime.date(2016, 1, 9)],
[datetime.date(2016, 1, 10), datetime.date(2016, 1, 11),
datetime.date(2016, 1, 12), datetime.date(2016, 1, 13),
datetime.date(2016, 1, 14), datetime.date(2016, 1, 15),
datetime.date(2016, 1, 16)]]
>>> ccy2 = cc.yeardays2calendar(2016)                     [23]
>>> ccy2[0][0][:3]                                        [24]
[[(0, 6), (0, 0), (0, 1), (0, 2), (0, 3), (1, 4), (2, 5)],
 [(3, 6), (4, 0), (5, 1), (6, 2), (7, 3), (8, 4), (9, 5)],
 [(10, 6), (11, 0), (12, 1), (13, 2), (14, 3), (15, 4),
(16, 5)]]
>>> ccyt = cc.yeardayscalendar(2016)                      [25]
>>> ccyt[0][0][:3]                                        [26]
[[0, 0, 0, 0, 0, 1, 2], [3, 4, 5, 6, 7, 8, 9], [10, 11,
12, 13, 14, 15, 16]]
```

Fig. 11.16 Python Interpreter sequence illustrating the features of calendar module

three separate months, each month of weeks starting on a Sunday. Here only the dates are included. The data for the first three weeks is accessed as **ccyt** [0][0][:3] in [26] and shown; these again correspond to the first three weeks in January 2016 (see also the calendar structure for January in Fig. 11.15).

There can be situations/application where one has to scan a calendar to identify a specific date/day like festivities or decide on a celebration of events and so on. In

```
>>> import calendar                                        [1]
>>> cc = calendar.Calendar(firstweekday = 6)              [2]
>>> ai0 = cc.iterweekdays()                                [3]
>>> list(ai0)                                              [4]
[6, 0, 1, 2, 3, 4, 5]
>>> aimd = cc.itermonthdates(2016, 3)#corresponds to
monthdatescalendar(2016,3)                                 [5]
>>> for jj in range(30):                                   [6]
...     an0  = next(aimd)
...     if an0.month == 3 and an0.day == 10:
...         jj0 = jj
...         break
...     continue
...
>>> jj0                                                    [7]
11
>>> ai1 = cc.itermonthdays2(2016, 3)#corresponds to
monthdays2(2016, 3)                                        [8]
>>> md1 = []
>>> kk = 1
>>> while kk < 8:
...     an1 = next(ai1)
...     if an1[0]:
...       md1.append(an1)
...       kk += 1
...
>>> md1                                                    [9]
[(1, 1), (2, 2), (3, 3), (4, 4), (5, 5), (6, 6), (7, 0)]
>>> ai2 = cc.itermonthdays(2016, 3)                       [10]
>>> mtd = []
>>> for jj in range(10):
...     mtd.append(next(ai2))
...
>>> mtd                                                    [11]
[0, 0, 1, 2, 3, 4, 5, 6, 7, 8]
>>>
```

Fig. 11.17 Python Interpreter sequence illustrating the use of iterators in the calendar module

such cases the full calendar need not be formed and used. An iterator is an effective alternative. A set of iterators are available in the calendar module which can be used in such cases. The Python Interpreter sequence in Fig. 11.17 accesses the iterators for specific cases and illustrates their use.

As earlier **cc** has been defined as a calendar in [2] with the week staring on a Sunday. **cc**.iterweeks() (=**ai0**) is an iterator for week days starting with Sunday [3]. list(**ai0**) in [4] is the full list of the corresponding week days. **cc**.itermonthdates(2016, 3) (=**aimd**) [5] is the iterator counterpart of monthdatescalendar(2016, 3) [19] in Fig. 11.16. The calendar for the month of March in 2016 is in focus here with **aimd** as the iterator for the datetime.date objects for all the dates of the month. It starts on the Sunday of the first week of the month. `Datetime.date`(2016, 2, 28) being the data for the first day of the week concerned, it forms the first element pointed by the `iterator`. An example illustrating the use of the `iterator` (though trivial) follows.

Example 11.1 Nevan who runs 'Royal Restaurant' left the station on the first day of March 2016 m and returned on the 10th of March. How many days was he out of station?

With **aimd** as **iterable** the routine from [6] counts the total number of days from the first up to the 10th of March 2016 (inclusive). 11 being the returned value [7], Nevan has been out of station for 12 days (the count starts with 0).

cc.itermonthdays2(2016, 3) in [8] is the `iterator` of all the (date, day) `tuples` formed in the `list` in [17] in Fig. 11.16. The (date, day) pairs for all the dates from the 1st to the 7th of March 2016 have been formed as a list and returned in [9]. It is done through a small routine here. The routine scans for the (date, day) `tuples`; as soon as the date becomes non-zero (=1) the routine starts appending the `tuples`; it continues until the 7th of March 2016. The list of `tuples` collected is returned. The first element in `list` is for the 1st of March on a Tuesday and the last—7th—for the following Monday.

itermonthdays(2016, 3) in [10] is the `iterable` representing the monthdayscalendar(2016, 3) in [15] in Fig. 11.16. (list of all the dates of the month of March starting on the first Sunday of the month). The routine from [10] in Fig. 11.17 returns the list of all the first 10 dates represented by the iterable.

All the illustrations above are centered on the calendar for the month of March 2016. Instead any month of any year in the admissible range can be used here.

A set of additional simple functions are available in the calendar module. The Python Interpreter sequence in Fig. 11.18 has the calendar module imported in [1]. calendar.setfirstweekday(calendar.WEDNESDAY) [2] directly sets the first week day as Wednesday. calendar.firstweekday() [3] returns the integer representing the firstweekday. It has been reset to Sunday in [4]. calendar. isleap(**y**) confirms whether '**y**' as an year is a leap year. 2016 in [5] as an example—it is confirmed as a leap year. calendar.leapdays(**y1**, **y2**) returns the total number of leap years in the interval (**y1**, **y2**) (inclusive). calendar. leapdays(2001, 2017) returns the number as four years [6] (2004, 2008, 2012, and 2016).

The weekday of any specified date can be obtained directly. calendar.weekday(2016, 3, 21) returns the day as a Sunday [7]. calendar.weekheader(5) returns the header of the calendar as a string having the abbreviated weekday names [8]. 5 is the width for each day set. This can be change to any other desired value.

calendar.monthcalendar(2016, 3) returns the calendar for the month of March 2016 [9] as a matrix with only the dates; successive weeks (starting with the first) are in successive rows. Days of the first week in the previous month and those of the last week in the succeeding month have zeros in place of the actual dates (similar to a typical month sheet in the calendar): compare this with.formatmonths() in [4] in Fig. 11.14. calendar.month(2016, 3) [10] returns the

```
>>> import calendar                                              [1]
>>> calendar.setfirstweekday(calendar.WEDNESDAY)                 [2]
>>> calendar.firstweekday()                                      [3]
2
>>> calendar.setfirstweekday(calendar.SUNDAY)                    [4]
>>> calendar.isleap(2016)                                        [5]
True
>>> calendar.leapdays(2001, 2017)                                [6]
4
>>> calendar.weekday(2016, 3, 21)                                [7]
0
>>> calendar.weekheader(5)                                       [8]
' Sun   Mon   Tue   Wed   Thu   Fri   Sat '
>>> calendar.monthcalendar(2016, 3)                              [9]
[[0, 0, 1, 2, 3, 4, 5], [6, 7, 8, 9, 10, 11, 12], [13,
14, 15, 16, 17, 18, 19], [20, 21, 22, 23, 24, 25, 26],
[27, 28, 29, 30, 31, 0, 0]]
>>> calendar.month(2016, 3)                                     [10]
'     March 2016\nSu Mo Tu We Th Fr Sa\n      1  2  3  4
5\n 6  7  8  9 10 11 12\n13 14 15 16 17 18 19\n20 21 22
23 24 25 26\n27 28 29 30 31\n'
>>> calendar.prmonth(2016, 3)                                   [11]
     March 2016
Su Mo Tu We Th Fr Sa
       1  2  3  4  5
 6  7  8  9 10 11 12
13 14 15 16 17 18 19
20 21 22 23 24 25 26
27 28 29 30 31
>>> calendar.prcal(2016, m = 2)                                 [12]
Similar to calendar in Fig. 12.15
>>> calendar.monthrange(2016, 3)                                [13]
(1, 31)
>>> import time                                                 [14]
>>> tg0 = time.gmtime(1455891360.1407747)                       [15]
>>> tg0                                                         [16]
time.struct_time(tm_year=2016, tm_mon=2, tm_mday=19,
tm_hour=14, tm_min=16, tm_sec=0, tm_wday=4, tm_yday=50,
tm_isdst=0)
>>> calendar.timegm(tg0)                                        [17]
1455891360
```

Fig. 11.18 Python Interpreter sequence illustrating the usage of the additional methods/functions in calendar module

calendar for the whole month of March 2016 as a formatted string. calendar.prmonth(2016, 3) [11] is its printed counterpart; compare this with [3] in Fig. 11.14 where the formatting has been changed by allocating a larger width for each date. calendar.prcal(2016, m = 2) [12] prints the calendar for the entire year—similar to pryear(2016, m = 2) [6] in Fig. 11.14 and shown in Fig. 11.15.

calendar.monthrange(2016, 3) returns a tuple of two quantities—the first day of March 2016 and the number of days in March 2016—as (1, 31) [13]. Similar data can be obtained for any month in any selected year.

In addition to all the above the calendar module has a method.timegm. It accepts the 9-tuple struct_time() object in the time module as an argument and returns the corresponding time from epoch in seconds. time module has been imported [14]. **tg0** is formed as time.gmtime() in [15]; its argument is the time from epoch obtained in [1] in Fig. 11.3. **tg0** can be seen to be time.struct_time() in [16]. calendar.timegm(**tg0**) returns the time from epoch in seconds.

11.5   timeit Module

Python (like other programming languages) offers different possible coding sequences for a given task. It becomes necessary to compare code segments for their speed to decide on alternatives for implementation. 'timeit' is a convenient module for such comparisons; its use is illustrated here.

timeit.timeit() is a function to test a brief code segment under specified conditions. Its structure is shown in Fig. 11.19a. If necessary an initialization can be carried out wherein the assignments prior to embarking on execution of the code segment under test, can be done; the initialization part is specified as 'setup' for this. Once this is done the code segment to be tested can be executed repeatedly a fixed number of times. The function returns the total time for execution. Division by the number of executions yields the time for a single loop execution. Referring to Fig. 11.20a Python has been opened [1] and timeit imported [2]. The string "Are you staring" is tested for the presence of the letter (substring) "**g**" in it in [3].

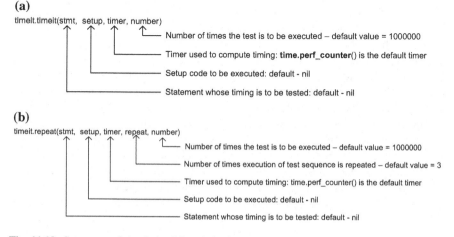

(a)

tImeit.tImeit(stmt, setup, timer, number)

— Number of times the test is to be executed – default value = 1000000

— Timer used to compute timing: **time.perf_counter()** is the default timer

— Setup code to be executed: default - nil

— Statement whose timing is to be tested: default - nil

(b)

timeit.repeat(stmt, setup, timer, repeat, number)

— Number of times the test is to be executed – default value = 1000000

— Number of times execution of test sequence is repeated – default value = 3

— Timer used to compute timing: time.perf_counter() is the default timer

— Setup code to be executed: default - nil

— Statement whose timing is to be tested: default - nil

Fig. 11.19 Structures of timeit.timeit() and timeit.repeat() functions

The test execution is carried out 10 000 times. The execution takes 844.11 μs—that is 844.11 ns per cycle. No 'setup' is required here. time.perfo_counter() is the timer clock (by default) used. If number = 10 000 were left out the default value of 1 000 000 will be used in its place. The same test is carried out in [4] with a setup operation preceding. **a1** and **b1** are assigned the strings "g", and "Are you staring" respectively as setup. The test '**a1** in **b1**' is carried out 10 000 times. The setup is done once at start and the time for it is not included in the test run. The test is repeated in the following line.

The time module is imported [5] and time.process_time() used as the timer clock in [6]. The function timeit.repeat() is similar to timeit.timeit() but the whole testing is repeated a specified number of times. The structure of timeit.repeat() is shown in Fig. 11.19b. The number of repeats has the default value three. If necessary it can be specified separately. Barring this timeit.repeat() is similar to timeit.timeit(). The timing test—"'**g**' in 'Are you staring'" is carried out three times (default value) and then five times in [7] and [8] respectively.

timeit.Timer() is a class defined in the module timeit. The defining statement with arguments and default options is shown in Fig. 11.21a. It is instantiated as **tt** in [9]. Timer.timeit(number = **xxx**) is a method in Timer which executes the test specified xxx times and returns the execution time. Default value for xxx is 1000,00. **tt**.timeit() is returned (for the default value of number = 1 000 000) in [10]. The method tt.repeat (r = 3, number = 1 000 000) executes the test repeatedly a specified number of times and returns the timings. Here again the default values are r = 3 and number = 1 000 000. **tt**.repeat() has been carried out for the default values in [11].

All the above timing tests have been done for testing whether "'**g**" in "Are you staring'" is True. The time per execution of the loop varies from 42.01 to 86.08 ns here. Even for the case of repeated tests (where the execution sequence and timing should be identical) the time durations vary. These variations are due to the interruptions in the program execution in the regular functioning of the processor. Hence the minimum execution time for the lot should be taken as the guiding value in any decision regarding comparison of the codes and their performance.

As another example a, b, c, and d are assigned values and $\sqrt{a+b+c+d}$ obtained in different ways in the lines following—with 10 000 000 runs (default number) in [12] and the same in the following line; the execution times per loop are 238.9 and 237.6 ns respectively. The function **chk**() in [13] (Fig. 11.20b) evaluates the same 1000 times repeatedly without invoking timeit or any of the functions within it. Increase in time.process_time() and time.perfo_time() (representing processing time) represent respective execution times. They are 538.5 and 538.4 ns respectively in the execution of **chk**() in [14]. The overheads here in terms of decrementing the counter variable **e** and checking its value in every loop add to the execution time; the increase in loop execution times here are mainly due to these. The sqrt function in the math module is used to evaluate $\sqrt{a+b+c+d}$

(a)

```
trp@trp-Veriton-Series:~$ python3.5 -q                    [1]
>>> import timeit                                         [2]
>>> timeit.timeit('"g" in "Are you staring"', number =
10000)                                                   [3]
0.0008441140000172709
>>> timeit.timeit('a1 in b1', setup = 'a1 = "g"; b1 =
"Are you staring"', number = 10000)                      [4]
0.0008608150000100068
>>> timeit.timeit('a1 in b1', setup = 'a1 = "g"; b1 =
"Are you staring"', number = 10000)
0.000842470999998568
>>> import time                                          [5]
>>> timeit.timeit('a1 in b1', setup = 'a1 = "g"; b1 =
"Are you staring"',timer = time.process_time, number=
10000)                                                   [6]
0.000843211
>>> timeit.repeat('a1 in b1', setup = 'a1 = "g"; b1 =
"Are you staring"', number = 10000)                      [7]
[0.0008424019997619325,
0.0008400020005865372,0.0008397960000365856]
[0.000861885999995593, 0.0008400990000154707,
0.000836861999971461]
>>> timeit.repeat('a1 in b1', setup = 'a1 = "g"; b1 =
"Are you staring"', number = 10000, repeat=5)            [8]
[0.000842976000001272, 0.0008368370000084724,
0.0008468860000334644, 0.0008398329999863563,
0.000839723000012782]
>>> tt = timeit.Timer('a1 in b1', setup = 'a1 = "g"; b1 =
"Are you staring"')                                      [9]
>>> tt.timeit()                                          [10]
0.050677361999987625
>>> tt.repeat()                                          [11]
[0.05228787999976703, 0.04205966100016667,
0.04201785000032032]
>>> timeit.timeit('(a+b+c+d)**0.5', setup = 'a=2; b=3;
c=4;d=5')                                                [12]
0.23894656800001712
>>> timeit.timeit('(a+b+c+d)**0.5', setup = 'a=2; b=3;
c=4;d=5')
0.237641372999974
```

Fig. 11.20 a Python Interpreter sequence to illustrate features of timeit module (continued in Fig. 11.20b). **b** Python Interpreter sequence to illustrate features of timeit module (continued in Fig. 11.20a)

in [15]. sqrt is imported from math module in setup prior to execution of the loop. The test returns 318 ns as timing per loop execution.

timeit module offers the facility to test code snippets for the execution times directly from the command line. The general format for the same is shown in

(b)

```
>>> def chk():                                              [13]
...     t1 = time.process_time(), time.perf_counter()
...     a, b, c, d, e = 2, 3, 4, 5, 10000
...     while e:
...         aa = (a+b+c+d)**0.5
...         e -= 1
...     t2 = time.process_time(), time.perf_counter()
...     return t2[0]-t1[0], t2[1]-t1[1]
...
>>> chk()                                                   [14]
(0.005385477999999999, 0.005383988000062345)
>>> timeit.timeit('sqrt(a+b+c+d)',setup = 'from math
import sqrt; a, b, c, d = 2, 3, 4, 5', number = 1000) [15]
0.0003181270000141012
```

Fig. 11.20 (continued)

(a)

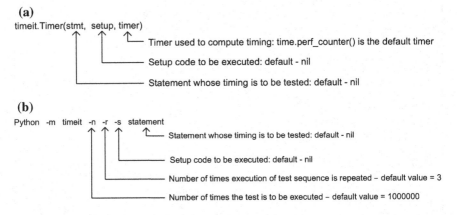

(b)

Fig. 11.21 Structures of **a** timeit.Timer() class and **b** Command line execution of timeit

Fig. 11.21b. Setup option, options for the number of runs and repetitions of the whole test are available. Timings of $\sqrt{a+b+c+d}$ are obtained in different ways in Fig. 11.22—all from the command line. The time for one execution is calculated and displayed directly here. In every case the best of three successive runs of the test is returned. a, b, c, and d are assigned values and $\sqrt{a+b+c+d}$ computed in [1] in every execution loop. The best execution time is 257 ns. math.sqrt is imported in every execution loop in [2]; in turn the best execution time extends to 1.98 μs. The assignment a, b, c, $d = 2$, 3, 4, 5 is done in setup in [3] and $\sqrt{a+b+c+d}$ computed in the execution loop—done 10 000 times; the test is repeated three times. The best execution time is 246 ns per loop; the same is 229 ns in [4] when done again.

```
trp@trp-Veriton-Series:~$ python3.5 -m timeit 'a, b, c, d =
2, 3, 4, 5; (a+b+c+d)**0.5'                                    [1]
1000000 loops, best of 3: 0.257 usec per loop
trp@trp-Veriton-Series:~$ python3.5 -m timeit 'a, b, c, d =
2, 3, 4, 5; from math import sqrt;sqrt(a+b+c+d)'      [2]
100000 loops, best of 3: 1.98 usec per loop
trp@trp-Veriton-Series:~$ python3.5 -m timeit  -n 10000 -r
3 -s 'a, b, c, d = 2, 3, 4, 5' '(a+b+c+d)**0.5'      [3]
10000 loops, best of 3: 0.246 usec per loop
trp@trp-Veriton-Series:~$ python3.5 -m timeit  -n 10000 -r
3 -s 'a, b, c, d = 2, 3, 4, 5' '(a+b+c+d)**0.5'      [4]
10000 loops, best of 3: 0.229 usec per loop
trp@trp-Veriton-Series:~$
```

Fig. 11.22 Command line execution of timeit

11.6 Exercises

1. A naïve scheme of archiving files is suggested here with a few possibilities of access alternatives. Implement the same for a set of 10 files through a program and test it with simulated data.

   For each file form a tuple (**fst**) with the file itself and a header as its two elements. The header as a tuple will have four fields as the file name assigned, the password supplied, date of creation, and the length of the file in bytes; the first two are supplied by the file owner; the date and file length computed by the program are added by the program. Use the hash value of the first three fields of the header together as the key and the tuple **fst** as the value. Form a dictionary of the (key, value) pairs. This forms the file archive. The file originator has to be queried using the input() function to provide the file name and the password when forming the file header.

   The file retrieval sequence is as follows:

   Query: Ask the file name and the password.

   Add the date of creation and form the hash value of the three.

   With the above hash value as the key scan the file set. If there is a match allow retrieval. Else deny access.

   On retrieval get the file length and compare it with the value in the header. In case of mismatch display a warning of '*file error*'.

   The three fields used at the time of creation (file name, date of creation, and the password) provide a rudimentary security to the file archive system. The same can be used for retrieval in different ways. Allow access on supplying any two of the three fields or a specific two of these fields. Implement all these.

2. Alternate formulations for solving the same problem have been used in the previous chapters in a number of cases. Compare their execution times using perfo_counter() as well as timeit(). Some of the cases are cited below:

   Cube root of 10 as in Example 3.10 and that using the pow() function

Ealuation of $5.1^{7.2}$ as in Exercise 3 (Sect. 5.3) and that using the pow() function $\sin(x)$, $\cos(x)$, and $\exp(x)$ as in Example 4.6 and those using the respective functions in the math module

Values π of using the four series in Exercise 6 (Sect. 4.3) and the value obtained using pi in the math module.

Scalar product of vectors with vectors given as lists as in Example 5.5 and the same taking the vectors as arrays.

Variance of a sample set as in Example 5.6 and the variance obtained using variance() in the statistics module. Do the same taking the sample set as an array.

Sorting of a data set using sort() and that using heapq() in a loop.

References

ITU (2002) Recommendation ITU-R TF.460–6* Standard-frequency and time-signal emissions
van Rossum G, Drake FL Jr (2014) The Python library reference, Python software foundation

Chapter 12
Functional Programming Aids

tuples, lists, dictionarys and their variants have been discussed in Chaps. 5–9. Ways of forming them, accessing them, and processing the data within have also been discussed. When a sequence like a dictionary becomes large in size it is stored in the disc and not in cache. Processing data within them using the constructs discussed thus far becomes cumbersome. Every access calls the full sequence concerned for the relevant operation. Iterators and generators prove to be more useful here. In general an iterator associated with a sequence points to a specific location in the sequence. As and when required the data in the specific location concerned is accessed and used for processing. The access here is on a 'on demand' basis and the full data is not called except when specifically demanded. Different iterator and generator functions are available in Python; some of them have been dealt with in Sect. 5.9; a number of additional ones are discussed here. They become handy and the benefits of their use show up only when the concerned data size is relatively large. However we have limited to their use for sequences of small size; this suffices to illustrate the applications concerned.

The standard library in Python has some additional modules with functions which are closely linked to iterators and generators (van Rossum and Drake 2014). These are also discussed here.

12.1 operator Module

The basic built-in functions for algebra and logic operations in Python have been defined as functions in the operator module. They can be used with appropriate arguments for compact coding in Python. The operations follow a pattern for a set in the lot. Hence only representative usages are illustrated. All items in the operator module have been imported [1] in Fig. 12.1. lt(**a**, **b**) returns True if

© Springer Nature Singapore Pte Ltd. 2016
T.R. Padmanabhan, *Programming with Python*,
DOI 10.1007/978-981-10-3277-6_12

```
>>> from operator import *                                    [1]
>>> lt(5,4),lt('aa','ab'),lt(['a','b'],['b','c','d']) [2]
(False, True, True)
>>> __lt__(5, 4), __lt__('aa', 'ab'), __lt__(['a', 'b'],
['b', 'c', 'd'])                                              [3]
(False, True, True)
>>> is_(3, 5-2), is_not(3, 5-2)                                [4]
(True, False)
>>> add(3, 5), add('God is god', add(' but ', 'Truth is
TRUTH'))                                                       [5]
(8, 'God is god but Truth is TRUTH')
>>> pos(0b1100001), pos(0b0011110), pos(-33), pos(0xab),
pos(0x54)                                                      [6]
(97, 30, -33, 171, 84)
>>> neg(0b1100001), neg(0b0011110), neg(-33), neg(0xab),
neg(0x54)                                                      [7]
(-97, -30, 33, -171, -84)
>>> aa, bb = 1, 0                                              [8]
>>> not_(aa), not_(bb), not_(0b1100001)                       [9]
(False, True, False)
>>> a, b c = 9, 2**3 + 1, 13                                   [10]
>>> truth(a==b), truth(a==c)                                   [11]
(True, False)
>>> inv(0b1100001), inv(0b0011110), inv(-33), inv(0xab),
inv(0x54)                                                      [12]
(-98, -31, 32, -172, -85)
>>> and_(0b1100001, 0b0011110), or_(0b1100001, 0b0011110),
xor(0b1100001, 0b1111000)                                      [13]
(0, 127, 25)
>>> lshift(21, 2), rshift(21, 2)                               [14]
(84, 5)
```

Fig. 12.1 Use of typical methods in operator module

a < b is satisfied. **a** and **b** can be numbers, or objects which can be compared in a Pythonic sense—as seen from [2]. __lt__(**a, b**) is an alternate representation of the same function as can be seen from [3]. le, gt, ge, ne, and eq are similar functions; these, their alternate forms, and their respective functions are given in Table 12.1. All of them return True/False as result. is_(**a, b**) corresponds to the test **a** is **b**; and is_not_ its negation. Both are illustrated in [4].

Details of algebraic operators are in Table 12.2. [5] illustrates the use of add. With more than two arguments—when three of them are to be added—add can be used in a chained sequence. Direct as well as the chained use is illustrated in [5]. Other algebraic operators with a pair of arguments in Table 12.2 can be used similarly. pos() operator returns the value of the object as an integer. [6] shows a few examples. neg() operator returns the negative value of the object as an integer [7].

The bit and logical operations in the operator module are given in Table 12.3 along with their alternate representations. not_(**a**) returns the logical inverse

Table 12.1 Methods for comparing objects in `operator` module; **a** and **b** are objects here. In each case if the condition is satisfied `True` is returned; else `False` is returned

Method	Alternate form	Direct equivalent	Condition tested
lt(**a**, **b**)	__ lt__ (**a**, **b**)	**a < b**	**a < b**
le(**a**, **b**)	__ le__ (**a**, **b**)	**a <= b**	**a ≤ b**
gt(**a**, **b**)	__ gt__ (**a**, **b**)	**a > b**	**a > b**
ge(**a**, **b**)	__ ge__ (**a**, **b**)	**a >= b**	**a ≥ b**
eq(**a**, **b**)	__ eq__ (**a**, **b**)	**a == b**	**a = b**
ne(**a**, **b**)	__ ne__ (**a**, **b**)	**a ≠ !b**	**a ≠ b**
is(**a**, **b**)	No alternate forms	**a** is **b**	a & b are the same?
is_not(**a**, **b**)		**a** is not **b**	a & b are different?

Table 12.2 Methods for algebra in **operator** module

Method	Alternate form	Direct equivalent	Operation done
add(**a**, **b**)	__ add__ (**a**, **b**)	**a + b**	**a + b**
sub(**a**, **b**)	__ sub__ (**a**, **b**)	**a − b**	**a − b**
mul(**a**, **b**)	__ mul__ (**a**, **b**)	**a * b**	**a × b**
truediv(**a**, **b**)	__ truediv__ (**a**, **b**)	**A / b**	**a ÷ b**
floordiv(**a**, **b**)	__ floordiv__ (**a**, **b**)	**a // b**	$\lfloor a/b \rfloor$
mod(**a**, **b**)	__ mod__ (**a**, **b**)	mod(**a**, **b**)	**a % b**
pow(**a**, **b**)	__pow__(**a**, **b**)	**a ** b**	a^b
abs(**a**)	__abs__(**a**)	abs(**a**)	|a|
neg(**a**)	__neg__(**a**)	**−a**	**−a**
pos(**a**)	__pos__(**a**)	**+a**	**+a**

Table 12.3 Methods for logical and bit-wise operations in `operator` module

Method	Alternate form	Direct equivalent	Operation done
not_(**a**)	__not__(**a**)	not **a**	Negation (Logical)
truth(obj)			Truth test
invert (**a**)	__invert__(**a**), inv(**a**), __invt__(**a**)	$\sim a$	Bitwise inversion
and_(**a**, **b**)	__and__(**a**, **b**)	a & b	Bitwise AND
or_(**a**, **b**)	__or__(**a**, **b**)	a | b	Bitwise OR
xor(**a**, **b**)	__xor__(**a**, **b**)	a ^ b	Bitwise exclusive OR
lshift(**a**, **b**)	__lshift__(**a**, **b**)	a ≪ b	Left shift
rshift(**a**, **b**)	__rshift__(**a**, **b**)	a ≫ b	Right shift

of **a**. If **a** is a Boolean variable its inverse (False or True as the case may be) is returned. Else True or False is returned depending on whether **a** is zero or not. With **aa** = 1 and **bb** = 0 as in [8] not_(**aa**) and not_(**bb**) are False and True respectively [9]. 0b1100001 being non-zero not_(0b1100001) is False. Truth (expression) tests whether expression is True or not (similar to the expression following 'if'. **a**, **b**, and **c** have been assigned values in [10]. truth(**a** == **b**) and truth(**a** == **c**) are returned as True and False respectively in [11].

The other operators in Table 12.2 are applicable only for integers. inverse() returns the bit-wise inverse of **a** (that is ∼**a**). With **a** as an integer –(**a** + 1) is returned. The inverses of numbers considered in [6] above are returned in [12]. and_(), or_(), and xor_() are respective bit-wise Boolean operations. [13] is a set of illustrative examples.

lshift(**a**, **b**) shifts integer a by b bits to the left; it is the equivalent of multiplying a by 2^b. Similarly rshift(**a**, **b**) shifts a by b bits to the right; it is equivalent to a // b operation; [14] are representative examples.

Table 12.4 has all the methods for operation on sequences. The possible alternate syntax as well as the operational details is also given in the table. Illustrative examples of their use are in Fig. 12.2. concat(**a**, **b**) concatenates **a** and **b**—which can be sequences of any type; but both are to be of the same type. **s1** and **s2** in [2] are two lists. concat(**s1**, **s2**) concatenates them in the same order [3]. **s3** and **s4** are two strings [4]. The concatenated string **s0** is formed as concat(**s3**, **s4**); it is in [5]. contains (**a**, '**b**') checks for the presence of '**b**' in the sequence **a**; if it is True (False) 'True ('False')' is returned. The method is the equivalent of 'b in a' test. [6] is an illustrative example (testing for the presence of letter '**V**' in **s0** both ways). countOf(**s0**, '**e**') returns the number of occurrences of the letter '**e**' in **s0** [7]. With string **s0** as a sequence each of its characters is an element here. Hence '**ee**' has no presence in **s0**. This explains countOf(**s0**, '**ee**') being zero in [8]. **s4** is a list of strings [9]. String '**aa**' is present in it three times. Hence countOf(**s4**, '**aa**') returns 3 in [10].

indexOf(**a**, '**b**') returns the index of first occurrence of letter '**b**' in list **a**. Illustrative examples are in [11]. getitem(**a**, '**bb**') does the reverse operation—the element at index **b** of sequence **a** is returned here. Here **b**—being an index—has to be an integer (or an object evaluating to an integer). The third item of string **s0**

Table 12.4 Methods for operations on sequences in operator module

Method	Alternate form	Direct equivalent	Operation done
concat(**a**, **b**)	__concat__(**a**, **b**)	a + b	Concatenate a & b
contains(**a**, **b**)	__contains__(**a**, **b**)	b in a	b in a?
countOf(**a**, **b**)		a.count(**b**)	Count of b in a
indexOf(**a**, **b**)		a.index(**b**)	Index of first occurrence of b in a
delitem(**a**, **b**)	__delitem__(**a**, **b**)		Delete b from a
getitem(**a**, **b**)	__getitem__(**a**, **b**)		Get value of a at index b
setitem(**a**, **b**, **c**)	__setitem__(**a**, **b**, **c**)		Set value of a at index b to c

```
>>> from operator import *                              [1]
>>> s1, s2 = [12, 34, 56], ['ab', 'cd']                 [2]
>>> concat(s1, s2)                                      [3]
[12, 34, 56, 'ab', 'cd']
>>> s3, s4 = 'Keep up, Vivek', '- Roshan screamed'      [4]
>>> s0 = concat(s3, s4)                                 [5]
>>> s0
'Keep up, Vivek- Roshan screamed'
>>> contains(s0, 'V'), 'V' in s0                        [6]
(True, True)
>>> countOf(s0, 'e')                                    [7]
5
>>> countOf(s0, 'ee')                                   [8]
0
>>> s4 = ['aa', 'bb', 'cc', 'dd', 'aa', 'aa']           [9]
>>> countOf(s4, 'aa')                                   [10]
3
>>> indexOf(s0, 'e'), indexOf(s4, 'aa')                 [11]
(1, 0)
>>> getitem(s0, 3), getitem(s4, 3)                      [12]
('p', 'dd')
>>> delitem(s4, 3)                                      [13]
>>> s4                                                  [14]
['aa', 'bb', 'cc', 'aa', 'aa']
>>> delitem(s0, 3)                                      [15]
Traceback (most recent call last):
  File "<stdin>", line 1, in <module>
TypeError: 'str' object doesn't support item deletion
>>> setitem(s4, 3, 'DD')                                [16]
>>> s4
['aa', 'bb', 'cc', 'DD', 'aa']                          [17]
```

Fig. 12.2 Methods for operations with sequences in **operator** module

('**p**') and the forth item of list **s4** ('**dd**') are returned in [12]. delitem(**a**, '**b**') deletes the item with index b (an integer) from sequence **a**. **S4**[3] is deleted in [13]. The truncated **s4** is in [14]. String **s0** is immutable and such selective deletion is not possible. Hence delete(**s0**, 3) [15] returns an error. setitem(**a**, **b**, **c**) has three arguments. **a** is an immutable sequence. The element **a**[**b**] is replaced by the element **c** (object **c**) in it. setitem(**s4**, 3, '**DD**') replaces **s4**[3] ('**aa**') by the new object —'**DD**' [16]. The modified **s4** is in [17].

12.1.1 Generic Methods

Three generic methods with varied possible uses are available in operator module. The Python Interpreter sequence in Fig. 12.3 brings out their uses.

```
>>> from operator import *                              [1]
>>> rr = [2, 3, 4, 5]                                   [2]
>>> gg = itemgetter(2)                                  [3]
>>> gg(rr)
4
>>> hh = itemgetter(3, 0)                               [4]
>>> hh(rr)                                              [5]
(5, 2)
>>> d0 = {'aa':22, 'bb':2.2, 'cc':220, 'dd':0.22}       [6]
>>> b0 = itemgetter('bb')                               [7]
>>> b0(d0)                                              [8]
2.2
>>> import math
>>> py0 = attrgetter('pi')                              [9]
>>> py0(math)                                           [10]
3.141592653589793
>>> ss = attrgetter('cos')                              [11]
>>> sf = ss(math)                                       [12]
>>> sf(0.25*py0(math))                                  [13]
0.7071067811865476
>>> qtt = '''What everybody echoes or in silence passes by
as true today may turn out to be falsehood tomorrow, mere
smoke of opinion, which some had trusted for a cloud that
would sprinkle fertilizing rain on their fields'''     [14]
>>> ff1 = methodcaller('index', 'or')                   [15]
>>> ff1(qtt)                                            [16]
22
>>> ff2 = methodcaller('index', 'or', 93)               [17]
>>> ff2(qtt)                                            [18]
146
```

Fig. 12.3 Generic methods related to sequences in the operator module

itemgetter (**x**, **y**, ***z**, ****w**) is one of them. **b** = itemgetter (**x**, **y**, ***z**, ****w**) defines **b** as an operator. **b**(**c**) with argument '**c**' as an object returns **c**(**x**), **c**(**y**), ... and so on. ***z** are a set of arguments, ****w**—a set of keys for respective arguments. The argument, the iterator ***z** and keywords ****ky** should occur in the same order. Types of **y**, ***z**, ****w** should be in line with the object whose features are being extracted/returned. **gg** in [3] has integer 2 as the assigned argument. With **rr** as a list [2] **gg**(**rr**) returns its second element. With any other sequence object in place of **rr**, **gg**() returns its second element. **hh** in [4] extracts the 3rd and 0th elements of its argument object. **hh**(**rr**) in [5] returns the tuple (**rr**[3], **rr**[0]). **b0** in [7] is an operator with '**bb**'—a key—as the specified item. Hence **b0**(**d0**) [8] returns the specific item in **d0** which has '**bb**' as its key. **d0** being a dictionary the value 2.2 for the specific key '**bb**' is returned [8]. To access items in **rr**—a list— the argument for itemgetter in [3] and [4] are integers. **d0** being a dictionary [6] the corresponding argument in [7] is a key. The arguments with itemgetter should correspond to the object to be accessed.

attrgetter(**a**) is an operator intended to return the specified attribute of the object concerned. With attrgetter('pi') assigned to **py0**, **py0**(math) returns the attribute math.pi [10] (the value of π). The math module has to be imported beforehand to make the access meaningful. **ss** in [11] (=.attrgetter('cos')) is an operator targeted to return the attribute cos in its argument. Hence **sf** = **ss** (math) [12] returns the math.cos() function from the math module. In turn **sf** (0.25***py0**(math)) returns cos(π/4) (as 0.7071067811865474).

The third generic method is methodcaller(); it returns an operator to execute the specified method. Its use is illustrated here for a string—string **qtt** [14] has been reproduced here from Chap. 6. **ff1** = methodcaller('index', '**or**') has two string arguments [15]. **ff1**(**qtt**) executes **qtt**.index('**or**') and returns the index of the first occurrence of '**or**' in **qtt**. Here the first argument—'index'—is the syntax of the method concerned. The rest of the arguments are those demanded by the method index()—here it is '**or**' (see Sect. 6.4). In a similar manner with **ff2** = methodcaller('index', '**or**', 93), **ff2**(**qh**) returns what **qtt**.index('**or**', 93) will return—index of the first occurrence of substring '**or**' in the slice **qtt**[93:].

12.1.2   Inplace Operators

Operations corresponding to the composite operations +=, −=, and the like also have the corresponding operators defined in the operator module. These are given in Table 12.5. As an illustration iadd(**a**, **b**) (representing +=) adds **b** to **a** in place; **a** has the enhanced value. **a** and **b** in [1] in Fig. 12.4 are two lists. iadd(**a**, **b**) in [2] adds list **b** to list **a** and **a** is the new and augmented list [3]. This is feasible only if **a** and **b** are of mutable type; else iadd(**a**, **b**) returns the added result but **a** remains unaltered. As an illustration **c** and **d** in [4] are numbers—immutable.

Table 12.5 Methods in operator module for in-place operations

Method	Alternate form	Direct equivalent
iadd(**a**, **b**)	__iadd__(**a**, **b**)	a += b
isub(**a**, **b**)	__isub__(**a**, **b**)	a −= b
imul(**a**, **b**)	__imul__(**a**, **b**)	a *= b
ipow(**a**, **b**)	__ipow__(**a**, **b**)	a **= b
itruediv(**a**, **b**)	__itruediv__(**a**, **b**)	a /= b
ifloordiv(**a**, **b**)	__ifloordiv__(**a**, **b**)	a //= b
imod(**a**, **b**)	__imod__(**a**, **b**)	a %= b
iand(**a**, **b**)	__iand__(**a**, **b**)	a &= b
ior(**a**, **b**)	__ior__(**a**, **b**)	a |= b
ixor(**a**, **b**)	__ixor__(**a**, **b**)	a ^= b
iconcat(**a**, **b**)	__iconcat__(**a**, **b**)	a += b
ilshift(**a**, **b**)	__ilshift__(**a**, **b**)	a <<= b
irshift(**a**, **b**)	__irshift__(**a**, **b**)	a >>= b

```
>>> from operator import *
>>> a, b = [2, 4, 6, 8], [1, 3,5]                         [1]
>>> iadd(a, b)
        [2]
[2, 4, 6, 8, 1, 3, 5]
>>> a, b
([2, 4, 6, 8, 1, 3, 5], [1, 3, 5])
        [3]
>>> c, d = 4.7, 2.1
        [4]
>>> iadd(c, d)
        [5]
6.800000000000001
>>> c, d
        [6]
(4.7, 2.1)
>>> br1, br2 = bytearray(b'1234'), bytearray(b'987')
        [7]
>>> iadd(br1, br2)
        [8]
bytearray(b'1234987')
>>> br1, br2
        [9]
(bytearray(b'1234987'), bytearray(b'987'))
>>>
```

Fig. 12.4 In-place operators in operator module

iadd(**c**, **d**) returns the added value (4.7 + 2.1 = 6.8) [5] but **c** and **d** remain the same [6]. **br1** and **br2** in [7] are two bytearrays (immutable). iadd(**br1**, **br2**) in [8] return the added bytesarray in [9]—analogous to 'adding' lists. Note the difference between adding integers and bytearrays as done by iadd() method.

12.2 itertools

A number of iterator functions are available in the itertools module. These are adaptations of their popular counterparts in other languages. The python Interpreter sequence in Fig. 12.5a–c illustrate their usage. The three of them in Table 12.6 continue ad infinitum and have to be stopped through other executable statements. count(**a**, **b**) is an iterator to run a counter. The count starts at number a and at every step increments count by number b. **a0** in [2] is an iterator to count starting with value 5 and increment count by 3 at every step. The first two values can be seen to be 5 [3] and 8 [4]. The subsequent five values are returned as list **b0** [7].

(a)

```
>>> from itertools import  *                               [1]
>>> a0 = count(5,3)                                        [2]
>>> next(a0)                                               [3]
5
>>> next(a0)                                               [4]
8
>>> b0 = []                                                [5]
>>> for jj in range(5):b0.append(next(a0))                 [6]
...
>>> b0                                                     [7]
[11, 14, 17, 20, 23]
>>> a1 = cycle('a0b1c2d3')                                 [8]
>>> c1 = ([],[])                                           [9]
>>> for jj in range(25):                                   [10]
...     c1[0].append(next(a1))
...     c1[1].append(next(a1))
...
>>> c1                                                     [11]
(['2', '3', '0', '1', '2', '3', '0', '1', '2', '3', '0',
'1', '2', '3', '0', '1', '2', '3', '0', '1', '2', '3',
'0', '1', '2'], ['d', 'a', 'b', 'c', 'd', 'a', 'b', 'c',
'd', 'a', 'b', 'c', 'd', 'a', 'b', 'c', 'd', 'a', 'b',
'c', 'd', 'a', 'b', 'c', 'd'])
>>> list(repeat('z1z2', 5))                                [12]
['z1z2', 'z1z2', 'z1z2', 'z1z2', 'z1z2']
>>> list(map(pow, range(10), repeat(2)))                   [13]
[0, 1, 4, 9, 16, 25, 36, 49, 64, 81]
>>> dd = [2, 4, 6, 8, 10]                                  [14]
>>> d0 = list(accumulate(dd))
>>> d0                                                     [15]
[2, 6, 12, 20, 30]
>>> import operator
>>> d1 = list((accumulate(dd, operator.mul)))              [16]
>>> d1                                                     [17]
[2, 8, 48, 384, 3840]
>>> d2 = list((accumulate(dd, operator.truediv)))          [18]
>>> d2                                                     [19]
[2, 0.5, 0.08333333333333333, 0.010416666666666666,
0.0010416666666666667]
```

Fig. 12.5 a Illustrative usages of iterators in **itertools** module (continued in Fig. 12.5b).
b Illustrative usages of iterators in **itertools** module (continued from Fig. 12.5a). **c** Illustrative
usages of iterators in **itertools** module (continued from Fig. 12.5b)

cycle (**a**) takes any iterable—a sequence—as an argument. Its elements are
returned in succession until exhaustion. Then the cycle repeats. As an illustration
with string—'**a0b1c2d3**'—a1 is formed as a cyclic iterator [8]. With this as basis
c1 is returned as a pair of sequences [11]—one of integers (0, 1, 2, 3, 0, 1, ...) and
the other as one of alphabets—(a, b, c, a, b, ...).

(b)

```
>>> zz, yy = (1, 3, 5), ('a0', 'b1', 'c2', 'd3')          [20]
>>> list(chain(zz, yy))                                   [21]
[1, 3, 5, 'a0', 'b1', 'c2', 'd3']
>>> xx = [zz, yy]                                         [22]
>>> bb = chain.from_iterable(xx)                          [23]
>>> list(bb)                                              [24]
[1, 3, 5, 'a0', 'b1', 'c2', 'd3']
>>> tt = combinations('mnop', 2)                          [25]
>>> list(tt)                                              [26]
[('m', 'n'), ('m', 'o'), ('m', 'p'), ('n', 'o'), ('n',
'p'), ('o', 'p')]
>>> list(combinations(yy, 3))                             [27]
[('a0', 'b1', 'c2'), ('a0', 'b1', 'd3'), ('a0', 'c2',
'd3'), ('b1', 'c2', 'd3')]
>>> ww = list(combinations_with_replacement(yy, 3))       [28]
>>> ww                                                    [29]
[('a0', 'a0', 'a0'), ('a0', 'a0', 'b1'), ('a0', 'a0',
'c2'), ('a0', 'a0', 'd3'), ('a0', 'b1', 'b1'), ('a0',
'b1', 'c2'), ('a0', 'b1', 'd3'), ('a0', 'c2', 'c2'),
('a0', 'c2', 'd3'), ('a0', 'd3', 'd3'), ('b1', 'b1',
'b1'), ('b1', 'b1', 'c2'), ('b1', 'b1', 'd3'), ('b1',
'c2', 'c2'), ('b1', 'c2', 'd3'), ('b1', 'd3', 'd3'),
('c2', 'c2', 'c2'), ('c2', 'c2', 'd3'), ('c2',
'd3', 'd3'), ('d3', 'd3', 'd3')]
```

Fig. 12.5 (continued)

repeat(**a**, **b**) is the iterator for the repeated sequence—**a, a, a**, ... it continues *b* times—*b* being an integer—and stops. If b is not specified the sequence continues non-stop. list(repeat('**z1z2**', 5)) [12] produces the list of five numbers of the string '**z1z2**'. As an additional illustration the sequence $\{a^a\}$ with ten entries is returned by list(map(pow, range(10), repeat(2))) in [13].

itertools has a set of iterators for sequences of limited size—size being decided by the argument. These are listed in Table 12.7. accumulate takes a sequence as an argument. With that it returns an iterator for the progressive accumulation of the elements in the argument starting with the first one. With **dd** as a list of numbers (=[2, 4, 6, 8, 10]) [14] list(accumulate(**dd**)) returns the progressive sums as a list [15]. Its elements are formed as—{2, 6 (=2 + 4), 12 (=6 + 6), 20 (=12 + 8), and 30 (=20 + 1). In the general form accumulate(**arg**, **function**) has two arguments—a sequence as the first one and a function as the second. With operator imported [16] operator.mul returns the product of the two concerned operands. **d1** = list((accumulate(**dd**, operator.mul))) outputs **d1** as a list—formed from **dd**. The elements of **d1** are formed as: **d1** [0] = **dd**[0]; **d1**[i] = **d1**[$i - 1$] * **dd**[i]. **d1** has as many elements as **dd** itself. Any other function of two arguments in the operator module can be used with accumulate in this manner. operator.truediv() is used in [18] to form **d2** as a

(c)

```
>>> yy0 = ('b1', 'c2', 'a0', 'd3')                        [30]
>>> list(combinations(yy0, 3))                            [31]
[('b1', 'c2', 'a0'), ('b1', 'c2', 'd3'), ('b1', 'a0',
'd3'), ('c2', 'a0', 'd3')]
>>> yy1 = ('b1', 'c2', 'a0', 'b1')                        [32]
>>> list(combinations(yy1, 3))                            [33]
[('b1', 'c2', 'a0'), ('b1', 'c2', 'b1'), ('b1', 'a0',
'b1'), ('c2', 'a0', 'b1')]
>>>
>>> list(permutations(yy, 3))                             [34]
[('a0', 'b1', 'c2'), ('a0', 'b1', 'd3'), ('a0', 'c2',
'b1'), ('a0', 'c2', 'd3'), ('a0', 'd3', 'b1'), ('a0', 'd3',
'c2'), ('b1', 'a0', 'c2'), ('b1', 'a0', 'd3'), ('b1', 'c2',
'a0'), ('b1', 'c2', 'd3'), ('b1', 'd3', 'a0'), ('b1', 'd3',
'c2'), ('c2', 'a0', 'b1'), ('c2', 'a0', 'd3'), ('c2', 'b1',
'a0'), ('c2', 'b1', 'd3'), ('c2', 'd3', 'a0'), ('c2', 'd3',
'b1'), ('d3', 'a0', 'b1'), ('d3', 'a0', 'c2'), ('d3', 'b1',
'a0'), ('d3', 'b1', 'c2'), ('d3', 'c2', 'a0'), ('d3', 'c2',
'b1')]
>>> xx = lambda x:x*x                                     [35]
>>> zz = map(xx, count(2,3))
>>> list(next(zz) for jj in range(20))                    [36]
[4, 25, 64, 121, 196, 289, 400, 529, 676, 841, 1024, 1225,
1444, 1681, 1936, 2209, 2500, 2809, 3136, 3481]
>>> list(islice(map(xx, count(2,3)), 10))                 [37]
[4, 25, 64, 121, 196, 289, 400, 529, 676, 841]
>>> list(islice(map(xx, count(2,3)),4, 40, 5)) [38]
[196, 841, 1936, 3481, 5476, 7921, 10816, 14161]
>>> list(islice(cycle('a0b1c2d3'), 20))                   [39]
['a', '0', 'b', '1', 'c', '2', 'd', '3', 'a', '0', 'b',
'1', 'c', '2', 'd', '3', 'a', '0', 'b', '1']
```

Fig. 12.5 (continued)

Table 12.6 Methods in itertools for iterators to be terminated separately

Method	Operation
count(**a**, **b**)	Run a counter starting with number a and incrementing in steps of number b ($a, a + b, a + 2 * b, a + 3 * b, \ldots$)
cycle (**a**)	Cyclically repeat elements of sequence **a** in the same order as in a
repeat(**a**, **b**)	Repeat **a** b times; continue endlessly if b is absent

sequence of ratios of successive elements of **dd**. This structure offers compact coding with first order recurrent sequences—typically first order difference equations. If necessary the function can be defined separately and used here.

chain(**a1**, **a2**, …) chains the sequences {**a1**, **a2**, …} in the same order to form a single combined sequence. The number of arguments here can be as many as desired. **zz** and **yy** are two sequence—one of numbers and the other of strings [20]

Table 12.7 Methods in operator module for in-place operations

Method	Arguments	Operation
accumulate()	p, f	f is optional; in its absence iterator for summing elements of p successively. If present, f is a function of two arguments and is used instead of sum
chain()	p_1, p_2,...	Sequentially combine p_1, p_2,... to form a single sequence
chain.from_iterable()	p_1	p_1 is a sequence of sequences which are chained
combinations()	p, n	All combinations of n-length sequences from p
combinations_with_replacement()	p, n	Similar to combinations allowing repeated use of elements in p
permutations()	p, n	All possible permutations of n elements from p
groupby()	p, key = None	Iterator to search sequence q with key as basis
islice()	p, a, b, c	a and c are optional. Iterator to return a slice using p: slice starts at a (default zero), proceeds in steps of c(default one) and stops at b
product()	*iterables, repeat = 1	Iterator for the Cartesian product of all iterables: with a single iterable repeat value dictates product size
tee	p, n	N Independent iterators are formed with elements of p.
zip_longest	*iterables, fillvalue = None	An iterator for sequentially aggregating elements of all iterables: continued until the longest iterable is exhausted. Missing positions are filled by fillvalue .

(Fig. 12.5b); they have been chained together in [21] to form a single list. chain. from_iterable() is a slightly altered version of chain. It takes a single argument—a sequence of sequences—list of strings, list of lists and so on. The elements are chained to form the iterator for a single sequence. Elements of the first sequence are chained first; after the same is exhausted chaining continues with the elements of the second sequence and so on until all the sequences are chained (called 'lazy evaluation'); as an example **xx** in [22] is a list of the two tuples **yy** and **zz**. **bb** [23] is formed as an iterator as chain.from_iterable (**xx**). The corresponding composite chain is returned in [24] as list(**bb**).

combinations (**a**, **n**) has **a** as a sequence and **n** as an integer. All combinations of elements of **a** taken **b** at a time—$\binom{len(a)}{b}$ in number—together form the object of the iterator here. With '**mnop**' as a sequence **tt** in [25] is an iterator for the set of $\binom{len(tt)}{2}$ such combinations. list (**tt**) is in [26]. **yy** [21] being a list of four strings all the four combinations of **yy** with three elements taken at a time ($\binom{len(yy)}{3}$ in number) are returned in [27].

combinations_with_replacement(**a**, **n**) is the counterpart of combinations(**a**, **n**) with replacement of each item in **a**. **ww** [28] is the combinations_with_replacement(**a**, **n**) counterpart. permutation(**a**, **n**) is the iterator for all possible permutations of n elements from **a**. [34] (Fig. 12.5c) is the list of possible permutations of 3 elements from sequence **yy**.

Two aspects of the iterators here are noteworthy:

- The iterator sequencing takes place in the same order as the elements in the iterable. **yy0**[30] has the same elements as **yy** in [20] but in a different order. Correspondingly list(combinations (**yy0**, 3)) [31] has a different order

(a)

```
trp@trp-Veriton-Series:~$ python3.5 -q
>>> from itertools import *                                    [1]
>>> pp = product('abc', '98')                                 [2]
>>> list(pp)                                                  [3]
[('a', '9'), ('a', '8'), ('b', '9'), ('b', '8'), ('c',
'9'), ('c', '8')]
>>> list(product('abc', '98', repeat = 2))                    [4]
[('a', '9', 'a', '9'), ('a', '9', 'a', '8'), ('a', '9',
'b', '9'), ('a', '9', 'b', '8'), ('a', '9', 'c', '9'),
('a', '9', 'c', '8'), ('a', '8', 'a', '9'), ('a', '8',
'a', '8'), ('a', '8', 'b', '9'), ('a', '8', 'b', '8'),
('a', '8', 'c', '9'), ('a', '8', 'c', '8'), ('b', '9',
'a', '9'), ('b', '9', 'a', '8'), ('b', '9', 'b', '9'),
('b', '9', 'b', '8'), ('b', '9', 'c', '9'), ('b', '9',
'c', '8'), ('b', '8', 'a', '9'), ('b', '8', 'a', '8'),
('b', '8', 'b', '9'), ('b', '8', 'b', '8'), ('b', '8',
'c', '9'), ('b', '8', 'c', '8'), ('c', '9', 'a', '9'),
('c', '9', 'a', '8'), ('c', '9', 'b', '9'), ('c', '9',
'b', '8'), ('c', '9', 'c', '9'), ('c', '9', 'c', '8'),
('c', '8', 'a', '9'), ('c', '8', 'a', '8'), ('c', '8',
'b', '9'), ('c', '8', 'b', '8'), ('c', '8', 'c', '9'),
('c', '8', 'c', '8')]
>>> list(product([1, 2, 3, 4], repeat = 2))                   [5]
[(1, 1), (1, 2), (1, 3), (1, 4), (2, 1), (2, 2), (2, 3),
(2, 4), (3, 1), (3, 2), (3, 3), (3, 4), (4, 1), (4, 2),
(4, 3), (4, 4)]
>>> a0 = 'pqrstuvwxyz'                                        [6]
>>> list(zip_longest(a0, range(6)))                           [7]
[('p', 0), ('q', 1), ('r', 2), ('s', 3), ('t', 4), ('u',
5), ('v', None), ('w', None), ('x', None), ('y', None),
('z', None)]
>>> list(zip_longest('elephant', 'marshall',
'beautiful'))                                                 [8]
[('e', 'm', 'b'), ('l', 'a', 'e'), ('e', 'r', 'a'), ('p',
's', 'u'), ('h', 'h', 't'), ('a', 'a', 'i'), ('n', 'l',
'f'), ('t', 'l', 'u'), (None, None, 'l')]
```

Fig. 12.6 a Python Interpreter sequence demonstrating usage of some iterators in the **itertools** module (continued in Fig. 12.6b). **b** Python Interpreter sequence demonstrating usage of some iterators in the **itertools** module (continued from Fig. 12.6a)

(b)

```
>>> list(enumerate(list(zip_longest('elephant',
'marshall', 'beautiful'))))                              [9]
[(0, ('e', 'm', 'b')), (1, ('l', 'a', 'e')), (2, ('e',
'r', 'a')), (3, ('p', 's', 'u')), (4, ('h', 'h', 't')),
(5, ('a', 'a', 'i')), (6, ('n', 'l', 'f')), (7, ('t',
'l', 'u')), (8, (None, None, 'l'))]
>>> list(zip(range(2, 6), range(1, 5)))                  [10]
[(2, 1), (3, 2), (4, 3), (5, 4)]
>>> import operator                                      [11]
>>> list(starmap(operator.sub,list(zip(range(2, 6),
range(1, 5)))))                                          [12]
[1, 1, 1, 1]
>>> list(starmap(pow,list(zip(range(12, 16),range(2,
6),list(repeat(7, 4))))))                                [13]
[4, 6, 0, 1]
>>> e1= enumerate('Elephant', 1)                         [14]
>>> list(starmap(operator.mul, e1))                      [15]
['E', 'll', 'eee', 'pppp', 'hhhhh', 'aaaaaa', 'nnnnnnn',
'tttttttt']
>>> ai = tee(a0, 3)                                      [16]
>>> for jj in range(len(a0)):print(next(ai[0]),
next(ai[1]), next(ai[2]))                                [17]
...
p p p
q q q
r r r
s s s
t t t
u u u
v v v
w w w
x x x
y y y
z z z
>>>
```

Fig. 12.6 (continued)

compared to list(combinations(**yy**, 3)) [27] though both have the same elements.

- The iterator generated treats each element in the argument iterables as a separate entity. It does not take cognizance of items being repeated. **yy1** in [32] has 'b1' repeated; but list(combinations(**yy1**, 3)) [33] treats the two 'b1's as separate items.

islice(**a**, **n**) is an iterator to extract a slice of **a** and stop extraction at **n**. A possible use is illustrated here. With **xx** defined as x^2 [36] map(**xx**, count(2, 3) is the iterator for the sequence of elements—4 (=22), 25 (=$(2 + 3)^2$), 64 (=(2 + 2 * $3)^2$), 121 (=$(2 + 3 * 3)^2$), ... list(islice(map(**xx**, count(2, 3), 10)) returns a list of the first 10 elements here [38]. The generalized version of the islice() iterator is islice(**a, b, c, d**) where **a** is the sequence and the slice comprises of the elements at b, $b + d$, $b + 2 * d$, $b + 3 * d$, ... until $b + k * d$ where $b + k * d \leq c < b + (k + 1) * d$. With b, c, and d being 4, 40, and 5 respectively the list in [39] starts with the 4th element (corresponding to 2 + 4 * 3) and includes every subsequent 5th element until the 39th—(2 + 4 * 3)th, (2 + 19 * 3)th, and (2 + 39 * 3)th.

As another example with a as a string ('**a0b1c2d3**'), list(islice(cycle ('**a0b1c2d3**', 20))) yields a list of 20 elements—the members of '**a0b1c2d3**' are sequentially cyclically repeated to produce a slice of length 20.

All the items in the itertools module have been imported into the Python Interpreter sequence in Fig. 12.6 [1]. product(*****aa**, repeat = 1) is an iterator for the Cartesian product of elements in the set of sequence represented by *****aa**. If the sequences are **aa1, aa2, aa3**, ... the items represented are (**aa1**[0], **aa2** [0], ,.), (**aa1**[1], **aa2**[1], **aa3**[12], ... ,), (**aa1**[2], **aa2**[2], **aa3**[2], ,.), ... This is true for the default value of the last argument (repeat = 1). If the repeat is specified as 2 each element set is duplicated to represent a corresponding sequence; same is true of other repeat values also. A few illustrative examples are shown in the figure. **pp** [2] is the iterator for the Cartesian products generated by '**abc**', and '**98**' without repetition. list(**pp**) [3] confirms this. With repeat = 2 in [4] each element set is duplicated. list(product('**abc**', '**98**', repeat = 2), is a list of 36 items; each item has four elements—all possible combinations generated by the set of six items in list(**pp**) taken two at a time. If product() has a single sequence of arguments the iterator is for the same sequence repeated repeat times. list(product([1, 2, 3, 4], repeat = 2)) [5] is the sequence of all possible integer pairs using [1, 2, 3, 4].

zip_longest(*****ai**, fillvalue = None) as an iterator, is a variant of zip (see Sect. 5.8). It points to the set of tuples formed by combining the corresponding elements of all the iterable argumets. The sequence continue until the longest iterable is exhausted. All deficiencies are filled by the specified fillvalue (with default None). Note that in contrast zip() stops when the shortest iterable is exhausted. With **a0** (='**pqrstuvwxyz**') as a string [6] list(zip_longest (**a0**, range(6))) produces a list of tuples [('**p**', 0), ('**q**', 1), ('**r**', 2), ('**s**', 3), ('**t**', 4), ('**u**', 5), ('**v**', None)' ('**w**', None), ('**x**', None), ('**y**', None), ('**z**', None)] [7]. list(zip_longest('**elephant**', '**marshal**', '**beautiful**')) [8] produces a list of tuples combining letters from all the three words-in the same order. The last of them is (None, None, '**l**') accommodating the last letter ('**l**') of **beautiful** with two Nones preceding it. Continuing with Fig. 12.6b list(enumerate(zip_ longest('**elephant**', '**marshal**', '**beautiful**')))) enumerates the above set of tuples starting at 0 and forms a corresponding list [9]. starmap(**ff, aa**) as an iterable is a variant of map. With **ff** as a function, it represents the sequence of functions **ff**(**aa**[0], **ff**(**aa**[1]), ... Here **aa**[i] is the ith element of **aa**; it constitutes the set of arguments for **ff** for the specific i value. Contrast with map (**ff, a, b, c** ...)

which is the iterator for the functions **ff(a**[0], **b**[0], **c**[0], ...), **ff(a**[1], **b**[1], **c**[1], ...).
In [10] list(zip(range(2, 6), range(5)) represents the list [(2, 1), (3, 2), (4, 3), (5, 4)]; in turn list(starmap(operator.sub, list(zip(range(2, 6), range(5))))) is a list of four ones representing [2-1, 3-2, 4-3, and 5-4] respectively [12]. Similarly list(starmap(pow, list(zip(range(12, 16), range(1, 5), list(repeat(7, 4)))))) leads to the list of integers [4 (=12^1 mod 7), 6(=13^2 mod 7), 0 (=14^4 mod 7), 1 (=15^5 mod 7)] [13]. With **e1** (=enumerate('**Elephant**', 1)) [14]—same as in [6] above list(starmap(operator.mul, **e1**)) forms the list {'E'(='**E**' * 1), 'll'(='l' * 2), ... 'tttttttt'(='**t**' * 8)] [15].

   tee(aa, n = 2) accepts argument **aa** as a sequence. With its elements *n* number of iterators is formed—all of them identical—all of them representing the elements of **aa** itself; the default value of n is two. **ai**(=**tee(a0**, 3)) forms a set of three identical iterators for the elements of **a0**[16]. The corresponding full sets of elements are printed out in [17].

12.2.1 Filtering

A set of four iterator functions are available in the itertools module to filter data out of sequences in different ways. The Python Interpreter sequence in Fig. 12.7 illustrates their use. compress(**aa, bb**) has **aa** as a sequence. In the

```
>>> from itertools import *
>>> ww = [('a0', 'a0', 'a0'), ('a0', 'a0', 'b1'), ('a0',
'a0', 'c2'), ('a0', 'a0', 'd3'), ('a0', 'b1', 'b1'),
('a0', 'b1', 'c2'), ('a0', 'b1', 'd3'), ('a0', 'c2',
'c2'), ('a0', 'c2', 'd3'), ('a0', 'd3', 'd3'), ('b1',
'b1', 'b1'), ('b1', 'b1', 'c2'), ('b1', 'b1', 'd3'),
('b1', 'c2', 'c2'), ('b1', 'c2', 'd3'), ('b1', 'd3',
'd3'), ('c2', 'c2', 'c2'), ('c2', 'c2', 'd3'),
('c2', 'd3', 'd3'), ('d3', 'd3', 'd3')]            [1]
>>> list(compress(ww,
[1,1,0,0,0,1,1,1,1,0,0,0,1,0,1,0,0,0,0,0]))        [2]
[('a0', 'a0', 'a0'), ('a0', 'a0', 'b1'), ('a0', 'b1',
'c2'), ('a0', 'b1', 'd3'), ('a0', 'c2', 'c2'), ('a0',
'c2', 'd3'), ('b1', 'b1', 'd3'), ('b1', 'c2', 'd3')]
>>> list(islice(dropwhile(lambda n:n<10, count(2,3)), 8))
                                                   [3]
[11, 14, 17, 20, 23, 26, 29, 32]
>>> list(islice(filterfalse(lambda n:n%3, count(2,5)),
10))                                               [4]
[12, 27, 42, 57, 72, 87, 102, 117, 132, 147]
>>> a0 = 'pqrstuvwxyz'
>>> list(takewhile(lambda n:n<'w', a0))            [5]
['p', 'q', 'r', 's', 't', 'u', 'v']
```

Fig. 12.7 Use of iterators for filtering from sequences

simplest case **bb** is a corresponding sequence of True and False values. The iterator filters and extracts only those elements of **aa** for which **bb** has a True value. Other elements in **aa** are ignored. [2] is an illustrative example where only a select set from argument **ww** [1] (obtained in [29] in Fig. 12.5b) is passed on to the list. dropwhile(**cc**, **aa**) is an iterator centred around sequence **aa**; **cc** is a condition to 'trigger' start of iterator. At start the iterator ignores the elements for which the condition **cc** is satisfied. Once an element which does not satisfy **cc** is detected the iterator is activated. The condition is not checked again. As an example [3] produces a list of eight elements in the sequence {2, 5, 8, ...} starting with the one greater than 10—decided by the function 'lambda n: $n < 10$'.

filterfalse(**cc**, **aa**) is an iterator to select elements of sequence **aa** which do not satisfy condition **cc**. n % 3 is zero for all n values divisible by 3; hence [4] produces a list of the first ten elements in the sequence {2, 5, 8, ... which are divisible by three.

takewhile(**cc**, **aa**) has two arguments with **cc** as a condition and **aa** as a sequence. The result is a sequence of elements in **aa** which satisfy the condition **cc**; here the test for **cc** starts at the left end of **aa** and continues until cc is not satisfied for the first time. takewhile() is an iterator for this target list. list (takewhile(lambda **n**: **n** < 'w', **a0**)) sifts out all letters in **a0** starting with the first one ('**p**') and until a letter as '**w**' or beyond is encountered [5].

Searching through sequences for specific information using specified keys is facilitated by groupby(**aa**, key = None) iterator. Here **aa** is the target sequence to be searched. If key is not specified a bland search is carried out using the supplied key directly. If key is specified as a function the supplied item is used to generate the key using the specified function; then with that as basis the search is carried out. A set of illustrative examples follow through the Python Interpreter sequence in Fig. 12.8a, b. **marks2.st** in the **demo_5** module is reproduced in Fig. 12.9. It has the marks data for a set of students—their names and marks obtained in a set of subjects. itemgetter and groupby have been imported from operator and itertools modules respectively [2] and [3]. itemgetter('**Name**') assigns string '**Name**' to **nm** [4]. The routine starting with [5] blindly accesses the sequence for each **Name** and prints out the name and the full sequence associated with it. The suite starting with [8] uses **nm**('**Name**') as key directly and accesses the data against each '**Name**' in **marks2.st**. The same is printed out and then the concerned marks is accessed and printed out. The task is carried out for all the **Name**s in **marks2.st**. The suite [11] to [13] sifts out the names and marks separately and produces corresponding lists [14] and [15]. The suite [17]–[19] returns (Fig. 12.8b) two lists—the list of **name**s as **nm0** [20] and the sum of marks obtained in all subjects by each object (**Name**) in **nm0** [21].

q0 [22] is an unorganized list of strings. **q0** is scanned for entries successively and types are identified and grouped blindly and directly in **q11**. Since 'a0' finds place repeatedly in two different locations these two are separately identified and listed in **q11**. It leads to the question—how to be more organized and club items like '**a0**' together. **q0** is sorted and returned as **q1** (sorted(**q0**)) [25].

(a)

```
trp@trp-Veriton-Series:~$ python3.5 -q
>>> from demo_5 import marks2                              [1]
>>> from operator import itemgetter                        [2]
>>> from itertools import groupby                    [3]
>>> nm = itemgetter('Name')                               [4]
>>> for ky, mk in groupby(marks2.st, nm):                 [5]
...     print(ky)                                         [6]
...     for mr in mk:print('    ', mr['Marks'])           [7]
...
Karthik
   [77, 78, 79, 80, 81]
Sarani
   [76, 78, 82, 83, 84]
Karun
   [85, 86, 87, 88, 89]
Kala
   [90, 86, 91, 92, 93]
Lan
   [65, 86, 66, 67, 68]
>>> for ky, mk in groupby(marks2.st, nm):                 [8]
...     print('NAME: ', ky)                               [9]
...     for rr in mk:print(rr)                            [10]
...
NAME:    Karthik
{'Marks': [77, 78, 79, 80, 81], 'Name': 'Karthik'}
NAME:    Sarani
{'Marks': [76, 78, 82, 83, 84], 'Name': 'Sarani'}
NAME:    Karun
{'Marks': [85, 86, 87, 88, 89], 'Name': 'Karun'}
NAME:    Kala
{'Marks': [90, 86, 91, 92, 93], 'Name': 'Kala'}
NAME:    Lan
{'Marks': [65, 86, 66, 67, 68], 'Name': 'Lan'}
>>> nms, mks = [], []
>>> for ky, mk in groupby(marks2.st, nm):                 [11]
...     nms.append(ky)                                    [12]
...     for mr in mk:mks.append(mr['Marks'])              [13]
...
>>> nms                                                   [14]
['Karthik', 'Sarani', 'Karun', 'Kala', 'Lan']
>>> mks                                                   [15]
[[77, 78, 79, 80, 81], [76, 78, 82, 83, 84], [85, 86, 87,
88, 89], [90, 86, 91, 92, 93], [65, 86, 66, 67, 68]]
```

Fig. 12.8 a Python Interpreter sequence illustrating the use of **groupby** (continued in Fig. 12.8b). **b** Python Interpreter sequence illustrating the use of **groupby** (continued from Fig. 12.8a)

(b)

```
>>> nm0, mk0 = [], []
>>> for ky,mk in groupby(marks2.mm,lambda nn:nn[0]):   [16]
...     for mb in mk:                                   [17]
...         nm0.append(mb[0])                           [18]
...         mk0.append(sum(mb[1]))                      [19]
...
>>> nm0                                                 [20]
['Kishore', 'Sanjay', 'Siva', 'Asha', 'Nisha']
>>> mk0                                                 [21]
[395, 391, 228, 418, 300]
>>> q0 = ['a0', 'b1', 'b1', 'b1', 'c2', 'c2', 'a0', 'a0',
'a0']                                                   [22]
>>> ql1 = [(x, list(y)) for x, y in groupby(q0)]        [23]
>>> ql1                                                 [24]
[('a0', ['a0']), ('b1', ['b1', 'b1', 'b1']), ('c2', ['c2',
'c2']), ('a0', ['a0', 'a0', 'a0'])]
>>> q1 = sorted(q0)                                     [25]
>>> q1
['a0', 'a0', 'a0', 'a0', 'b1', 'b1', 'b1', 'c2', 'c2']
>>> ql2 = [(x, list(y)) for x, y in groupby(q1)]        [26]
>>> ql2                                                 [27]
[('a0', ['a0', 'a0', 'a0', 'a0']), ('b1', ['b1', 'b1',
'b1']), ('c2', ['c2', 'c2'])]
```

Fig. 12.8 (continued)

```
dta = ['name', 'physics', 'chemistry', 'maths',
'mechanics', 'english']
s1 =  {'Name':'Kishore', 'Marks':[75, 66, 91, 87, 76]}
s2 =  {'Name':'Sanjay', 'Marks':[81, 62, 95, 91, 62]}
s3 =  {'Name':'Siva', 'Marks':[41, 51, 45, 39, 52]}
s4 =  {'Name':'Asha', 'Marks':[88, 78, 97, 83, 72]}
s5 =  {'Name':'Nisha', 'Marks':[50,61, 68, 40, 81]}
ss = [s1, s2, s3, s4, s5]
s6 =  {'Name':'Karthik', 'Marks':[77, 78, 79, 80, 81]}
s7 =  {'Name':'Sarani', 'Marks':[76, 78, 82, 83, 84]}
s8 =  {'Name':'Karun', 'Marks':[85, 86, 87, 88, 89]}
s9 =  {'Name':'Kala', 'Marks':[90, 86, 91, 92, 93]}
s10 = {'Name':'Lan', 'Marks':[65, 86, 66, 67, 68]}
st = [s6, s7, s8, s9, s10]
```

Fig. 12.9 Marks details of a few students used to illustrate use of **groupby**()

A subsequent access of **q1** through groupby using the strings in **q1** as keys in [26] returned the more organized list as **q12** [27]. Such sorting of a sequence prior to access with groupby using the same key is often necessary to ensure orderly grouping.

12.3 `generator` Using `yield`

A function can be converted to a corresponding `generator` using `yield` in place of `return`. Two features characterize the `generator` here.

- Being a `generator` it is an `iterator`. The values can be computed and returned through `next`, `list`, their combinations & c.
- On the first call the evaluation continues until the first `yield` is encountered. Execution halts on 'as is where is' basis and the desired output returned. Every subsequent call resumes at the point left off at the previous call and continues to next `yield`. The resumption is always with the status/values left frozen earlier. This continues to the last possible value of the `iterator`.

Contrast this with a function with a `return` where every call is a fresh one (past/latest values of variables/entities are not retained or carried forward). A few illustrative examples to highlight the potential of 'yield' are considered here.

def **life(qq, rr)** [2] is defined as a `generator` in the Python Interpreter sequence in Fig. 12.10; the `yield` **kk, jj** statement [9] signifies this. The arguments **qq** and **rr** are strings, **rr** being a single character `string`. **life()** points to the occurrence of character '**rr**' in the string. The three `print` statements after initialization—[3], [4], [5]—are essentially for monitoring the execution flow. The loop starting with `while` [6] identifies the location of character **rr** in the `string` **qq**. `print`(**kk, b**) [8] prints the location of **rr** identified. '**b**' is a flag to distinguish this **kk** value from that earlier—`print`(**kk, a**) [4]. After the printout the (**kk, jj**) pair—location of next rr and its latest count—is returned through `yield` [9]. Values of **kk** and **jj** remain frozen. At next call, execution resumes with these values and proceeds from the next executable statement—(**kk + = 1**) [10]. **pp** in the figure is a string extending to a few lines [1]. **life(pp, 'e')** is assigned to **a5** in [11]. `next` (**a5**) calls life at [12].

The following three lines ('0', ('0', 'a'), '**Hello**') are the printouts corresponding to execution of [3], [4], and [5]. With the `while` loop the first occurrence of '**e**' is identified as the 27th character in **pp**. 27, **b** [13] signifies this. Execution stops at `yield` [9] and the (27, 1) pair as a `tuple` (location of next '**e**' and the count of '**e**') is returned. `next`(**a5**) [12] continues search for the next occurrence of '**e**'. It is the 62nd character in **pp**. (62, **b**) is printed out [16] and the pair—(62, 2) signifying the location and count of the second '**e**'—is returned [17]. Execution resumption at [10] (**kk** +=1) implies that `print`(**jj**) [3], print (**kk, a**) [4], and print('**Hello**') [5] are not executed. Same is true of `next`(**a5**) [18]. Rest of the generator progress is through `list`(**a5**); it continues until the full search is over.

Example 12.1 Prepare a program to compute exp(x) and evaluate exp(1.2). Use the generator function to compute the successive terms of the series for exp(x).

The `generator` function **exp_f(x)** in Fig. 12.11 [1] computes $\underline{x}^n/n!$ from $\underline{x}^{n-1}/(n-1)!$. **exp_f(a0)** with **a0** = 1.2 [2] has been assigned to **aa** in [3]. The first three approximate values of the function are in [4] (These correspond to the evaluation of $1 + x$, $1 + \underline{x} + \underline{x}^2/2!$, and $1 + x + x^2/2! + x^3/3!$) (Zwillinger 2003).

Fig. 12.10 A Python suite to
illustrate use of **yield** to
form a **generator**

```
>>> pp = '''Burn, burn, burn          [1]
...            Shed your rays
...            Hot, fast, wide
...            The moon in front
...            Gulps it all
...            And puts forth
...            A tiny mean bit
...            Lo - The Sun burns,
...            The moon sooooths'''
>>> def life(qq, rr):                  [2]
...     jj, kk, lq = 0, 0,len(qq)
...     print(jj)                      [3]
...     print(kk, 'a')                 [4]
...     print('Hello')                 [5]
...     while kk < lq:                 [6]
...         if qq[kk] == rr:           [7]
...             jj += 1
...             print(kk, 'b')         [8]
...             yield kk, jj           [9]
...         kk += 1                    [10]
...
>>> a5 = life(pp, 'e')                 [11]
>>> next(a5)                           [12]
0
0 a
Hello
27 b                                   [13]
(27, 1)                                [14]
>>> next(a5)                           [15]
62 b                                   [16]
(62, 2)                                [17]
>>> next(a5)                           [18]
74 b
(74, 3)
>>> list(a5)                           [19]
150 b
173 b
196 b
[(150, 4), (173, 5), (196, 6)]         [20]
>>>
```

exp_f(a0) (with **a0** = 1.2) is assigned afresh to **a1** in [5]. The program suite in the following lines evaluates exp (1.2) to an accuracy of 1.0^{-10} by successively invoking next(**a1**) until the required accuracy is achieved (if achievable in 30 iterative cycles) [7]. The value obtained for exp (1.2) is 3.320116922735597 (compare with the value from the calculator as 3.320116923) [8].

Use of generator with yield in **exp_f** makes the computation elegant. Every new term—$(i + 1)$th—is evaluated by multiplying the previous one (ith) by $x/(i + 1)$. Every recurring series can be evaluated similarly (recursively).

```
>>> def exp_f(x):                                          [1]
...     "yield exp(x) to different approximations"
...     e_p, xp, jj = 1.0, 1.0, 1
...     while jj < 100:
...         xp *= (x/jj)
...         e_p += xp
...         jj += 1
...         yield e_p
...
>>> a0 = 1.2                                               [2]
>>> aa = exp_f(a0)                                         [3]
>>> next(aa), next(aa), next(aa)                           [4]
(2.2, 2.92, 3.2079999999999997)
>>> a1 = exp_f(a0)                                         [5]
>>> b1, b2, jj = next(a1), next(a1), 1                     [6]
>>> while True:
...     b1 = b2
...     b2, jj = next(a1), jj+1
...     if(abs(b1-b2)<1.0e-10) or (jj > 30):break          [7]
...
>>> b2, b2-b1, jj#(calculatorvalue:3.320116923)           [8]
(3.320116922735597, 1.17821308826532011e-11, 14)
>>>
```

Fig. 12.11 The Python Interpreter sequence for Example 13.1

Example 12.2 Realize the random number generator considered in Exercise 6.8 using yield.

The random number generator is defined as function **rny** in Fig. 12.12; its arguments **a**, **c**, **m**, and **sd** are assigned default values as specified (1 103 515 245, 12 345, 2 147 483 648 and 753 respectively). **xn** is defined recursively in [2] and yield **xn** [3] returns the generator for the next **xn**. The function is assigned to **ay** in [4] with the default seed value (**sd** = 753). next(**ay**) in [5] returns the first random number value; the subsequent three random numbers are in [6]; additional random numbers can be obtained in the same manner. With the seed set to 234, the first four random numbers obtained are in [8]. **ryd**() in [9] is an enhanced version of **rny**() considered above. If a **d** value is specified the generator corresponds to the random number sequence in the range (0, **d** − 1) [10]. If **d** is not specified, by default **ryd**() returns a random number in the range (0, **m** − 1) itself [11]. **ryd**() has been assigned to **cy** in [13]. When **d** is not specified, with the default **seed** value (753) the sequence returned [14] is identical to that in [5] and [6] with **ay**. Similarly with **sd** = 234 as seed [15] the random number sequence returned [16] is the same as in [8]. With **d** = 257 [17], the random number sequence has range (0, 256). The first four values are in [18].

The generator functions formed through yield can be chained together to accommodate multiple sequences. The Python interpreter sequence in Fig. 12.13 shows two illustrative examples. **nn1**, **nn2**, and **nn3** in [1], [2], and [3]

```
>>> def rny(a = 1103515245, c = 12345, m = 2147483648, sd
= 753):                                                     [1]
...     xn = sd
...     while True:
...         xn = (a*xn + c)%m                                [2]
...         yield xn                                         [3]
...
>>> ay = rny()                                               [4]
>>> next(ay)                                                 [5]
2018303702
>>> next(ay), next(ay), next(ay)                             [6]
(1411663191, 417085508, 2004933933)
>>> bb = rny(sd = 234)                                       [7]
>>> next(bb), next(bb),next(bb),next(bb)                     [8]
(524541915, 1014839928, 435332433, 1750417846)
>>> def
ryd(a=1103515245,c=12345,m=2147483648,sd=753,d=None):[9]
...     xn = sd
...     while True:
...         if d:xn = ((a*xn + c)%m)%d                       [10]
...         else:xn = (a*xn + c)%m                           [11]
...         yield xn                                         [12]
...
>>> cy = ryd()                                               [13]
>>> next(cy), next(cy), next(cy), next(cy)                   [14]
(2018303702, 1411663191, 417085508, 2004933933)
>>> cc = ryd(sd = 234)                                       [15]
>>> next(cc), next(cc), next(cc), next(cc)                   [16]
(524541915, 1014839928, 435332433, 1750417846)
>>> cd = ryd(d = 257)                                        [17]
>>> next(cd), next(cd), next(cd), next(cd)                   [18]
(205, 38, 192, 94)
```

Fig. 12.12 Random number realizations for Example 12.2

(Fig. 12.13a) form three sets of tuples. Correspondingly **wish_n** [4] defines a sequence of generator functions to wish the set in **nn1**, **nn2**, and **nn3** respectively. The set in **nn1** is wished first [5] and the yield in [6] returns the wished name ('Lava'). Similar wishes follow for those in **nn2** and **nn3** in the same order. list(**wish_n**()) in [9] prints the wishes in the desired sequence. '*Hello Lava Good day to you*' is printed out in the first call since '**Lava**' is the first element in **nn1**. Since yield returns '**Lava**' [6], the same is added to the list [9]. Similarly at the second call '*Hello Kusha good day to you*' is printed out since **Kusha** is the next element in **nn1**. In turn '**Kusha**' is added to the list [9]. With **nn1** is exhausted control is transferred to the next set [7]. Execution continues in the same manner with the third set in [8] and then to completion. The list in [10] has seven names corresponding to their successive returns in a sequence—the first two are from **nn1**, the following three from **nn2**, and the rest two from **nn3**.

(a)

```
>>> nn1 = 'Lava', 'Kusha'                                    [1]
>>> nn2 = 'Tom', 'Dick', 'Harry'                             [2]
>>> nn3 = 'Queen of Spades', 'King of Hearts'                [3]
>>> def wish_nn():                                           [4]
...     for jj in range(len(nn1)):                           [5]
...         print('Hello {}, Good day to you!'.format(nn1[jj]))
...         yield nn1[jj]                                    [6]
...     for jj in range(len(nn2)):                           [7]
...         print('Hello {}, Good day to you!'.format(nn2[jj]))
...         yield nn2[jj]
...     for jj in range(len(nn3)):                           [8]
...         print('Hello {}, Good day to you too,
dear!'.format(nn3[jj]))
...         yield nn3[jj]
...
>>> list(wish_nn())                                          [9]
Hello Lava, Good day to you!
Hello Kusha, Good day to you!
Hello Tom, Good day to you!
Hello Dick, Good day to you!
Hello Harry, Good day to you!
Hello Queen of Spades, Good day to you too, dear!
Hello King of Hearts, Good day to you too, dear!
['Lava', 'Kusha', 'Tom', 'Dick', 'Harry', 'Queen of
Spades', 'King of Hearts']                                   [10]
```

Fig. 12.13 a Illustration of direct use of **yield** to chain generator functions (continued in Fig. 12.13b). **b** Illustration of direct use of **yield** to chain generator functions (continued from Fig. 12.13a)

The three generator functions in **wish_n**() have been separated out as **wish_1**() [11], **wish_2**() [12], and **wish_3**() [13] respectively (Fig. 12.13b); all these three are combined into a composite generator function **wish_g**() in (14). list (**wish_g**()) in [15] invokes the full set. The output can be seen to be identical to that obtained earlier.

The use of 'yield from' as done in the generator **wish_g**() in [14] facilitates chaining of generators and transfer of execution from one generator to another. Further (if desired) the generator functions **wish_1**(), **wish_2**(), and **wish_3**() can be altered at a later date without the need to 'touch' the master generator **wish_g**(). With this (when the application demands), one can decide the overall structure of a program and get into the details separately later.

(b)

```
>>> def wish_1():                                          [11]
...   for jj in range(len(nn1)):
...     print('Hello {}, Good day to you!'.format(nn1[jj]))
...     yield nn1[jj]
...
>>> def wish_2():                                          [12]
...   for jj in range(len(nn2)):
...     print('Hello {}, Good day to you!'.format(nn2[jj]))
...         yield nn2[jj]
...
>>> def wish_3():                                          [13]
...   for jj in range(len(nn3)):
...     print('Hello {}, Good day to you too,
dear!'.format(nn3[jj]))
...         yield nn3[jj]
...
>>> def wish_g():                                          [14]
...     yield from wish_1()
...     yield from wish_2()
...     yield from wish_3()
...
>>> list(wish_g())                                         [15]
Hello Lava, Good day to you!
Hello Kusha, Good day to you!
Hello Tom, Good day to you!
Hello Dick, Good day to you!
Hello Harry, Good day to you!
Hello Queen of Spades, Good day to you too, dear!
Hello King of Hearts, Good day to you too, dear!
['Lava', 'Kusha', 'Tom', 'Dick', 'Harry', 'Queen of
Spades', 'King of Hearts']
```

Fig. 12.13 (continued)

12.4 **iterator** Formation

The __iter__() and __next__() methods can be built into a user-defined class and iterator action imparted to it. Starting with a basic set of parameters an iterator can be generated in this manner. The Python Interpreter sequence in Fig. 12.14 carries a few illustrative examples.

As a class **Ff_0** returns an iterator for a sequence—'an arithmetic progression in a finite field' [1]. An integer sequence starts at **ms** and continues with successive increments of **me** until the integer value reaches **md**. With **v10** as an element of this sequence **v10**(mod 11) is returned for every **v10** to form the desired progression. def__init__() [2] assigns the argument values—**ms**, **me**, and **md** —to corresponding instance variables. If the next method is present in the class

```
>>> class Ff_0:                                            [1]
...     def __init__(self, ms, me, md):                    [2]
...         self.vl0 = ms - md
...         self.edm = me
...         self.ic0 = md
...     def __iter__(self):return self                     [3]
...     def __next__(self):                                [4]
...         if self.vl0 > self.edm:raise StopIteration     [5]
...         self.vl0 += self.ic0                           [6]
...         return self.vl0 % 11                           [7]
...
>>> z1 = Ff_0(2, 22, 3)                                    [8]
>>> list(z1)                                               [9]
[2, 5, 8, 0, 3, 6, 9, 1]
>>> z0 = Ff_0(2, 22, 3)                                    [10]
>>> for jj in z0:print(jj, end = ' ')                     [11]
...
2 5 8 0 3 6 9 1 >>>
>>> class Ff_1:                                            [12]
...     def __init__(self, ms, me, md):
...         self.vl0 = ms - md
...         self.edm = me
...         self.ic0 = md
...     def __iter__(self):                                [13]
...         while self.vl0 < self.edm:
...             self.vl0 += self.ic0
...             yield self.vl0 % 11                        [14]
...
>>> z2 = Ff_1(3, 30, 4)                                    [15]
>>> [jj for jj in z2]                                      [16]
[3, 7, 0, 4, 8, 1, 5, 9]
>>> zz2 = Ff_1(3, 30, 4)                                   [17]
>>> for jj in zz2:print(jj, end = ' ')                    [18]
...
3 7 0 4 8 1 5 9 >>>
>>> z3 = Ff_1(3, 30, 4)                                    [19]
>>> next(z3)                                               [20]
Traceback (most recent call last):
  File "<stdin>", line 1, in <module>
TypeError: 'Ff_1' object is not an iterator
>>> z3i = iter(z3)                                         [21]
>>> next(z3i)                                              [22]
3
>>> list(z3i)                                              [23]
[7, 0, 4, 8, 1, 5, 9]
>>>
```

Fig. 12.14 Examples to illustrate iterator formation from a class

definition as here [4] the __iter__() method [3] need return only self or a desired variant of self. When the class is instantiated the next element value is automatically computed (transparent to the instance) and returned through the __next__() method. In the example here if the value of **v10** exceeds the set limit the iteration is stopped [5]; else the next element value is computed as explained above and returned [7]. The __iter_() and the __next__() methods together play the role of next(iter()) with a sequence. **z1** [8] is an instance of **Ff_0**. list(**z1**) [8] returns the full list of the integer sequence desired. As another instance **Ff_0** (2, 27, 3) is assigned to **z0** in [10]; functionally **z0** is identical to **z1** in [8]. for **jj** in **z0** print(**jj**, end = ' ') outputs the same set of numbers [11]. The example also brings out the basic operations with for. The for statement calls the iter() on the sequence. Following this the element in the concerned object is accessed through the next() method. Once the number of items in the sequence is exhausted the for loop terminates.

Class **Ff_1**() [12] has been defined with an iterator method in it but without the associated __next__() method. Hence the __iter__() method yields the desired value (it does not return) [14]. With an instance of **Ff_1**, at every access iter() for the next element is returned. **z2** [15] and **zz2** [17] are instances of **Ff_1** ()—similar to **z1** and **z0** above. The for based loops in [16] and [18] return the corresponding full sequences. In both cases 'for' loop accesses the next method with the iterator. It obviates the need for defining a separate __next__() method in the class (as was done with **Ff_0**()). **z3** [19] is again an instance of **Ff_1** (). Attempt to extract next(**z3**) [20] fails because **z3** has not been defined as an iterator. Iterator formation using iter (**z3**) as in [21] and its use the subsequent lines can be seen to be the correct usage.

12.5 decoratorS

Nested functions, a function forming an argument to another being defined, and one function returning another function—all these have been discussed in Sect. 4.1. Decorators provide a template with an elegant and flexible syntax for many nested function structures.

The Python Interpreter sequence in Fig. 12.15 has a few examples to facilitate understanding of decorators. Two functions **jj1**() [1] and **ff1**() [2] have been defined; function **jj1**(**yy**) [1] returns **yy** * **yy**. Function **ff1**(**gg1**, **xx**) has **gg1** (a function) and **xx** (a number or an object returning number) as its arguments [2]. It returns (**gg1**(**xx**) + 5.0)$^{0.5}$ [3]. **ff1**(**jj1**, 3.0) [4] uses **jj1** as the function argument, invokes function **ff1** for the number 3.0 and returns (3.0 * 3.0 + 5.0)$^{0.5}$ (=3.7416573867739413). In a typical application functions **jj1**() and **ff1**() can be more involved and **ff1** can be defined independently of **jj1** itself. The decorator based implementation of this function pair follows from [5] to [11] with **ff2**, **jj2** and **hh2** used in place of **ff1** and jj 1respectively. @**ff2** [9] implies that the function following (**jj2**()) 'has been decorated' by function **ff2**; here **ff2** is the decorator

```
>>> def jj1(yy):                                       [1]
...     ww = yy*yy
...     return ww
...
>>> def ff1(gg1, xx):                                  [2]
...     import math
...     return = math.sqrt(gg1(xx) + 5.0)              [3]
...
>>> ff1(jj1, 3.0)                                      [4]
3.7416573867739413
>>> def ff2(gg2):                                      [5]
...     def hh2(xx):                                   [6]
...         import math
...         return = math.sqrt(gg2(xx) + 5.0)          [7]
...     return hh2                                     [8]
...
>>> @ff2                                               [9]
... def jj2(yy):                                       [10]
...     ww = yy*yy
...     return ww                                      [11]
...
>>> jj2(3.0)                                           [12]
3.7416573867739413
>>> ff2                                                [13]
<function ff2 at 0x7f0899e12598>
>>> jj2                                                [14]
<function ff2.<locals>.hh2 at 0x7f0899e126a8>
>>> if __name__ == '__main__':
...     def pnt0(gg):                                  [15]
...         def nn():                                  [16]
...             n1=input("What is Grand-pa's choice?\n")   [17]
...             n2=gg()                                [18]
...             n3=input("What is Grand-ma's choice?\n")   [19]
...             print("The boy's name is: "+n1+' '+n2+' '+n3)[20]
...             print("The boy's pet name is: "+n1[:3]+n3[:2])
...             return
...         return nn
...     @pnt0                                          [21]
...     def fnl1():                                    [22]
...         n0 = input("What is Parents's choice?\n")  [23]
...         return n0                                  [24]
...
>>> fnl1()                                             [25]
What is Grand-pa's choice?
Veera
What is Parents's choice?
Venkat
What is Grand-ma's choice?
Kumar
The boy's name is: Veera Venkat Kumar                  [26]
The boy's pet name is: VeeKu                           [27]
```

Fig. 12.15 Illustrative examples for decorator

function. Thanks to the '@**ff2**' usage the linked pair—**ff2** and **jj2**—behave in the same manner as the pair **jj1** and **ff1** above. Functionally the two pairs are equivalent. [13] and [14] clarify this further. Function **jj2** takes the place of function **hh2** within **ff2** and hence it is local to **ff2**.

As an additional illustration **fn11** [22] has been decorated by **pnt0**() [21], [15]. The two together decide the name of a new born baby confirming to traditional family customs. Parents and grandparents contribute their own to the name and all these are combined into a single string to form the name and decide a pet name too. Function **fn11**() [22] prompts the parents [23] to return their contributions to the name as **n0** [24]. The function **pnt0**() [15] forms the full name [20], forms the pet name, and returns these through the function **nn**() [16] defined within it. With the decoration through @**pnt0** [21] the queries are made in the desired sequence to form the name and the pet name. As an example **fnl1**() is invoked in [25] and the full name and pet name are formed and returned (as 'Veera Venkata Kumar' [26], and 'Veeku' [27] respectively).

12.6 functools

The functools module has a set of readymade decorators and functions. Functions or classes defined otherwise can be simplified, enhanced, or overloaded in different ways using these.

12.6.1 total_ordering

The total_ordering decorator simplifies the implementation of comparison operation with similar objects. The comparison operations are six in number (see Table 12.1)—__lt__, __le__, __eq__, __ne__, __gt__, and __ge__ representing operations <, , <=, ==, !=, > an >= respectively. A class definition to compare two objects can be decorated by total_ordering. One can define the equal operation and any one of the remaining five. All others will be implemented implicitly without the need for additional definitions for them. An illustration is shown in the Python Interpreter sequence in Fig. 12.16. The class **Rank**[2] instantiates student data with name and marks in two subject [3]. It has two comparison methods—__eq__ and __gt__ defined and has been decorated by total_ordering. The decoration implies that all the other comparison operations are also valid and can be used. **saa** [6] and **sbb** [7] are two instances of Rank class for '**Gopan**' and '**Deepa**' respectively. Validity of all the comparison operations is checked in [8].

```
>>> from functools import total_ordering
>>> @total_ordering                          [1]
... class Rank():                            [2]
...     def __init__(self, an, am,
ae):self.name , self.mm, self.me = an,
am, ae                                       [3]
...     def __eq__(self, other):return
((self.mm, self.me) == (other.mm,
other.me))                                   [4]
...     def __gt__(self, other):return
((self.mm, self.me) > (other.mm,
other.me))                                   [5]
...
>>> saa = Rank('Gopan', 95, 76)   [6]
>>> sbb = Rank('Ramya', 75, 96)   [7]
>>> saa > sbb, saa == sbb, saa >= sbb,
saa < sbb, saa <= sbb, saa != sbb[8]
(True, False, True, False, False, True)
>>>
```

Fig. 12.16 Use of **total_ordering** decorator for comparison operations

12.6.2   *single dispatch* Generic Function

len(), iter() are examples of generic functions in Python. The actual functional implementation differs depending on the argument types. But the function returns an object with a predictable uniform pattern. The single dispatch decorator transforms a function to such a generic one. The first argument of the function statement and its type together, decide the alternate definition implemented—hence the term 'Single Dispatch Generic Function'. The register attribute of the generic function is used to do the desired overloading. The procedure is illustrated through an example in the Python Interpreter sequence in Fig. 12.17.

Function **ff(aa, bb)** [3] has **aa**—a string and **bb**—a list of strings as its two arguments. It returns **cc** as a single string joining aa to the string formed by joining the elements of strings in **bb**. Illustrative invocation of **ff** follows in [4] where the string '**pp**' is joined to the string formed by joining the set of strings '**qq**', '**rr**', and '**ss**'; the result is the single string '**ppqqrrss**'. Presence of the single dispatch decorator [2] transforms **ff** into a 'Single Dispatch Generic Function'. For an integer type argument the desired overloading is enabled [6] through the register attribute. With **cc** as an integer type the second argument (**dd**) is selected as a list of integers; the elements of **dd** are summed up to form an integer which is added to **cc** and the sum is returned in hex form. [7] is an illustration of its use.

Another example of a similar overloading follows from [8]. With **gg** as a floating point type number and **hh** as a list of similar floating point numbers, the

```
>>> from functools import singledispatch        [1]
>>> @singledispatch                             [2]
... def ff(aa, bb):                             [3]
...     cc = ''.join([aa, ''.join(bb)])
...     return cc
...
>>> ff('pp', ['qq', 'rr', 'ss'])               [4]
'ppqqrrss'
>>> @ff.register(int)                           [5]
... def _(cc, dd):return hex(sum([cc, sum(dd)]))
                                                [6]
...
>>> ff(11, [22, 33, 44])                        [7]
'0x6e'
>>> @ff.register(float)                         [8]
... def _(gg, hh):return sum([gg, sum(hh)]).hex()
                                                [9]
...
>>> ff(11.11, [22.22, 33.33, 44.44])           [10]
'0x1.bc66666666666p+6'
>>> ff.registry.keys()                          [11]
dict_keys([<class 'int'>, <class 'float'>, <class
'object'>])
>>> ff.registry[object], ff.registry[int],
ff.registry[float]                              [12]
(<function ff at 0x7fa8c0d75048>, <function _ at
0x7fa8bf78b598>, <function _ at 0x7fa8bf78b620>)
>>> ff.dispatch(dict), ff.dispatch(int),
ff.dispatch(float)                              [13]
(<function ff at 0x7fa8c0d75048>, <function _ at
0x7fa8bf78b598>, <function _ at 0x7fa8bf78b620>)
```

Fig. 12.17 Single dispatch decorator transforming a function into the generic form

elements of **hh** are summed up and added to **gg** and the sum expressed in hex form and returned [9]. An illustrative example is in [10].

In all the above three invocations of **ff** [4], [7], and [10], the dispatch attribute of **ff** steers the implementation to the appropriate function. **ff**.registry.keys [11] returns all the registered implementations of **ff**. The attributes **ff**.registry(object), **ff**.registry(int), and **ff**.registry(float) show the respective distinct function IDs [12]. **ff**.dispatch() in [13] confirm the steering done based on the type of argument. The keys also point to the respective dispatch locations.

ff can be seen to be a family of generic functions with three implementations. In both cases of overloading done here the function execution pattern remains the same as the basic function—combining the elements of the sequence (second argument) to that of the first argument. Such similar overloading definition makes use of the generic function meaningful (although this is not a syntactic constraint).

12.6.3 *partial Objects*

A function which has been defined elaborately can be used to yield a curtailed function with the curtailed portion assigned implicitly. The curtailed function can be used separately. The partial function in functools facilitates this. The Python Interpreter sequence in Fig. 12.18 has an illustrative application. With **p**, **q**, **r** as the components of a 3-D vector the function **VVCC** [1] returns its Euclidean magnitude $(=\sqrt{p^2+q^2+r^2})$. The vector 2.0i + 3.1j + 4.2k has the magnitude 5.5901699437494745. partial has been imported in [3] from functools. **vc2_0** has **r** in **VVCC** frozen at zero [4]. This makes **vc2_0** as a function to return the 2-D vector magnitude $(=\sqrt{p^2+q^2})$. **vc2_0**(2.1, 3,1) in [5] returns $\sqrt{2.0^2+3.1^2}$ as 3.6891733491393435.

The general form of partial usage is partial(**ff**, ***agg**, ****kka**); (***agg**, ****kka**) forms the frozen set here.

```
>>> def vvcc(p, q, r):return pow((pow(p, 2) + pow(q, 2) +
pow(r, 2)), 0.5)                                              [1]
...
>>> vvcc(2.0, 3.1, 4.2)                                        [2]
5.5901699437494745
>>> from functools import partial              [3]
>>> vc2_0 = partial(vvcc, r = 0)                              [4]
>>> vc2_0(2.0, 3.1)                                           [5]
3.6891733491393435
>>> from functools import reduce                             [6]
>>> reduce(lambda p, q:p*q, range(1, 7))                     [7]
720
>>> from operator import mul                                 [8]
>>> reduce(mul, range(1, 7))                                 [9]
720
```

Fig. 12.18 Illustrations of using partial and reduce functions in **functools**

12.6.4 Reduction Functions

The reduce function in the functools module has the functional form reduce(**ff**, **aa**, **bb**). Here **ff** is a function and **aa** an iterable. **bb** is optional. ff() has to be a function of two arguments. The function is applied to all the element of **aa** in succession. If **bb** is specified **ff**(**bb**, aa[0]) is done first; the result forms the first argument for the next **ff**() and **ff**(**ff**(**bb**, **aa**[0]), aa[1]) done next. The sequence of such reduction operations is continued with all the elements of **aa** and the final reduced result returned. If **bb** (initializer) is not specified the function starts with **aa** [0] and **aa**[1] as the two arguments. The resulting reduction sequence is **ff**(aa[0], **aa**[1]), **ff**(**ff**(**aa**[0], **aa**[1]), **aa**[2]), **ff**(ff(ff(**aa**[0], **aa**[1]), **aa**[2]), **aa**[3]), … until completion. As an illustration reduce is imported [6] in Fig. 12.18 to compute and return 7! The lambda function in [7] returns the product of the two arguments; the initialization is not specified. It is taken as unity—the first element of range (1, 7). Multiplication is done in succession up to seven, 7! (=720) is computed and returned.

12.7 Exercises

1. The suite starting with [1] in Fig. 12.19 is a generator—a modified version of the random number generator program for Example 12.2. Run the program and explain its behaviour. Do the same with the modified version starting with [2].
2. In Fig. 12.13 replace yield **nn1**[jj], **nn2**[jj], and **nn3**[jj] by yield in each case; run the programs and explain respective outputs.
3. Modify **pnt0**() in Fig. 12.15 to include contributions from great grandparents. Also accommodate separate print output for the baby being a boy or a girl through an additional query for it.
4. Repeat the above with two decorator functions—one for grandparents and the other for great grandparents.

```
def rny(a = 1103515245, c = 12345, m = 2147483648, xn =
753):                                                    [1]
    while True:
        xn = (a*xn + c)%m
        yield xn

def rny(a = 1103515245, c = 12345, m = 2147483648, xn =
753):                                                    [2]
    while True:
        xn = (a*xn + c)%m
```

Fig. 12.19 (pseudo-) Random number generators

5. The perf_counter (in the time module can be used to ascertain time duration for the execution of routines invoking decoration.

Define function timing(ff) as
def timing(ff):
    from time import perf_counter
    t0 = perf_counter
    gg = ff(*arg, **karg)
    t1 = perf_counter
    del_t = t1 − t0
return del_t
Use timing(ff) inside a decorator function tdr. With
@tdr
def jj(. .)
    . . .
    return time of execution of jj.

Write a program to generate Fibbonacci number recursively from $f(n) = f(n − 1) + f(n − 2)$ and get the execution time for $f(6)$ with $f(0) = 2$ and $f(1) = 5$.

6. Marks data for a set of students is given as in Fig. 5.16. Rank the students with the following criteria:

- The rank is decided by the total marks obtained in all the subjects.
- In case of a tie the student with higher marks in mathematics has the higher rank.
- In case of a tie with equal total marks and marks in mathematics as well, marks obtained in physics is taken as the next one for comparison and rank assignment.
- Similar resolution of multiple ties is carried out with priority in the order: total marks, marks in mathematics, physics, chemistry, and then English.
- Prepare student mark lists using random numbers as in Exercise 5 in Chap. 9. Test the program with this data.
- Adapt the merge-sort algorithm (Exercise 13(b) in Chap. 6) to carry out the ranking

7. The decision to procure a refrigerator of a given size is to be made by comparing the closely similar products offered by 10 companies. The refrigerators differ marginally in their specifications, price etc. Write a program to carry out a comparison and do ranking. The criteria to be used in the order of decreasing importance are: cooling size (volume), warranty period, warranty for the cooling system, input voltage range, price, brand name (assign an index in a scale of one to five for brand).
Modify the above by assigning weights to individual criterion.
Do a comparison with actual data.

(Similar comparison may be done with other products: The procedure can be adopted to compare strategies, compare candidates for selection to a position & c.).

8. The overload to a generic function can be used with different types of arguments as discussed in Sect. 12.6.2. With (a_1, a_2, a_3, a_4) as a 4-D vector the Euclidean vector magnitude $v_m = (a_1^2 + a_2^2 + a_3^2 + a_4^2)^{0.5}$.
   Given a vector as a tuple write a program to get the magnitude of the vector. As illustrated in Sect. 12.6.2 use the tuple as the argument and the function for v_m as the additional argument in the overloading scheme. Use the program to get the vector magnitude for the vector (9.1, 8.2, 7.3, 6.4).

9. With v_a (a_1, a_2, a_3) and v_b (b_1, b_2, b_3) as two vectors the angle θ between v_a and v_b can be obtained as follows (Anton and Rorres 2005):
   Get the unit vectors along v_a and v_b as
   $a_u = (a_{1u}, a_{2u}, a_{3u})$
   and
   $b_u = (b_{1u}, b_{2u}, b_{3u})$
   where
   $$a_{ju} = \frac{a_j}{\sqrt{a_1^2 + a_2^2 + a_3^2}}$$
   for all j and similarly for all b_{ju}. $\cos \theta = a_{1u} b_{1u} + a_{2u} b_{2u} + a_{3u} b_{3u}$. Given v_a and v_b write a program to get $\cos\theta$.
   Make the two vectors as a list of the two tuple vectors. Get $\cos \theta$ by overloading as illustrated in Sect. 12.6.2. Evaluate $\cos \theta$ for $v_a = [2.3, -3.4, 4.5, 6.8]$ and $v_b = [7.9, 9.1, -1.2, -3.4]$.

10. Let v_a and v_b be two four dimensional vectors each being given as a list of numbers representing the component magnitudes. Define a single dispatch generic function which will add the two vectors and return the sum vector of four components. Test it with $v_a = [2.3, -3.4, 4.5, 6.8]$ and $v_b = [7.9, 9.1, -1.2, -3.4]$.

11. v_a and v_b are two four dimensional vectors each being given as a tuple of the four vector component magnitudes. Define a single dispatch generic function to return the dot product of the two vectors (The dot product is $\sum_j a_j b_j$). Test it with $v_a = (-11.2, 12.3, 9.4, 8.7)$ and $v_b = (22.4, 35.6, -42.3, -9.87)$. Note that the dot product is also equal to $v_{ma} \cdot v_{mb} \cos \theta$ with v_{ma} and v_{mb} being the vector magnitudes (as in Exercise 8 above) and θ the angle between the vectors (as in Exercise 9 above).

12. Let v represent a 5-D vector $(v_1, v_2, v_3, v_4, v_5)$. With $v_a, v_b, v_c, v_d,$ and v_e as five 5-D vectors define functions to get vector magnitude, unit vectors, and the angle between two vectors. Define a 5-D orthogonal reference base unit vector set; for this start with v_a and form the rest of the unit vector set with $v_b, v_c, v_d,$ and v_e in that order as follows (*Gram-ScHmidt procedure*) (Anton and Rorres 2005):

- Form the unit vector along v_a as u_1.—this is the first component of the reference base unit vector set.
- $u_1 \cdot v_b$ (dot product of u_1 and v_b) is the projection of v_b on v_a. Form the vector $v_b - u_1 \cdot v_b$ and the unit vector u_2 along this. This is the second component of the reference base unit vector set.
- Starting with v_c subtract components along u_1 and u_2 from it; form the unit vector u_3 along this as the third component of the reference base unit vector set.
- Proceed similarly to get u_4 and u_5. to complete the 5-D orthogonal reference base unit vector set.
- Write a program to get the 5-D orthogonal reference base unit vector set. Test it with a specific vector set.
- Use *arg and **kwarg constructs to generalize the program to an n-D vector set.

13. Start with the program for the 5-D vector set in the forgoing exercise. With `partial` define a new 3-D limited vector set and its corresponding functions. Test it with $v_a = [2.3, -3.4, 4.5]$ and $v_b = [7.9, 9.1, -1.2]$ and making the limited set with the fourth and the fifth components as (2, 2).

14. Let $\{x_i\}$ be a given sequence of numbers (can be regular samples of a continuous signal). A corresponding smoothened (filtered) sequence $\{y_i\}$ can be obtained from $\{x_i\}$ by using a '*moving window*' filter. The simplest moving window filter of length l (an odd integer) takes the average of the sample set $(x_{i-b}, x_{i-b-1}, \ldots x_i, x_{i+1}, \ldots x_{i+b}\}$ where $b = (l - 1)/2$ and assigns it to y_i. Note that if x_i has the range zero to n (inclusive) y_i has the range $-b$ to $n + b$. Two routines to do window filtering are given in Fig. 12.20 (**yy0**() and **yy2**()) where l is taken as 11. The former program computes y_i directly. In the latter case y_i for any i is computed using the already computed y_{i-1} and modifying it. Get $\{y_i\}$ for $\{x_i\} = [\text{range}(15)]$ and $\{x_i\} = \text{list}(2 \text{ for } j \text{ in range}(15))$. The function **mtr**() is a monitoring function to find the time for execution of the function inside it. It is used as a decorator for function **yy0**(). Assign it as decorator for **yy2**() also and find the time for execution of for both sets of $\{x_i\}$. Explain why takes conspicuously less time for execution with **yy2**().

15. Use the `timeit` module (Vide Sect. 11.5) to measure execution times for **yy0**() and **yy2**() in the programs of the last exercise and compare the results.

```
import time
def mtr(ff0):
    def spvr0(*args):
        ts = time.perf_counter()
        rr = ff0(*args)
        dt = time.perf_counter() - ts
        print('[%0.6fs]'%(dt))
        return rr
    return spvr0

@mtr
def yy0(xx):
    'Moving window filter of length ll'
    aa, ll = len(xx), 11
    bb = (ll-1)//2
    y0 = []
    for jj in range(-bb-2,aa+bb+2):
        sp = 0
        for kk in range(-bb, bb+1):
            if 0 <= jj+kk < aa:sp += xx[kk+jj]
        y0.append((round(sp/ll, 4), jj))
    return y0

def yy2(xx):
    'Moving window filter of length ll'
    aa, ll = len(xx), 11
    bb = (ll-1)//2
    y1 = [0]*(aa+ll)
    for jj in range(aa+ll):
        if jj == 0:y1[jj] = xx[0]/ll
        elif jj < ll:y1[jj] = y1[jj-1]+ xx[jj]/ll
        elif jj < aa:y1[jj] = y1[jj-1] + (xx[jj]-xx[jj-ll])/ll
        else:y1[jj] = y1[jj-1] - xx[jj-ll]/ll
    y2 = [round(jj, 4) for jj in y1]
    return [(y2[kk], kk - bb) for kk in range(len(y2))]
```

Fig. 12.20 Moving window filter routines for Exercises 14 and 15

References

Anton H, Rorres C (2005) Elementary linear algebra. Wiley, New Jeresy

van Rossum G, Drake FL Jr (2014) The Python library reference. Python software foundation

Zwillinger D (ed) (2003) Standard mathematical tables and formulae. Chapman & Hall/CRC, New York

Index

© Springer Nature Singapore Pte Ltd. 2016
T.R. Padmanabhan, *Programming with Python*,
DOI 10.1007/978-981-10-3277-6

Printed in the United States
By Bookmasters